Introductory
QUATTRO PRO 5.0 FOR WINDOWS

Introductory
QUATTRO PRO 5.0 FOR WINDOWS

David Auer
Western Washington University

June Jamrich Parsons
Northern Michigan University

Dan Oja
GuildWare, Inc.

A Susan Solomon Book

Course Technology, Inc. *One Main Street, Cambridge, MA 02142*

Introductory Quattro Pro 5.0 for Windows is published by Course Technology, Inc.

Vice President, Publisher	Joseph B. Dougherty
Series Consulting Editor	Susan Solomon
Managing Editor	Marjorie Schlaikjer
Project Editor	Joan Carey
Director of Production	Myrna D'Addario
Production Editor	Cynthia H. Anderson
Desktop Publishing Supervisor	Debbie Masi
Composition and Illustrations	Gex, Inc.
Production Assistant	Christine Spillett
Copyeditor	Kathleen Finnegan
Proofreader	Elyse Demers
Indexer	Alexandra Nickerson
Product Testing and Support Supervisor	Jeff Goding
Student Testers	Isabel González
	Chris Greacen
	Snehal Shah
	James Valente
Prepress Production	Gex, Inc.
Manufacturing Manager	Elizabeth Martinez
Text Designer	Sally Steele
Cover Designer	John Gamache

Introductory Quattro Pro 5.0 for Windows © 1994 Course Technology, Inc.

Trademarks

Course Technology and the open book logo are registered trademarks of Course Technology, Inc.

Quattro is a registered trademark of Borland International, Inc. and Windows is a trademark of Microsoft Corporation.

Some of the product names and company names used in this book have been used for identification purposes only and may be trademarks or registered trademarks of their respective manufacturers and sellers.

Disclaimer

Course Technology, Inc. reserves the right to revise this publication and make changes from time to time in its content without notice.

ISBN 1-56527-162-9 (text)

Printed in the United States of America

10 9 8 7 6 5 4 3 2 1

From the Publisher

At Course Technology, Inc., we believe that technology will transform the way that people teach and learn. We are very excited about bringing you, college professors and students, the most practical and affordable technology-related products available.

The Course Technology Development Process

Our development process is unparalleled in the higher education publishing industry. Every product we create goes through an exacting process of design, development, review, and testing.

Reviewers give us direction and insight that shape our manuscripts and bring them up to the latest standards. Every manuscript is quality tested. Students whose backgrounds match the intended audience work through every keystroke, carefully checking for clarity, and pointing out errors in logic and sequence. Together with our own technical reviewers, these testers help us ensure that everything that carries our name is error-free and easy to use.

Course Technology Products

We show both *how* and *why* technology is critical to solving problems in college and in whatever field you choose to teach or pursue. Our time-tested, step-by-step instructions provide unparalleled clarity. Examples and applications are chosen and crafted to motivate students.

The Course Technology Team

This book will suit your needs because it was delivered quickly, efficiently, and affordably. In every aspect of our business, we rely on a commitment to quality and the use of technology. Every employee contributes to this process. The names of all of our employees are listed below:

Tim Ashe, David Backer, Stephen M. Bayle, Josh Bernoff, Erin Bridgeford, Ann Marie Buconjic, Jody Buttafoco, Kerry Cannell, Jim Chrysikos, Susan Collins, John M. Connolly, David Crocco, Myrna D'Addario, Lisa D'Alessandro, Howard S. Diamond, Kathryn Dinovo, Katie Donovan, Joseph B. Dougherty, MaryJane Dwyer, Chris Elkhill, Don Fabricant, Kate Gallagher, Laura Ganson, Jeff Goding, Laurie Gomes, Eileen Gorham, Andrea Greitzer, Cathie Griffin, Tim Hale, Roslyn Hooley, Tom Howes, Nicole Jones, Matt Kenslea, Susannah Lean, Suzanne Licht, Laurie Lindgren, Kim Mai, Elizabeth Martinez, Debbie Masi, Dan Mayo, Kathleen McCann, Jay McNamara, Mac Mendelsohn, Laurie Michelangelo, Kim Munsell, Amy Oliver, Kristine Otto, Debbie Parlee, Kristin Patrick, Charlie Patsios, Jodi Paulus, Darren Perl, Kevin Phaneuf, George J. Pilla, Cathy Prindle, Nancy Ray, Marjorie Schlaikjer, Christine Spillett, Susan Stroud, Michelle Tucker, David Upton, Mark Valentine, Renee Walkup, Lisa Yameen.

Preface

Course Technology, Inc. is proud to present this new book in its Windows Series. *Introductory Quattro Pro 5.0 for Windows* is designed for a first course on Quattro Pro for Windows. This book capitalizes on the energy and enthusiasm students have for Windows-based applications and clearly teaches students how to take full advantage of Quattro Pro's power. It assumes students have learned basic Windows skills and file management from *An Introduction to Microsoft Windows 3.1* by June Jamrich Parsons or from an *equivalent* book.

Organization and Coverage

Introductory Quattro Pro 5.0 for Windows contains six tutorials that provide hands-on instruction. In these tutorials students learn to plan, build, test and document spreadsheets contained in Quattro Pro Spreadsheet Notebooks.

The text emphasizes the ease-of-use features included in the Quattro Pro software: SpeedBar buttons, SpeedMenus, Object Inspectors, and graphing tools. Using this book, students will learn how to do more advanced tasks sooner than they would using other introductory texts; a perusal of the table of contents affirms this. By the end of the book, students will have learned "advanced" tasks such as consolidating results from several spreadsheets, using block names to facilitate database queries, and controlling apparent spreadsheet errors caused by the displayed rounding of a formatted value.

Approach

Introductory Quattro Pro 5.0 for Windows distinguishes itself from other Windows books because of its unique two-pronged approach. First, it motivates students by demonstrating *why* they need to learn the concepts and skills. This book teaches Quattro Pro using a task-driven rather than a feature-driven approach. By working through the tutorials—each motivated by a realistic case—students learn how to use Quattro Pro in situations they are likely to encounter in the workplace, rather than learn a list of features one-by-one, out of context. Second, the content, organization, and pedagogy of this book make full use of the Windows environment. What content is presented, when it's presented, and how it's presented capitalize on Quattro Pro's power to perform complex modeling tasks earlier and more easily than was possible under DOS.

Features

Introductory Quattro Pro 5.0 for Windows is an exceptional textbook also because it contains the following features:

- **"Read This Before You Begin" Page** This page is consistent with Course Technology's unequaled commitment to helping instructors introduce technology into the classroom. Technical considerations and assumptions about hardware, software, and default settings are listed in one place to help instructors save time and eliminate unnecessary aggravation.

- **Tutorial Case** Each tutorial begins with a spreadsheet-related problem that students could reasonably encounter in business. Thus, the process of solving the problem will be meaningful to students.

- **Step-by-Step Methodology** The unique Course Technology, Inc. methodology keeps students on track. They click or press keys always within the context of solving the problem posed in the Tutorial Case. The text constantly guides students, letting them know where they are in the process of solving the problem. The numerous screen shots include labels that direct students' attention to what they should look at on the screen.

- **Page Design** Each *full-color* page is designed to help students easily differentiate between what they are to *do* and what they are to *read*. The steps are easily identified by their color background and numbered bullets. Windows default colors are used in the screen shots so instructors can more easily assure that students' screens look like those in the book.

- **TROUBLE?** TROUBLE? paragraphs anticipate the mistakes that students are likely to make and help them recover from these mistakes. This feature facilitates independent learning and frees the instructor to focus on substantive conceptual issues rather than common procedural errors.

- **Reference Windows and Task Reference** Reference Windows provide short, generic summaries of frequently used procedures. The Task Reference appears at the end of the book and summarizes how to accomplish tasks using the SpeedBar buttons, the menus, and the keyboard. Both of these features are specially designed and written so students can use the book as a reference manual after completing the course.

- **Questions, Tutorial Assignments, and Case Problems** Each tutorial concludes with meaningful, conceptual Questions that test students' understanding of what they learned in the tutorial. The Questions are followed by Tutorial Assignments, which provide students with additional hands-on practice of the skills they learned in the Tutorial. Finally, each tutorial ends with three or more complete Case Problems that have approximately the same scope as the Tutorial Case.

- **Exploration Exercises** The Windows environment encourages students to learn by exploring and discovering what they can do. The Exploration Exercises are Questions, Tutorial Assignments, or Case Problems designated by an **E** that encourage students to explore the capabilities of the computing environment they are using and to extend their knowledge using the Windows on-line Help facility and other reference materials.

The CTI WinApps Setup Disk

The CTI WinApps Setup Disk bundled with the instructor's copy of this book contains an innovative Student Disk generating program designed to save instructors time. Once this software is installed on a network or standalone workstation, students can double-click the "Make Quattro Pro 5.0 Student Disk" icon in the CTI WinApps group window. Double-clicking this icon transfers all the data files students need to complete the tutorials, Tutorial Assignments, and Case Problems to a high-density disk in drive A or B. Tutorial 1 provides complete step-by-step instructions for making the Student Disk.

Adopters of this text are granted the right to install the CTI WinApps group window on any standalone computer or network used by students who have purchased this text.

For more information on the CTI WinApps Setup Disk, see the section in this book called, "Read This Before You Begin."

The Supplements

■ **Instructor's Manual** The Instructor's Manual is written by the authors and is quality assurance tested. It includes:

  • Answers and solutions to all the Questions, Tutorial Assignments, and Case Problems. Suggested solutions are also included for the Exploration Exercises.

  • A disk (3.5-inch or 5.25-inch) containing solutions to all the Questions, Tutorial Assignments, and Case Problems.

  • Tutorial Notes, which contain background information from the authors about the Tutorial Case and the instructional progression of the tutorial.

  • Technical Notes, which include troubleshooting tips as well as information on how to customize the students' screens to closely emulate the screen shots in the book.

  • Transparency Masters of key concepts.

■ **Test Bank** The Test Bank contains 50 questions per tutorial in true/false, multiple choice, and fill-in-the-blank formats, plus two essay questions. Each question has been quality assurance tested by students to achieve clarity and accuracy.

■ **Electronic Test Bank** The Electronic Test Bank allows instructors to edit individual test questions, select questions individually or at random, and print out scrambled versions of the same test to any supported printer.

Acknowledgments

Through their contributions, many people are responsible for the successful completion of this book, and the authors would like to express their gratitude to an excellent production team.

We want to thank the reviewers of this text—Danielle Bernstein of Kean College of New Jersey, John Leschke of the University of Virginia, and John Ross of Fox Valley Technical College. Our thanks also go to our developmental editor Joan Carey and the Course Technology production and product testing staff—particularly Cynthia Anderson, Kathy Finnegan, Marjorie Schlaikjer, and Jeff Goding and his team of student testers Isabel González, Chris Greacen, Snehal Shah, and James Valente for working tirelessly under tight deadlines to produce a quality, professional product. Finally, our thanks to our series editor Susan Solomon.

David Auer, June Jamrich Parsons and Dan Oja

Brief Contents

Contents

TUTORIAL 2   Planning, Building, Testing, and Documenting Notebooks

TUTORIAL 3   Formatting and Printing

TUTORIAL 4   **Functions, Formulas, and Absolute References**

TUTORIAL 5   Graphs and Graphing

TUTORIAL 6 Managing Data with Quattro Pro

Reference Windows

Quattro Pro 5.0 for Windows Tutorials

Read This Before You Begin

To the Student

To use this book, you must have a Student Disk. Your instructor will either provide you with one or ask you to make your own by following the instructions in the section "Your Student Disk" in Tutorial 1. See your instructor or lab manager for further information. If you are going to work through this book using your own computer, you need a computer system running Microsoft Windows 3.1, Quattro Pro 5.0 for Windows, and a Student Disk. *You will not be able to complete the tutorials and exercises in this book using your own computer until you have a Student Disk.*

To the Instructor

Making the Student Disk To complete the tutorials in this book, your students must have a copy of the Student Disk. To relieve you of having to make multiple Student Disks from a single master copy, we provide you with the CTI WinApps Setup Disk, which contains an automatic Student Disk generating program. Once you install the Setup Disk on a network or standalone workstation, students can easily make their own Student Disks by double-clicking the "Make Quattro Pro 5.0 Student Disk" icon in the CTI WinApps icon group. Double-clicking this icon transfers all the data files students will need to complete the tutorials, Tutorial Assignments, and Case Problems to a high-density disk in drive A or B. If some of your students will use their own computers to complete the tutorials and exercises in this book, they must first get the Student Disk. The section called "Your Student Disk" in Tutorial 1 provides complete instructions on how to make the Student Disk.

Installing the CTI WinApps Setup Disk To install the CTI WinApps icon group from the Setup Disk, follow the instructions inside the disk envelope that was bundled with your book. By adopting this book, you are granted a license to install this software on any computer or computer network used by you or your students.

README File A README.TXT file located on the Setup Disk provides additional technical notes, troubleshooting advice, and tips for using the CTI WinApps software in your school's computer lab. You can view the README.TXT file using any word processor you choose.

System Requirements

The minimum software and hardware requirements for your computer system are as follows:
- Microsoft Windows Version 3.1 or later on a local hard drive or a network drive.
- A 386 or higher processor with a minimum of 4 MB of RAM (6 MB or more is strongly recommended).
- A mouse supported by Windows 3.1.
- A printer supported by Windows 3.1.
- A VGA 640 x 480 16-color display is recommended; an 800 x 600 or 1024 x 768 SVGA, VGA monochrome, or EGA display is acceptable.
- At least 10 MB of free hard disk space for a minimum installation with Help. A full installation of the Workgroup Edition with the Workgroup Desktop requires 28 MB of free hard disk space.
- Student workstations with at least 1 high-density disk drive. If you need a 5.25-inch CTI WinApps Setup Disk, contact your CTI sales rep or call customer service at 1-800-648-7450. In Canada call Times Mirror Professional Publishing/Irwin Dorsey at 1-800-268-4178.
- If you want to install the CTI WinApps Setup Disk on a network drive, your network must support Microsoft Windows.

Using Spreadsheets to Make Business Decisions

Evaluating Sites for a World-Class Golf Course

OBJECTIVES

In this tutorial you will:

- Make a Quattro Pro for Windows Student Disk
- Launch and exit Quattro Pro
- Discover how Quattro Pro is used in business
- Open, explore, save, and close a Quattro Pro notebook
- Print a Quattro Pro spreadsheet
- Correct mistakes and use the Undo command
- Scroll a spreadsheet and a notebook
- Learn about values, labels, formulas and functions
- Learn about Quattro Pro objects and their properties
- Find information with the Quattro Pro Help system

CASE

InWood Design Group   In Japan golf is big business. Spurred by the Japanese passion for the sport, golf is enjoying unprecedented popularity. But in that small mountainous country of 12 million golfers, there are less than 2,000 courses, the average fee for 18 holes on a public course is between $200 and $300, and golf club memberships are bought and sold like stock shares. The market potential is phenomenal, but building a golf course in Japan is expensive because of inflated property values, difficult terrain, and strict environmental regulations.

InWood Design Group is planning to build a world-class golf course, and one of the four sites under consideration for the course is in Chiba Prefecture, Japan. The other possible sites are Kauai, Hawaii; Edmonton, Canada; and Scottsdale, Arizona. Mike Mazzuchi and Pamela Kopenski are members of the InWood Design Group site selection team. The team is responsible for collecting information on the sites, evaluating that information, and recommending the best site for the new golf course.

The team identified five factors that are likely to determine the success of a golf course: climate, competition, market size, topography, and transportation. The team collected information on these factors for each of the four potential golf course sites. The next step is to analyze the information and make a site recommendation to management.

Using Borland's Quattro Pro 5.0 for Windows, Pamela created a Quattro Pro notebook that the team can use to evaluate the four sites. She will bring the notebook to the next meeting to help the team evaluate the sites and reach a decision.

In this tutorial you will learn how to use Quattro Pro 5.0 for Windows as you work along with the InWood team to select the best site for the golf course.

What Is Quattro Pro for Windows?

Quattro Pro for Windows is a computerized spreadsheet program. A **spreadsheet** or worksheet (the two terms are interchangeable) is a business tool that helps you analyze and evaluate information. A spreadsheet displays data on a grid so that you can see how each piece of data relates to other data on the spreadsheet. Spreadsheets are often used for cash flow analysis, budgeting, decision making, cost estimating, inventory management, and financial reporting. For example, an accountant might use a spreadsheet for a budget like the one in Figure 1-1.

	Cash Budget Forecast	
	January Estimated	January Actual
Cash in Bank (Start of Month)	$1,400.00	$1,400.00
Cash in Register (Start of Month)	100.00	100.00
Total Cash	$1,500.00	$1,500.00
Expected Cash Sales	$1,200.00	$1,420.00
Expected Collections	400.00	380.00
Other Money Expected	100.00	52.00
Total Income	$1,700.00	$1,852.00
Total Cash and Income	$3,200.00	$3,352.00
All Expenses (for Month)	$1,200.00	$1,192.00
Cash Balance at End of Month	$2,000.00	$2,160.00

Figure 1-1
A budget
spreadsheet

Spreadsheets were originally created using multicolumn analysis paper, and calculations were done by hand. When computer spreadsheet programs were developed, multicolumn paper was reproduced on the screen, complete with rows and columns. Spreadsheet programs are also referred to as spreadsheet applications, electronic spreadsheets, computerized spreadsheets, or just spreadsheets.

Quattro Pro groups spreadsheets into a **notebook**, which contains 256 spreadsheet pages and a Graphs page. In this book, the term "notebook" refers to a Quattro Pro notebook, and the term "spreadsheet" refers to one page in a notebook.

Borland International produces Quattro Pro as its spreadsheet program, and Quattro Pro 5.0 is the fifth version of this program. There are two variants of Quattro Pro: Quattro Pro for DOS, which runs without using Microsoft Windows, and Quattro Pro for Windows, which runs under Microsoft Windows and features full Windows functionality and power. This book teaches you about Quattro Pro 5.0 for Windows, and references to "Quattro Pro" are to Quattro Pro 5.0 for Windows unless otherwise noted.

Using the Tutorials Effectively

The tutorials will help you learn about Quattro Pro. They are designed to be used at your computer. You will begin by reading text that explains the concepts and techniques you need to know. When you come to the numbered steps, follow the steps on your computer. Read each step carefully and completely before you try it.

In the tutorials you'll find figures with important parts of the screen display labeled. These figures show you what to look for on your screen. As you work, compare your screen with the figures to verify your results. Don't worry if what you see on your screen differs slightly from the figures, but make sure that the important parts of the screen display match those in each figure.

Don't worry about making mistakes—that's part of the learning process. **TROUBLE?** paragraphs identify common problems and explain how to get back on track. You should complete the steps in the **TROUBLE?** paragraph *only* if you are having the problem described.

After you read the conceptual information and complete the steps, you can do the exercises found at the end of each tutorial in the sections entitled "Questions," "Tutorial Assignments," and "Case Problems." The exercises are carefully structured to help you review what you learned in the tutorials and apply your knowledge to new situations.

Throughout the tutorials, you will find Reference Window boxes, which provide you with short summaries of frequently used procedures. When you are doing the exercises, refer back to the Reference Window boxes. You can also use the Task Reference at the end of the tutorials, which summarizes how to accomplish tasks using the mouse, the menus, and the keyboard.

Before you begin the tutorials, you should know how to use the menus, dialog boxes, Help facility, Program Manager, and File Manager in Microsoft Windows. Course Technology, Inc. publishes two excellent texts for learning Windows: *A Guide to Microsoft Windows* and *An Introduction to Microsoft Windows*, both available in current releases.

Your Student Disk

To complete the tutorials and exercises in this book, you must have a Student Disk. The Student Disk contains all the practice files you need for the tutorials, the Tutorial Assignments, and the Case Problems. If your instructor or technical support person provides you with your Student Disk, you can skip this section and go to the section entitled "Launching Quattro Pro." If your instructor asks you to make your own Student Disk, you need to follow the steps in this section.

To make your Student Disk, you need:
- a blank, formatted, high-density 3.5-inch or 5.25-inch disk
- a computer with Microsoft Windows 3.1, Quattro Pro 5.0 for Windows, and the CTI WinApps group icon installed on it

If you are using your own computer, the CTI WinApps group icon will not be installed on it. Before you proceed, you must go to your school's computer lab and find a computer with the CTI WinApps group icon installed on it. Once you have made your own Student Disk, you can use it to complete all the tutorials and exercises in this book on any computer you choose.

To make your Quattro Pro for Windows Student Disk:

❶ Launch Windows and make sure the Program Manager window is open.

TROUBLE? The exact steps you follow to launch Microsoft Windows 3.1 might vary depending on how your computer is set up. On many computer systems, you type WIN at the DOS prompt and then press [Enter] to launch Windows. If you don't know how to launch Windows, ask your technical support person or instructor for assistance.

❷ Label your formatted disk "Quattro Pro for Windows Student Disk" and place it in drive A.

TROUBLE? If your computer has more than one disk drive, drive A is usually on top. If your Student Disk does not fit into drive A, then place it in drive B and substitute "drive B" anywhere you see "drive A" in the tutorial steps.

❸ Look for an icon labeled "CTI WinApps" like the one in Figure 1-2 or a window labeled "CTI WinApps" like the one in Figure 1-3.

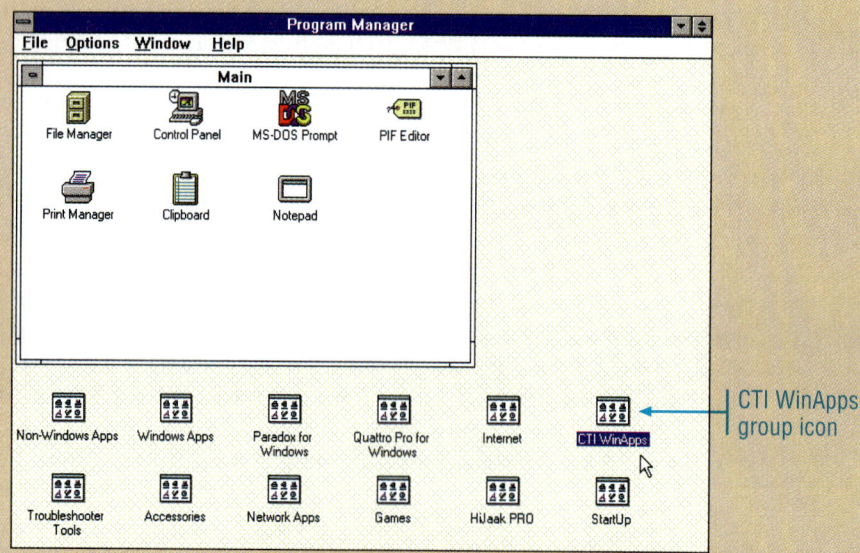

Figure 1-2
The CTI WinApps group icon

TROUBLE? If you cannot find anything labeled "CTI WinApps," the CTI software might not be installed on your computer. If you are in a computer lab, ask your technical support person or instructor for assistance.

If you are using your own computer, you will not be able to make your Student Disk. To make it you need access to the CTI WinApps group icon, which is, most likely, installed on your school's lab computers. Ask your instructor or technical support person for further information on where to locate the CTI WinApps group icon. Once you create your Student Disk, you can use it to complete all the tutorials and exercises in this book on any computer you choose.

❹ If you see an icon labeled "CTI WinApps," double-click it to open the CTI WinApps group window, shown in Figure 1-3. If the CTI WinApps window is already open, go to Step 5.

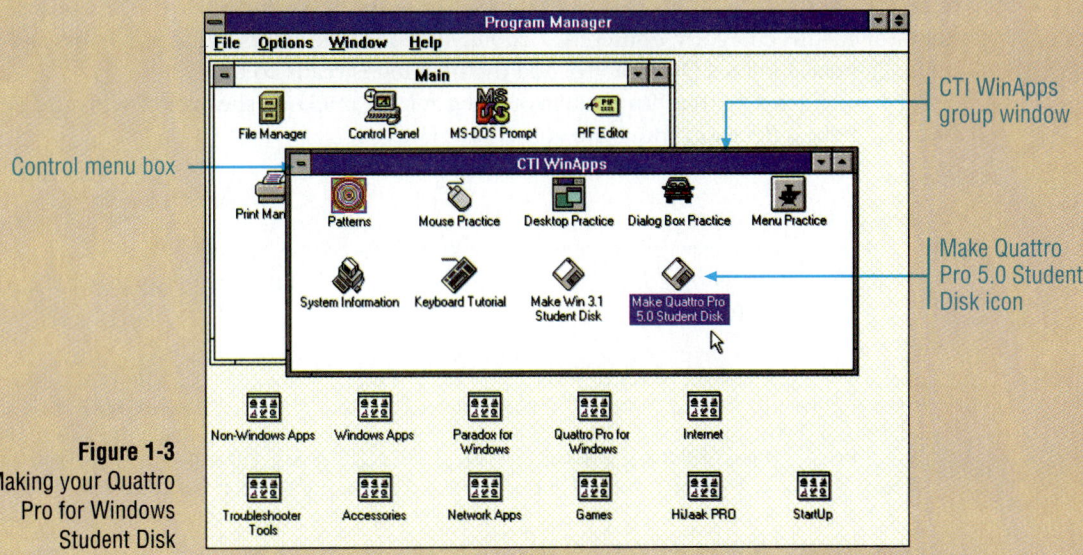

Figure 1-3
Making your Quattro Pro for Windows Student Disk

❺ Double-click the **Make Quattro Pro 5.0 Student Disk** icon. The Make Quattro Pro 5.0 Student Disk dialog box opens, shown in Figure 1-4.

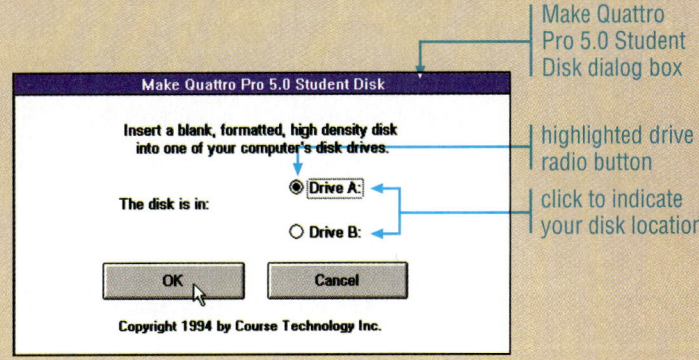

Figure 1-4
Indicating the drive that contains your disk

❻ Make sure the drive that contains your formatted disk corresponds to the drive radio button that is highlighted in the dialog box on your screen.

❼ Click **OK** to copy the practice files to your formatted data disk.

❽ When the copying is complete, a message indicates the number of files copied to your disk. Click **OK**.

❾ To close the CTI WinApps window, double-click the **Control menu box** on the CTI WinApps window, shown in Figure 1-3.

Launching Quattro Pro

Now we'll join Pamela Kopenski at the InWood team meeting. Pamela has arrived a few minutes early so she can open her laptop computer and connect it to the large screen monitor in the company conference room. In a few moments Windows is up and running, Pamela launches Quattro Pro, and the meeting is ready to begin.

Let's launch Quattro Pro to follow along with Pamela as she works with the design team to make a decision about the golf course site.

To launch Quattro Pro:

❶ Look for an icon or window titled "Quattro Pro for Windows." Figure 1-5 shows both the group icon and the group window, which contains the program-item icon that starts Quattro Pro.

TROUBLE? The icon or window on your screen might have a slightly different name, perhaps just "Quattro Pro" or "Quattro Pro 5.0." If you don't see anything called "Quattro Pro for Windows" or a slight variation of that name, click Window on the Program Manager menu bar. If you find Quattro Pro for Windows in the list of windows, click it. If you still can't find anything called "Quattro Pro for Windows," ask your technical support person or instructor for help on how to launch Quattro Pro for Windows. If you are using your own computer, make sure the Quattro Pro for Windows software has been installed correctly.

❷ Double-click the **Quattro Pro for Windows group icon** to open the group window. If you see the Quattro Pro for Windows *group window* instead of the *group icon*, go to Step 3, because your group window is already open.

❸ Double-click the **Quattro Pro for Windows program-item icon**, found in the group window. After a short pause, copyright information appears in a box and remains on the screen until Quattro Pro is ready for use. Quattro Pro is ready when your screen

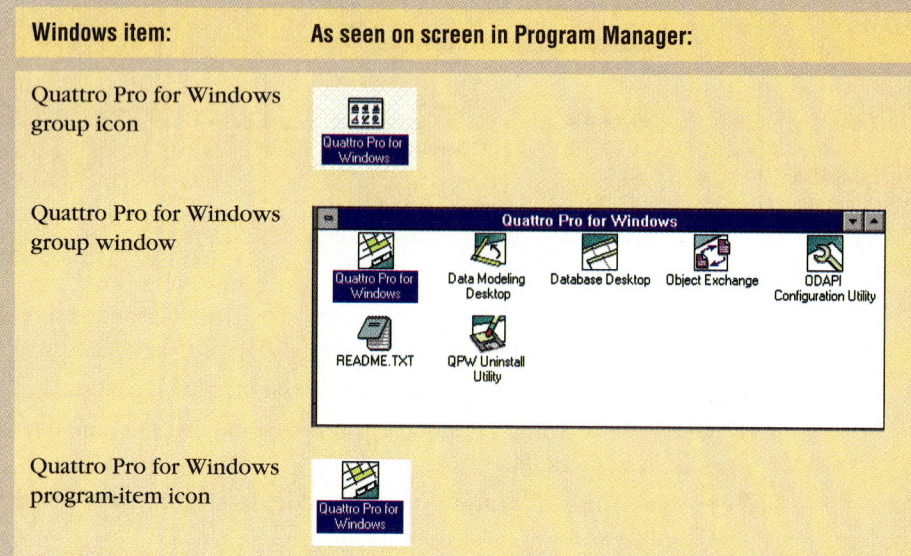

Windows item:	As seen on screen in Program Manager:
Quattro Pro for Windows group icon	
Quattro Pro for Windows group window	
Quattro Pro for Windows program-item icon	

Figure 1-5
Quattro Pro for Windows icons and window in Program Manager

looks similar to Figure 1-6. Don't worry if your screen doesn't look *exactly* the same as Figure 1-6. You are ready to continue when you see the Quattro Pro for Windows title bar and the NOTEBK1.WB1 notebook window title bar.

Quattro Pro for Windows title bar

application window

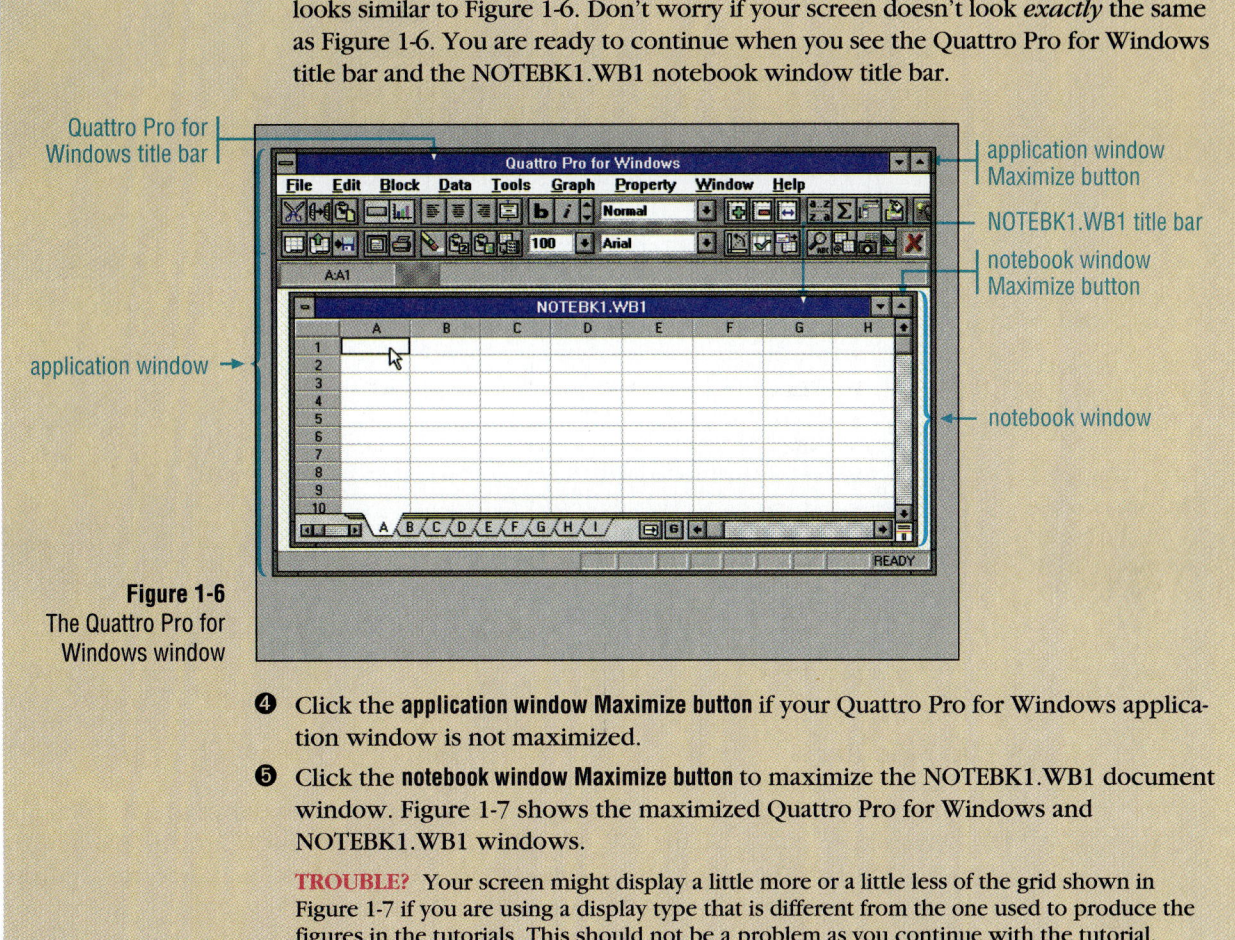

application window Maximize button

NOTEBK1.WB1 title bar

notebook window Maximize button

notebook window

Figure 1-6
The Quattro Pro for Windows window

❹ Click the **application window Maximize button** if your Quattro Pro for Windows application window is not maximized.

❺ Click the **notebook window Maximize button** to maximize the NOTEBK1.WB1 document window. Figure 1-7 shows the maximized Quattro Pro for Windows and NOTEBK1.WB1 windows.

TROUBLE? Your screen might display a little more or a little less of the grid shown in Figure 1-7 if you are using a display type that is different from the one used to produce the figures in the tutorials. This should not be a problem as you continue with the tutorial.

The Quattro Pro for Windows Window

Quattro Pro operates like most other Windows programs. If you have used other Windows programs, many of the Quattro Pro window controls will be familiar. Figure 1-7 shows the main components of the Quattro Pro window. Let's take a look at these components so that you're familiar with their location.

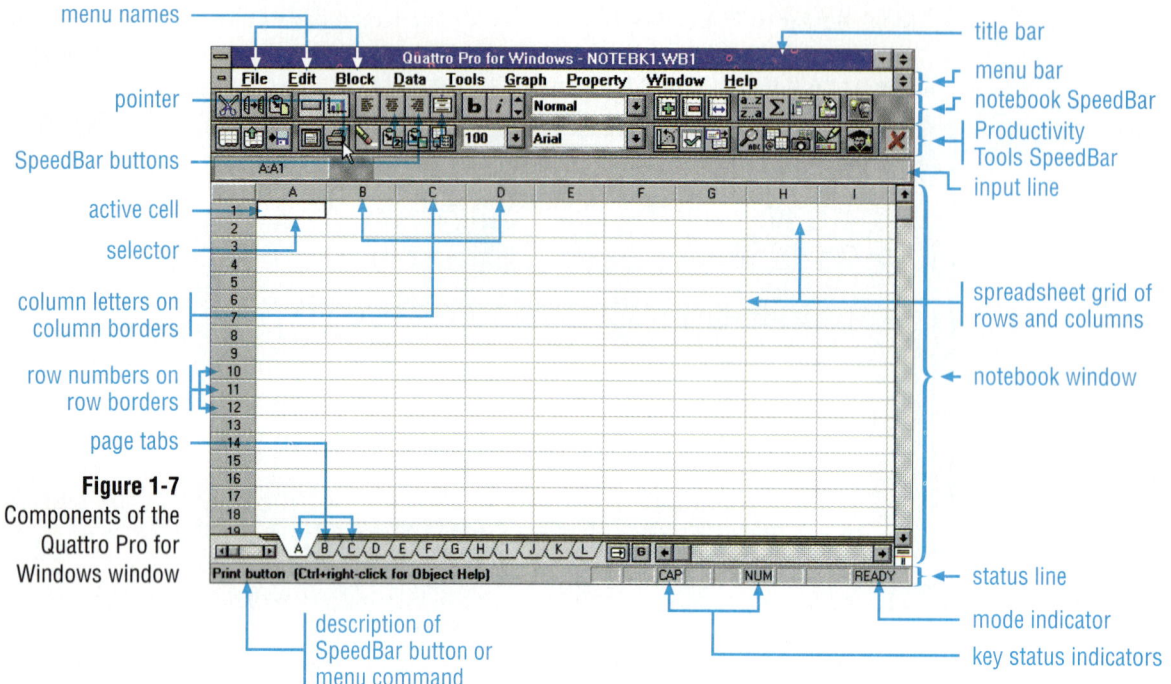

Figure 1-7
Components of the
Quattro Pro for
Windows window

The Title Bar

The **title bar**, which runs across the top of a window, identifies the window's contents. On your screen and in Figure 1-7 the title bar displays "Quattro Pro for Windows – NOTEBK1.WB1." The title of the *application* is "Quattro Pro for Windows," and the title of the *notebook* is "NOTEBK1.WB1." Because the notebook window for NOTEBK1.WB1 is maximized, the title of the notebook is displayed in the title bar for the application window. Look back at Figure 1-6 to see the notebook window within the application window, each with its own title bar.

The Menu Bar

Most Windows applications have a **menu bar**, which is located directly below the title bar. Each word in the menu bar is the name of a menu, a collection of commands and options. The menu bar provides easy access to all the features of Quattro Pro.

The Notebook SpeedBar

The Quattro Pro **notebook SpeedBar** is the row of square buttons located below the menu bar. The tools and buttons on the notebook SpeedBar provide shortcuts for accessing the most commonly used features of Quattro Pro.

The Productivity Tools SpeedBar

Quattro Pro can display secondary SpeedBars in addition to the notebook SpeedBar. The **Productivity Tools SpeedBar** is a secondary SpeedBar that is automatically displayed below the notebook SpeedBar when you start Quattro Pro. The buttons on the Productivity Tools SpeedBar provide more shortcuts to commonly used features.

The Input Line

The input line is located immediately below the Productivity Tools SpeedBar. The **input line** tells you where you are on the spreadsheet and displays the data you enter or edit.

The Notebook Window

The **notebook window** contains the notebook you are creating, editing, or using. Each page in the notebook is an individual spreadsheet. Each spreadsheet page in a notebook is initially named with a letter on a tab at the bottom of the spreadsheet. (You will learn how to change the spreadsheet name later.) For example, the A tab indicates the first spreadsheet page in the notebook, B the second, and so on. The spreadsheet page that you are working with is the **active spreadsheet** or **active page**.

A spreadsheet consists of a set of vertical **columns**, each labeled with a letter on the **column border**, and a set of horizontal **rows**, each labeled with a number on the **row border**. A **cell** is the rectangular area at the intersection of a column and row. Within a spreadsheet, each cell is identified by a **cell address**, which consists of its column and row coordinates. For example, the cell address B6 indicates the cell at the intersection of column B and row 6. The column letter is always specified first in the cell address: B6 is a correct cell reference, but 6B is not.

The complete cell address consists of the spreadsheet page name followed by the cell location within the spreadsheet. For example, the cell address A:B6 indicates cell B6 in the spreadsheet page named A. To keep the cell address notation simple, you can usually omit the spreadsheet page name when referring to cells on the active spreadsheet. You'll use the complete cell address whenever it's necessary to identify clearly the spreadsheet page containing the cell or cells that you're working with. For example, in Figure 1-8 the complete cell address of the cell indicated by a black outline is A:A1, which you can refer to as just A1 because spreadsheet page A is the active page (indicated by the A tab).

The cell with a black outline is the **active cell**, which is the cell most recently clicked or selected. The black outline is called the **selector**. You can change the active cell when you want to work in a different location on the spreadsheet.

The Pointer

The **pointer** is the indicator that moves on your screen as you move your mouse. Any action you take with the mouse causes a reaction on the screen at the location of the pointer. The pointer changes shape to indicate the type of task you can perform at a location. In Figure 1-7 the pointer, which is located over the Print button on the Productivity Tools SpeedBar, has its most common shape, which is ⌖. You'll learn about other pointer shapes as you use Quattro Pro features that cause changes in the shape of the pointer.

The Status Line

The **status line** is located at the bottom of the Quattro Pro window. The left side of the status line provides a brief description of the action associated with a command or option. The right side of the status line shows the status of important keys such as Caps Lock and Num Lock, and, at the far right, the current **mode** that Quattro Pro is operating in. In Figure 1-7 the status line shows that the Num Lock key is in effect, which means you use your numeric keypad to enter numbers rather than move the cursor; that the Caps Lock key is in effect, which means that letters you type will appear in uppercase; and that Quattro Pro is in Ready mode, which means that Quattro Pro is waiting for you to do something.

Opening a Notebook

When you want to use a notebook that you have previously created, you must first open it. When you open a notebook, a copy of the notebook file is transferred into the random access memory (RAM) of your computer and displayed on your screen. Figure 1-8 shows that when you open a notebook named "GOLF.WB1," Quattro Pro copies the notebook file from a disk or hard drive into RAM. The notebook name "GOLF.WB1" consists of a filename ("GOLF") and a filename extension (".WB1"). The filename extension helps you identify different types of files, and the extension ".WB1" tells you that this is a Quattro Pro notebook file.

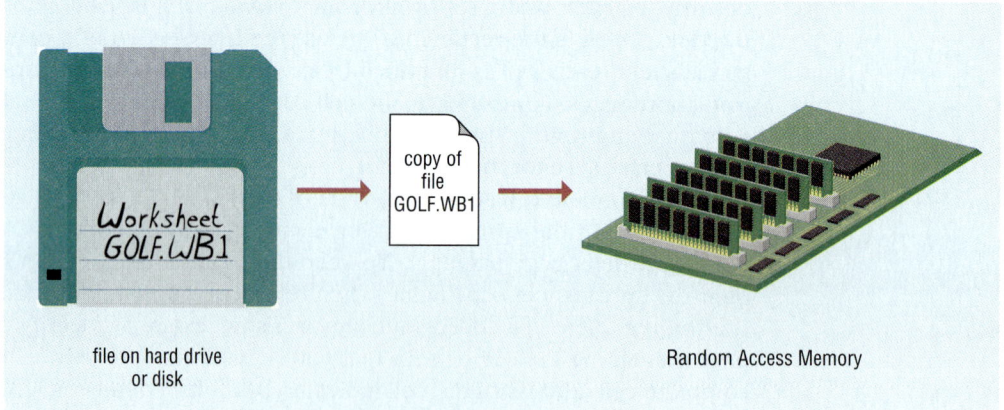

Figure 1-8
Opening a
notebook

file on hard drive
or disk

copy of
file
GOLF.WB1

Random Access Memory

Worksheet
GOLF.WB1

When the notebook is open, GOLF.WB1 exists both in RAM and on the disk. Changes you make to the spreadsheets in the notebook are made only in RAM until you save those changes to your disk. When you turn off your computer, anything in RAM is lost because RAM needs electrical power to maintain the data storage (think of a light bulb—when you switch off the power, there's no more light). It's a good idea to save your changes to the disk regularly—an unexpected power failure will cause you to lose any unsaved changes.

REFERENCE WINDOW

Opening a Notebook

- Click the Open Notebook button on the Productivity Tools SpeedBar (or click File, then click Open...).

- Make sure that the Drives list box displays the name of the drive that contains the notebook you want to open.

- If necessary, make sure that you have selected the correct directory in the Directories list.

- Double-click the filename of the notebook you want to open (or click the filename, then click OK).

The InWood site selection team has to consider several factors as part of its decision about the best location for InWood's new world-class golf course. Pamela has created a notebook to help the site selection team evaluate the four potential locations for the golf course. The notebook, GOLF.WB1, is stored on your Student Disk. Let's open this file to display Pamela's notebook.

To open the GOLF.WB1 notebook:

❶ Make sure your Quattro Pro for Windows Student Disk is in drive A.

TROUBLE? If you don't have a Student Disk, then you need to get one. Your instructor will either give you a copy or ask you to make your own by following the instructions earlier in this tutorial in the section called "Your Student Disk." See your instructor for information.

❷ Click the **Open Notebook button** 📖 on the Productivity Tools SpeedBar (or click **File**, then click **Open...**) to display the Open File dialog box. Figure 1-9 shows the location of the Open Notebook button and the correct Open File dialog box settings to open the GOLF.WB1 notebook.

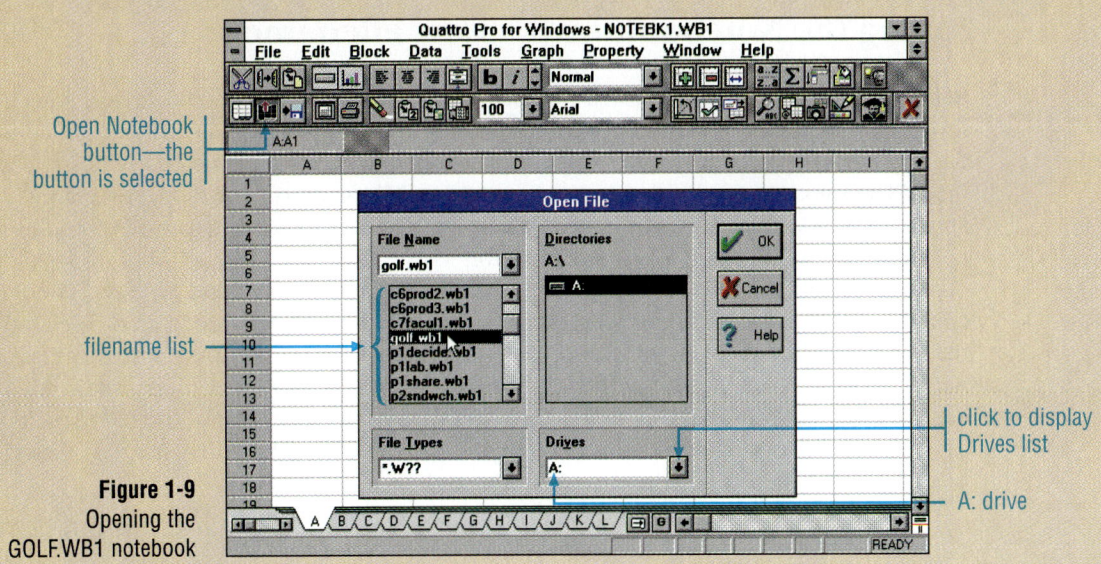

Figure 1-9
Opening the
GOLF.WB1 notebook

❸ If the A: drive name is not displayed in the Drives list box, click the **drop-down list arrow button** on the Drives list box; then in the list of drives, click the A: drive.

TROUBLE? If your disk is in a different drive, such as B:, then click that drive instead.

❹ Double-click the filename **GOLF.WB1** in the filename list. The GOLF.WB1 spreadsheet appears. See Figure 1-10.

TROUBLE? If you do not see GOLF.WB1 in the list, use the scroll bar next to the filenames list to view additional filenames.

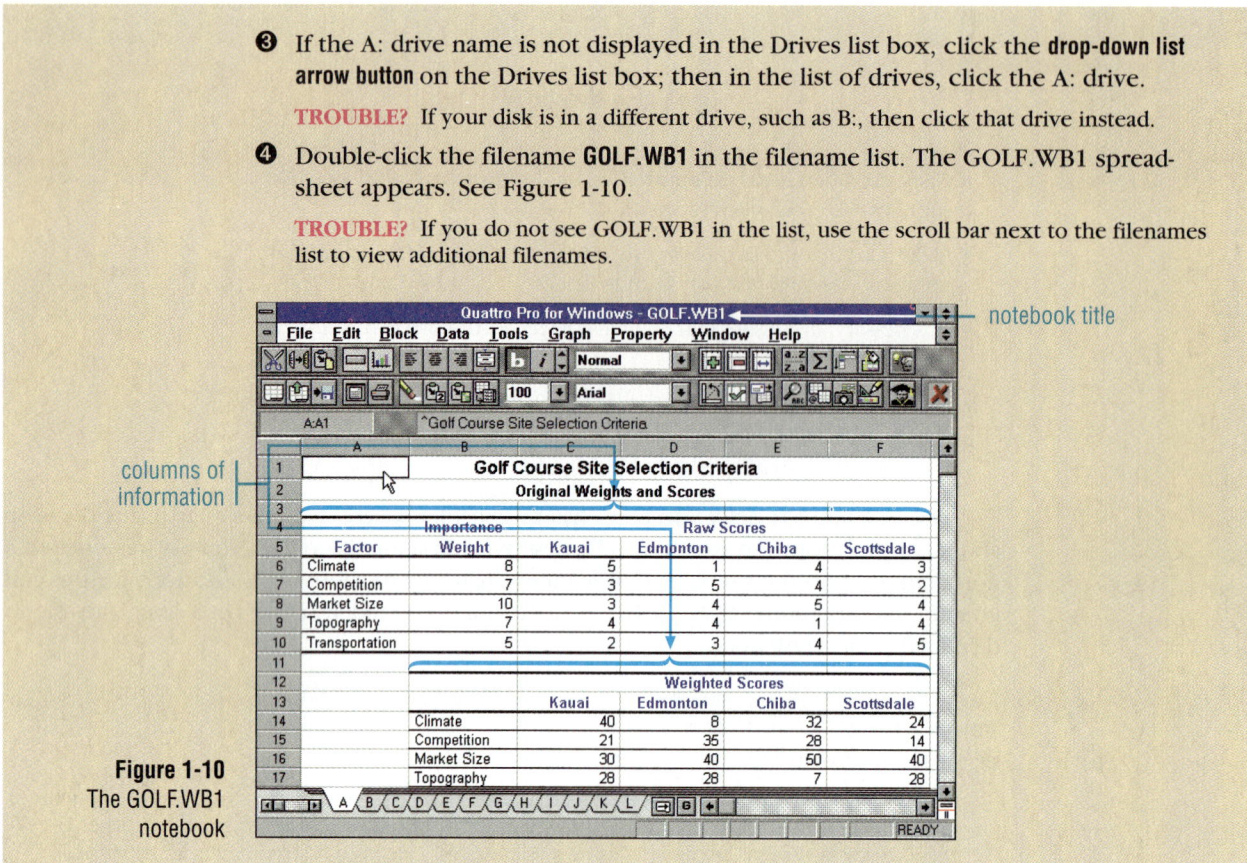

Figure 1-10
The GOLF.WB1
notebook

The first spreadsheet in Pamela's notebook, page A, contains columns of information and a graph (in a minute you'll scroll the spreadsheet to see the graph).

Saving the Notebook with a New Filename

Before you work through a tutorial that uses a previously created notebook, you'll need to save a copy of the notebook under a different name to maintain the integrity of the original file. This allows you to rework the tutorial starting with the original notebook file at a later time. When you save a notebook, it is copied from RAM onto your disk. Any graphs that appear in the notebook are also saved. When you save a notebook, Quattro Pro copies the notebook file from RAM to a disk or hard drive.

Quattro Pro has two save commands on the File menu: Save and Save As. The **Save** command copies the notebook onto a disk using the current filename. If an old version of the file exists, the new version will replace the old one. The **Save As** command asks for a filename before copying the notebook onto a disk. When you enter a new filename, the current file is saved under that new name, and the previous version of the file remains on the disk under its original name. Figure 1-11 shows a flowchart that helps you decide whether to use the Save or the Save As command.

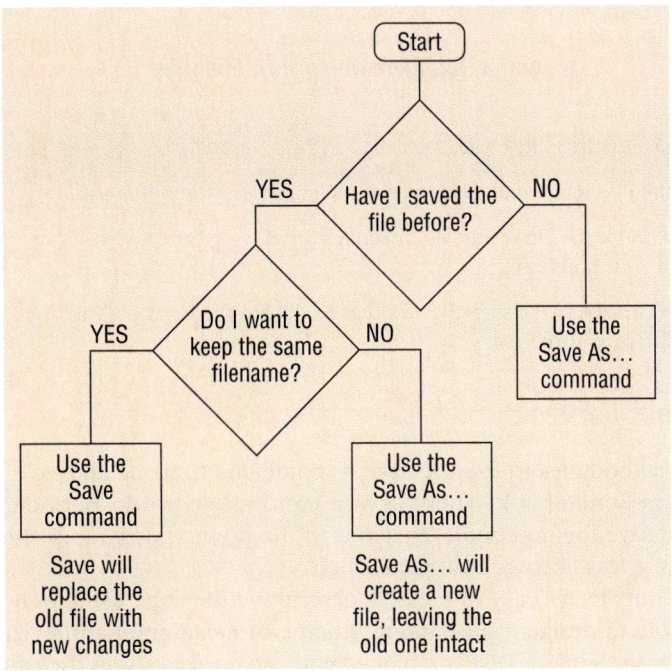

Figure 1-11
Deciding whether
to use Save
or Save As

As a general rule, use the Save As command the first time you save a file or whenever you have modified a file and want to save both the old and new versions. Use the Save command when you have modified a file and want to save only the current version.

In this case, you want to use the Save As command to save the file under a new filename. Quattro Pro filenames can contain up to eight characters. These characters can be letters, numbers, and some symbols such as "-" (hyphen) and "_" (underscore). Filenames *cannot* include spaces. When you type a filename, you can use either uppercase or lowercase letters, but Quattro Pro will always save the name with only lowercase letters. Don't worry if you save a notebook using a filename typed in uppercase and later see the filename in lowercase in a filename list in one of Quattro Pro's dialog boxes. In this book, you'll always see filenames in uppercase in the text.

Quattro Pro will add the extension "WB1" to the filename to identify the type of file. You don't need to type the extension because Quattro Pro adds it automatically when saving the file.

You type the filename in a dialog box area that's called an edit field in Quattro Pro. An **edit field** is an area where you can type and edit text information for use in Quattro Pro procedures. This area is also known as a **text box** in other Windows applications.

Saving a Notebook with a New Filename

- Click File then click Save As....
- In the File Name edit field, type the filename for the notebook.
- Make sure the Drives list box displays the drive where you want to save your notebook.
- If necessary, make sure that you have selected the correct directory in the Directories list.
- Click OK.

It's a good idea to use the Save As command to name and save your file soon after you open a new notebook. Then, as you continue to work, periodically use the Save command to save the notebook. That way, if the power goes out or the computer stops working, you're less likely to lose your work.

It's not always easy to create a descriptive filename using only eight characters, but it is possible to design a file-naming scheme of meaningful abbreviations. For example, the files on your Student Disk are named and categorized using the first letter of the filename, as shown in Figure 1-12.

First Character of Filename	File Category	Description of File Category
C	Tutorial **Case**	The files you use to work through each tutorial
T	**T**utorial Assignments	The files that contain the notebook you need to complete the Tutorial Assignments at the end of each tutorial
P	Case **P**roblems	The files that contain the notebooks you need to complete the Case Problems at the end of each tutorial
S	**S**aved Notebook	Any notebook that you save

Figure 1-12
Categories of files on the Student Disk

The second character in each filename on your Student Disk indicates the tutorial in which the file is created or used. For example, a filename that begins with C1 is a notebook you open in Tutorial 1; a filename that begins with S2 is a notebook you save in Tutorial 2. The remaining three to six characters of the filename relate to the content of the notebook.

The notebook you opened is named GOLF.WB1. To make a copy of this notebook for your work in this tutorial, you will save a copy of the notebook as S1GOLF.WB1 (using the naming convention, this is a version of the GOLF notebook you saved in Tutorial 1) on your disk in drive A. Then you will have two copies of the notebook on the disk—the original notebook named GOLF.WB1 and a copy of the notebook named S1GOLF.WB1 for use during this tutorial.

To save a copy of the notebook as S1GOLF.WB1:

❶ Click **File** then click **Save As...** to display the Save File dialog box.

❷ Type **S1GOLF** in the File Name edit field, *but don't press [Enter]*. You can use lower-case or uppercase to type the filename.

Before you proceed, check the rest of the dialog box specifications to ensure that you save the notebook on the correct disk.

❸ Make sure the A: drive name (or the name of the drive you're using) is displayed in the Drives list box. If it isn't, click the **Drives drop-down list arrow button**, then click A: in the list, as in Figure 1-13.

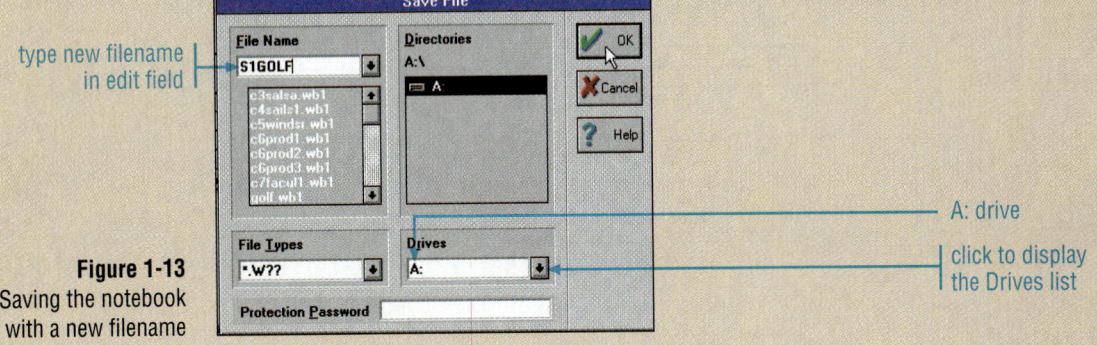

type new filename in edit field

A: drive

click to display the Drives list

Figure 1-13
Saving the notebook with a new filename

❹ When your Save File dialog box looks like the one in Figure 1-13, click **OK**. The Save File dialog box closes, and the notebook is saved. Your notebook is still displayed in the notebook window, but the notebook title is now S1GOLF.WB1. The window title bar changes to display the new file name.

Now let's scroll the first spreadsheet in Pamela's notebook to see what it contains.

Scrolling a Spreadsheet

The notebook window has a horizontal scroll bar and a vertical scroll bar, as shown in Figure 1-14. The **vertical scroll bar** allows you to move up and down through the spreadsheet. The **horizontal scroll bar** allows you to move left and right across the spreadsheet.

You click the scroll arrow buttons at the ends of the vertical or horizontal scroll bar to move the spreadsheet one row or column at a time. You drag the scroll box to move the spreadsheet more than one row or column at a time. Let's scroll through the spreadsheet to view the graph.

To scroll the spreadsheet to view the graph:

❶ Drag the scroll box on the vertical scroll bar down the screen, as shown in Figure 1-14. Release the mouse button. The spreadsheet window displays the section of the spreadsheet that contains the graph.

TROUBLE? To drag the scroll box, first position the pointer on the scroll box, then hold the mouse button down as you move the mouse toward you on the desk.

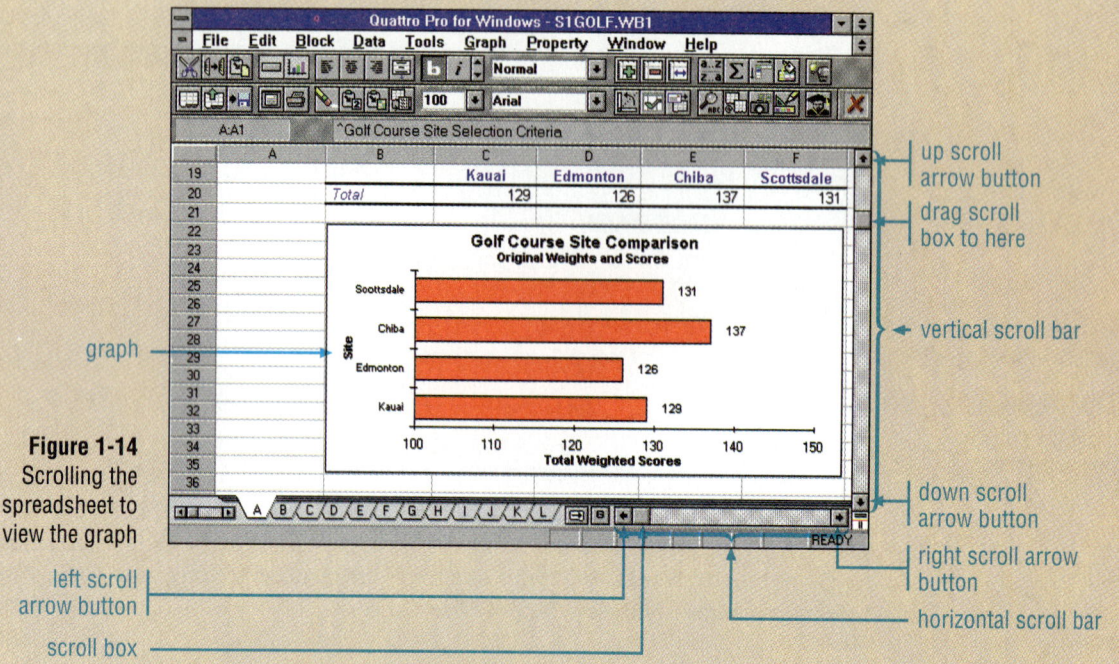

Figure 1-14
Scrolling the spreadsheet to view the graph

❷ If the graph is not positioned like the one in Figure 1-14, use the scroll arrow buttons or scroll box to position it correctly.

❸ After you view the graph, scroll back up the spreadsheet until you can see rows 4 through 20, as in Figure 1-15.

You might see fewer rows and columns in your spreadsheet window, depending on your computer's display type. Now that you know how to scroll the spreadsheet, you can scroll whenever you need to view an area of the spreadsheet that is not visible.

Using a Decision Support Spreadsheet

Pamela explains the general layout of the decision support spreadsheet, which is shown in Figure 1-15, to the rest of the team. Cells A6 through A10 contain the five factors on which the team is basing its decision: climate, competition, market size, topography, and transportation. The team assigned an **importance weight** to each factor, using a scale from 1 to 10, to show its relative importance to the success of the golf course. Pamela entered the weights in cells B6 through B10. Market size, with an importance weight of 10, is the most important factor. The least important factor is transportation.

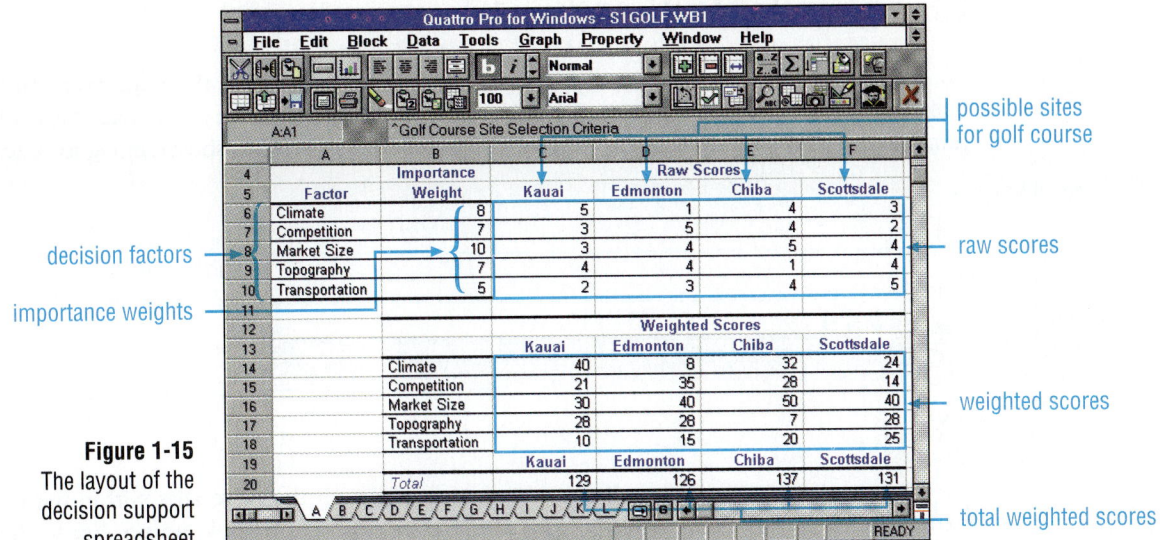

Figure 1-15
The layout of the decision support spreadsheet

Cells C5 through F5 list the four sites under consideration. The team used a scale of 1 to 5 to assign a **raw score**, unadjusted for importance, to each location for climate, competition, market size, topography, and transportation. Larger raw scores indicate the site is very strong in that factor. Smaller raw scores indicate the site is weak in that factor. For example, the raw score for Kauai's climate is 5. The other locations have scores of 1, 4, and 3 so it appears that Kauai, with warm, sunny days for 12 months of the year, has the best climate for the golf course. Edmonton, on the other hand, has cold weather and received a climate raw score of only 1.

The raw scores do not take into account the importance of each factor. Climate is important, but the team considers market size to be the most important factor. Therefore, the raw scores are not used for the final decision but are instead multiplied by the importance weight to produce **weighted scores**. Which site has the highest weighted score for any factor? If you look at the scores in cells C14 through F18, you will see that Chiba's score of 50 for market size is the highest weighted score for any factor.

Cells C20 through F20 contain the total weighted scores for each location. With the current weighting and raw scores, it appears that Chiba is the most promising site, with a total score of 137.

As the team examines the spreadsheet, Pamela reminds the group that these scores reflect their discussion at the previous meeting, and that they are going to consider revisions to the weights and scores before making a final decision. To keep a record of their revisions, Pamela has copied the current information to spreadsheet B, the second page in the notebook.

Changing the Active Spreadsheet

To change the active spreadsheet page, you click the name tab of the page you want to make active. Because there are 256 pages in a notebook, you can't see all the page tabs at the same time. To see other page tabs, you use the notebook tab scroller shown in Figure 1-16.

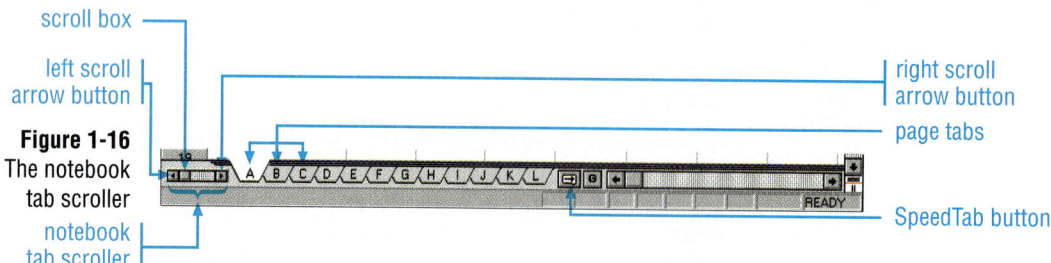

Figure 1-16
The notebook
tab scroller

scroll box
left scroll
arrow button
notebook
tab scroller
right scroll
arrow button
page tabs
SpeedTab button

The notebook tab scroller allows you to move through the page tabs within the notebook. You click the scroll arrow buttons at the ends of the notebook tab scroller to move through the notebook one spreadsheet at a time. You drag the scroll box to move through the notebook more than one spreadsheet at a time. Clicking the **SpeedTab button** just to the right of the last visible tab will move you to the Graphs page at the end of the notebook (if you're at the Graphs page, the SpeedTab button will return you to the spreadsheet that was active before you went to the Graphs page).

Let's change to spreadsheet page B along with Pamela. When you switch to a different spreadsheet in a notebook, Quattro Pro makes the spreadsheet active and displays the information on that spreadsheet.

To change to spreadsheet page B in the notebook:

❶ Make sure that the tab for page B is visible at the bottom of the notebook window. If the tab isn't visible, use the notebook tab scroller to make it visible.

❷ Click the **B** tab to make spreadsheet B the active spreadsheet. The window displays the second spreadsheet in the notebook, which has the subheading "Revised Weights and Scores."

❸ Use the vertical scroll bar to scroll through spreadsheet B until the area from row 4 to row 20 is visible on the screen.

Changing Values and Observing Results

Mike tells the group about a recent news story describing a competing design group that has announced plans to build a $325 million golf resort just 10 miles away from InWood's Chiba site. He suggests that they revise Chiba's raw score for competition to reflect this market change. The team decides to lower the competition raw score for the Chiba site from 4 to 2.

When you change a value in a spreadsheet, Quattro Pro enters the change into the spreadsheet and then recalculates the spreadsheet to display updated results.

Pamela now revises the cell containing Chiba's raw score for competition.

To change the competition raw score for Chiba from 4 to 2:

❶ Click cell **E7**. The selector (a black outline) appears around cell E7 indicating it is the active cell. The input line shows B:E7 is the active cell and shows that the current value of cell E7 is 4. Notice that the input line always shows the complete cell address including the page.

   TROUBLE? If you have trouble finding cell E7, recall that the cell address "E7" means column E, row 7 on the active spreadsheet.

❷ Type **2**. Notice that 2 appears in the input line, shown in Figure 1-17.

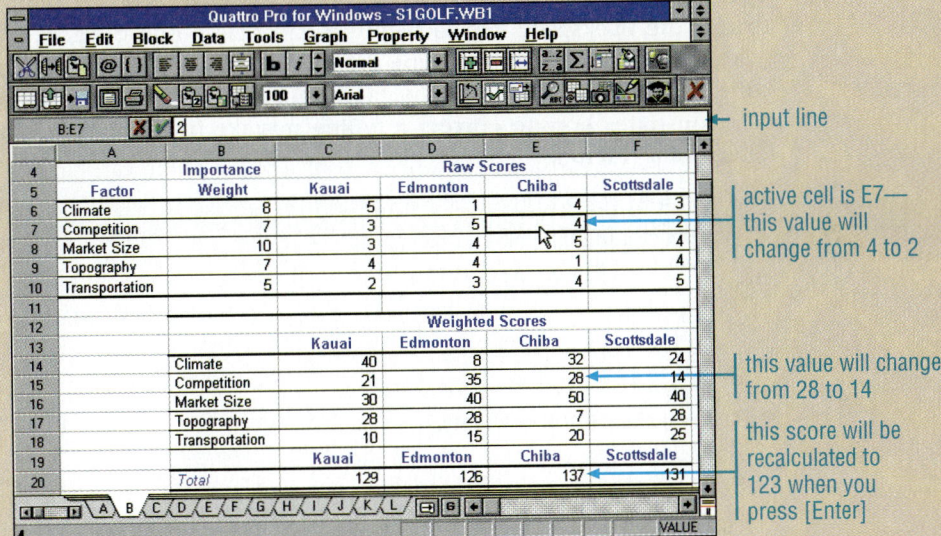

Figure 1-17
Changing the
contents of a cell

❸ Press **[Enter]**. The number 2 appears in cell E7. The spreadsheet recalculates the weighted competition score for Chiba in cell E15 as 14, and the total weighted score for Chiba in cell E20 as 123. Although you can't see it on the screen at this time, the graph has also been redrawn.

The team takes another look at the total weighted scores in row 20. Scottsdale just became the top-ranking site, with a total weighted score of 131.

As the team continues to discuss the spreadsheet, several members express their concern over the importance weight used for transportation, which on the current spreadsheet has an importance weight of 5. Mike thinks they had agreed to use an importance weight of 2 at their last meeting. He asks Pamela to change the importance weight for transportation.

To change the importance weight for transportation:

❶ Click cell **B10** to make it the active cell.

❷ Type **2** and press **[Enter]**. Cell B10 now contains the value 2 instead of 5, and the rest of the spreadsheet is recalculated to reflect this change.

With the change in the transportation importance weight, it appears that Kauai has pulled ahead as the most favorable site, with a total weighted score of 123.

Mike, who has never used a spreadsheet program, asks Pamela about mistakes. Pamela explains that a common mistake to make on a spreadsheet is a typing error. Typing mistakes are easy to correct, so Pamela asks the group if she can take just a minute to demonstrate.

Correcting Mistakes

It's easy to correct a mistake when you're typing information in a cell and before you press the Enter key. If you need to correct a mistake as you're typing information in a cell, press the Backspace key to back up and delete one or more characters until you've deleted the error, and then type the correct information. When you're typing, don't use the cursor arrow keys to edit because they move the cell pointer to another cell. Pamela demonstrates how to correct a typing mistake by starting to type the word "Faktors" instead of "Factors."

To correct a mistake as you're typing:

❶ Click cell **B13** to make it the active cell.

❷ Type **Fak** to make an intentional error, *but don't press [Enter]*. Your entry appears on the input line (not the cell).

❸ Press **[Backspace]** to delete the *k*.

❹ Type **ctors** and press **[Enter]**.

Now the word "Factors" is in cell B13, but Pamela really wants the word "Factor" in the cell. She explains that after you press the Enter key (or click the check mark button on the input line), you use a different method to change the contents of a cell. The F2 key puts Quattro Pro into **Edit mode**, which lets you use [Home], [End], [←], [→], and the mouse to move around on the input line and make changes to the cell contents. To cancel the edit without changing the cell contents, you can click the X button on the input line or press [Esc] once or, if necessary, twice, until the mode indicator on the right side of the status line says READY.

Pamela uses Edit mode to demonstrate how to change *Factors* to *Factor* in cell B13.

To change the word *Factors* to *Factor* in cell B13:

❶ If B13 is not the active cell, click it to make it the active cell.

❷ Press **[F2]** to begin Edit mode and display *Factors* in the input line.

❸ Press **[Backspace]** to delete the *s*.

❹ Press **[Enter]** to complete the edit.

Pamela points out that sometimes you might inadvertently enter the wrong value in a cell. To cancel that type of error, Quattro Pro provides an Undo command.

The Undo Command

The Undo command on the Edit menu lets you cancel the last change you made to the spreadsheet. This command is also available as the Undo/Redo button on the Productivity Tools SpeedBar. You can use Undo not only to correct typing mistakes, but to correct almost anything you did to the spreadsheet that you wish you hadn't. For example, Undo cancels font changes, deletions, and cell entries. If you make a mistake, use Undo to put things back the way they were.

Pamela intentionally types the wrong label *Faktors* into cell B13, and uses the Undo command to restore the label *Factor*.

To practice canceling a mistake using the Undo command:

❶ If B13 is not the active cell, click it.

❷ Type **Faktors** to make an intentional error, then press **[Enter]**.

❸ To undo the typing, click the **Undo/Redo button** ▧ on the Productivity Tools SpeedBar (or click **Edit** then click **Undo Entry**).

Now that you know how to correct typing mistakes and use the Undo command to cancel your last entry or command, you can apply these skills as you need them.

The InWood team is glad to see that correcting errors is so easy. Mike reviews his notes from the previous meetings and finds that the team had a long discussion about the importance of transportation, but eventually agreed to use 5 as the importance weight. Now Pamela needs to restore the original importance weight for transportation.

To change the importance weight in the spreadsheet:

❶ Click cell **B10** to make it the active cell.

❷ Type **5** then press **[Enter]**.

Scottsdale once again ranks highest with a weighted score total of 131. Kauai ranks second with a total score of 129. Edmonton ranks third with a total score of 126, and Chiba ranks last with a total score of 123. Pamela asks if everyone is satisfied with the current weightings and scores. The team agrees that the current spreadsheet is a reasonable representation of the factors that need to be considered for each site.

Making and Documenting the Decision

Mike asks if the team is ready to recommend a final site. Pamela wants to recommend Scottsdale as the primary site and Kauai as an alternative location. Mike asks for a vote, and the team unanimously agrees with Pamela's recommendation.

The notebook will document the decision process because it will show both the original factor weights and ratings showing Chiba with the highest score on the spreadsheet on page A, and the modified factor weights and scores showing Scottsdale with the highest score on the spreadsheet on page B.

Saving the Notebook with the Same Filename

Pamela decides that it's time to save a copy of the revised notebook to the disk. This will store the changes Pamela has made to the notebook in RAM to the copy of the notebook on the disk. Because Pamela is saving the notebook with the same filename, S1GOLF.WB1, she'll use the Save command on the File menu instead of the Save As... command. The new version of the notebook will replace the old one on her disk. Because you use the Save command frequently, the Productivity Tools SpeedBar has a **Save Notebook button**, which provides you with a single mouse-click shortcut for saving your notebook.

To save the S1GOLF.WB1 notebook with the same filename:
❶ Click the **Save Notebook button** 🖫 on the Productivity Tools SpeedBar as shown in Figure 1-18 (or click **File** then click **Save**).

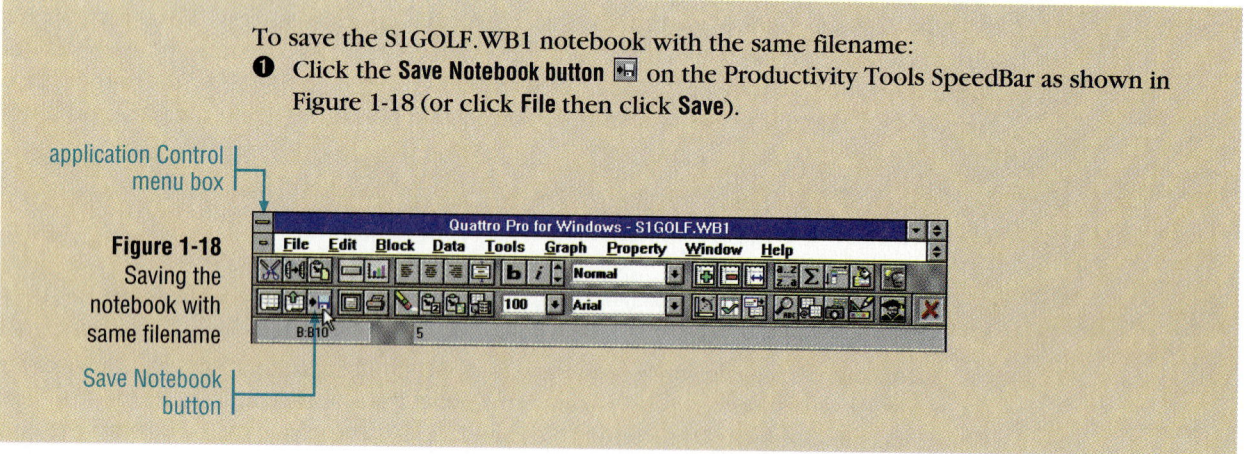

application Control
menu box

Figure 1-18
Saving the
notebook with
same filename

Save Notebook
button

If you want to take a break and resume the tutorial at a later time, you can exit Quattro Pro by double-clicking the Quattro Pro application Control menu box in the upper-left corner of the screen as shown in Figure 1-18 (or by clicking File then clicking Exit). When you want to resume the tutorial, launch Quattro Pro, maximize the Quattro Pro and NOTEBK1.WB1 windows, place your Student Disk in the disk drive, open the file S1GOLF.WB1, and make spreadsheet page B active. Then scroll the spreadsheet until rows 4 to 20 are visible. You can then continue with the tutorial.

Mike wants to have complete documentation for the team's written recommendation, so he asks Pamela to print the spreadsheet and graph.

Printing the Spreadsheet and Graph

You can initiate the Print command using the File menu or the Print button on the Productivity Tools SpeedBar. When you initiate printing, a dialog box lets you specify the area of the spreadsheet you want to print, which pages of the spreadsheet within that area you want to print, and the number of copies you want to print.

A group of cells is referred to as a **block** in Quattro Pro (in some other electronic spreadsheets the equivalent term **range** is used). For example, you can refer to cells B4, B5, and B6 as "the block B4 through B6." Quattro Pro displays this block in the input line as B4..B6. The double period indicates cells B4, B5, and B6. The area of the spreadsheet you print is called **print block**.

Pamela wants to print the entire spreadsheet and graph.

To check the print settings then print the spreadsheet and graph on page B of the S1GOLF.WB1 notebook:

❶ Make sure your printer is turned on and contains paper.

❷ Click the **Print button** 🖨 on the Productivity Tools SpeedBar (or click **File** then click **Print...**) to display the Spreadsheet Print dialog box.

TROUBLE? If your screen display changed to a picture of the printed page, you clicked the Print Preview button 🔲 instead of 🖨. Quattro Pro's Print Preview feature has started, and the Print Preview SpeedBar is now at the top of the screen. Click the Close SpeedBar button 🗙 on the right end of the Print Preview SpeedBar to return to the spreadsheet, then repeat Step 2. You'll use Print Preview in Tutorial 3.

❸ Make sure your Spreadsheet Print dialog box settings for Print block(s), Print Pages, and Copies are the same as those in Figure 1-19.

TROUBLE? If your Print block(s) edit field doesn't read B:A1..F36, type B:A1..F36 so that it does. The double period indicates a block of cells. Notice that the *complete* block address *including the spreadsheet page name* must appear in the Print block(s) edit field box.

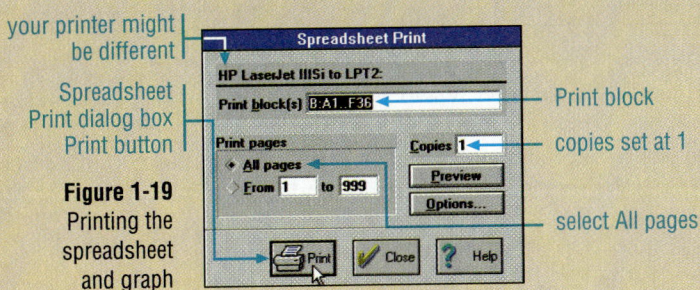

your printer might be different

Spreadsheet Print dialog box Print button

Figure 1-19
Printing the spreadsheet and graph

Print block

copies set at 1

select All pages

❹ Click the **Print button** in the Spreadsheet Print dialog box to print the spreadsheet and graph. The printout is shown in Figure 1-20.

TROUBLE? If the spreadsheet and graph do not print, contact your technical support person or instructor.

Golf Course Site Selection Criteria
Revised Weights and Scores

Factor	Importance Weight	Raw Scores			
		Kauai	Edmonton	Chiba	Scottsdale
Climate	8	5	1	4	3
Competition	7	3	5	2	2
Market Size	10	3	4	5	4
Topography	7	4	4	1	4
Transportation	5	2	3	4	5

	Weighted Scores			
Factor	Kauai	Edmonton	Chiba	Scottsdale
Climate	40	8	32	24
Competition	21	35	14	14
Market Size	30	40	50	40
Topography	28	28	7	28
Transportation	10	15	20	25
	Kauai	Edmonton	Chiba	Scottsdale
Total	129	126	123	131

Golf Course Site Comparison
Revised Weights and Scores

(Bar graph — Total Weighted Scores)
- Scottsdale: 131
- Chiba: 123
- Edmonton: 126
- Kauai: 129

Figure 1-20
The printed spreadsheet and graph

Pamela volunteers to put together the report with the team's final recommendation, and the meeting adjourns. After the meeting Mike mentions to Pamela that he is impressed with the way the spreadsheet program helped the team analyze the data and make a decision, but he admits that he doesn't really understand how it works. Pamela offers to explain the basic concepts.

Values, Labels, Formulas, and Functions

Pamela explains that a Quattro Pro spreadsheet is a grid consisting of 256 columns and 8,192 rows. A spreadsheet notebook has 256 spreadsheet pages and one additional page for graphs. As noted earlier, the rectangular areas at the intersections of each column and row are called cells. A cell can contain a value, a label, or a formula. Pamela tells Mike that to understand how the spreadsheet program works, he must understand how Quattro Pro manipulates values, labels, formulas, and functions.

Values

Values are numbers, dates, and times that Quattro Pro can use for calculations. For example, 378, 11/29/95, and 4:40:31 are values. As you type information into a cell, Quattro Pro determines if the characters you're typing can be used as a value. For example, if you type *456*, Quattro Pro recognizes it as a value and displays it on the right side of the cell. Pamela shows Mike that cells B6 through B10 contain values.

To examine the contents of cells B6 through B10:

❶ If rows 4 through 20 are not visible, scroll the spreadsheet until they are.

❷ Click cell **B6** to make it the active cell. The input line at the top of the screen displays B:B6 and its contents, as in Figure 1-21.

input line shows
active cell and
cell contents

cell B6 is active

Figure 1-21
Examining the
contents of cell B6

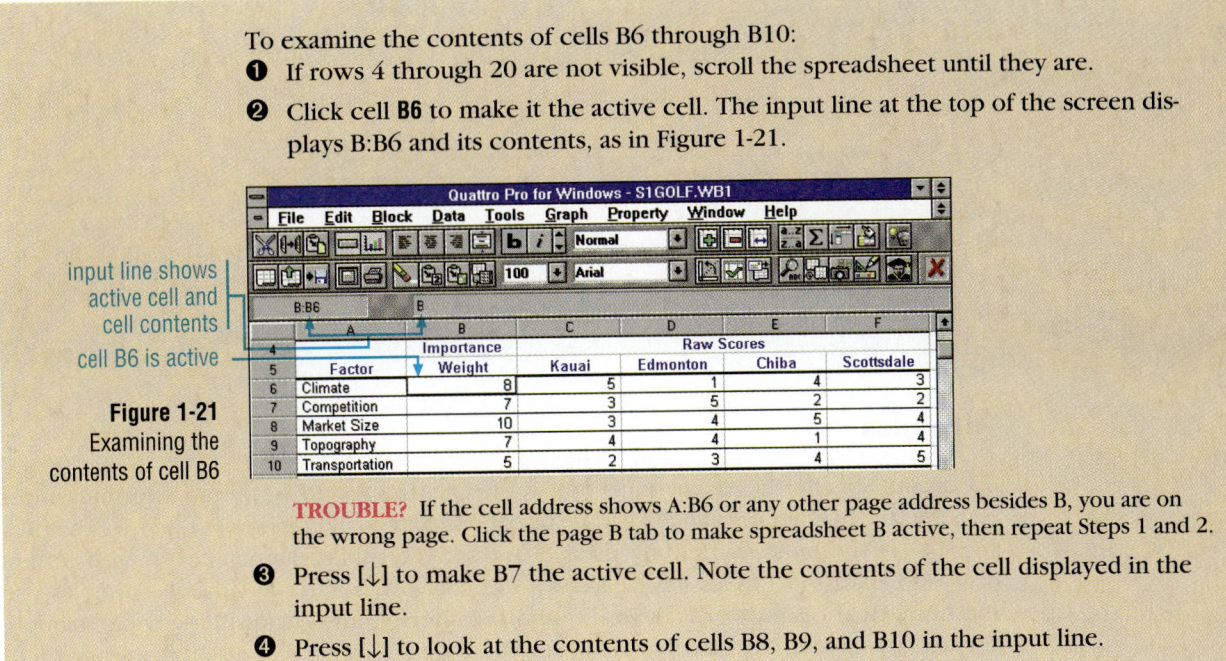

TROUBLE? If the cell address shows A:B6 or any other page address besides B, you are on the wrong page. Click the page B tab to make spreadsheet B active, then repeat Steps 1 and 2.

❸ Press [↓] to make B7 the active cell. Note the contents of the cell displayed in the input line.

❹ Press [↓] to look at the contents of cells B8, B9, and B10 in the input line.

Labels

A **label** is any set of characters that Quattro Pro does not interpret as a value. Labels are often used as headings for the columns and rows in the spreadsheet, such as "Total Sales," "Acme Co.," and "Eastern Division."

Labels are preceded by a **label-prefix**. The most common label-prefix is the apostrophe ('), which indicates a left-aligned label. Quattro Pro automatically puts a label-prefix before any label that starts with a letter, but you have to put the label-prefix before labels that don't start with a letter. Some data commonly referred to as "numbers" must be entered as labels in Quattro Pro. For example, you should enter a telephone number such as 227-1240 or a social security number such as 372-70-9654 as labels by preceding them with a label-prefix. If you don't use the label-prefix, Quattro Pro treats these numbers as calculations, and will display -1,013 (227 minus 1240) instead of 227-1240 and -9,352 (372 minus 70 minus 9654) instead of 372-70-9654. Labels cannot be used for calculations. Pamela shows Mike that cells A6 through A10 contain labels.

To examine the contents of cells A6 through A10:

1. Click cell **A6** to make it the active cell. The input line displays the cell address A6 and the cell contents, 'Climate. Notice the apostrophe before this label, which indicates that the label is left-aligned in the cell. See Figure 1-22.

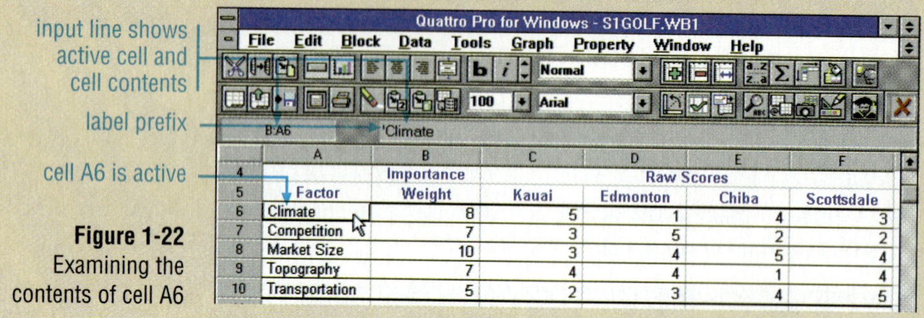
input line shows active cell and cell contents
label prefix
cell A6 is active
Quattro Pro for Windows - S1GOLF.WB1
File Edit Block Data Tools Graph Property Window Help
Normal
100
Arial
B:A6
'Climate
Importance
Raw Scores
Factor
Weight
Kauai
Edmonton
Chiba
Scottsdale
Climate 8 5 1 4 3
Competition 7 3 5 2 2
Market Size 10 3 4 5 4
Topography 7 4 4 1 4
Transportation 5 2 3 4 5

Figure 1-22
Examining the contents of cell A6

2. Press [↓] to make A7 the active cell. Note the contents of the cell displayed in the input line.
3. Press [↓] to look at the contents of cells A8, A9, and A10.

Formulas

Formulas specify the calculations you want Quattro Pro to perform. A formula must begin with a number or one of a set of special characters, including = + (and @. The plus sign (+) is the most commonly used character. Formulas cannot begin with letters because Quattro Pro treats any cell entry starting with a letter as a label. Formulas use **mathematical operators** such as + - * and / to specify how Quattro Pro should manipulate the numbers in the calculation. When you type a formula, you use the asterisk (*) to indicate multiplication and the slash (/) to indicate division.

The numbers used in formulas can be either **constants** (for example, 20 or 0.057) or references to cells containing numbers (for example, B6, or A:B6, or B:C10). If you are using a cell reference in your formula, you can omit the spreadsheet page name if the reference is on the same page as the formula. For example, you can refer to cell B:B6 simply as B6 in any of the formulas you enter on spreadsheet B. Some examples of formulas are +20+10, +G9/2, and +C5*B5. The formula +C5*B5 instructs Quattro Pro to multiply the contents of cell C5 by the contents of cell B5.

The result of the formula is displayed in the cell in which you entered the formula. To view the formula in a cell, you must first make that cell active, and then look at the input line. Pamela shows Mike how to view formulas and their results.

To view the formula in cell C14:

❶ Click cell **C14** to make it the active cell. The input line shows +C6*B6 as the formula for cell C14 (the weighted score). This formula multiplies the contents of cell C6 (the raw score) by the contents of cell B6 (the weight). See Figure 1-23.

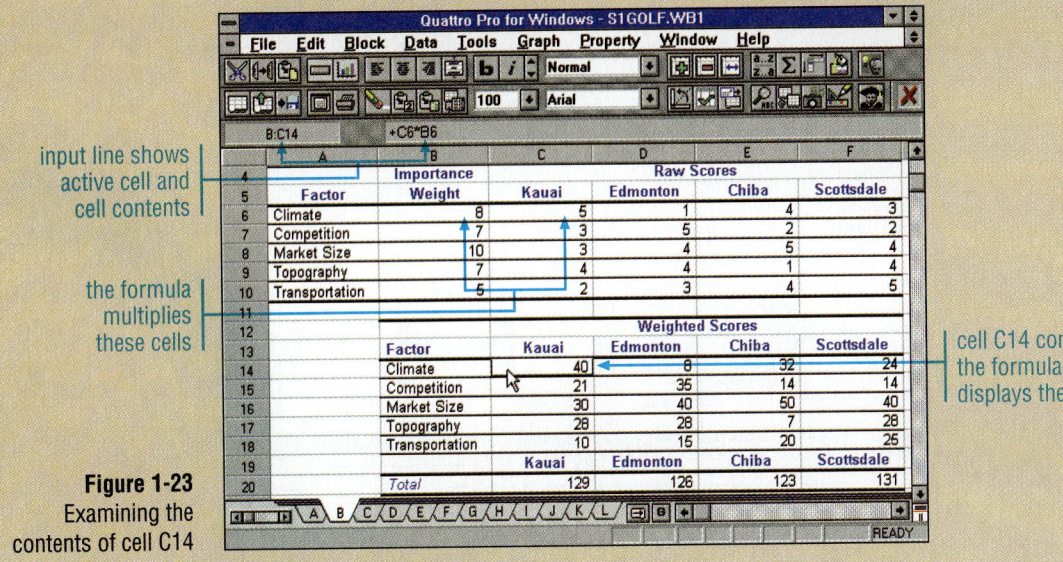

input line shows active cell and cell contents

the formula multiplies these cells

cell C14 contains the formula but displays the result

Figure 1-23
Examining the contents of cell C14

❷ Look at cell C6. The number in this cell is 5.

❸ Look at cell B6. The number in this cell is 8.

❹ Look at the input line. Multiplying the contents of C6 by B6 means to multiply 5 by 8. The result of this formula is the number 40, displayed in cell C14.

Functions

A **function** is a special prewritten formula that provides a shortcut for commonly used calculations. In Quattro Pro, functions always start with the "at" sign (@) and are called **@functions** ("at-functions"). For example, you can use the @SUM function to create the formula @SUM(D14..D18) instead of typing the longer formula +D14+D15+D16+D17+D18. The @SUM function in this example sums the block D14..D18. Other functions include @AVG, which calculates the average value, @MIN, which finds the smallest value, and @MAX, which finds the largest value of a group of cells.

To view the function in the formula in cell C20:

❶ Click cell **C20** to make it the active cell. See Figure 1-24.

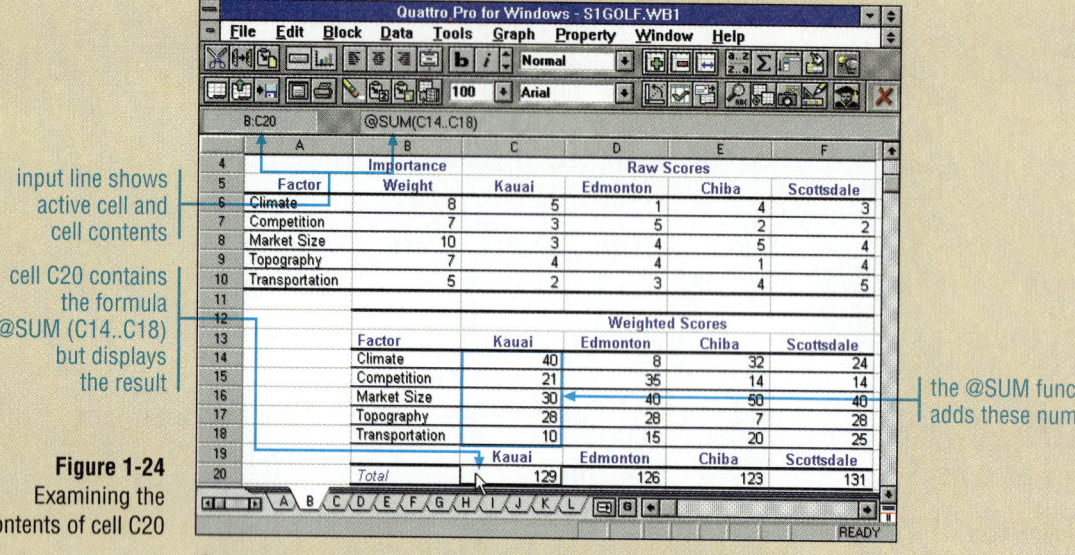

input line shows active cell and cell contents

cell C20 contains the formula @SUM (C14..C18) but displays the result

Figure 1-24
Examining the contents of cell C20

the @SUM function adds these numbers

❷ Look at the formula displayed in the input line, @SUM(C14..C18). The @SUM function adds the contents of cells C14 through C18.

❸ Look at the result of this formula in cell C20. The sum of the numbers in cells C14 through C18 is 129.

Remember that the input line shows the *contents* of the cell, the formula @SUM(C14..C18). The spreadsheet cell displays the *result* of the formula. To determine the actual contents of a cell, you must make that cell the active cell and view the contents on the input line.

Automatic Recalculation

Pamela explains that any time a value in a spreadsheet cell is changed, Quattro Pro automatically recalculates all the formulas. Changing a number in only one cell might result in many changes throughout the spreadsheet. Pamela demonstrates by changing the importance weight for climate from 8 to 2.

To change the importance weight for climate:

❶ Note the current importance weight for climate (8) in cell B6, the weighted scores for climate in each location (Kauai 40, Edmonton 8, Chiba 32, and Scottsdale 24) in cells C14..F14, and the total weighted scores for each location (Kauai 129, Edmonton 126, Chiba 123, and Scottsdale 131) in cells C20..F20.

❷ Click cell **B6** to make it the active cell.

❸ Type **2** then press **[Enter]**. Watch the spreadsheet update the results of the formulas in cells C14 through F14 and cells C20 through F20.

Note the updated results for the climate weighted scores (10, 2, 8, and 6) and the weighted totals (99, 120, 99, and 113). *Remember, when a value is changed in a spreadsheet, every cell that depends on that value is recalculated.*

Quattro Pro Objects

Pamela explains to Mike that there are many spreadsheet programs to choose from, but she prefers Quattro Pro because its notebook structure makes it easy to organize information. She also likes Quattro Pro's use of objects that make it easy to modify parts of the notebook.

An **object** is an identifiable part of the Quattro Pro program. For example, a notebook is an object, a spreadsheet page is an object, the active cell is an object, and a button on a SpeedBar is an object. Aspects of objects that you can change are called **properties**. For example, the name of a spreadsheet page is a property of the page object, and you can change the page name.

To change a property of an object, you use the **Object Inspector** for that object. You open Object Inspectors by positioning the pointer on the object and right-clicking (clicking with the right mouse button instead of the left mouse button). Depending on the object, either a SpeedMenu or the Object Inspector for the object appears. A **SpeedMenu** is a short menu of commands that you might want to use with the object. If a SpeedMenu appears, you use it to open the Object Inspector. When the Object Inspector is displayed, you select which property you want to change from the **Object Inspector menu**, which lists the different properties that you can change.

REFERENCE WINDOW

Using the Object Inspector

- Position the pointer on the object whose properties you want to modify.

- Right-click the object.

- If a SpeedMenu appears, click the Block Properties... command to display the Object Inspector.

- To modify a property, click the property name in the Object Inspector menu.

- Change the property settings, as necessary, then click OK.

Pamela shows Mike how to use the Object Inspector to change a page name in the notebook. Assigning names to spreadsheet pages in a notebook enables you to distinguish pages easily and quickly. Page names can contain up to 15 characters or numbers but cannot contain spaces.

To change the name of page B to "Revised":

❶ Position the pointer on the B page tab.

❷ Right-click the **B** page tab. The Active Page Object Inspector appears, shown in Figure 1-25.

TROUBLE? If the SpeedMenu appeared with the command Block Properties... at the top, you probably right-clicked the cell *above* the page tab. Press [Esc], then repeat Step 2.

TROUBLE? If nothing happened when you right-clicked, you probably right-clicked *below* the page tab. Repeat Step 2.

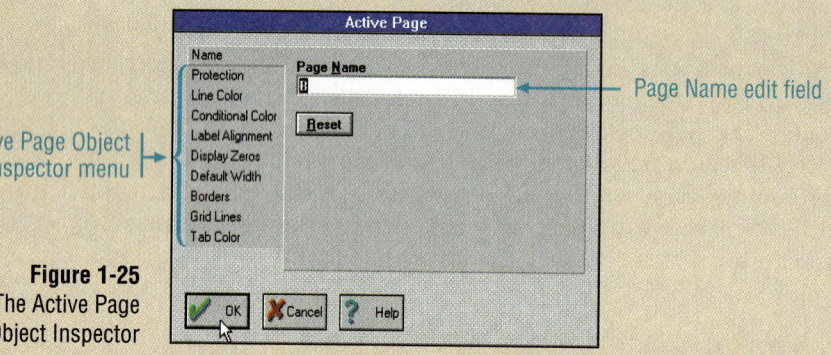

Active Page Object Inspector menu

Page Name edit field

Figure 1-25
The Active Page Object Inspector

❸ The property "Name" is at the top of the Object Inspector menu, and should be selected. If it isn't, click **Name** in the Object Inspector menu to select it.

❹ The current page name "B" is highlighted in the Page Name edit field, and the box is active. Press **[Backspace]** to remove the current page name.

❺ Type **Revised** in the Page Name edit field as the new page name. If you make any mistakes, edit your typing until "Revised" is spelled correctly.

❻ Look at the word "Name" at the top of the property list. Notice that it has changed color to blue to indicate that this property has been modified.

TROUBLE? If you have a monochrome monitor, you will not be able to see the change in the color of the property in the Object Inspector menu.

❼ Click **OK**. The new name appears on the page tab, as in Figure 1-26.

new page name on page tab

Figure 1-26
The renamed page tab

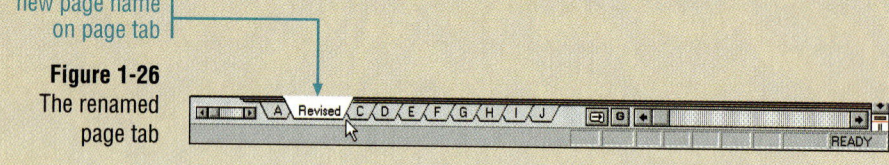

Quattro Pro Help

Pamela tells Mike that another feature she especially likes is the Quattro Pro on-line Help system. The easiest feature to use in the Help system is Object Help. **Object Help** identifies each SpeedBar button and field, allows you to see an Object Help window for each item in the SpeedBar and for any object with an Object Inspector, and gives you access to the full Quattro Pro Help system.

To get help on a SpeedBar button, you simply move the pointer to the button. When the pointer is over the button, the button name appears on the left side of the status line. To open an Object Help window, hold down the Ctrl key and right-click the button. You can then click the Help button in the Object Help window to access Quattro Pro's complete Help system. When you are finished using the Quattro Pro Help system, double-click the Control menu box for the Quattro Pro Help window (or click File then click Exit on the Quattro Pro Help window menu bar).

Pamela shows Mike how he can use Object Help to learn the function of the Save Notebook button on the SpeedBar.

To use Object Help to learn the function of the Save Notebook button:

❶ Move the pointer to the Save Notebook button 🔲 on the Productivity Tools SpeedBar. In the status line at the bottom of the screen, Quattro Pro displays the message, "Save Notebook button (Ctrl+right-click for Object Help)."

❷ Press and hold down [Ctrl] and right-click 🔲. The Object Help window appears. See Figure 1-27.

TROUBLE? If the Object Help window doesn't appear, you probably weren't holding down the Ctrl key when you right-clicked the button. Repeat Step 2.

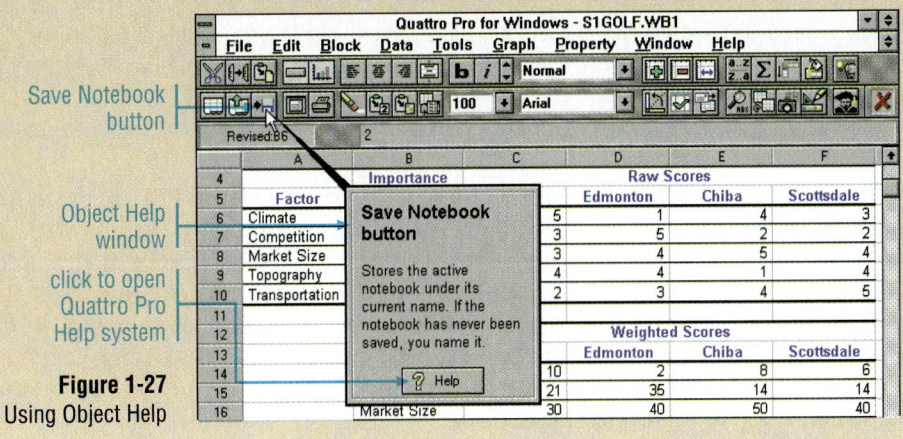

Save Notebook button

Object Help window

click to open Quattro Pro Help system

Figure 1-27
Using Object Help

❸ Read the information about the Save Notebook button, then click the **Help button** in the Object Help window to access the full Quattro Pro Help system. The Quattro Pro Help window appears and displays a page titled "Saving Files." See Figure 1-28.

TROUBLE? If your Quattro Pro Help window is not the same size as the one in Figure 1-28, drag the borders to make it the same size.

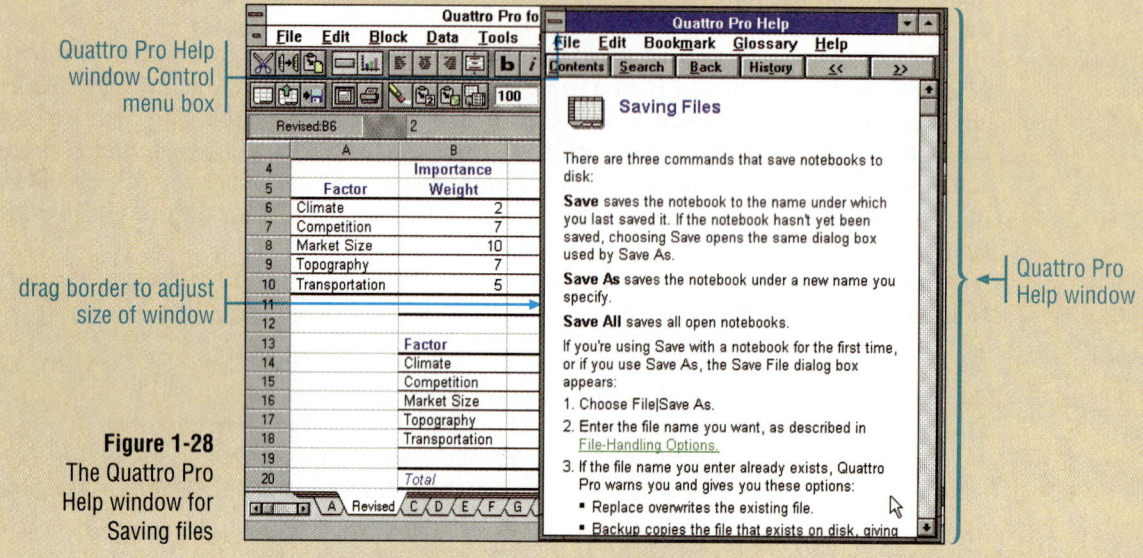

Quattro Pro Help window Control menu box

drag border to adjust size of window

Quattro Pro Help window

Figure 1-28
The Quattro Pro Help window for Saving files

❹ Read through the information about saving files. (The Quattro Pro Help system uses a standard Microsoft Windows Help window. See your Microsoft Windows guide for an explanation of the various features available in the Help window.)

❺ Double-click the **Quattro Pro Help window Control menu box** shown in Figure 1-28 (or click **File** then click **Exit** on the Quattro Pro Help window menu bar) to close the Quattro Pro Help window.

Pamela explains to Mike that help on the commands in Quattro Pro's menu system is available by using the F1 function key. To get help about a specific command, you click the name of the menu containing the command in the menu bar. When the menu drops down, you use the [↓] and the [↑] to highlight the command you want help on (don't use the mouse to click the command because you will activate the command instead of getting help), and then press the F1 function key to access Quattro Pro's Help system.

Pamela shows Mike how he can use the F1 function key to get help on the Save command, which is listed on the File menu.

To use the F1 function key to access the Quattro Pro Help system for information on the Save command:
❶ Click **File** on the menu bar. The drop-down File menu appears.
❷ Use the [↓] to move the highlight to the Save command. See Figure 1-29.

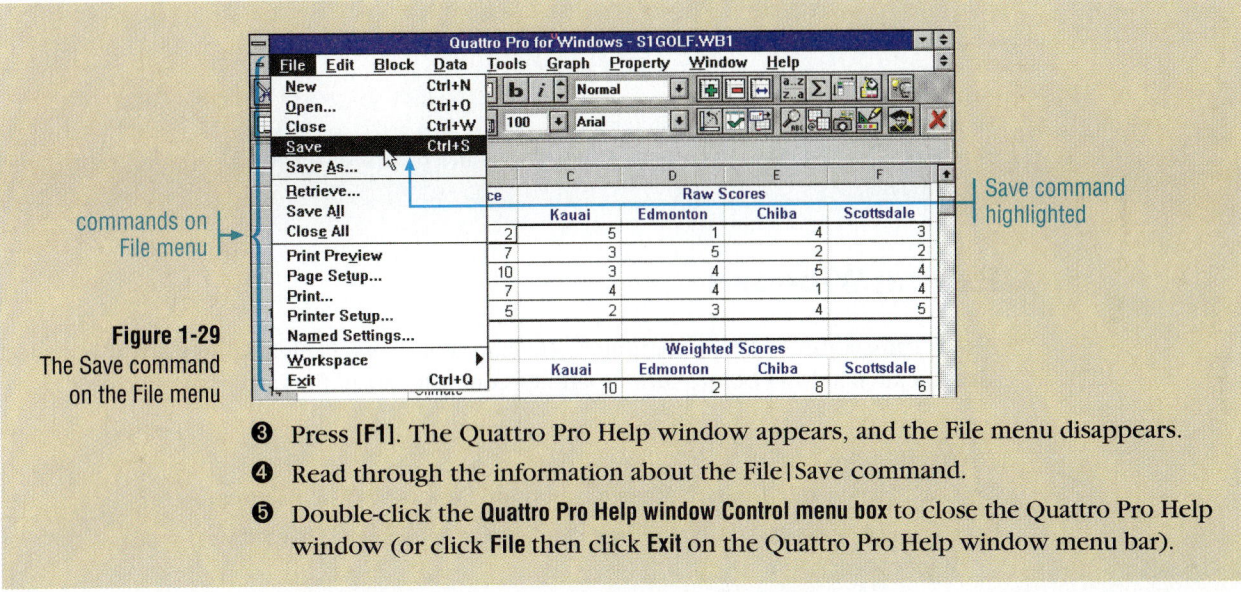

commands on
File menu

Save command
highlighted

Figure 1-29
The Save command
on the File menu

❸ Press **[F1]**. The Quattro Pro Help window appears, and the File menu disappears.

❹ Read through the information about the File|Save command.

❺ Double-click the **Quattro Pro Help window Control menu box** to close the Quattro Pro Help window (or click **File** then click **Exit** on the Quattro Pro Help window menu bar).

Pamela tells Mike that the Help menu on the menu bar also provides access to the Quattro Pro Help system, which works like most Windows Help systems. Pamela doesn't have time to show Mike how to use the Help menu, but assures him that he can easily explore its options.

Closing the Notebook

Pamela is ready to close the notebook window. She does not want to save the changes that she made while demonstrating the spreadsheet to Mike, so she does not use the Save command or the Save As command. Instead, she uses the Close command on the File menu.

When Pamela tries to close the notebook window, a message asks if she wants to save the changes she has made. Pamela responds by clicking the No button.

To close the S1GOLF.WB1 notebook without saving changes:
❶ Click **File** then click **Close**. A dialog box displays the message, "Save changes in A:\S1GOLF.WB1?"
❷ Click **No** to close the notebook without saving the changes.

The Quattro Pro window remains open so Pamela could open or create another notebook. She doesn't want to do this, so her next step is to exit Quattro Pro.

Exiting Quattro Pro

To exit Quattro Pro, you can double-click the application Control menu box or use the Exit command on the File menu.

Pamela generally uses the Exit command.

To exit Quattro Pro using the File menu:
❶ Click **File** then click **Exit** to exit Quattro Pro and return to the Windows Program Manager.

Exiting Windows

Before Pamela turns off her computer, she exits Windows. Pamela knows that it is a good idea to exit Windows before turning off her computer so all files are properly closed.

To exit Windows:
❶ Click **File** on the Program Manager menu bar to display the File menu.
❷ Click **Exit Windows....** A dialog box displays the message, "This will end your Windows session."
❸ Click **OK** to exit Windows and return to the DOS prompt.

■   ■   ■

The InWood site selection team has completed its work. Pamela's decision support notebook helped the team analyze the data and recommend Scottsdale as the best site for InWood's next golf course. Although the Japanese market was a strong factor in favor of locating the course in Japan's Chiba Prefecture, the mountainous terrain and competition from nearby courses reduced the desirability of this location and, therefore, it was not the final choice.

Questions

1. In your own words describe what a spreadsheet program does.
2. List three uses of spreadsheets in business.
3. Identify each of the numbered components of the Quattro Pro window shown in Figure 1-30.

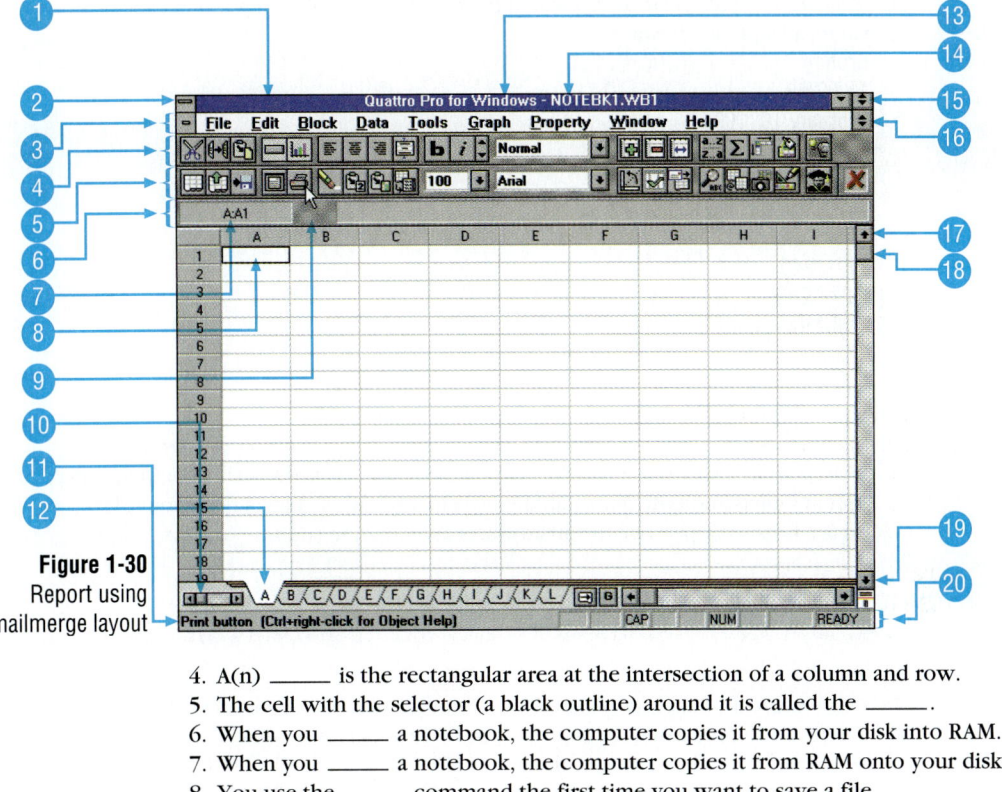

Figure 1-30
Report using
mailmerge layout

4. A(n) _____ is the rectangular area at the intersection of a column and row.
5. The cell with the selector (a black outline) around it is called the _____.
6. When you _____ a notebook, the computer copies it from your disk into RAM.
7. When you _____ a notebook, the computer copies it from RAM onto your disk.
8. You use the _____ command the first time you want to save a file.
9. If you want to save the new version of a file in place of the old version, you use the _____ command.
10. The _____ command is useful if you enter an incorrect value and want to restore the original value.
11. Numbers, dates, and times that Quattro Pro uses for calculations are called _____.
12. How can you tell exactly what a cell contains?
13. A set of characters that you use as a row or column heading is called a(n) _____.
14. Cell B3 contains *'New Sales*. The apostrophe before the word "New" is the _____ and indicates that the label is _____.
15. A(n) _____ specifies the calculations you want Quattro Pro to make.
16. In the formula +B5*125, 125 is a(n) _____.
17. In the formula +B5*125, B5 is a(n) _____.
18. Special prewritten formulas that provide shortcuts for commonly used calculations are _____, and in Quattro Pro these prewritten formulas always start with a(n) _____ and are called _____.
19. How do you write the equivalent of the formula +A1+A2+A3+A4 using an @ function?

20. Indicate whether Quattro Pro would treat each of the following cell entries as a value, a label, or a formula:
Profit
11/09/95
February 10, 1995
@AVG(B5..B20)
11:01:25
+B9*225
+A6*D8
227-1240
'227-1240
@SUM(C1..C10)
372-80-2367
'372-80-2367

21. The two periods in the notation B4..B6 indicate a(n) _____ .

 22. Use the resources in your library to find information on decision support systems. Write a short paper (no more than two pages) that describes what a decision support system is and how one might be used in a business. Also include your ideas on the relationship between spreadsheets and decision support systems.

Tutorial Assignments

The other company that had planned a golf course in Chiba, Japan, has run into financial difficulties. There are rumors that the project might be canceled. A modified copy of the final InWood site selection team notebook is stored on your Student Disk in the file T1GOLF2.WB1. In this notebook, the analysis and graph on page B have been copied to page C. Do the Tutorial Assignments below to modify this notebook to show the effect that the cancellation of the other project would have on the site selection. Print your results for Tutorial Assignment 10. Write your answers to Tutorial Assignments 11 through 13.

1. Launch Windows and Quattro Pro. Make sure your Student Disk is in the disk drive.
2. Open the notebook T1GOLF2.WB1.
3. Use the Save As command to save the notebook as S1GOLF2.WB1 (make sure you save this file with the "2" after "GOLF") so you don't modify the original notebook file for this set of Tutorial Assignments (or the S1GOLF.WB1 file you created while working through Tutorial 1).
4. Use the Object Inspector to name page A as "Original," page B as "Revision1," and page C as "Revision2." (*Hint:* Remember that you *cannot* use spaces in page names, so the name of page B is "Revision1" [without a space] instead of "Revision 1" [with a space].)

All of the following tutorial assignments are done on page Revision2.

5. Make Revision2 the active page.
6. Change the competition raw score for Chiba from 2 to 4.
7. Use the vertical scroll bar to view the effect on the graph showing the Golf Course Site Comparison.
8. Enter the text "Scores if the Competing Project in Chiba, Japan, is Canceled" in cell A2.
9. Save the notebook and graph with the same filename.
10. Print the entire spreadsheet page Revision2, including the graph. (*Hint:* Use the print block Revision2:A1..F36 to print the spreadsheet.)
11. Use Object Help to learn the function of the three buttons shown in Figure 1-31. (*Hint:* One of the buttons actually performs two different, but related, actions.)

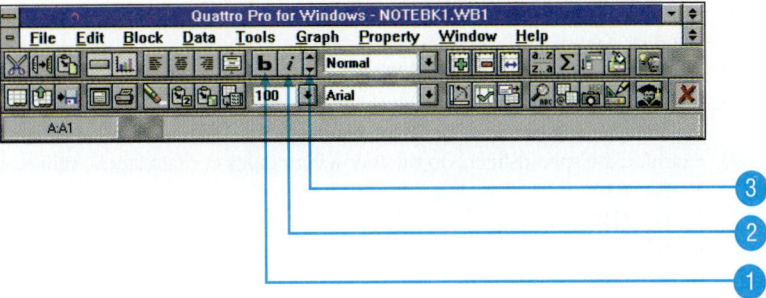

Figure 1-31

12. Use [F1], the Help function key, to learn more about the Print command on the File menu.

E   13. Use the Help menu to search for information about graphs.
   a. How many graph types does Quattro Pro offer? What are they?
   b. Quattro Pro groups the graph types into graph categories. How many categories are there? What are they?

14. Exit Quattro Pro.

Case Problems

1. Selecting a Hospital Laboratory Computer System for Bridgeport Medical Center

David Choi is on the Laboratory Computer Selection Committee for the Bridgeport Medical Center. After an extensive search, the committee identified three vendors with products that appear to meet its needs. The committee prepared a Quattro Pro spreadsheet to help evaluate the strengths and weaknesses of the three potential vendors. The raw scores for two of the vendors, LabStar and Health Systems, have already been entered. Now the raw scores must be entered for the third vendor, MedTech. Which vendor's system is best for the Bridgeport Medical Center? Complete the following to find out:

1. If necessary, launch Windows and Quattro Pro. Make sure your Student Disk is in the disk drive.
2. Open the notebook P1LAB.WB1.
3. Use the Save As command to save the notebook as S1LAB.WB1 so you don't modify the original notebook for this case.
4. Enter the following raw scores for MedTech:
   Cost = 5, Compatibility = 6, Vendor Reliability = 5, Size of Installed Base = 4, User Satisfaction = 5, Critical Functionality = 9, Additional Functionality = 7
5. Use the Save command to save the modified spreadsheet.
6. Print the spreadsheet. (*Hint:* Use the print block A:A1..E25.)
7. Which vendor should be selected? Write a memo reporting the committee's decision.

2. Market Share Analysis at Aldon Industries

Helen Shalala is the Assistant to the Regional Director for Aldon Industries, a manufacturer of corporate voice mail systems. Helen prepared an analysis of the market share of the top vendors with installations in the region. Helen is on her way to a meeting with the Marketing staff, where she will use her spreadsheet to plan a new marketing campaign. Help Helen and her team evaluate the options and plan the best advertising campaign for Aldon Industries. Write a memo to your instructor with your responses to Steps 4 through 10. Attach the spreadsheet you are asked to print in Step 12 to your memo.

1. If necessary, launch Windows and Quattro Pro. Make sure your Student Disk is in the disk drive.
2. Open the notebook P1SHARE.WB1.
3. Use the Save As command to save the notebook as S1SHARE.WB1 so you don't modify the original notebook for this case.
4. Examine the spreadsheet. Do the following ranges contain labels, values, or formulas?
    a. A3..A10
    b. G3..G10
    c. B13..F13
    d. C3..C10
5. What is Aldon Industries' overall share of the market? The spreadsheet extends to column H, which might not be visible on your screen, depending on your monitor type.
6. Examine the spreadsheet to determine in which state Aldon Industries currently has the highest market share.
7. Aldon Industries currently runs localized marketing campaigns in each state.
    a. In which state does Aldon Industries appear to have the most successful marketing campaign?
    b. In which state does Aldon Industries appear to have the least successful marketing campaign?
8. Which company is the overall market leader?
9. What is Aldon Industries' overall ranking in total market share (1st, 2nd, 3rd, etc.)?
10. Which companies rank ahead of Aldon Industries in total market share?
11. Save the spreadsheet on your Student Disk.
12. Print the spreadsheet. (*Hint:* Use the print block A:A1..H14.)

E 3. Completing Your Own Decision Analysis

Think of a decision that you are trying to make. It might be choosing a new car, selecting a major, deciding where to go for vacation, or accepting a job offer. Use the notebook P1DECIDE.WB1 to evaluate up to three options on the basis of up to five factors. Write a memo to your instructor containing your responses to Steps 9 through 12. Attach a printed copy of the spreadsheet to the memo.

1. If necessary, launch Windows and Quattro Pro. Make sure your Student Disk is in the disk drive.
2. Open the notebook P1DECIDE.WB1.
3. Use the Save As command to save the notebook as S1DECIDE.WB1.
4. Click cell A1 and type a spreadsheet title.
5. Type titles for up to three choices in cells C4, D4, and E4.
6. Type titles for up to five factors in cells A6..A10.
7. Type importance weights for each of the five factors in cells B6..B10.
8. Type raw scores for each of your choices in columns C, D, and E.
9. Write a paragraph explaining your choice of factors and assignment of importance weights.
10. On the basis of the current importance weights and raw scores, which option appears most desirable?
11. How confident are you that the spreadsheet shows the most desirable choice?
12. Write a paragraph explaining your reaction to the results of the spreadsheet.
13. Save the spreadsheet on your Student Disk.
14. Print the spreadsheet.

Planning, Building, Testing, and Documenting Notebooks

Creating a Standardized Income and Expense Notebook Template for Regional Offices

OBJECTIVES

In this tutorial you will:

- Plan, document, build, and test a notebook
- Enter labels, values, and formulas
- Change column widths and row heights
- Create a series using SpeedFill
- Copy data and formulas
- Enter formulas using the @SUM function and the SpeedSum feature
- Insert a row in a spreadsheet
- Combine data from more than one spreadsheet
- Create groups of spreadsheets

CASE

SGL Business Training and Consulting   SGL Business Training and Consulting, headquartered in Springfield, Massachusetts, provides consulting services and management training for small businesses. SGL has three regional offices in the United States, and within each region there are several branch offices. The managers of the branch offices report their results to the managers of the regional offices. The regional managers in turn prepare a quarterly report called an "Income and Expense Summary" and send it to Otis Nunley, a staff accountant who works at SGL headquarters.

Each quarter Otis must compile the income and expense information from the three reports. This task has not been easy because the regional managers do not use the same categories for income and expenses. For example, one of the regional managers lists advertising as an expense, while the other regional managers do not.

Otis knows that he can simplify the task of consolidating the branch office information if he can convince the regional managers to use a standardized form for their reports. He gets approval from management to create a Quattro Pro notebook template as the standardized form that the regional managers will use to report income and expenses.

A **template** is a notebook with one or more preformatted spreadsheet pages that contain labels and formulas, but do not contain any values. Otis's idea is to create a template notebook that contains only one preformatted spreadsheet. Otis will send a copy of the template to each of the regional managers. The managers will fill in the template with income and expense information, and then send it back to Otis. With all the information in a standard format, Otis will be able to consolidate it easily into a company-wide report.

In this tutorial, you will work with Otis as he plans, documents, builds, and tests the standardized spreadsheet for reporting income and expenses in his notebook template for the SGL regional managers.

Developing Effective Spreadsheets

An effective spreadsheet is well planned, carefully built, thoroughly tested, and comprehensively documented. When you develop a spreadsheet, therefore, you should do each of the following activities:

- *Plan* the spreadsheet by identifying the overall goal of the project; listing the requirements for input, output, and calculations; and sketching the layout of the spreadsheet.
- *Build* the spreadsheet by entering labels, values, and formulas, and then format the spreadsheet so it has a professional appearance.
- *Test* the spreadsheet to make sure that it provides correct results.
- *Document* the spreadsheet by recording the information others will need to understand, use, and revise the spreadsheet.

Although planning is generally the first activity of the spreadsheet development process, the four development activities are not necessarily sequential. After you begin to enter labels, values, and formulas for the spreadsheet, you might need to revise your original plan. You are also likely to rebuild the spreadsheet by changing some values or formulas after you have tested the spreadsheet. Documentation activities are very important; they can and should take place throughout the process of spreadsheet development. For example, you might jot down some documentation notes as you are planning the spreadsheet, or you might enter documentation on the spreadsheet itself as you are building it.

Planning the Notebook

Because each spreadsheet you develop will be one page in a notebook, you should also plan how you will use different notebook pages. One effective plan is to use page A for notebook documentation and page B for the first spreadsheet. If you are planning a notebook with more than one spreadsheet, the second spreadsheet can go on page C, the third on page D, and so on.

Otis decides that he'll use Quattro Pro's notebook organization to his advantage by using page A for documentation and page B for his spreadsheet. He documents this with a notebook plan, which is shown in Figure 2-1.

Notebook Plan for Income and Expense Report Notebook Template

My Goal:
To develop a Quattro Pro notebook template containing a spreadsheet for regional income and expense reports

What notebook pages will I use?

Page A	Notebook documentation
Page B	Income and Expense Report spreadsheet

Figure 2-1
Otis's notebook plan

Now Otis considers how to structure his spreadsheet.

Planning the Spreadsheet

To create a plan for the spreadsheet for the SGL template, Otis first studies the content and format of the reports from the regional managers. He notices that each regional manager uses a different report format, so that there are three different formats in use.

The reports from Region 1 look similar to the sample report in Figure 2-2. On these reports the labels for each quarter are arranged on the left side of the report. The column titles, arranged across the top of the report, are Income, Expenses, and Profit. The profit for each quarter is calculated by subtracting the expenses from the income. Annual totals are displayed at the bottom of the report.

	Income	Expenses	Profit
Quarter 1	$45,350	$39,421	$5,929
Quarter 2	$47,893	$38,878	$9,015
Quarter 3	$45,988	$36,689	$9,299
Quarter 4	$63,222	$41,011	$22,211
	----------	-----------	--------
Annual Total	$202,453	$155,999	$46,454

column titles
row labels
total profit for each quarter
annual profit
annual expenses
annual income

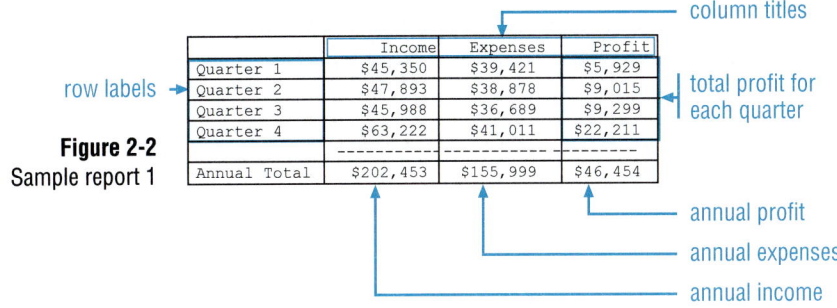

Figure 2-2
Sample report 1

The reports from Region 2 look similar to the sample report in Figure 2-3. The format of sample report 2 is very different from sample report 1. On sample report 2 the quarters are listed across the top as Q1, Q2, Q3, and Q4, rather than down the side. The income and expense categories are referred to as *revenue* and *expenses* and are listed down the left side of the report. This report has one revenue category and six expense categories. For each revenue or expense category, the sum of the amounts for each quarter produces the year-to-date totals shown on the right side of the report. The profit, shown at the bottom of the report, is calculated by subtracting the total expenses from the total revenue.

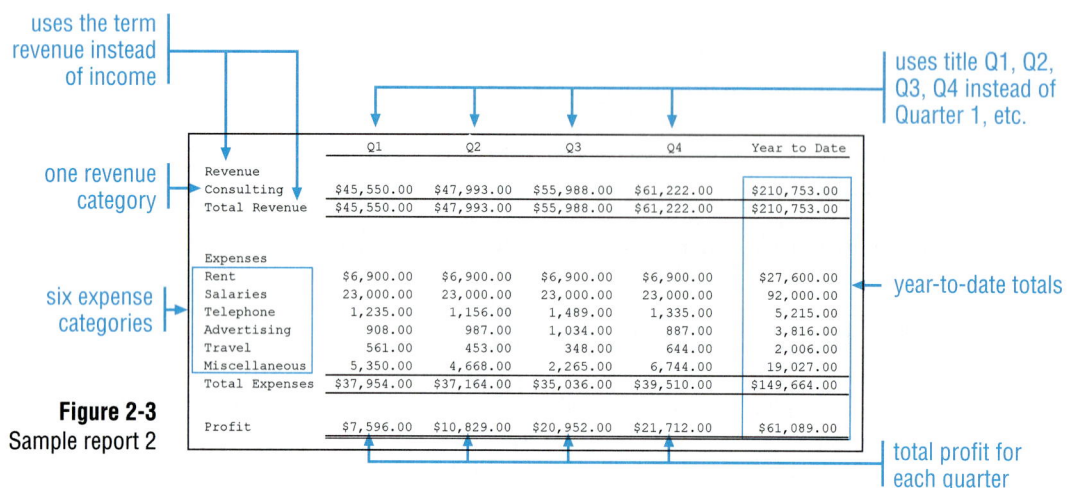

Figure 2-3
Sample report 2

The reports from Region 3 look similar to sample report 3 in Figure 2-4. Notice the two income categories and eight expense categories. The titles for each quarter are listed across the top of the report. For each income or expense category, the sum of the amounts for each quarter produces the year-to-date totals shown on the right side of the report. The total profit for each quarter is shown in the last row of the report.

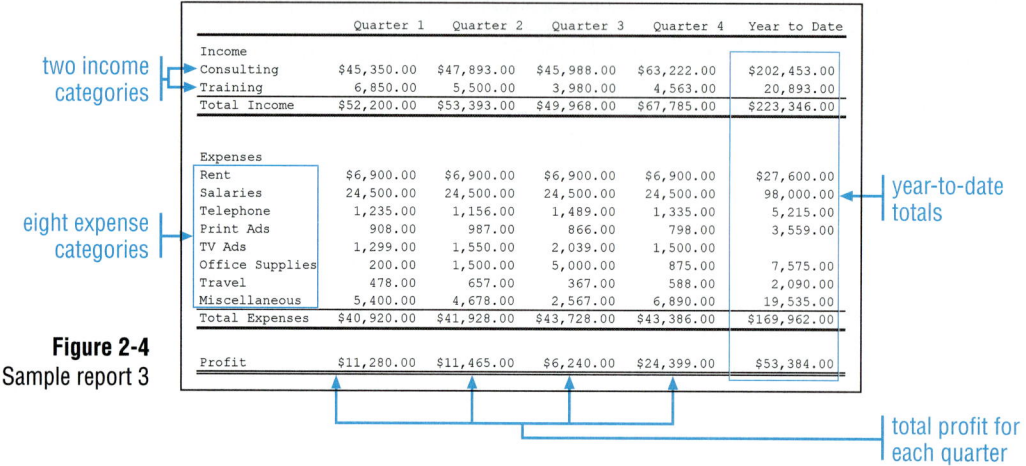

Figure 2-4
Sample report 3

After he studies the reports, Otis writes out a spreadsheet plan that:
- lists the goal(s) for the spreadsheet
- identifies the results, or **output**, that the spreadsheet must produce
- lists the information, or **input**, that is required to construct the spreadsheet
- specifies the calculations that use the input to produce the required output

The spreadsheet plan, shown in Figure 2-5, will guide Otis as he builds and tests the spreadsheet.

Spreadsheet Plan for Income and Expense Report Spreadsheet

<u>My Goal</u>:
To develop a Quattro Pro spreadsheet that regional managers can use to submit income and expense reports

<u>What results do I want to see?</u>
Income categories for consulting and training
Expense categories for rent, salaries, telephone, advertising, office supplies, travel, and miscellaneous
Income and expenses for each quarter
Total income for each quarter
Total expenses for each quarter
Total profit for each quarter

<u>What information do I need?</u>
The amount for each income and expense category

<u>What calculations will I perform?</u>
Total income = consulting income + training income
Total expenses = rent + salaries + telephone + advertising + office supplies + travel + miscellaneous
Profit = total income - total expenses

Figure 2-5
Otis's spreadsheet plan

After he completes the spreadsheet plan, Otis draws a sketch of the planned spreadsheet, indicating the spreadsheet titles, row labels, column headings, and formulas. His sketch is shown in Figure 2-6.

Income and Expense Report

	Quarter 1	Quarter 2	Quarter 3	Quarter 4
Income				
Consulting	99,999.99	99,999.99	99,999.99	99,999.99
Training	:	:	:	:
Total Income	{total income formula}	{total income formula}	{total income formula}	{total income formula}
Expenses				
Rent	99,999.99	99,999.99	99,999.99	99,9 99.99
Salaries	:	:	:	:
Telephone	:	:	:	:
Advertising	:	:	:	:
Office Supplies	:	:	:	:
Travel	:	:	:	:
Miscellaneous	:	:	:	:
Total Expenses	{total expenses formula}	{total expenses formula}	{total expenses formula}	{total expenses formula}
Profit	{profit formula}	{profit formula}	{profit formula}	{profit formula}

Figure 2-6
Otis's spreadsheet sketch

Otis decides to list the income and expense categories down the left side of the spreadsheet and list the quarters across the top. The numbers 99,999.99 indicate that values must be entered into the spreadsheet, and show the largest number that can be entered into a cell. Planning for the largest value that a cell can hold will help determine how wide these columns must be on the final version of the spreadsheet.

Otis indicates formulas by using "curly brackets" {}. The formulas are described in the calculation section of the spreadsheet plan in Figure 2-5. For example, the {total income formula} shown on the spreadsheet sketch is described in the spreadsheet plan as:

total income = consulting income + training income

Look in the calculation section of the spreadsheet plan in Figure 2-5 to find the descriptions for the rest of the formulas on Otis's spreadsheet sketch.

Now that Otis has completed the notebook plan, the spreadsheet plan, and the spreadsheet sketch, he is ready to start documenting, building, and testing the notebook. Let's launch Quattro Pro and work along with Otis.

To launch Quattro Pro and maximize the notebook window:

❶ Launch Windows and Quattro Pro following your usual procedure.

❷ Make sure your Student Disk is in the disk drive.

❸ Make sure the Quattro Pro for Windows and NOTEBK1.WB1 windows are maximized.

Otis knows that he should not wait until the notebook is complete to begin his documentation. There is some basic information about the notebook and the spreadsheets in it that Otis can record immediately.

Documenting the Notebook

The purpose of documenting a notebook is to provide the information necessary to use and modify the notebook. The documentation for your notebook can take many forms. Many companies will have a standard procedure for documentation, but if you work for a company that does not, you must decide what type of documentation is most effective for your notebooks.

Your notebook plan, spreadsheet plan, and spreadsheet sketch provide one type of notebook documentation: a "blueprint" to follow as you build and test the notebook and the spreadsheets in it. This can be useful information for someone who needs to modify one of your notebooks because the "blueprint" states your goals, describes your notebook's organization, specifies the required input, describes the output, and indicates the calculations you used to produce the output.

You can include documentation as part of a spreadsheet. This documentation might be as simple as a header with your name and the date you created the spreadsheet. More complete documentation might include the information from your notebook plan and spreadsheet plan typed onto a page in the notebook.

The notebook plan that Otis created uses page A for documentation and page B for the income and expense report spreadsheet. Otis decides to begin his documentation by including:

- A title identifying the company
- A subtitle naming the notebook
- The filename for the notebook
- The name of the person who created the notebook
- The date the notebook was created
- The purpose of the notebook
- The contents of the notebook

Figure 2-7 shows Otis's sketch of how this documentation will appear in the spreadsheet on page A.

Company name
Notebook name

Filename: Put filename here
Created by: Put the name of the person who created the notebook here
Date: Put the date the notebook was created here

Purpose: Put a short statement that describes the purpose of the
               notebook here

Contents: List each page in the notebook here, followed by a description of the
               spreadsheet on that page

Figure 2-7
Otis's sketch of the
planned documentation

Otis will enter all the documentation information as labels.

Entering Labels

When you type a label in a cell, Quattro Pro automatically aligns the label at the left side of the cell and adds a **label-prefix** indicating that the label is left-aligned. If you want to enter a centered, right-aligned, or repeating label, you have to type the label-prefix when you type the label. The label-prefixes used in Quattro Pro are shown in the spreadsheet in Figure 2-8.

One label, the word "Cat," is shown entered with each label-prefix, so that the effect of each label-prefix can be seen. Figure 2-8 also illustrates that labels that are too long to fit in a cell spill over into the adjacent cell or cells to the right if those cells are empty. If the next cell to the right is not empty, Quattro Pro displays only as much of the label as fits in the cell containing the label.

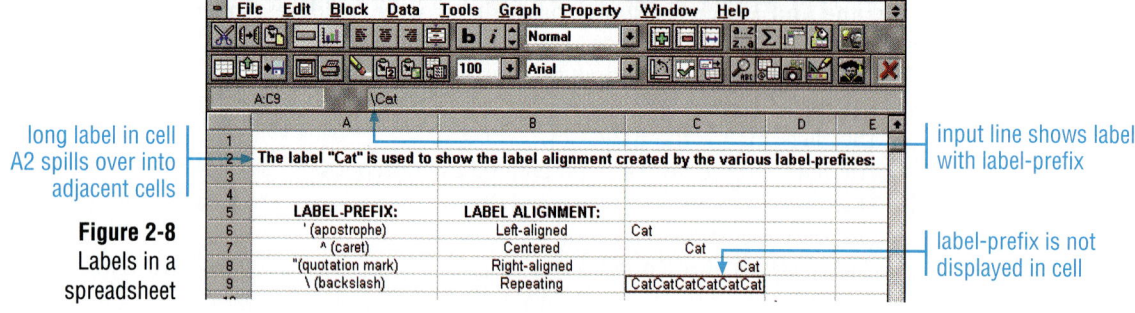

long label in cell
A2 spills over into
adjacent cells

Figure 2-8
Labels in a
spreadsheet

input line shows label
with label-prefix

label-prefix is not
displayed in cell

Otis decides to use left-aligned labels for the documentation. He begins by entering the company name and notebook title.

To enter the company name and notebook title:

❶ Click cell **A1** to make it the active cell.

❷ Type **SGL BUSINESS TRAINING AND CONSULTING** (all capital letters) then press **[Enter]**. You do not need to use a label-prefix because Quattro Pro automatically left-aligns labels unless you use a label-prefix that changes the alignment. The label appears in cell A1 and spills over into cells B1, C1, D1, and E1.

   TROUBLE? If you made a mistake in typing the label, correct it using the editing techniques you learned in Tutorial 1.

❸ Press [↓] to move to cell A2.

   TROUBLE? If the number 2 appeared in the input line when you pressed [↓], you pressed [↓] on the numeric keypad with [Num Lock] engaged. Press [Esc] to remove the number 2 from the input line. Press [Num Lock] to turn the numeric keypad lock off and then press [↓] on the numeric keypad.

❹ Type **Regional Income and Expense Notebook** then press **[Enter]**. Again, the label spills over into the adjoining cells.

Otis continues working in column A to enter the identifying labels for the other parts of the documentation. He knows that he can: (1) type each label in a cell, (2) press [Enter], then (3) use [↓] or the mouse to move to the next cell. But Otis also knows a shortcut for entering labels. He can save a step by: (1) typing the label, then (2) pressing [↓] to both enter the label and move to the next cell. Let's see how this works.

To enter the remaining labels using [↓]:

❶ Click cell **A4** to make it the active cell.

❷ Type **Filename:** (be sure to include the colon) then press [↓] to complete the entry and move to cell A5.

❸ In cell A5 type **Created by:** then press [↓].

❹ In cell A6 type **Date:** then press [↓].

❺ Press [↓] to leave a blank row and move to cell A8.

❻ In cell A8 type **Purpose:** then press [↓] four times to leave cells A9 through A11 blank and move to cell A12.

❼ In cell A12 type **Contents:** then press **[Enter]**. The completed set of labels is shown in Figure 2-9.

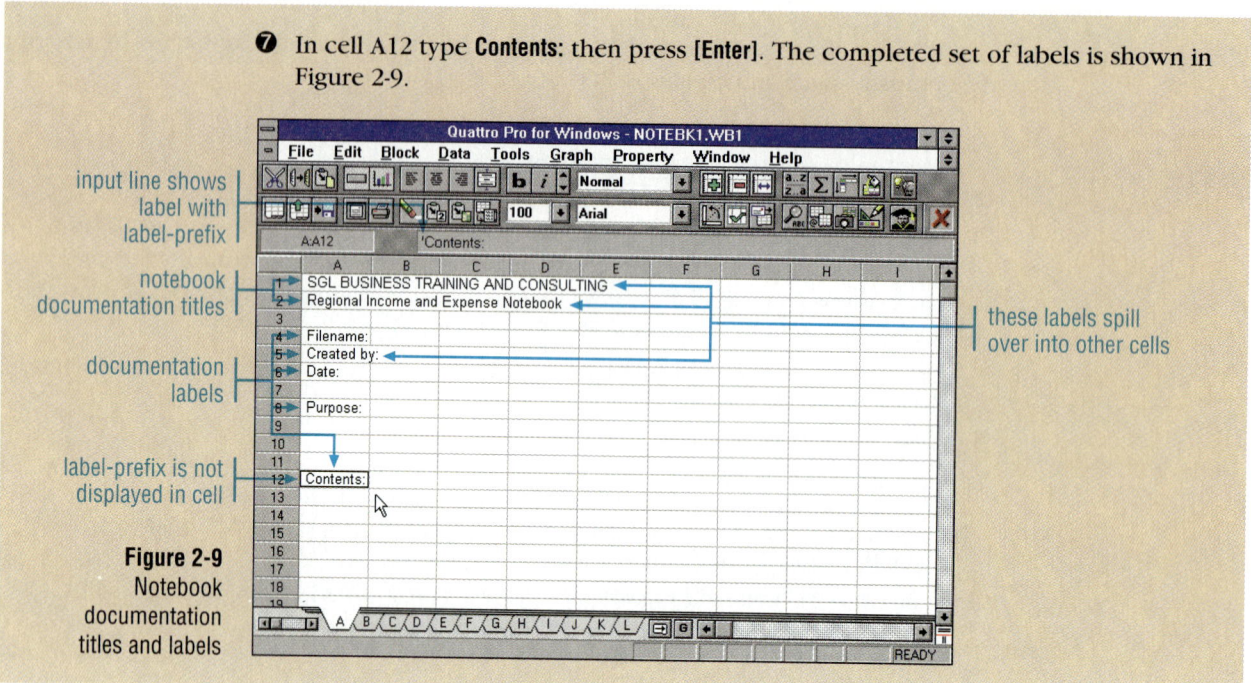

input line shows label with label-prefix

notebook documentation titles

documentation labels

label-prefix is not displayed in cell

these labels spill over into other cells

Figure 2-9
Notebook documentation titles and labels

Otis notices that the "Created by:" label spills over into column B, so he decides to increase the width of column A.

Changing Column Width

The number of letters or numbers that Quattro Pro displays in a cell depends on the font, size, and style of the text you are using and on the width of the column. If you do not change the width of the columns on your spreadsheet, Quattro Pro automatically uses a nine-character column width.

As shown in Figure 2-10, Quattro Pro provides several methods for changing column width. One method is to drag the right edge of a column border or any column border within a highlighted series of columns. The **column border** is the shaded area at the top of each column containing the identifying letter of the column. When you move the pointer to the right edge of a column border, it changes shape to ↔, and you use this pointer to drag the right edge to a new location. Another method is to select the column, then click the Fit button on the notebook SpeedBar. Quattro Pro will then adjust the column width to fit the longest label or number in the column. A third method is to right-click a column border to select the column and open the SpeedMenu at the same time. From the SpeedMenu, you open the Active Block Object Inspector and use it to modify the Column Width property. As you learned in Tutorial 1, Quattro Pro treats cells or blocks of cells as an object. You can change the property settings using the Object Inspector for the active block. All three methods can be used to change the width of more than one column at the same time if you select the set of columns (by dragging the pointer across the column borders) before you change the column width.

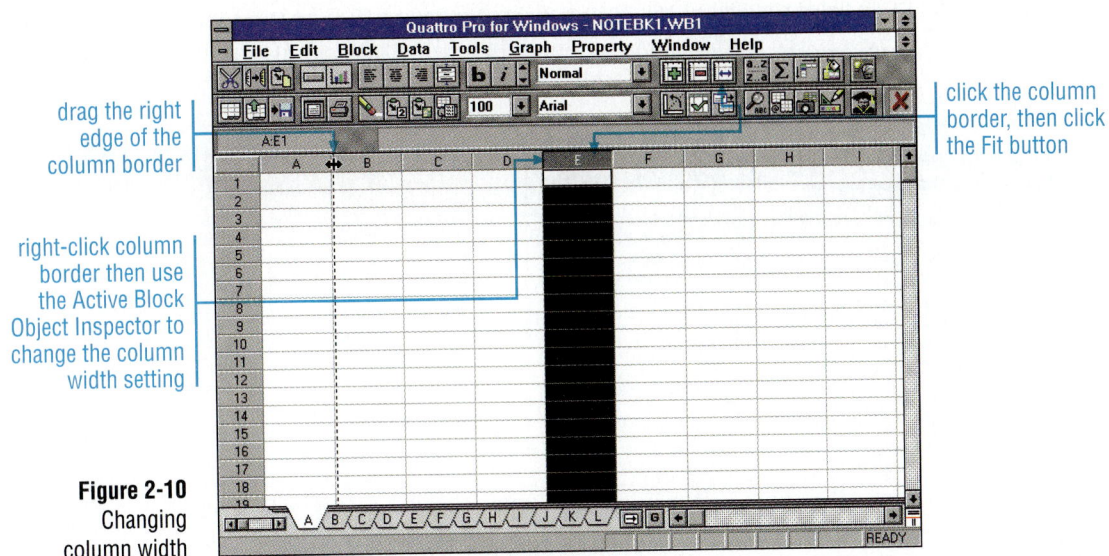

drag the right
edge of the
column border

click the column
border, then click
the Fit button

right-click column
border then use
the Active Block
Object Inspector to
change the column
width setting

Figure 2-10
Changing
column width

Otis wants to change the width of column A so that all the identifying labels fit within the boundary of column A. He decides to widen the column to a width of 15 characters.

To change the width of column A using the Object Inspector:

❶ Right-click the column border of **column A** to select the column and open the SpeedMenu. Quattro Pro highlights the column border of column A and all cells in column A, and the SpeedMenu appears. See Figure 2-11.

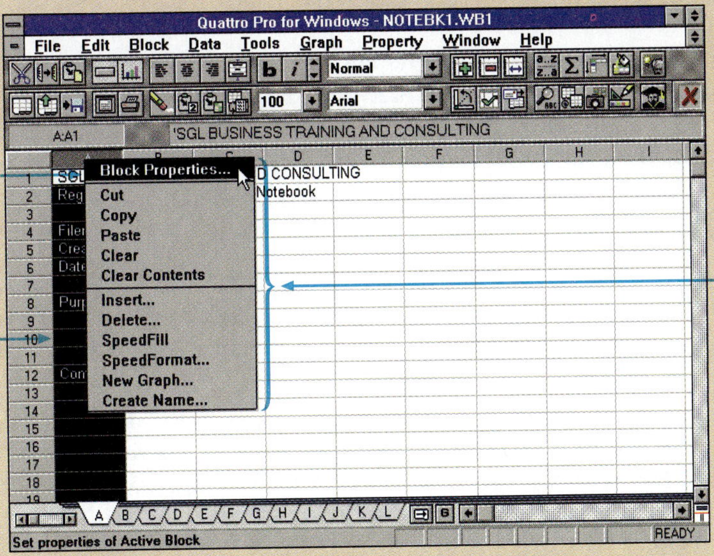

click Block
Properties... to
open Active Block
Object Inspector

column A is
highlighted

SpeedMenu

Figure 2-11
The SpeedMenu

❷ Click **Block Properties....** The Active Block Object Inspector appears.

❸ Click **Column Width** in the Object Inspector menu. The column width settings appear in the settings pane to the right of the menu, as shown in Figure 2-12. Notice that the Set Width option is selected.

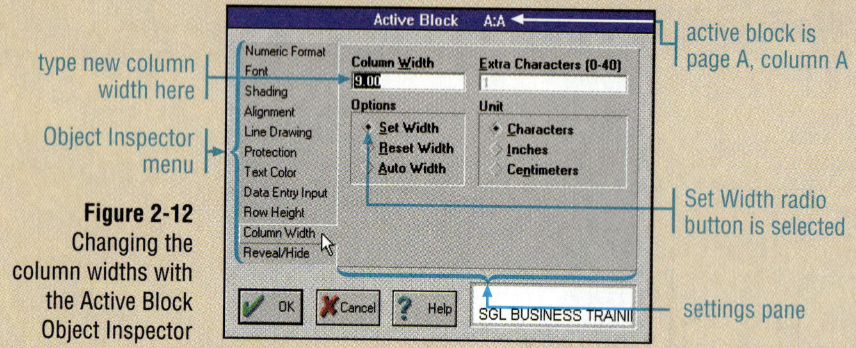

type new column width here

Object Inspector menu

Figure 2-12
Changing the column widths with the Active Block Object Inspector

active block is page A, column A

Set Width radio button is selected

settings pane

Active Block   A:A

Numeric Format
Font
Shading
Alignment
Line Drawing
Protection
Text Color
Data Entry Input
Row Height
Column Width
Reveal/Hide

Column Width
9.00

Extra Characters (0-40)

Options
♦ Set Width
◇ Reset Width
◇ Auto Width

Unit
♦ Characters
◇ Inches
◇ Centimeters

✓ OK   ✗ Cancel   ? Help   SGL BUSINESS TRAINII

❹ Type **15** in the Column Width edit field.

❺ Click **OK**. The width of column A changes to 15 characters.

❻ Click cell **A1** (or any other cell) to remove the column highlighting.

Otis is ready to fill in the rest of the initial documentation for this notebook. He will put this information in column B. The first item Otis needs to fill in is the notebook file-name. Otis decides that this is a good time to choose a filename and save the notebook.

Saving the New Notebook

Because this is the first time he has saved this notebook, Otis will use the Save As command to name the notebook S2INC.WB1. The "S" signifies a file that you saved, the "2" means that you used the file in Tutorial 2, and "INC" refers to "income" to remind you that the file contains an income and expense report notebook. Let's save the file now.

To save the notebook as S2INC.WB1:

❶ Click **File** then click **Save As...** to display the Save File dialog box.

❷ Type **S2INC** *but don't press [Enter] yet because you need to check some additional settings.* When you type the filename S2INC, you can use either uppercase or lowercase.

❸ Make sure the Drives box displays the name of the drive that contains your Student Disk. If the correct drive name is not shown, click the Drives drop-down list arrow button to display the list of drives. Your Save As dialog box should look like the dialog box in Figure 2-13 (your drive might be different if your Student Disk is in another drive).

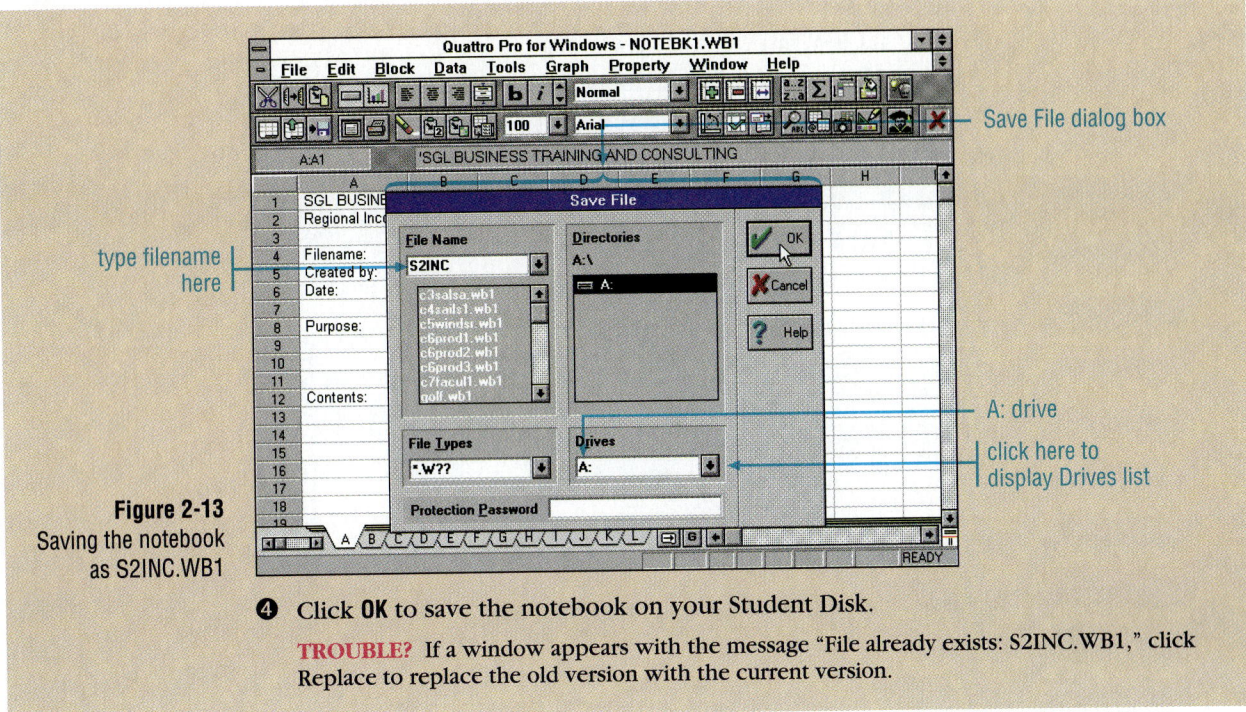

Figure 2-13
Saving the notebook
as S2INC.WB1

❹ Click **OK** to save the notebook on your Student Disk.

    TROUBLE? If a window appears with the message "File already exists: S2INC.WB1," click
    Replace to replace the old version with the current version.

Otis is now ready to enter the filename in his documentation.

To enter the filename in the documentation:
❶ Click cell **B4** to make it the active cell.
❷ Type **S2INC.WB1** then press [↓] to complete the entry and move to cell **B5**.

Otis now completes the rest of the initial documentation. The finished documentation is shown in Figure 2-14, and you can check your work against this figure as you enter
the rest of the documentation in the following steps.

To complete the documentation:
❶ In cell B5 type **Otis Nunley** then press [↓] to move to cell B6.
❷ Type **August 1, 1996** then press [Enter].
Next, Otis enters the purpose for the notebook.
❸ Click cell **B8**, type **This notebook will be used by SGL regional managers** then press [↓] to
    move to cell B9.
❹ Type **to report quarterly income and expense information to** then press [↓] to move to
    cell B10.

❺ Type **SGL headquarters.** then press **[Enter]**.

Finally, Otis enters information about the contents of the notebook.

❻ Click cell **B12**, type **Page A** then press **[→]** to move to cell C12.

❼ Type **Notebook documentation** then press **[Enter]**.

❽ Press **[←]** then press **[↓]** to move to cell B13.

❾ Type **Page B** then press **[→]** to move to cell C13.

❿ Type **Income and Expense Report spreadsheet** then press **[Enter]**.

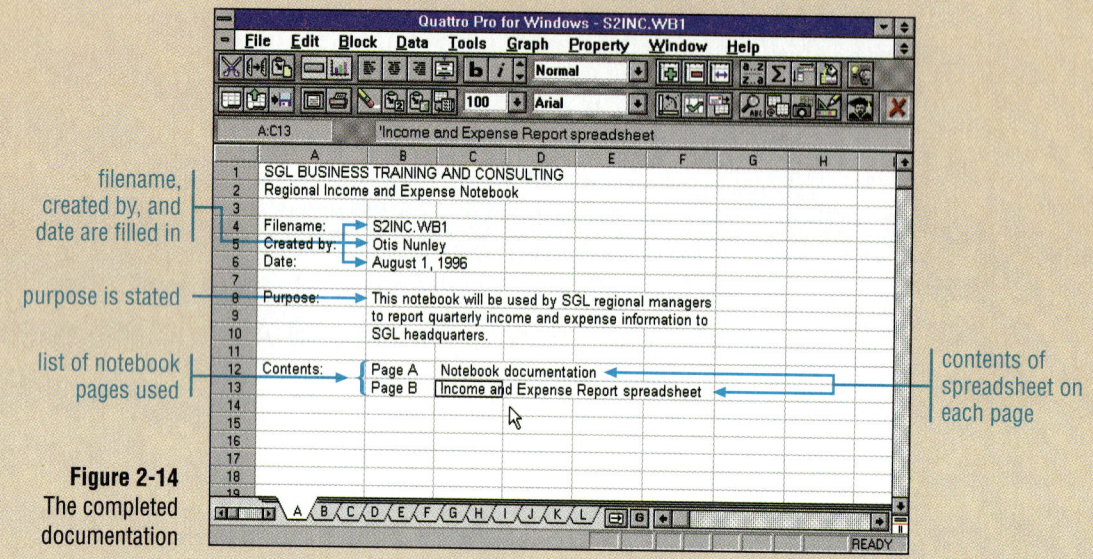

filename, created by, and date are filled in

purpose is stated

list of notebook pages used

contents of spreadsheet on each page

Figure 2-14
The completed documentation

Otis decides that it's time to save a copy of the revised notebook. Because Otis is saving the notebook with the same filename, he'll use the Save Notebook button on the Productivity Tools SpeedBar.

To save the S2INC.WB1 notebook with the same filename:
❶ Click the **Save Notebook button** 📑 on the Productivity Tools SpeedBar (or click **File** then click **Save**).

If you want to take a break and resume the tutorial at a later time, you can exit Quattro Pro by double-clicking the Quattro Pro application Control menu box (or by clicking File then clicking Exit). When you want to resume the tutorial, launch Quattro Pro, maximize the Quattro Pro and NOTEBK1.WB1 windows, place your Student Disk in the disk drive, and open the file S2INC.WB1. You can then continue with the tutorial.

Building the Spreadsheet

Otis is ready to start building his spreadsheet on page B.

To make page B the active spreadsheet:

❶ Make sure that the tab for page B is visible at the bottom of the notebook window. If it is not, use the notebook tab scroller to make it visible.

❷ Click **page tab B** to make spreadsheet B the active spreadsheet. The notebook window displays the second spreadsheet in the notebook.

As you learned in Tutorial 1, a spreadsheet generally contains values, labels that describe the values, and formulas that perform calculations using the values. When you build a spreadsheet, you usually enter the labels first, followed by values and formulas. You should also format the spreadsheet so that the information it contains is displayed in a clear and understandable way.

When you build a spreadsheet, the first step is to enter the labels you defined in the planning stage. Otis decides to use left-aligned labels for the spreadsheet title, the income category labels, and the expense category labels. He begins by entering the spreadsheet title.

To enter the spreadsheet title:

❶ Click cell **A1** on page B to make it the active cell. This cell is empty.

   TROUBLE? If cell A1 contains the label "SGL BUSINESS TRAINING AND CONSULTING" you are on page A. Switch to page B then repeat Step 1.

❷ Type **Income and Expense Report** then press **[Enter]**. You do not need to use a label-prefix because Quattro Pro automatically left-aligns labels unless you use a label-prefix that changes the alignment. The title appears in cell A1 and spills over into cells B1 and C1.

Otis continues working in column A to enter the labels for the income and expense categories he defined on his spreadsheet sketch in Figure 2-6. First he enters the labels for the income categories.

To enter the labels for the income categories:

❶ Click cell **A3** to make it the active cell.

❷ Type **Income** then press [↓] to complete the entry and move to cell A4.

❸ In cell A4 type **Consulting** then press [↓].

❹ In cell A5 type **Training** then press [↓].

❺ In cell A6 type **Total Income** then press **[Enter]**.

Next, Otis enters the labels for the expense categories.

To enter the labels for the expense categories:

❶ Click cell **A8** to make it the active cell.

❷ Type **Expenses** then press [↓] to complete the entry and move to cell A9.

❸ Refer to Figure 2-15 and type the labels for cells A9 through A16: Rent, Salaries, Telephone, Advertising, Office Supplies, Travel, Miscellaneous, Total Expenses.

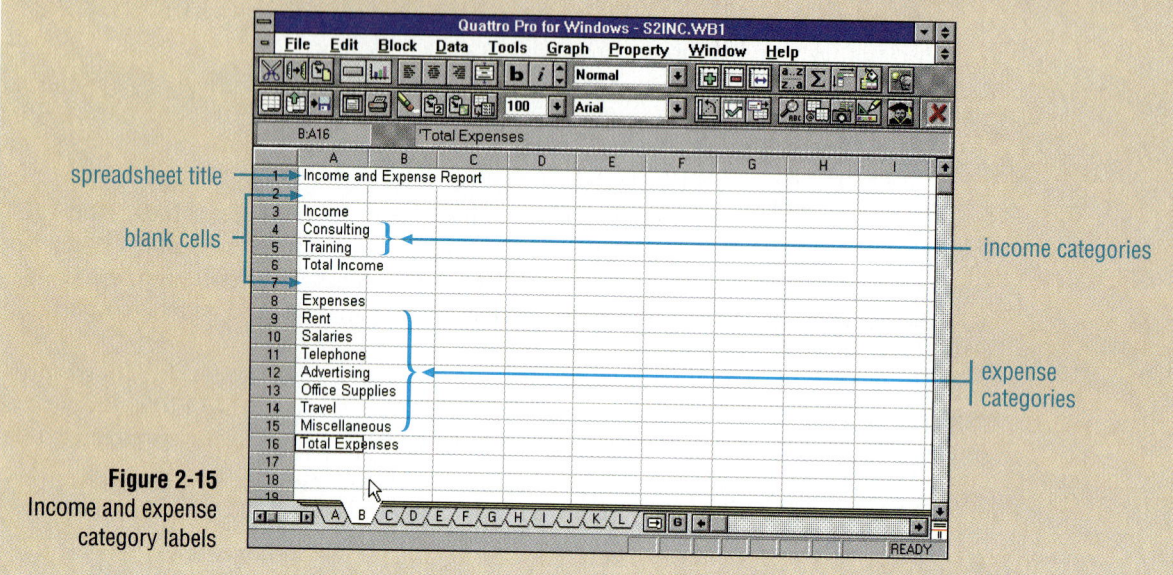

Figure 2-15
Income and expense category labels

Otis wants to leave a blank row after the "Total Expenses" label and put the label "Profit" in cell A18.

To enter the label "Profit" in cell A18:

❶ Press [↓] until the active cell is A18.

❷ Type **Profit** then press [**Enter**].

Otis notices that the text in some of the cells spills over into column B, so he decides to increase the width of column A so that all the labels fit within the boundary of column A. He decides to drag the edge of the column border to the right, past the end of the title "Income and Expense Report."

To increase the width of column A:

❶ Make sure that you can see cell A1. If you can't, press [Home] to move the selector (the outline around the active cell) to cell A1. You can press [Home] anytime you want to make cell A1 the active cell.

❷ Position the pointer on the column border for column A.

❸ Move the pointer slowly to the right until it is positioned over the right edge of the border of column A—the dividing line between column A and column B. Notice how the pointer changes to ↔.

❹ Drag the pointer to the right, past the end of the title "Income and Expense Report." See Figure 2-16.

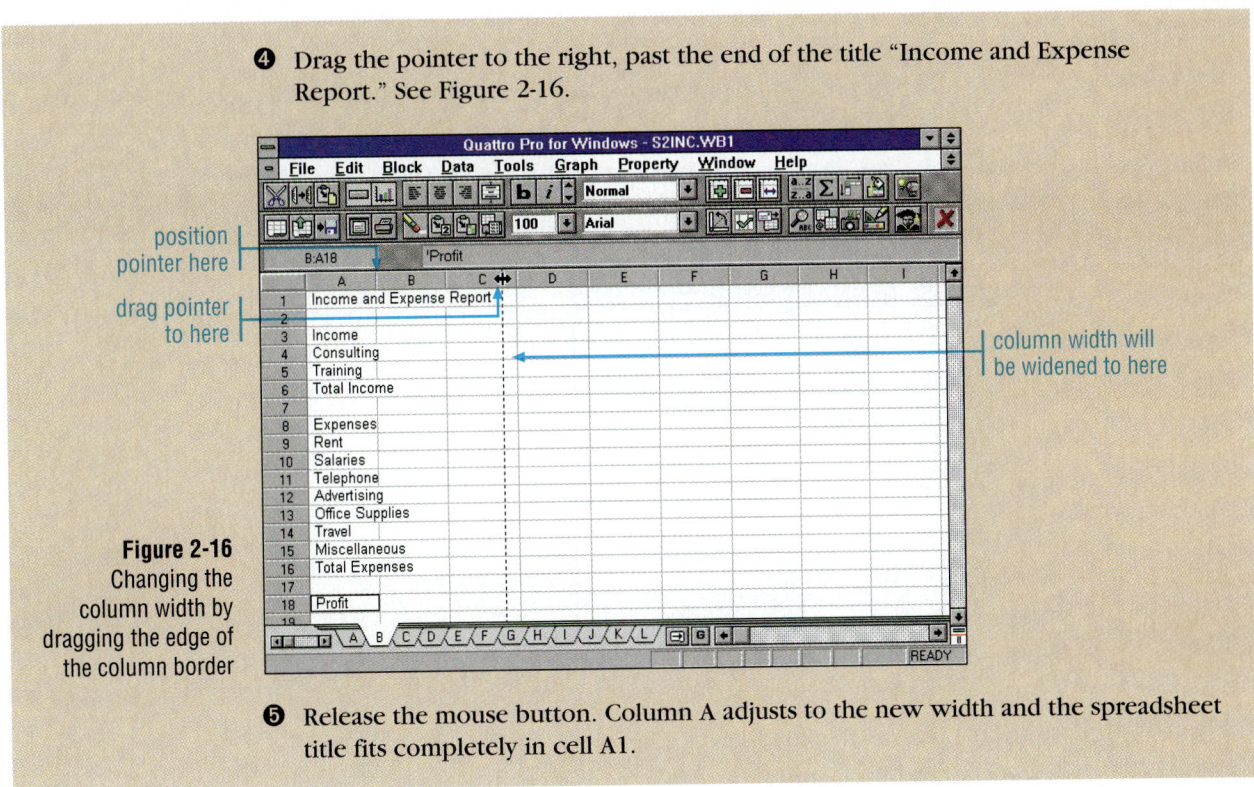

Figure 2-16
Changing the column width by dragging the edge of the column border

❺ Release the mouse button. Column A adjusts to the new width and the spreadsheet title fits completely in cell A1.

Looking at the spreadsheet he has created so far, Otis decides that although he wants to leave a blank row between "Total Income" and "Expenses" and between "Total Expenses" and "Profit," he doesn't want these rows to be as tall as the other rows in the spreadsheet.

Changing Row Height

Just as you can adjust column widths, you can adjust row heights. Using thin empty rows can help you visually separate the parts of your spreadsheets, or you might need to adjust a row height if you decide to use a larger type (font) size for your spreadsheet title. (You'll learn about different fonts and font sizes in Tutorial 3.)

Quattro Pro lets you quickly adjust row heights by dragging the bottom edge of the row border. The **row border** is the shaded area at the left of each row containing the row number. When you move the pointer over the bottom edge of the row border, the pointer changes to ✥, and you use it to drag the bottom edge to a new position. If you want an exact adjustment of the row height, you right-click the row border to select the row and open the SpeedMenu. From the SpeedMenu, you open the Active Block Object Inspector and use it to modify the Row Height property.

Otis wants to change the height of rows 7 and 17 so that they are about one-third as tall as the rows containing the income and expense category labels. Because he wants rows 7 and 17 to have exactly the same height, Otis decides to use the Object Inspector to make the row height adjustments.

To change the height of rows 7 and 17:

❶ Right-click the **row border** of row 7 to select the row and open the SpeedMenu.

❷ Click **Block Properties...** to open the Active Block Object Inspector.

❸ Click **Row Height** in the Object Inspector menu. The row height settings appear in the settings pane to the right of the menu, as shown in Figure 2-17. Notice that the Set Height option is selected.

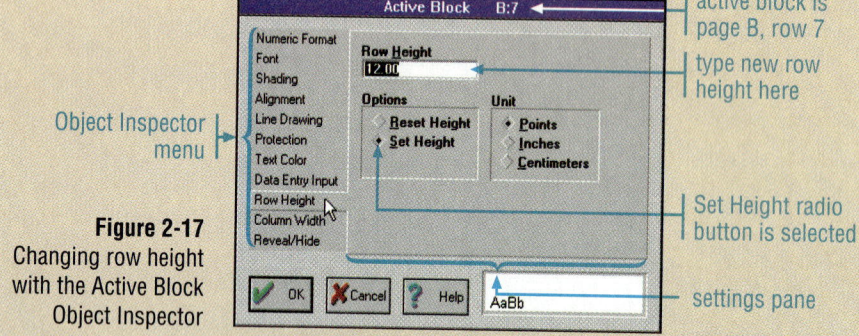

Figure 2-17
Changing row height with the Active Block Object Inspector

Otis wants the row height to be one-third of the current row height, 12.00. One-third of 12 is 4.

❹ Type **4** in the Row Height edit field.

❺ Click **OK**. Quattro Pro adjusts the row height.

❻ Right-click the **row border** of row 17 to select the row and open the SpeedMenu.

❼ Click **Block Properties...** to open the Active Block Object Inspector.

❽ Click **Row Height** in the Object Inspector menu. The row height settings appear in the settings pane to the right of the menu.

❾ Type **4** in the Row Height edit field, then click **OK**. Quattro Pro adjusts the row height.

❿ Click any cell to remove the highlighting from row 17.

Now Otis needs to enter the column titles for each quarter. Otis decides that he wants these titles to be centered instead of left-aligned.

Entering Centered Labels

Otis starts by entering the label "Quarter 1" in cell B2. He remembers that he must start the label with the label-prefix "^" to create a centered label.

To enter the centered label "Quarter 1" in cell B2:

❶ Click cell **B2** to make it the active cell.

❷ Type **^Quarter 1** then press **[Enter]**.

Otis is not a fast typist. He wonders if there is any way to avoid typing the name of the next three quarters across the top of the spreadsheet. Then he remembers a Quattro Pro feature called SpeedFill.

Creating a Series with SpeedFill

SpeedFill is a Quattro Pro feature that automatically fills areas of the spreadsheet with a series of values or text. To use this feature you type one or two initial values or text entries, then SpeedFill does the rest. SpeedFill evaluates the initial entry or entries, determines the most likely sequence to follow, and completes the remaining entries in the block of cells you specify.

SpeedFill recognizes many series of numbers, dates, times, and certain labels, but it won't recognize every series. For example, SpeedFill can't complete a list of the states for the United States or a list of the presidents of the United States. Figure 2-18 shows a selection of series that SpeedFill recognizes and completes.

Initial Series	SpeedFill Sequence
1, 2, 3	4, 5, 6 ...
1, 3, 5	7, 9, 11...
1st	2nd, 3rd, 4th ...
1st Quarter	2nd Quarter, 3rd Quarter, 4th Quarter ...
Jan	Feb, Mar, Apr...
January	February, March, April ...
Mon	Tue, Wed, Thu ...
Monday	Tuesday, Wednesday, Thursday ...
1993	1994, 1995, 1996 ...
10/15/96	10/16/96, 10/17/96, 10/18/96 ...
12:00 PM	1:00 PM, 2:00 PM, 3:00 PM ...
12:00 PM, 12:15 PM	12:30 PM, 12:45 PM, 1:00 PM, 1:15 PM ...

Figure 2-18
Examples of series completed by SpeedFill

If you use a repeating series such as months or days of the week, you can begin anywhere in the series. If there are cells that need to be filled after the series ends, SpeedFill repeats the series again from the beginning. For example, if you enter "October," SpeedFill completes the series by entering "November" and "December," then it continues the series with "January," "February," and so on.

To use SpeedFill, you select the block of cells containing your initial entry and the cells you want to fill, then you select the SpeedFill command. You select the block of cells by positioning the pointer on the cell that will be the upper-left corner of the block. Next, you hold down the mouse button while you drag the pointer to the cell in the lower-right corner of the block. This selects all the cells in the block, which is shown on the screen by **highlighting** the block. Highlighted cells are shown with a different background color, usually black. The cell in the upper-left corner of the block is the active cell, so it does not appear highlighted, but it is included in the block.

REFERENCE WINDOW

Using SpeedFill to Complete a Series

- Click the cell that will contain the first label, number, or date in the series.

- Type the first label, number, or date in the first cell of the series, then press [Enter].

- If Quattro Pro will need more than one label, number, or date to interpret the sequence, add additional labels, numbers or dates in adjacent cells until the series can be interpreted.

- Drag the pointer to highlight the block that includes the cell(s) with the initial label(s), number(s) or date(s) and the cells that you want SpeedFill to complete.

- Click the SpeedFill button on the notebook SpeedBar (or right-click any cell in the highlighted block to open the SpeedMenu, then click SpeedFill).

Otis uses SpeedFill to enter the labels for the remaining quarters.

To fill in the labels for the rest of the quarters using SpeedFill:

❶ Position the pointer on cell B2.

❷ Click and hold down the **left mouse button** while you drag the pointer to cell E2.

❸ Release the mouse button. The block of cells from B2 to E2 is highlighted, except for cell B2, which is the active cell and so is not highlighted but is part of the block, shown in Figure 2-19.

TROUBLE? If your highlight does not correspond to Figure 2-19, repeat Steps 1 through 3. You might have released your mouse button too soon.

TROUBLE? If the cursor changed to 🖑 and moved the contents of cell B2 to another cell, you held the left mouse button down too long before you started to drag the pointer. This activated the Drag and Drop feature. Click the Undo/Redo button 🔲 then repeat Steps 1 through 3. You'll learn to use the Drag and Drop feature later in this tutorial.

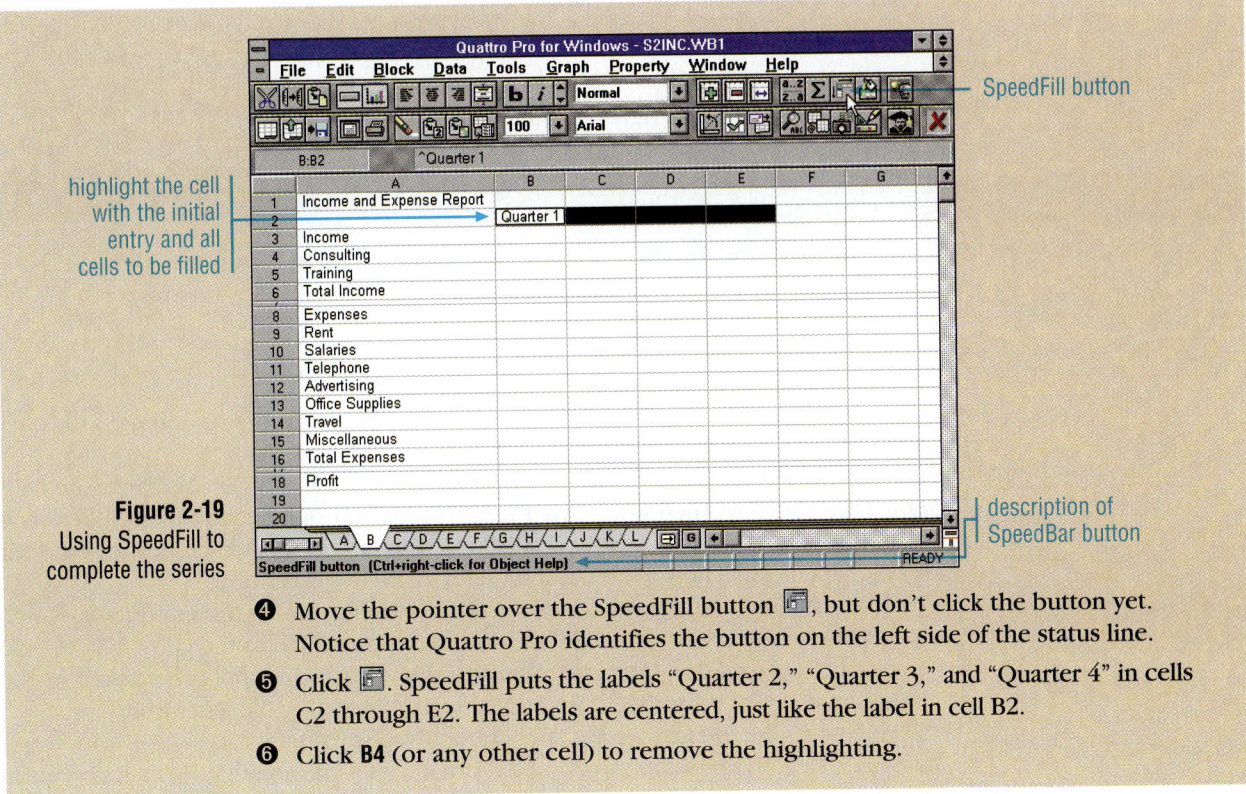

highlight the cell with the initial entry and all cells to be filled

SpeedFill button

description of SpeedBar button

Figure 2-19
Using SpeedFill to complete the series

④ Move the pointer over the SpeedFill button, but don't click the button yet. Notice that Quattro Pro identifies the button on the left side of the status line.

⑤ Click. SpeedFill puts the labels "Quarter 2," "Quarter 3," and "Quarter 4" in cells C2 through E2. The labels are centered, just like the label in cell B2.

⑥ Click **B4** (or any other cell) to remove the highlighting.

Now that Otis has entered the labels for his spreadsheet, he's ready to build the formulas. Because the spreadsheet will be used as a template, Otis knows that the final spreadsheet will not have any values in it. The branch managers will enter the values when they use the spreadsheet. Although Otis could build the formulas without values, he prefers to build the formulas using test values in the spreadsheet so that he can see the results of his formulas and verify that the formulas work correctly.

Testing the Spreadsheet

Test values are numbers that generate a known result. You enter test values in your spreadsheet to determine if your formulas are accurate. If the results on your spreadsheet don't match the known results, you have probably made an error. You can enter test values as you build the spreadsheet or after you've completed it. Either way, the test values give you a quick check on the accuracy of your work.

Test values can be numbers from a real sample or simple numbers that make it easy to determine if the spreadsheet is calculating correctly. Otis could use numbers from an income and expense report that he knows has been calculated correctly, or he could enter a simple value like 1 in all the cells. Then it would be easy to do the calculations "in his head" to verify that the formulas are accurate. Otis decides to use the number 100 as a test value because he can easily check the accuracy of the formulas he will build in the spreadsheet.

To enter the test value 100 in cells B4 and B5:

❶ Click cell **B4** to make it the active cell.

❷ Type **100** then press [↓] to move to cell B5.

❸ Type **100** then press **[Enter]**.

Otis decides to copy the test values from cells B4 and B5 to columns C, D, and E.

Copying Cells

You can copy the information in a cell (the cell contents and property settings) to other cells using several methods:

- One method is to use Quattro Pro's Drag and Drop feature. You highlight the cells you want to copy, then hold down [Ctrl] while you point at the block. Press and hold down the left mouse button until the pointer changes to ⍟. Drag the cell or block of cells to its new location, then release the mouse button.
- Another method is to use the Copy and Paste commands on the Edit menu, which are common commands in all Windows programs. Highlight the cell or block you want to copy, click the Copy button, click the cell (or the upper-left corner or the block) where you want the information copied, then click the Paste button.
- You can also use the Copy command on the Block menu.

Otis wants to copy the values in B4 and B5 to cells C4 through E5. He starts by using Drag and Drop to copy the value in B4 to cells C4 through E4.

To copy the test value to cells C4 through E4 using Drag and Drop:

❶ Click cell **B4** to make it the active cell.

❷ Position the pointer over B4.

❸ Press and hold **[Ctrl]**, then press and hold the **left mouse button**. The pointer changes to ⍟ and the cell is outlined, as shown in Figure 2-20.

   TROUBLE? Make sure that you press and hold down [Ctrl] before you press the mouse button. If you don't, you will *move* the information in the cell rather than *copy* it.

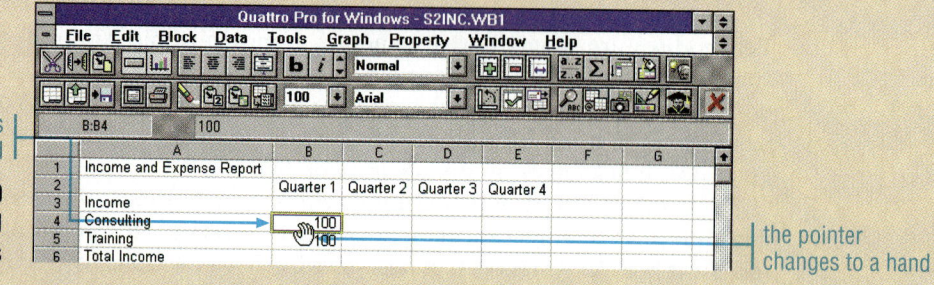

cell B4 is outlined

Figure 2-20
Using Drag and Drop to copy cells

the pointer changes to a hand

❹ Drag the pointer to cell C4 (you can release [Ctrl] once you start dragging). Quattro Pro displays an outline so you can see when the pointer is positioned correctly.

❺ Release the mouse button. The value 100 appears in C4.

TROUBLE? If the value 100 disappeared from cell B4, you moved the information instead of copying it. Click the Undo/Redo button 🔲 on the Productivity Tools SpeedBar, then repeat Steps 1 through 5.

❻ Repeat Steps 1 through 5 to use the Drag and Drop feature to copy the information in B4 to cells D4 and E4.

Now Otis will use Copy and Paste to copy the value in B5 to cells C5 through E5.

To copy the test value to cells C5 through E5 using Copy and Paste:

❶ Click cell **B5** to make it the active cell.

❷ Click the **Copy button** 🔳 on the notebook SpeedBar, as shown in Figure 2-21.

❸ Drag the pointer across cells C5 to E5. The block C5..E5 is highlighted. See Figure 2-21.

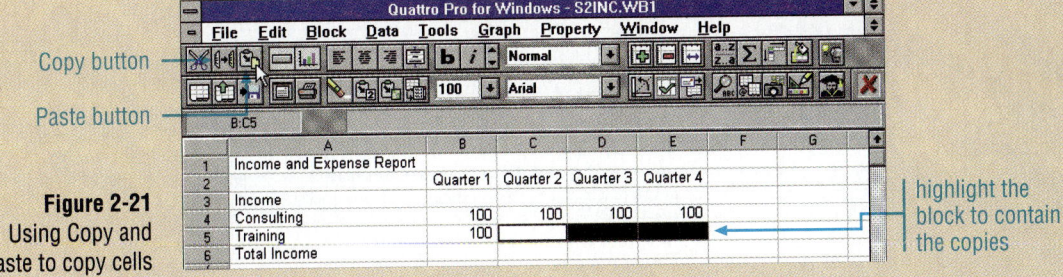

Figure 2-21
Using Copy and Paste to copy cells

❹ Click the **Paste button** 🔳 on the notebook SpeedBar. The value 100 appears in cells C5 through E5.

❺ Click any cell to remove the highlighting. The spreadsheet now looks like Figure 2-22.

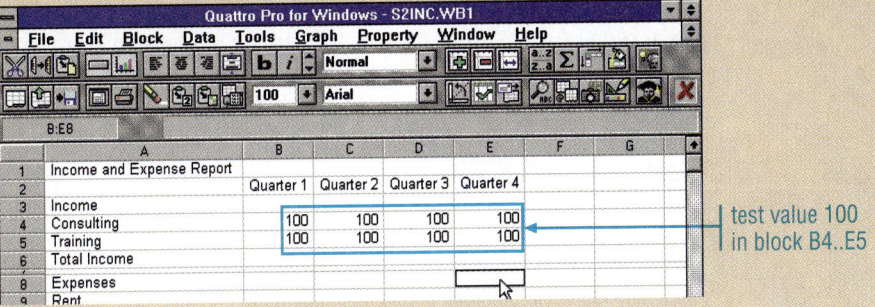

Figure 2-22
The spreadsheet with copied income test values

Whenever you use the Copy command, Windows saves what you have copied, in this case the value 100, in a location called the **Clipboard**, and keeps it there until you replace it with something else. Because the value 100 is still in the Clipboard, Otis can paste the value in as many cells as he wants, without having to recopy it. He decides to paste the test value 100 in the cells for the expense categories.

To paste the contents of the Clipboard, the value 100, in cells B9 through E15:

❶ Drag the pointer across cells B9 to E15. The block B9..E15 is highlighted.

❷ Click the **Paste button** 📋 on the notebook SpeedBar. The value 100 appears in cells B9 through E15.

❸ Click any cell to remove the highlighting. The spreadsheet now looks like Figure 2-23.

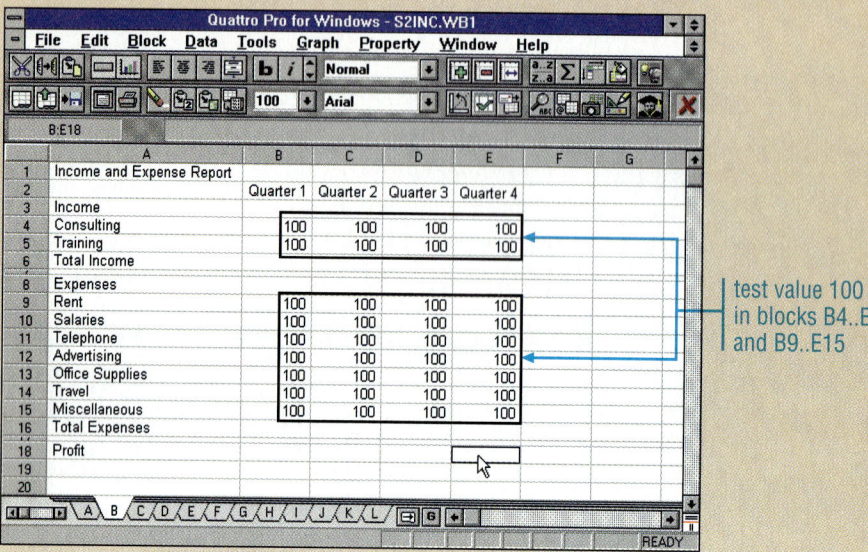

Figure 2-23
The spreadsheet with the copied expense test values

Otis is now ready to enter his formulas.

Entering Formulas

You will recall from Tutorial 1 that formulas tell Quattro Pro what to calculate. You begin entering a formula in a cell by typing one of the characters that Quattro Pro recognizes as starting a formula. These characters are shown in Figure 2-24.

Character	Description
=	Equal sign
0 1 2 3 4 5 6 7 8 9	Numbers
.	Decimal point
+	Plus sign
−	Minus sign
(	Left parenthesis
@	At sign
#	Number or pound sign
$	Dollar sign

Figure 2-24
Characters that can start a formula

Although you could use any of the characters shown in Figure 2-24 to start a formula, in this text you will always use the equal sign because it is the quickest way to tell Quattro Pro to expect a formula under any circumstances. The ability to start formulas with the equal sign is new in Quattro Pro 5.0. To maintain compatibility with other software, Quattro Pro rewrites formulas that you start with an equal sign. Figure 2-25 shows how Quattro Pro will convert the formula.

Formula with Equal Sign	Quattro Pro Conversion
=100+A6	100+A6
=.25*A7	.25*A7
=(A5+A6)	(A5+A6)
=@SUM(A6..B7)	@SUM(A6..B7)
=A6+B7	+A6+B7

Figure 2-25
Quattro Pro equal
sign conversions

Don't worry when Quattro Pro converts an equal sign that you just entered in a formula. You'll quickly get used to this. You've sent the signal you needed to send, and Quattro Pro interprets your entry as a formula.

Formulas can contain values, functions, and operators. As you learned in Tutorial 1, values can be numbers or cell references (such as A1 and G14). For values that include cell references, such as B5 or D38, you can type the cell reference or you can use the mouse or arrow keys to point to the cells. **Functions** are prewritten formulas that give you shortcuts for certain calculations. Remember from Tutorial 1 that functions always start with the @ (at) symbol, and are called @functions ("at functions"). **Operators** (such as + and *) tell Quattro Pro what calculations to perform. Figure 2-26 shows some examples of the numbers, cell references, and operators you can include in a formula. You'll use the @SUM function in this tutorial, and learn more about @functions in Tutorial 4.

Example	Description
101	A number
A1	Cell reference
A1..E5	Reference to a block of cells
+	Addition operator
–	Subtraction operator
/	Division operator
*	Multiplication operator
^	Exponentiation operator
>	Greater than sign
<	Less than sign

Figure 2-26
Examples of numbers,
cell references, and
operators

When Quattro Pro calculates the results of a formula that contains more than one operator, it follows the precedence of operations shown in Figure 2-27. This is the normal mathematical order of precedence.

Operator	Description	Precedence Order
( )	Parentheses	1
^	To the power of (exponentiation)	2
- +	Negative, positive	3
* /	Multiplication, division	4
+ -	Addition, subtraction	5
= <>	Equal, not equal	6
< >	Less than, greater than	6
<=	Less than or equal	6
>=	Greater than or equal	6

Figure 2-27
Precedence of
operations

In accordance with the precedence of operations, Quattro Pro performs calculations by first doing any operations contained in parentheses, then any exponentiation, then any multiplication or division, and so on. For example, the result of the formula 3+4*5 is 23 because Quattro Pro completes the multiplication before the addition. The result of the formula (3+4)*5 is 35 because Quattro Pro calculates the operation in the parentheses first.

REFERENCE WINDOW

Entering a Formula

- Click the cell where you want the result to appear.
- Type = then enter the rest of the formula.
- Press [Enter] or click the check mark on the input line.

Otis decides to enter the formulas to calculate the total income for each quarter. The basic formula for total income is:

total income = consulting income + training income

Otis starts with Quarter 1. The first quarter consulting income goes in cell B4, and the first quarter training income goes in cell B5. Therefore, the formula for the first quarter total income must add the contents of cells B4 and B5. Otis will enter this formula as =B4+B5. Otis wants the total income displayed in cell B6, so this is the cell in which he enters the formula.

To enter the formula for first quarter total income:

❶ Click cell **B6** because this is where you want the total income displayed.

❷ Type **=B4+B5**, *but do not press [Enter]*. As shown in Figure 2-28, the formula =B4+B5 appears in the input line. Notice that two of the buttons on the notebook SpeedBar have changed. When you enter a formula, the @Functions button ⬚ and the Macros button ⬚ appear. You won't use these buttons in this tutorial, but do note the change in the notebook SpeedBar.

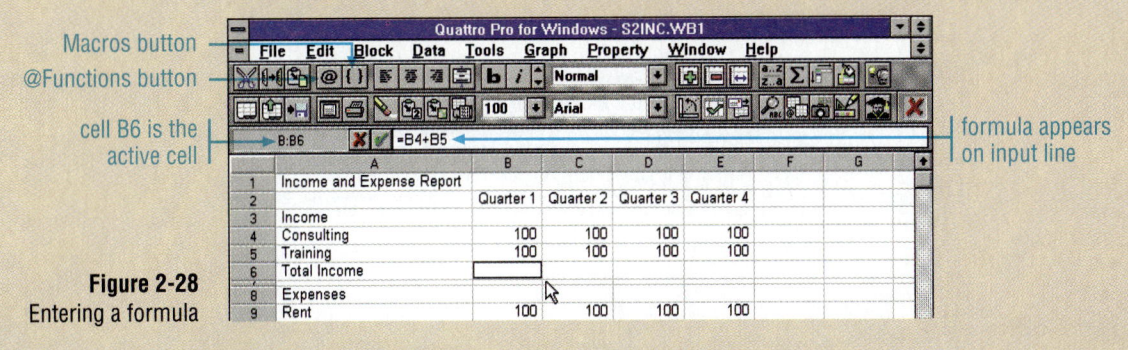

Macros button —
@Functions button —
cell B6 is the active cell —
formula appears on input line

Figure 2-28
Entering a formula

❸ Press **[Enter]**. The result 200 appears in cell B6.

Otis wants to enter the total income formulas for Quarters 2, 3, and 4. He could type the formula =C4+C5 in cell C6, then type the formula =D4+D5 in cell D6, and finally type the formula =E4+E5 in cell E6. Instead, Otis decides to copy the formula he entered in B6 to cells C6 through E6.

To copy the formula in cell B6 to cells C6 through E6:

❶ If cell B6 is not the active cell, click cell B6 to make it the active cell.

❷ Click the **Copy button** ⬚ on the notebook SpeedBar.

❸ Drag the pointer across cells C6 through E6. The block C6..E6 is highlighted.

❹ Click the **Paste button** ⬚ on the notebook SpeedBar. The formula is copied to cells C6 through E6, and the value 200 appears in cells C6 through E6.

❺ Click cell **B6** (or any other cell) to remove the highlighting.

Otis now uses his test values of 100 to check the spreadsheet. He knows that 100 plus 100 equals 200. Because this result is displayed as the total income for each of the four quarters, it appears that the formulas are making the correct calculation.

But Otis wonders if he might have made a mistake. The formula in B6 is =B4+B5. Because he copied this formula to cells C6, D6, and E6, Otis is concerned that Quarters 2, 3, and 4 will show the same total income as Quarter 1 when the branch managers enter their data. Otis decides to look at the formulas in cells C6, D6, and E6.

To examine the formulas in cells C6, D6, and E6:

❶ Click cell **B6**. The formula +B4+B5 appears in the input line. Remember that although you typed the formula as =B4+B5, Quattro Pro converted the equal sign (=) to a plus sign (+).

❷ Click cell **C6**. The formula +C4+C5 appears in the input line.

When the formula from cell B6 was copied to cell C6, the cell references changed. The formula +B4+B5 became +C4+C5 when Quattro Pro copied it to column C. See Figure 2-29.

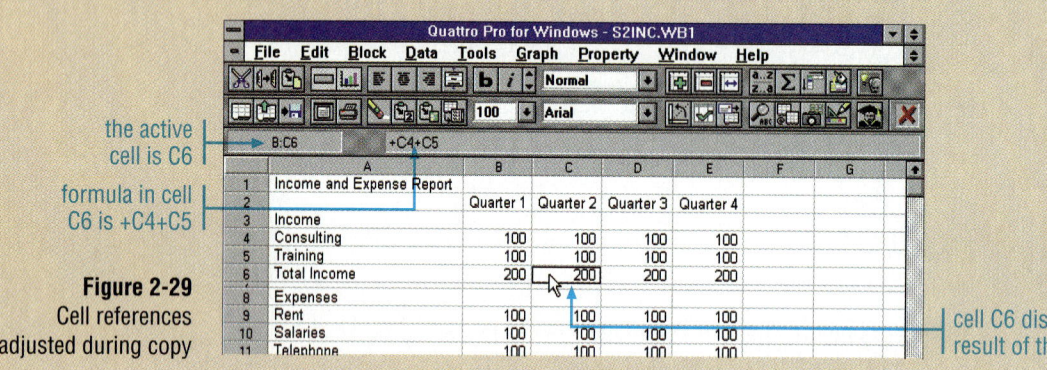

Figure 2-29
Cell references
adjusted during copy

the active cell is C6

formula in cell C6 is +C4+C5

cell C6 displays the result of the formula

❸ Click cell **D6**. The formula +D4+D5 appears in the input line. When Quattro Pro copied the formula to column D, the cell references changed from B to D.

❹ Click cell **E6**. The formula +E4+E5 appears in the input line. When Quattro Pro copied the formula to column E, the cell references changed from B to E.

When Otis copied the formula from cell B6, Quattro Pro automatically changed the cell references in the formulas to reflect the new position of the formulas in the spreadsheet. This is called relative referencing.

Relative References

A **relative reference** tells Quattro Pro which cell to use based on its location *relative* to the cell containing the formula. When you copy or move a formula that contains a relative reference, Quattro Pro changes the cell references so they refer to cells located in the same position relative to the cell that contains the new copy of the formula. Figure 2-30 shows an example of how this works.

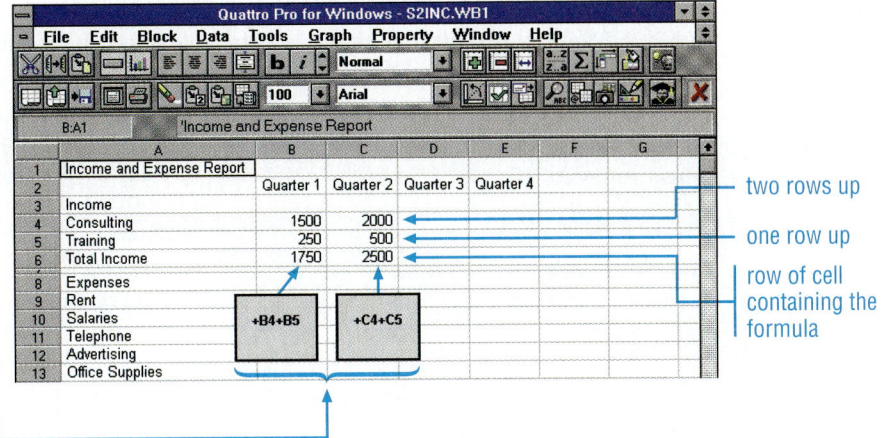

Figure 2-30
Relative references

Otis's original formula =B4+B5 contains relative references. Quattro Pro interpreted this formula to mean add the value from the cell two rows up from B6 (cell B4) to the cell one row up from B6 (cell B5) and display the result in the active cell (B6).

When Otis copied this formula to cell C6, Quattro Pro created the new formula to perform the same calculation, but starting at cell C6 instead of B6. The new formula adds the value from the cell two rows up from C6 (cell C4) to the cell one row up from C6 (cell C5) and displays the result in the active cell (C6).

All references in formulas are relative references unless you specify otherwise. Most of the time, you will want to use relative references. From time to time, however, you might need to create a formula that refers to a cell in a fixed location on the spreadsheet. A reference that always points to the same cell is an **absolute reference**. Absolute references contain a dollar sign before the column letter and/or the row number. Examples of absolute references include $A$4, $C$27, $A17, and D$32. You will learn more about absolute references in Tutorial 4.

Otis continues to enter the other formulas he planned to put in the spreadsheet template. Next he wants to enter the formula to calculate total expenses.

Using the @SUM Function

The **@SUM** function provides you with a shortcut for entering formulas that add the values in rows or columns. You can use @SUM to replace a lengthy formula such as =B9+B10+B11+B12+B13+B14+B15 with the more compact formula =@SUM(B9..B15).

Otis wants to enter a formula in cell B16 that calculates the total expenses (rent, salaries, and so forth). He uses @SUM to do this.

To calculate the total expenses using @SUM:

❶ Click cell **B16** because this is where you want to display the result of the formula.

❷ Type **=@SUM(** to begin the formula. Notice that the opening parenthesis is shown in red (on a color monitor) in the input line. See Figure 2- 31. The opening parenthesis will stay red until you type the closing parenthesis—then both parentheses will appear in green.

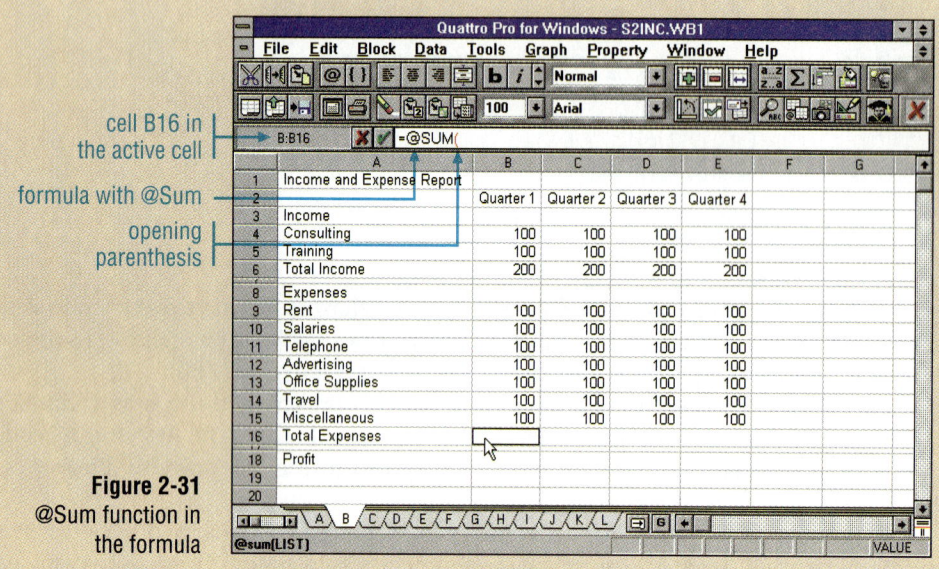

cell B16 in the active cell

formula with @Sum

opening parenthesis

Figure 2-31
@Sum function in the formula

❸ Type **B9..B15**.

❹ Type **)** to complete the formula. Notice that the parentheses now appear in green to indicate that both parentheses are in the formula.

❺ Press **[Enter]**. The result 700 appears in cell B18.

Now Otis can copy the formula in B16 to cells C16, D16, and E16.

To copy the formula in cell B16 to cells C16, D16, and E16:

❶ Make sure that cell B16 is the active cell.

❷ Click the **Copy button** 🖼 on the notebook SpeedBar.

❸ Drag the pointer across cells C16 to E16. The block C16..E16 is highlighted.

❹ Click the **Paste button** 🖼 on the notebook SpeedBar. The formula is copied to cells C16 through E16, and the value 700 appears in cells C16 through E16.

❺ Click any cell to remove the highlighting.

Otis again uses his test values to check the results of the formulas. There are seven expense categories, and Otis knows that 7 * 100 = 700. This agrees with the result displayed for the quarterly total expenses.

Otis reviews his spreadsheet plan and sketch and determines that he needs to enter the profit formula next; he considers how to do this.

Using the Mouse to Select Cell References

Quattro Pro provides several ways for you to enter cell references in a formula. One way is to type the cell references directly, as Otis did when he created the formula =B4+B5. Another way is to select the cell using the mouse. To use this method to enter the formula =B4+B5, Otis would type the equal sign, then click cell B4, type the plus sign, then click cell B5. Using the mouse to select cell references is often the preferred method because it minimizes typing errors.

Otis wants to calculate the profit for the first quarter as follows:

profit = total income – total expenses

Otis looks at the spreadsheet to locate the cell references for the first quarter profit formula. Cell B6 contains the total income and cell B16 contains the total expenses, so Otis knows that the formula should be =B6–B16. Let's see how Otis creates the formula to calculate profit by selecting the cell references with the mouse.

To create the formula to calculate first quarter profit by selecting cell references:

❶ Click cell **B18** because this is where you want the result of the formula displayed.

❷ Type **=** to begin the formula.

❸ Click cell **B6**. Notice that a box appears around cell B6. Also notice that B6 is added to the formula in the input line, as shown in Figure 2-32.

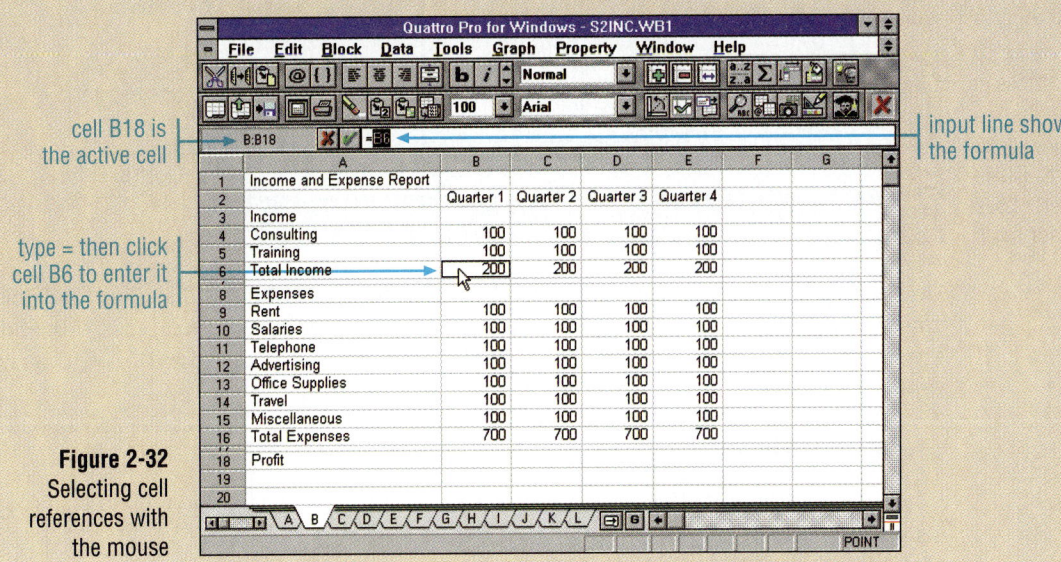

Figure 2-32
Selecting cell references with the mouse

❹ Type **–** (minus sign). Notice that the box disappears from cell B6. The input line now displays =B6– (the minus sign appears in the formula).

❺ Click cell **B16**. The box appears around cell B16, and the input line displays the entire formula =B6–B16.

❻ Press **[Enter]** to complete the formula. The result –500 appears in cell B18.

Now Otis copies the formula in B18 to cells C18, D18, and E18.

To copy the formula in B18 to cells C18, D18, and E18:

❶ Make sure cell B18 is the active cell because it contains the formula you want to copy.

❷ Click the **Copy button** ⊞ on the notebook SpeedBar.

❸ Drag the pointer across cells C18 to E18. The block C18..E18 is highlighted.

❹ Click the **Paste button** ⊟ on the notebook SpeedBar. The formula is copied to cells C18 through E18, and the value –500 appears in cells C18 through E18.

❺ Click any cell to remove the highlighting.

Otis has completed entering his test values and formulas, and the spreadsheet appears as shown in Figure 2-33.

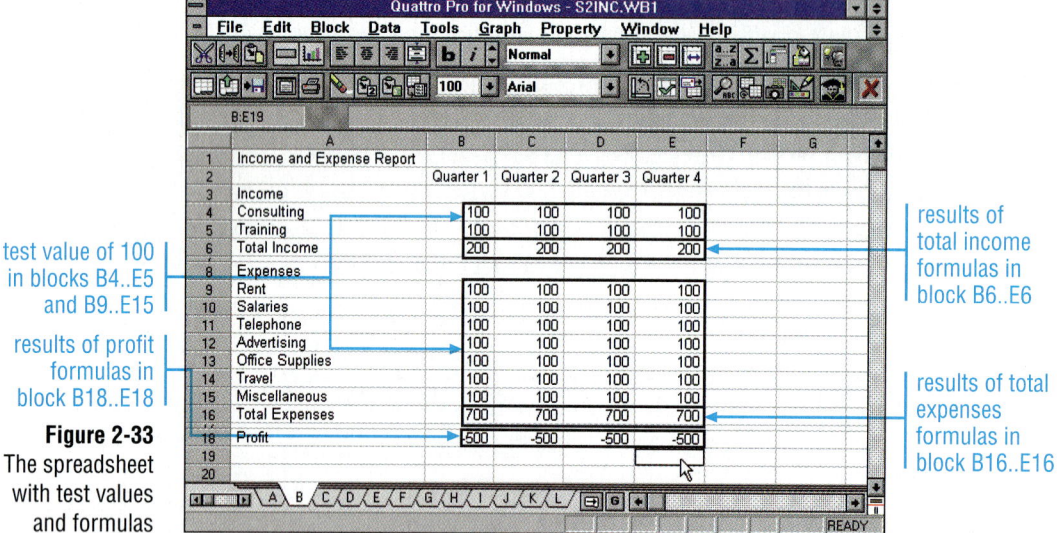

test value of 100 in blocks B4..E5 and B9..E15

results of profit formulas in block B18..E18

results of total income formulas in block B6..E6

results of total expenses formulas in block B16..E16

Figure 2-33
The spreadsheet with test values and formulas

Otis again uses his test values for his next check of the results. The total income amount in each quarter is 200. The total expenses amount in each quarter is 700, and Otis knows that 200 – 700 = –500. This checks with the result displayed for the quarterly profit. It looks like all the formulas are working correctly.

Now that all the formulas are entered in the spreadsheet, Otis decides it's a good time to save the notebook.

To save the notebook:

❶ Click the **Save Notebook button** ⊞ on the Productivity Tools SpeedBar (or click **File** then click **Save**).

If you want to take a break and resume the tutorial at a later time, you can exit Quattro Pro by double-clicking the Quattro Pro application Control menu box (or by clicking File then clicking Exit). When you want to resume the tutorial, launch Quattro Pro, maximize the Quattro Pro and NOTEBK1.WB1 windows, place your Student Disk in the disk drive, and open the file S2INC.WB1. You can then continue with the tutorial.

■   ■   ■

Otis is pleased with his spreadsheet, but he realizes that he forgot to include a row for the regional managers to type in their region numbers, and a column to display year-to-date totals. He revises his spreadsheet plan, as shown in Figure 2-34.

Spreadsheet Plan for Income and Expense Report Spreadsheet

My Goal:
To develop a Quattro Pro spreadsheet that regional managers can use to submit income and expense reports

What results do I want to see?
Income categories for consulting and training
Expense categories for rent, salaries, telephone, advertising, office supplies, travel, and miscellaneous
Income and expenses for each quarter
Total income for each quarter
Total expenses for each quarter
Total profit for each quarter

What information do I need?
The amount for each income and expense category

What calculations will I perform?
Total income = consulting income + training income
Total expenses = rent + salaries + telephone + advertising + office supplies + travel + miscellaneous
Profit = total income - total expenses
Year-to-date = Quarter 1 + Quarter 2 + Quarter 3 + Quarter 4

Figure 2-34
Otis's revised spreadsheet plan

Otis also revises his spreadsheet sketch to show the SGL region number and the title and formulas for the Year to Date column, as shown in Figure 2-35.

SGL Region Number
Income and Expense Report

	Quarter 1	Quarter 2	Quarter 3	Quarter 4	Year to Date
Income					
Consulting	99,999.99	99,999.99	99,999.99	99,999.99	{year-to-date formula}
Training					
	:	:	:	:	:
Total Income	{total income formula}	{total income formula}	{total income formula}	{total income formula}	{year-to-date formula}
Expenses	99,999.99	99,999.99	99,999.99	99,999.99	{year-to-date formula}
Rent	:	:	:	:	:
Salaries	:	:	:	:	
Telephone	:	:	:	:	:
Advertising	:	:	:	:	
Office Supplies	:	:	:	:	:
Travel	:	:	:	:	:
Miscellaneous	:	:	:	:	:
Total Expenses	{total expenses formula}	{total expenses formula}	{total expenses formula}	{total expenses formula}	{year-to-date formula}
Profit	{profit formula}	{profit formula}	{profit formula}	{profit formula}	{year-to-date formula}

Figure 2-35
Otis's revised spreadsheet sketch

Otis needs to use row 1 for the region number, but the spreadsheet title is in the row. Fortunately, he can easily insert a blank row.

Inserting a Row or Column

When you insert rows or columns, Quattro Pro repositions the other rows and columns in the spreadsheet and automatically adjusts the cell references in formulas to reflect the new location of values used in calculations. You can use the Insert command on the Block menu to insert one ore more rows or columns.

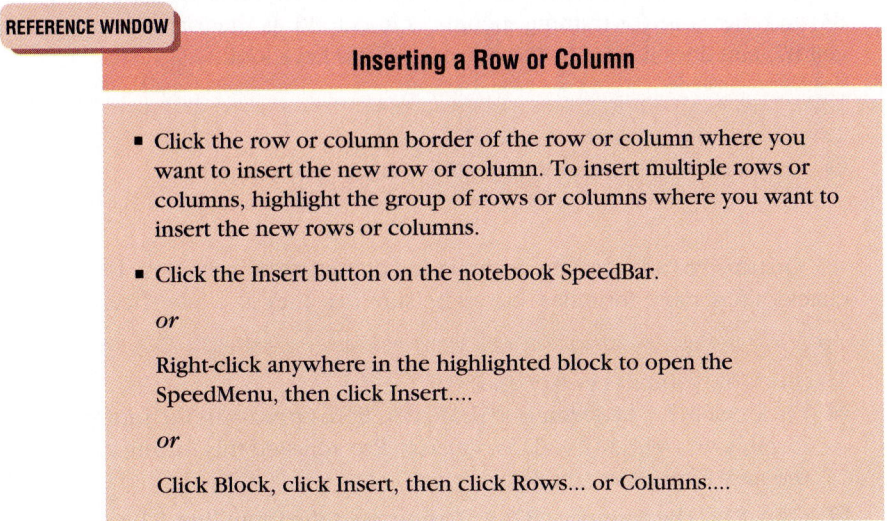

REFERENCE WINDOW

Inserting a Row or Column

- Click the row or column border of the row or column where you want to insert the new row or column. To insert multiple rows or columns, highlight the group of rows or columns where you want to insert the new rows or columns.

- Click the Insert button on the notebook SpeedBar.

 or

 Right-click anywhere in the highlighted block to open the SpeedMenu, then click Insert....

 or

 Click Block, click Insert, then click Rows... or Columns....

Otis decides to insert a row at the top of the spreadsheet. He doesn't want to type a region number in the new row because this template will be used by three different regions. Instead, he decides to enter "SGL Region Number" in the new row. The regional managers can then type in their region numbers when they use the spreadsheet. Let's see how Otis inserts a row for the region number.

To insert a row at the top of the spreadsheet:

❶ Click the **row border** (row number) for row 1. The entire row is highlighted, as shown in Figure 2-36.

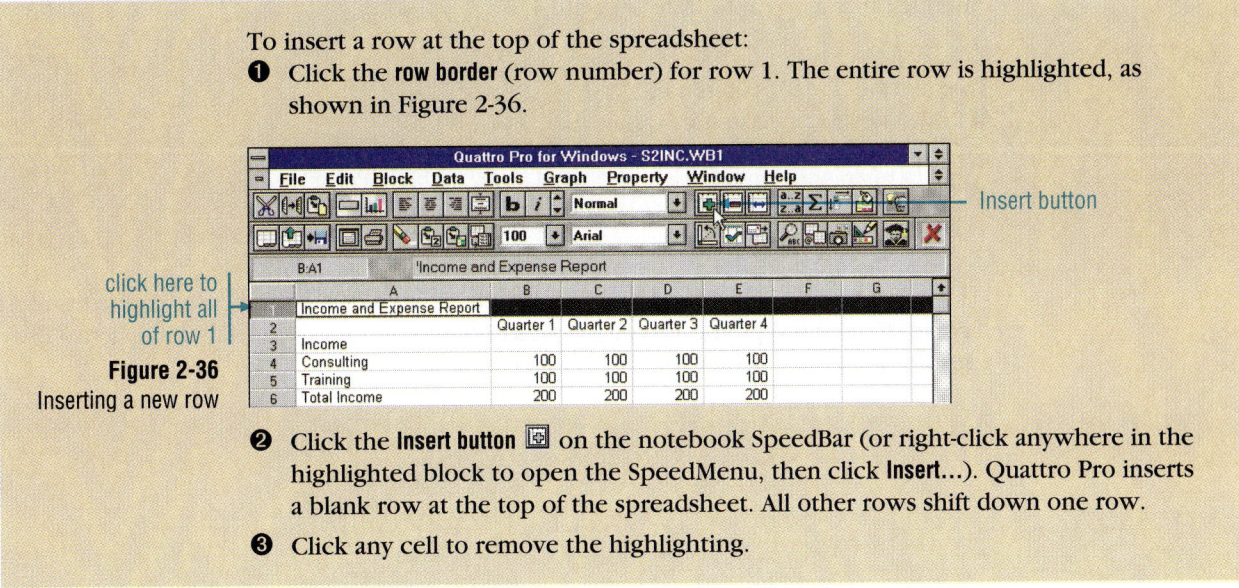

click here to highlight all of row 1

Figure 2-36
Inserting a new row

❷ Click the **Insert button** ⊞ on the notebook SpeedBar (or right-click anywhere in the highlighted block to open the SpeedMenu, then click **Insert...**). Quattro Pro inserts a blank row at the top of the spreadsheet. All other rows shift down one row.

❸ Click any cell to remove the highlighting.

Now Otis can add the title "SGL Region Number" in row 1.

To add the title in row 1:

❶ Click cell **A1** to make it the active cell.

❷ Type **SGL Region Number** then press **[Enter]**.

Adding a row changed the location of the data in the spreadsheet. The formula in cell B6 to calculate total income was +B4+B5. Now the value for consulting income is in cell B5, and the value for training income is in cell B6. Is the formula for total income now in cell B7, and does it refer to the correct values? Let's look.

To examine the contents of cell B7:

❶ Click cell **B7**. The formula +B5+B6 appears in the input line.

Quattro Pro adjusted the formula to compensate for the new location of the data. Otis checks a few more formulas, just to be sure that they also have been adjusted.

To check the formulas in B17 and B19:

❶ Click cell **B17**. The formula @SUM(B10..B16) appears in the input line. The original formula was @SUM(B9..B15). Quattro Pro adjusted this formula to compensate for the new location of the data.

❷ Click **B19**. The formula +B7–B17 appears in the input line. This formula used to be +B6–B16.

After he examines the formulas in his spreadsheet, Otis concludes that Quattro Pro automatically adjusted all the formulas when he inserted the new row.

Otis is ready to add the year-to-date information to the spreadsheet, and he begins by entering the title "Year to Date" in cell F3.

To enter the title for column F:

❶ Click cell **F3** to make it the active cell.

❷ Type **^Year to Date**. Make sure you include the caret (^).

❸ Press **[Enter]**.

Next, Otis needs to enter a formula in cell F5 to calculate the year-to-date consulting income. He could type the formula =@SUM(B5..E5), but he decides to use Quattro Pro's SpeedSum feature to eliminate some extra typing.

Using SpeedSum

SpeedSum automatically creates formulas that use @SUM. You highlight the block of cells you want to sum plus one extra cell for the total (at the bottom of the block for a column of numbers or at the right end of the block for a row of numbers). SpeedSum creates the formula, places it in the blank cell, and displays the result.

Otis uses SpeedSum to enter the formula for year-to-date consulting income in cell F5.

To enter the formula in cell F5 using SpeedSum:

❶ Drag the pointer to highlight cells B5 through F5. The block B5..E5 contains the numbers you want to add, and cell F5 is the blank cell for the formula. See Figure 2-37.

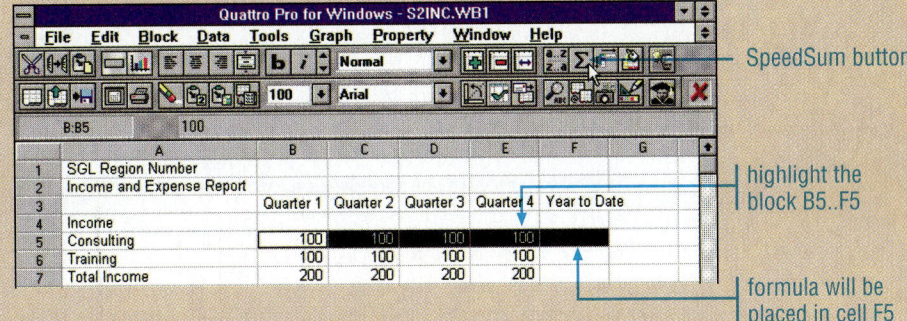

Figure 2-37
Using SpeedSum

❷ Click the **SpeedSum button** ∑ on the notebook SpeedBar. Quattro Pro builds the formula @SUM(B5..E5) in cell F5, and the result 400 appears in cell F5.

Otis would like to use the same formula to calculate the year-to-date totals for all income and expense categories as well as the totals. He decides to copy the formula in cell F5 to cells F6 through F19.

To copy the formula in cell F5 to cells F6 through F19:

❶ Click cell **F5** because this cell contains the formula you want to copy.

❷ Click the **Copy button** 📋 on the notebook SpeedBar.

❸ Highlight cells F6 through F19.

❹ Click the **Paste button** 📋 on the notebook SpeedBar. The formula is copied to cells F6 through F19.

❺ Click any cell to remove the highlighting, then view the results of the copy. See Figure 2-38.

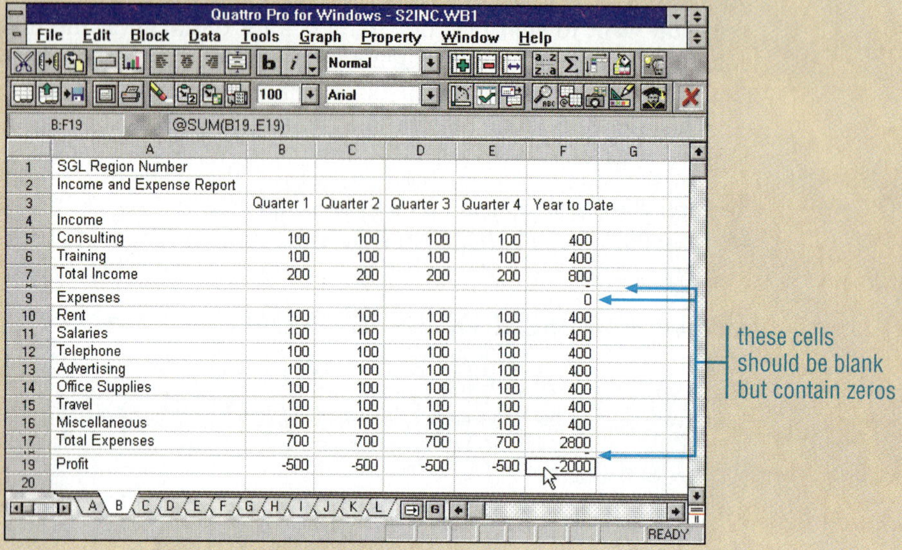
Quattro Pro for Windows - S2INC.WB1
File Edit Block Data Tools Graph Property Window Help
Normal
100
Arial
B:F19
@SUM(B19..E19)
A B C D E F G
1 SGL Region Number
2 Income and Expense Report
3 Quarter 1 Quarter 2 Quarter 3 Quarter 4 Year to Date
4 Income
5 Consulting 100 100 100 100 400
6 Training 100 100 100 100 400
7 Total Income 200 200 200 200 800
9 Expenses 0
10 Rent 100 100 100 100 400
11 Salaries 100 100 100 100 400
12 Telephone 100 100 100 100 400
13 Advertising 100 100 100 100 400
14 Office Supplies 100 100 100 100 400
15 Travel 100 100 100 100 400
16 Miscellaneous 100 100 100 100 400
17 Total Expenses 700 700 700 700 2800
19 Profit -500 -500 -500 -500 -2000
20
A B C D E F G H I J K L
READY
these cells should be blank but contain zeros

Figure 2-38
The spreadsheet after copying the formula from cell F5

As shown in Figure 2-38, cells F8, F9, and F18 should be blank. Instead they contain zero as a result of the @SUM function now in these cells. Otis decides to clear the formulas from the cells in column F that should be blank.

Clearing Cell Contents

Cells have both contents (labels, values, or formulas) and properties (text alignment, color, borders, numeric format, etc.). If you want to erase just the contents of a cell, this is called **clearing the cell contents**. Clearing cell contents is different from both clearing a cell and deleting a cell. When you clear *cell contents*, the contents of the cell are erased, but all property settings of the cell remain unchanged. When you *clear* a cell, the cell contents are erased, and its property settings are reset to the spreadsheet default settings. When you *delete* a cell, the cell (including its property settings) is actually removed from the spreadsheet and adjacent cells move to fill in the space left by the deleted cell.

To clear just the cell contents, you use the Clear Contents command on the Edit menu or the equivalent Clear Contents command on the SpeedMenu. You can also use [Del] to clear cell contents. If you want to clear both the cell contents and the cell's property settings, use the Clear command instead of the Clear Contents command.

Otis decides to clear the formula from cell F18 first. Then he'll highlight cells F8 and F9 and clear both formulas at the same time. Because Otis wants to clear the formula but not any other attributes from these cells, he'll use the Clear Contents command.

To clear the formula from cells F18, F8, and F9:

❶ Click cell **F18** because this is the first cell you want to clear.

   TROUBLE? You might have trouble clicking cell F18 because the row height is so short. If you do, click cell F19 then press [↑] to move the pointer to cell F18.

❷ Press **[Del]**. The contents of the cell are removed.

   TROUBLE? If a period appeared on the input line, you pressed [Del] on the numeric keypad and you have [Num Lock] engaged. Notice that there are two delete keys on the keyboard: [Del] on the numeric keypad and [Delete] in the set of keys above the cursor movement keys. Press [Esc] to clear the entry on the input line. Now either press [Delete] , or press [Num Lock] to disengage the numeric keyboard lock then press [Del] on the numeric keypad.

❸ Highlight cells F8 through F9, then release the mouse button.

   TROUBLE? You might have trouble highlighting cell F8 because the row height is so short. If you do, click cell F9 then hold down [Shift] and press [↑] to extend the highlight to cell F8.

❹ Right-click anywhere on the highlighted block. The SpeedMenu appears.

❺ Click **Clear Contents** to clear the formulas from the cells.

Otis realizes that his test values of 100 don't verify if the spreadsheet will handle numbers as large as he included in his spreadsheet plan. There, income and expense figures could be as large as $99,999.99. Otis decides to use 99,999.99 as a test figure.

Testing the Spreadsheet with Extreme Numbers

Otis enters 99,999.99 as income and expense values to check for spreadsheet problems when using large values.

To enter 99,999.99 as income and expense values:

❶ Click cell **B5** to make it the active cell.

❷ Type **99999.99** *without commas* then press **[Enter]**.

❸ Click the **Copy button** 📋 on the notebook SpeedBar.

❹ Highlight cells B5 through E6.

❺ Check to make sure you have the correct block highlighted, otherwise you might copy over some formulas. If the block B5..E6 is not highlighted, repeat Step 4.

❻ Click the **Paste button** 📋 on the notebook SpeedBar. The number 99999.99 is copied to cells B5 through E6.

   TROUBLE? If you pasted the value in the wrong place, remember that you can use the Undo/Redo button 🔄 to undo your mistake.

❼ Highlight cells B10 through E16.

❽ Check to make sure you have the correct block highlighted, otherwise you might copy over some formulas. If the block B10..E16 is not highlighted, repeat Step 7.

❾ Click 🔳. The number 99999.99 is copied to cells B10 through E16.

❿ Click any cell to remove the highlighting. The spreadsheet appears as shown in Figure 2-39.

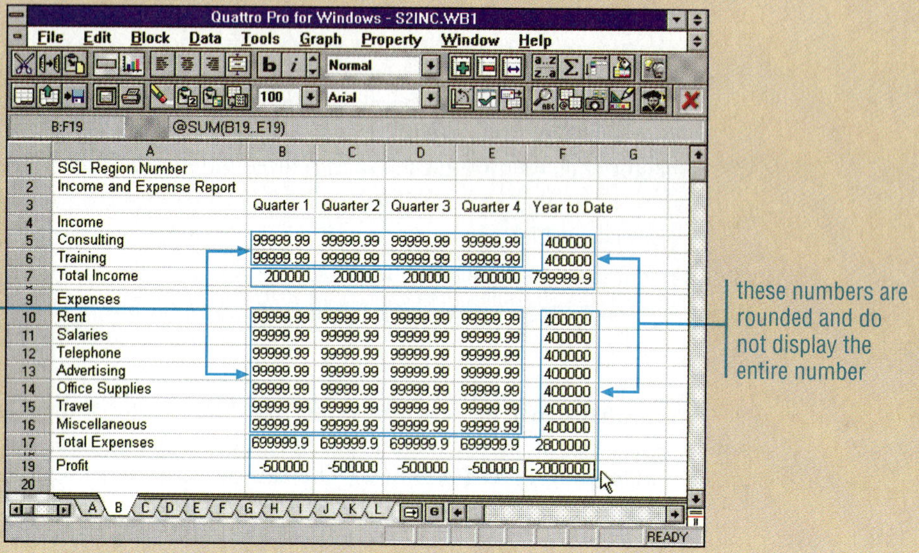

99,999.99 in blocks
B5..E6 and B10..E16

these numbers are
rounded and do
not display the
entire number

Figure 2-39
The spreadsheet
with the extreme
test values

Otis notices that the numbers in the spreadsheet are not maintaining a uniform appearance. Some show two decimal places, some show one, and some show none. Fortunately, Quattro Pro provides an easy way to change how numbers are displayed (you'll learn more about formatting numbers in Tutorial 3).

Otis decides to change how the numbers are displayed in his spreadsheet.

Using the Style List

Quattro Pro provides a group of ready-to-use formats called **styles** in the Style list on the notebook SpeedBar. The available styles are shown in Figure 2-40.

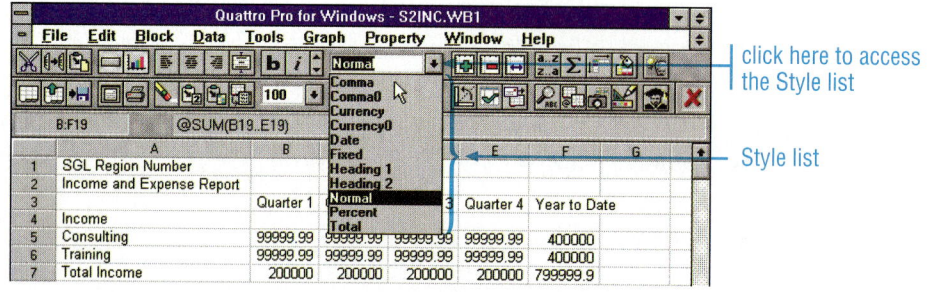

click here to access
the Style list

Style list

Figure 2-40
Styles in the Style list

Quattro Pro uses the Normal style to display the contents of all cells unless you change the style or change the settings of any cell properties (cell alignment, numeric format, text color, and others) that make up the style. Styles are discussed in detail in Tutorial 3. In this tutorial, you'll just use styles to change the appearance of parts of the spreadsheet.

Otis decides to display the numbers in the **Comma** style, which specifies commas to separate groups (hundreds, thousands, and so on), two decimal places, and negative numbers shown in parentheses.

To format the numbers in the spreadsheet with the Comma style:

❶ Highlight cells B5 through F19.

❷ Click the **drop-down list arrow button** to the right of the Style list to display the available styles.

❸ Click **Comma**.

❹ Click any cell to remove the highlighting. The spreadsheet appears as shown in Figure 2-41. Notice that all the cells with numbers are now filled with asterisks (***).

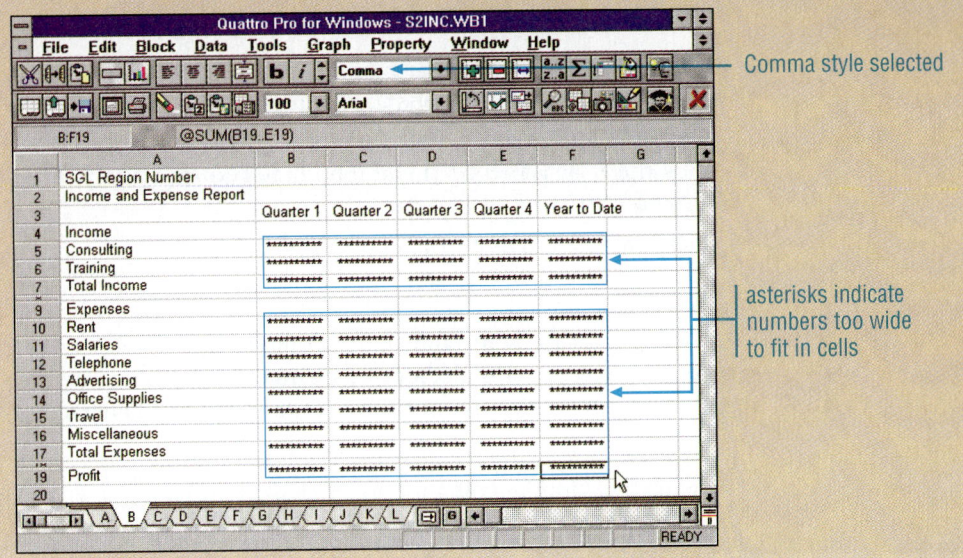

Figure 2-41
The spreadsheet with the Comma style

The asterisks indicate that the cells are not wide enough to display the numbers. This means that Otis will have to adjust the widths of those columns.

What to Do When Asterisks Appear in Cells

Whenever a number is too large to appear within the cell width, Quattro Pro either converts it to scientific notation or fills the cell with asterisks (***) to signal that the number of digits in the value exceeds the width of the cell.

Scientific notation appears in the form 2.2E+02. Scientific notation, which is also known as "power of tens" notation, is used to express a large number as a small number (2.2 in this example) multiplied by 10 raised to some power (the "exponent" of the number 10). The E in the notation stands for the exponent of the number ten, and the number +02 in this example means that 10 is raised to the 2nd power, or squared. Therefore, $2.2E+02 = 2.2 * 10^2 = 2.2 * 100 = 220$.

If a cell has been formatted in a format that Quattro Pro won't convert to scientific notation, Quattro Pro displays asterisks when a number is too large to fit in a cell width. Because Otis formatted the cells with the Comma style, Quattro Pro displays asterisks.

Why does Quattro Pro display asterisks? Because it would be misleading to display only some of the digits of the value. For example, suppose you enter the value 5129 in a cell that is wide enough to display only two digits. Should Quattro Pro display the first two digits or the last two digits? You can see that either choice would be misleading, so Quattro Pro displays the asterisks instead. The values, formats, and formulas have *not* been erased from the cells. To display the numbers, you just need to increase the column widths.

Otis needs to widen columns B, C, D, E, and F. He decides to change the column width using Quattro Pro's ability to fit a column width based on the largest label or value in the column.

To widen columns B, C, D, E, and F based on the largest label or value in the column:
❶ Drag the pointer on the column headings from B to F. Columns B through F are highlighted.
❷ Click the **Fit button** 🔲 on the notebook SpeedBar. Quattro Pro changes the column widths.
❸ Click any cell to remove the highlighting.

The asterisks are gone, and all the numbers are visible, but part of column F can't be seen on the screen. Otis decides to change the width of column A so that the entire spreadsheet can be seen. He decides to try a width of 20 characters.

To change the width of column A to 20 characters:
❶ Click the **column border** for column A. Column A is highlighted.
❷ Right-click anywhere in the highlight to open the SpeedMenu. The SpeedMenu appears.
❸ Click **Block Properties...** to open the Active Page Object Inspector.

❹ Click **Column Width** in the Object Inspector menu. The column width settings appear in the settings pane to the right of the menu.

❺ Type **20** in the Column Width edit field.

❻ Click **OK**. The width of column A changes to 20 characters.

❼ Click cell **A1** (or any other cell) to remove the highlighting.

Otis likes the appearance of his spreadsheet, but decides to add a row of the same height as rows 8 and 18 to separate the main titles from the headings in row 4.

To add a row between rows 2 and 3 and adjust its height:

❶ Click the **row border** of row 3. The entire row is highlighted.

❷ Click the **Insert button** 🔲 on the notebook SpeedBar (or right-click anywhere in the highlighted block to open the SpeedMenu, then click **Insert...**). Quattro Pro inserts a blank row at row 3, and all other rows shift down one row.

❸ Right-click anywhere in the highlighted row to open the SpeedMenu, then click **Block Properties...** to open the Active Block Object Inspector.

❹ Click **Row Height** in the Object Inspector menu. The row height settings appear in the settings pane to the right of the menu.

❺ The row height of rows 8 and 18 is 4, so type **4** in the Row Height box.

❻ Click **OK**. Quattro Pro adjusts the row height.

❼ Click any cell to remove the highlighting. Figure 2-42 shows the completed spreadsheet.

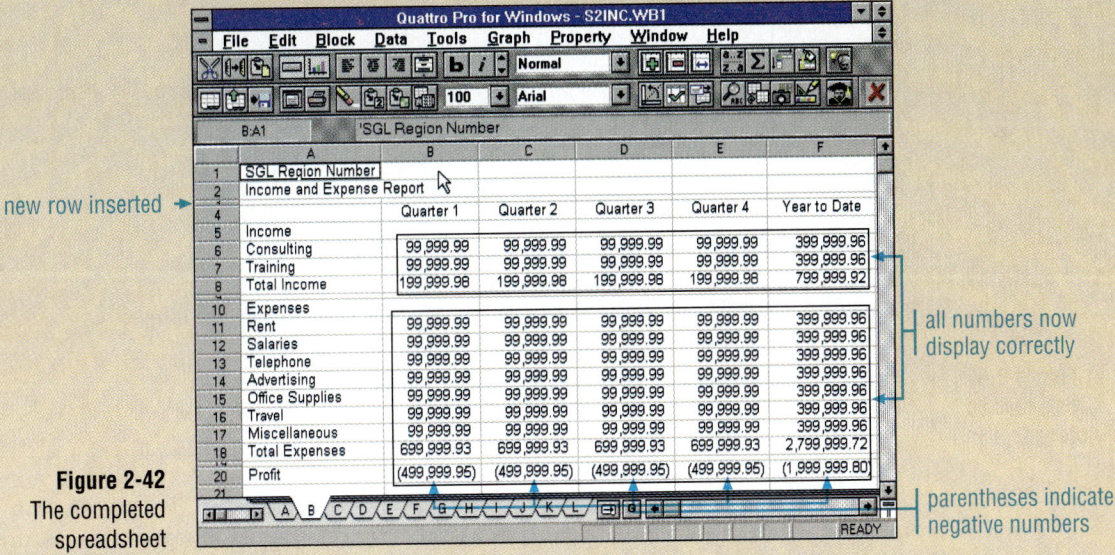

Figure 2-42
The completed
spreadsheet

Otis is satisfied with the spreadsheet's final appearance, and decides that it's time to save a copy of the revised notebook.

To save the S2INC.WB1 notebook with the same filename:
❶ Click the **Save Notebook button** 🖫 on the Productivity Tools SpeedBar (or click **File** then click **Save**).

If you want to take a break and resume the tutorial at a later time, you can exit Quattro Pro by double-clicking the Quattro Pro application Control menu box (or by clicking File, then clicking Exit). When you want to resume the tutorial, launch Quattro Pro, maximize the Quattro Pro and NOTEBK1.WB1 windows, place your Student Disk in the disk drive, and open the file S2INC.WB1. You can then continue with the tutorial.

■   ■   ■

Using the Notebook to Consolidate the Regional Reports

Otis realizes that if he collects three different notebooks from the three regional managers, he'll still have to combine the data himself. It occurs to him that by using several pages in one notebook, he can have Quattro Pro do the combining, or **consolidation,** of the regional reports into the final SGL company report for him. To do this, Otis will need to use four pages in the notebook—one page for the consolidated company report and three pages for the three regional reports. Otis will leave the documentation on page A and use pages B, C, D, and E for the income and expense spreadsheets he needs. Otis's revised plan is shown in Figure 2-43.

Notebook Plan for Income and Expense Report Notebook Template

My Goal:
To develop a Quattro Pro notebook template containing a spreadsheet for regional income and expense reports for each of the three regions and a consolidated spreadsheet to report total SGL income and expenses

What notebook pages will I use?

Page A	Notebook documentation
Page B	SGL Consolidated Income and Expense Report spreadsheet
Page C	Region 1 Income and Expense Report spreadsheet
Page D	Region 2 Income and Expense Report spreadsheet
Page E	Region 3 Income and Expense Report spreadsheet

Figure 2-43
Otis's revised
notebook plan

One of the advantages of Quattro Pro's notebook organization is that you can easily combine information from different spreadsheet pages. A common use of this feature is to have one spreadsheet page that shows the totals of similar cells in other pages. For example, the SGL company first quarter consulting income is the sum of the first quarter consulting income for the three regions.

Otis plans to use page B for the SGL company totals, page C for Region 1, page D for Region 2, and page E for Region 3. When you refer to cells on different pages, you include the page name in the cell reference. For example, if the first quarter consulting income is in cell B6 on each page, then the company income will be in cell B:B6 and would be calculated as =C:B6+D:B6+E:B6. This is shown in Figure 2-44.

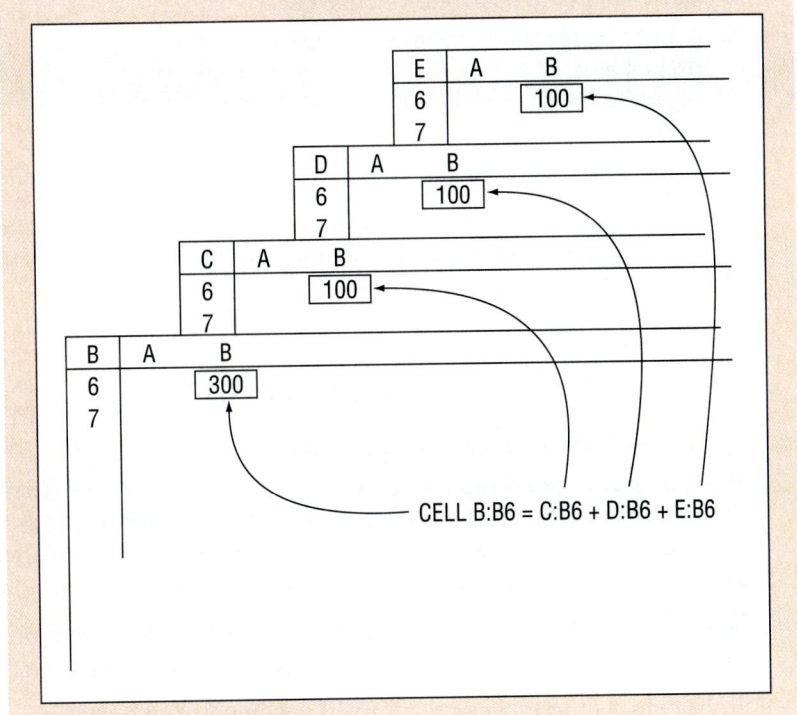

CELL B:B6 = C:B6 + D:B6 + E:B6

Figure 2-44
Calculating first
quarter consulting
income by combining
information from
different spreadsheets

Otis's first step is to revise the documentation in the notebook so that it accurately reflects the changes he's making.

Revising the Notebook Documentation

When you modify an existing notebook, you should revise any documentation to reflect the changes. Users of the notebook will rely on the documentation, and out-of-date or incomplete documentation can waste time and effort.

Otis needs to revise the purpose statement to show that the notebook also consolidates the regional reports, and revise the contents to show that the notebook now contains one consolidated report and three regional reports.

To revise the notebook documentation purpose statement:
❶ If the page tab for page A is not visible, scroll the notebook to make it visible. Click **page tab A** to make spreadsheet page A the active page.
❷ Drag the pointer across the row borders for rows 11 and 12 to highlight rows 11 and 12.
❸ Click the **Insert button** 🔲 on the notebook SpeedBar (or right-click anywhere in the highlighted area to open the SpeedMenu, then click **Insert...**). Two blank rows are inserted as rows 11 and 12. The information that was in row 12 is now in row 14.

❹ Click cell **B11** to make it the active cell.

❺ Type **This notebook will be used by SGL company headquarters** then press **[Enter]**.

❻ Click cell **B12** to make it the active cell.

❼ Type **to consolidate the regional information.** (be sure to include the period) then press **[Enter]**.

Next Otis will update the contents section of the documentation.

To revise the notebook contents documentation:

❶ Click cell **B16** to make it the active cell.

❷ Type **Page C** then press **[↓]**.

❸ In cell B17 Type **Page D** then press **[↓]**.

❹ In cell B18 type **Page E** then press **[Enter]**.

❺ Click cell **C15** to make it the active cell.

❻ Press **[F2]** to begin Edit mode and edit the label to read **SGL Consolidated Income and Expense Report spreadsheet** then press **[Enter]**, then press **[↓]**. This entry replaces the original contents of the cell, "Income and Expense Report spreadsheet."

❼ In cell C16 type **Region 1 Income and Expense Report spreadsheet** then press **[↓]**.

❽ In cell C17 type **Region 2 Income and Expense Report spreadsheet** then press **[↓]**.

❾ In cell C18 type **Region 3 Income and Expense Report spreadsheet** then press **[Enter]**.

The final appearance of the revised documentation is shown in Figure 2-45. Compare your screen with the figure, and make any necessary changes.

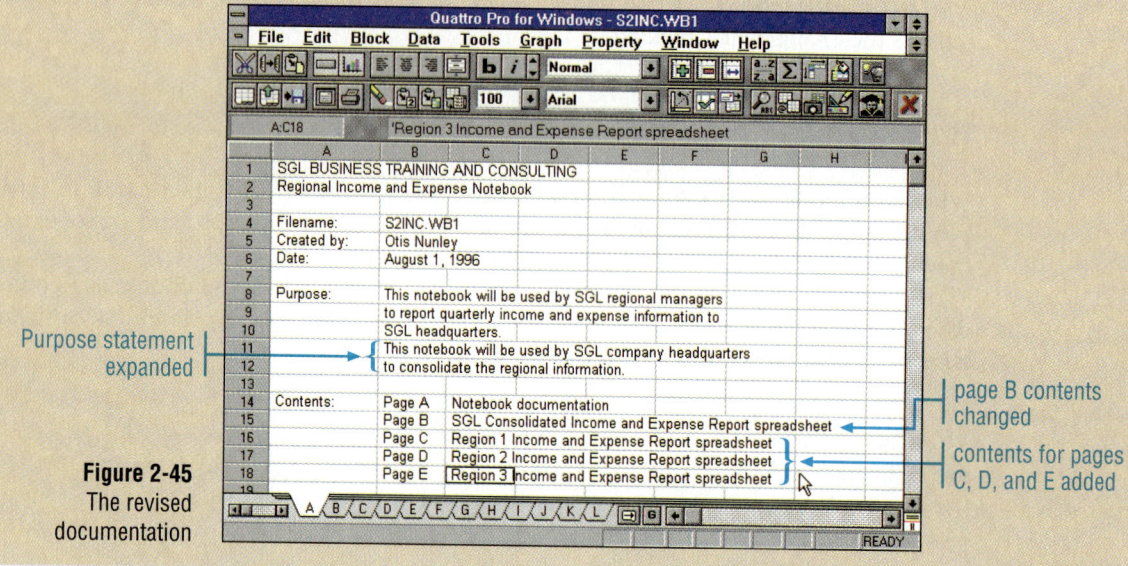

Purpose statement expanded

page B contents changed

contents for pages C, D, and E added

Figure 2-45
The revised documentation

Now Otis is ready to create the income and expense spreadsheets for each of the three regions. Because each region's spreadsheet is identical, Otis can copy the spreadsheet he's already created to pages C, D, and E. Then he'll just type the region number on each page. Originally, Otis planned to have the regional managers type in the region numbers, but his revised notebook plan requires him to do it.

Copying the Spreadsheet to Other Pages

When you want to copy a large block or an entire spreadsheet to another page and keep the column widths, row heights, etc., intact, you use the **Model copy option** of the Copy command on the Block menu. The copy methods you used earlier in this tutorial will not maintain column widths or row heights; therefore, they are not efficient ways to copy an entire spreadsheet.

Copying Blocks to Other Pages

- Make sure that the page containing the block you want to copy is the active page.

- Highlight the block you want to copy.

- Click Block then click Copy.

- To copy to the same block of cells on another page, edit the block address in the To edit field by changing the page name to the name of the new page.

or

To copy to a different block of cells on another page, edit the block address in the To edit field to the complete block address on the new page *including the name of the new page*.

- Click the Model copy check box.

- Click OK.

Otis wants to copy the spreadsheet on page B to pages C, D, and E.

To copy the spreadsheet on page B to page C:
❶ Click **page tab B** to make page B the active page.
❷ Highlight cells A1 through F20.
❸ Click **Block** then click **Copy**. The Block Copy dialog box appears.
❹ In the To edit field, change the page name to **C**. The full block address should read C:A1..F20.

❺ Click the **Model copy** check box. The Block Copy dialog box now appears as shown in Figure 2-46.

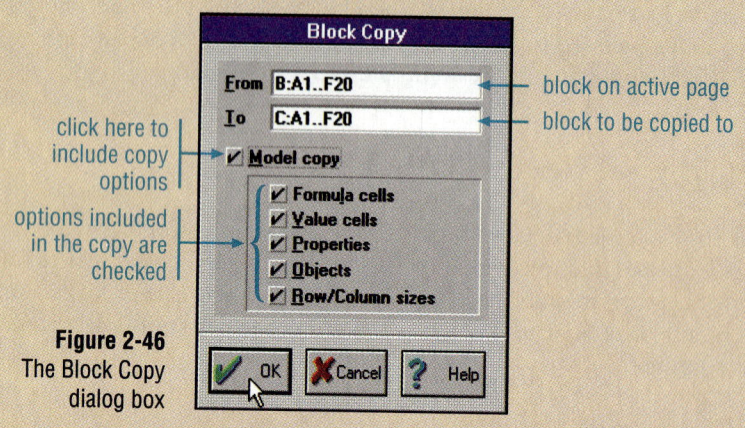

click here to include copy options

options included in the copy are checked

Figure 2-46
The Block Copy dialog box

❻ Click **OK**. The spreadsheet is copied to page C.

❼ Click any cell to remove the highlighting.

Otis wants to make sure that the spreadsheet was copied correctly. He also needs to enter the region number for page C.

To see the spreadsheet on page C and enter the region number:

❶ Click **page tab C** to make C the active page. Notice that the spreadsheet was copied correctly, and that all column widths and row heights have been maintained.

❷ Click cell **A1** to make it the active cell.

❸ Type **SGL Region 1** then press **[Enter]**.

Now Otis needs to copy the spreadsheet to pages D and E. To do this, he can copy the spreadsheet on the active page, page C.

To copy the spreadsheet on page C to pages D and E:

❶ Highlight cells A1 through F20.

❷ Click **Block** then click **Copy**. The Block Copy dialog box appears.

❸ In the To edit field, change the page name to **D**. The full block address should read D:A1..F20.

❹ Click the **Model copy** check box.

❺ Click **OK**. The spreadsheet is copied to page D. The block from A1 through F20 should still be highlighted.

TROUBLE? If the block is no longer highlighted, you might have clicked a cell or some other object. Drag the pointer to highlight the block from A1 through F20.

❻ Click **Block** then click **Copy**. The Block Copy dialog box appears.

❼ In the To edit field, change the page name to **E**. The full block address should read E:A1..F20.

❽ Click the **Model copy** check box.

❾ Click **OK**. The spreadsheet is copied to page E.

Otis has copied the spreadsheet and now he needs to edit the region numbers so each spreadsheet is correctly identified.

To edit the region numbers on pages D and E:

❶ Click **page tab D** to make D the active page.

❷ Click cell **A1** to make it the active cell.

❸ Press **[F2]** to edit the contents of cell A1. " 'SGL Region 1" appears on the input line.

❹ Edit the contents of cell A1 by changing the number 1 to the number **2**. The input line should read **'SGL Region 2** (remember to leave the label-prefix where it is), as shown in Figure 2-47.

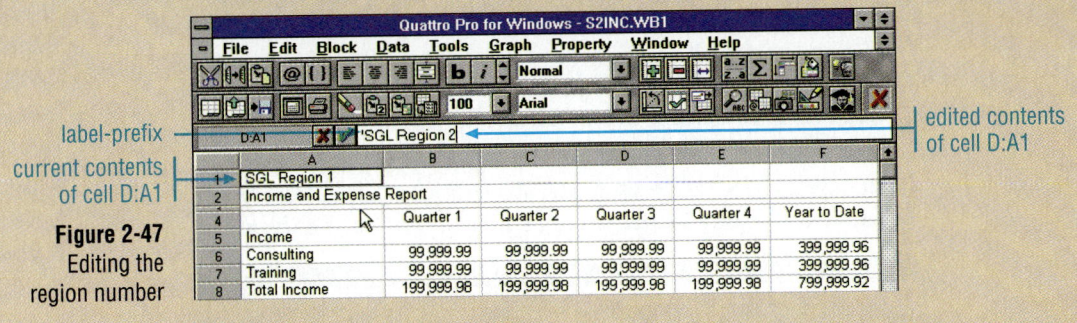

label-prefix —
current contents of cell D:A1

edited contents of cell D:A1

Figure 2-47
Editing the region number

❺ Press **[Enter]**.

❻ Click **page tab E** to make E the active page.

❼ Click cell **A1** to make it the active cell.

❽ Press **[F2]** to edit the contents of cell A1. " 'SGL Region 1" appears on the input line.

❾ Edit the contents of cell A1 by changing the number 1 to the number **3**. The input line should read **'SGL Region 3** (remember to leave the label-prefix where it is).

❿ Press **[Enter]**.

Otis has completed setting up the three spreadsheets for the regions. Now he's ready to change the title of the spreadsheet on page B and build the formulas that will consolidate the information from the regions into the company totals.

To change the spreadsheet title on page B:

❶ Click **page tab B** to make B the active page.

❷ Click cell **A1** to make it the active cell.

❸ Type **SGL Consolidated Quarterly Income and Expense Report** then press **[Enter]**.

Now Otis needs to build the consolidation formulas.

Entering the Consolidation Formulas

Building formulas that use values in different spreadsheets is easy in Quattro Pro. The only difference is that you have to include the spreadsheet page name in the cell references in the formula.

Otis starts by building the formula to combine the first quarter consulting income of the three regions.

To enter the formula to combine the first quarter consulting income for the three regions:

❶ Make sure that page B is the active page.

❷ Click cell **B6** to make it the active cell.

❸ Enter the formula **=C:B6+D:B6+E:B6** then press **[Enter]**. As shown in Figure 2-48, the value 299,999.97 appears in cell B6. This value is the sum of the values for first quarter consulting income in the spreadsheets for the three regions.

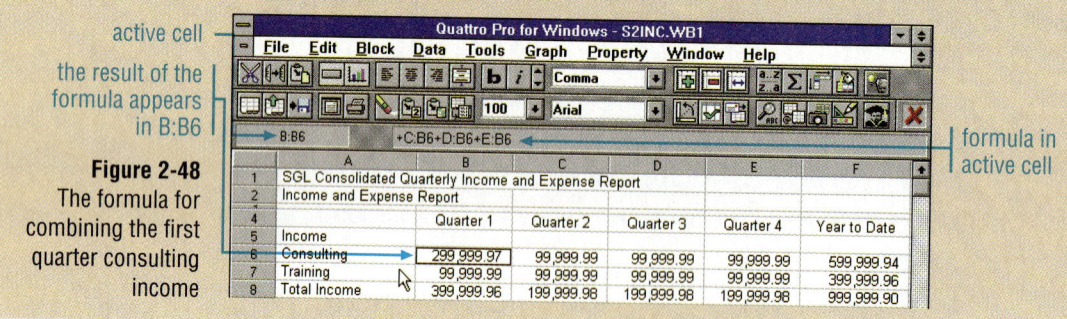

active cell

the result of the formula appears in B:B6

Figure 2-48
The formula for combining the first quarter consulting income

formula in active cell

Otis can now simply copy this formula to the other cells in the consolidation spreadsheet on page B where he needs to add the values from the regions. These cells are the income and expense categories for the four quarters. Otis will *not* replace the total income, total expenses, profit, and year-to-date formulas that are already in spreadsheet page B. Now these formulas will calculate the combined total income, total expenses, profit, and year-to-date amounts for the entire SGL company.

Otis copies his formula to all other cells where he wants to add the values in the regional spreadsheets.

To copy the formula in B:B6 to the other cells that combine the values in spreadsheets C, D, and E:

❶ Make sure that page B is the active page.

❷ Click cell **B6** to make it the active cell.

❸ Click the **Copy button** 🖳 on the notebook SpeedBar.

❹ Highlight cells B6 through E7.

❺ Make sure you have the correct block highlighted, otherwise you might copy over some formulas. If block B6..E7 is not highlighted, repeat Step 4.

❻ Click the **Paste button** 🖳 on the notebook SpeedBar. The formula in B6 is copied to cells B6 through E7.

❼ Highlight cells B11 through E17.

❽ Make sure you have the correct block highlighted, otherwise you might copy over some formulas. If block B11..E17 is not highlighted, repeat Step 7.

❾ Click 🖳 on the notebook SpeedBar. The formula in cell B6 is copied to cells B11 through E17.

❿ Click **B11** (or any other cell) to remove the highlighting. The spreadsheet appears as shown in Figure 2-49. Notice that some cells have asterisks, indicating that the columns are not wide enough to display the numbers.

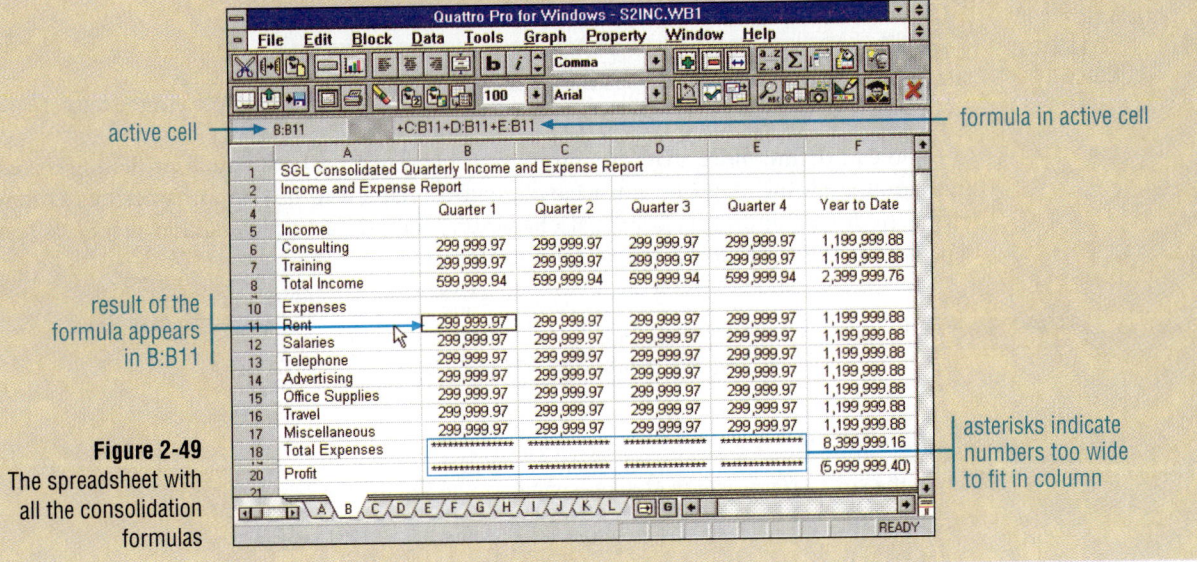

Figure 2-49
The spreadsheet with all the consolidation formulas

Otis realizes that he'll have to adjust the column widths again to correct the cells filled with asterisks. He wants to keep all the column widths the same on the consolidation page and the regional spreadsheet pages. He can adjust the column width on all four pages at the same time by using Quattro Pro's Group mode.

Using Group Mode

Quattro Pro lets you define a set of spreadsheet pages as a group so that you can make changes to all the pages in the group at the same time using **Group mode**. You define a group using the Define Group... command on the Tools menu. You activate Group mode by clicking the Group button, as shown in Figure 2-50.

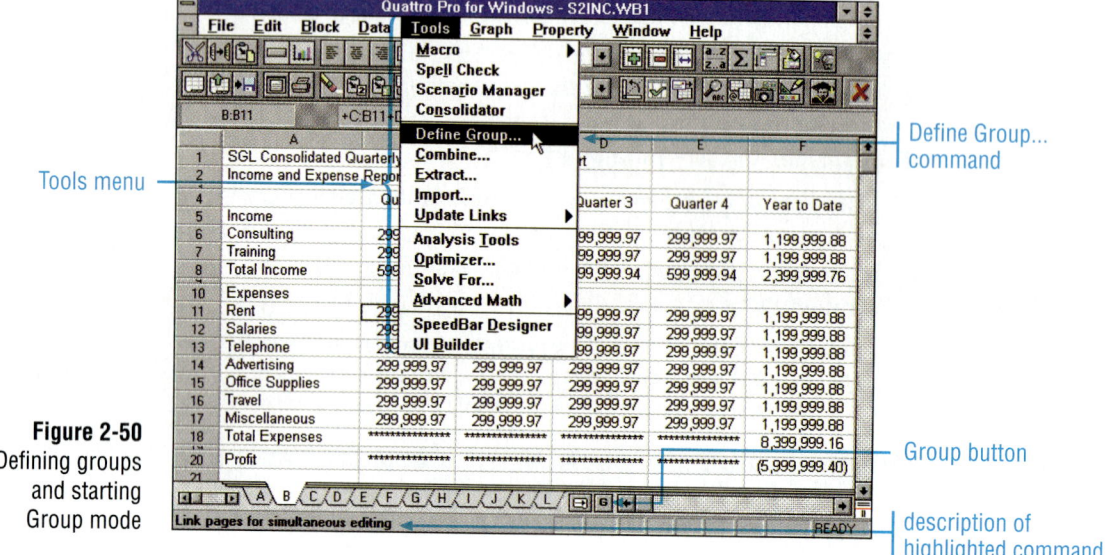

Figure 2-50
Defining groups
and starting
Group mode

You can define more than one group, but each spreadsheet page can belong to only one group at a time. A group must have a name assigned to it. Group names can contain letters, numbers, and certain special characters, including ! (exclamation mark), % (percent sign), and ? (question mark). Group names cannot contain spaces.

To use a group, you start Group mode by clicking the Group button. When Group mode is activated, a line appears below the G on the Group button and below the page tabs of the pages in the defined groups (the line will be blue on a color monitor). All defined groups become active when Group mode is on. When Group mode is active, any change made to one of the pages in a group is applied to all the other pages in the group, and a two-dimensional selection in one page (rows and columns) becomes a three-dimensional selection across the pages (rows, columns, and pages) in the group.

If you are entering labels, values, or formulas in a spreadsheet, you must hold down [Ctrl] when you press [Enter] if you want the entry to be placed in all the spreadsheets in the group. Similarly, if you are clearing cell contents using [Del], you must also hold down [Ctrl] when you press [Del] if you want the deletion to affect all the spreadsheets in the group.

The Group button works as a toggle; to deactivate Group mode, you simply click the Group button again.

Otis wants to create a group consisting of the consolidation spreadsheet and the spreadsheets for the three regions, so his group will include pages B, C, D, and E. Otis decides to name his group "Consolidation."

To define the group consisting of pages B, C, D, and E then activate Group mode:
❶ Make sure that page B is the active page. This step is *not* necessary to define the group, but do it to be consistent with the steps.
❷ Click **Tools** then click **Define Group…**. The Define/Modify Group dialog box appears.
❸ In the Group Name edit field, type **Consolidation** *but do not press [Enter]*.
❹ Click the **First Page edit field** (or press [Tab]) to move to the First Page edit field, then type **B** *but do not press [Enter]*.
❺ Click the **Last Page edit field** (or press [Tab]) to move to the Last Page edit field, then type **E** *but do not press [Enter]*. The dialog box now shows the group name, the first page in the group, and the last page in the group, as shown in Figure 2-51. Make sure your settings match those shown in the figure.

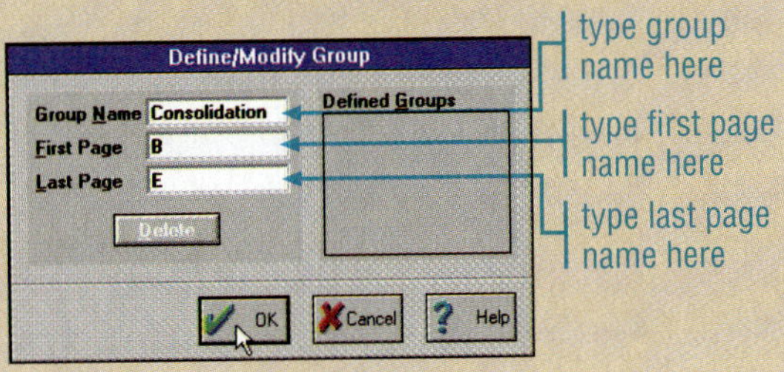

Figure 2-51
The Define/Modify Group dialog box settings

❻ Click **OK** or press [Enter].
Now Otis activates Group mode.
❼ Click the **Group button** ▣. A line appears below the letter G on the Group button and below the page tabs for pages B, C, D, and E.

With Group mode active, any changes that Otis makes to one of the spreadsheets will also be made to all the other spreadsheets in the group. Otis is ready to change the column widths in the columns containing asterisks. After trying several different column widths, Otis decides to make column A 16 characters wide, and columns B, C, D, E, and F 14 characters wide. With these widths, all the columns appear on his screen.

To change the column widths:

❶ Make sure page B is the active page.

❷ Right-click **column border A** to open the SpeedMenu.

❸ Click **Block Properties...** to open the Active Page Object Inspector.

❹ Click **Column Width** in the Object Inspector menu. The column width settings appear in the settings pane to the right of the menu.

❺ Type **16** in the Column Width edit field, then click **OK**. The width of column A changes to 16 characters.

❻ Highlight the borders for columns B through F.

❼ Right-click anywhere in the highlight to open the SpeedMenu.

❽ Click **Block Properties...** then click **Column Width** in the Object Inspector menu.

❾ Type **14** in the Column Width edit field, then click **OK**. The width of columns B, C, D, E, and F changes to 14 characters.

❿ Click cell **A1** (or any other cell) to remove the highlighting. All columns in the spreadsheet can now be seen on the screen.

Otis wants to make sure that the column width adjustments were made to the other spreadsheets in the group.

To check the column width adjustments of the other spreadsheets in the group:

❶ Click **page tab C** to make C the active page. The spreadsheet appears as shown in Figure 2-52. Notice that the column widths were adjusted correctly.

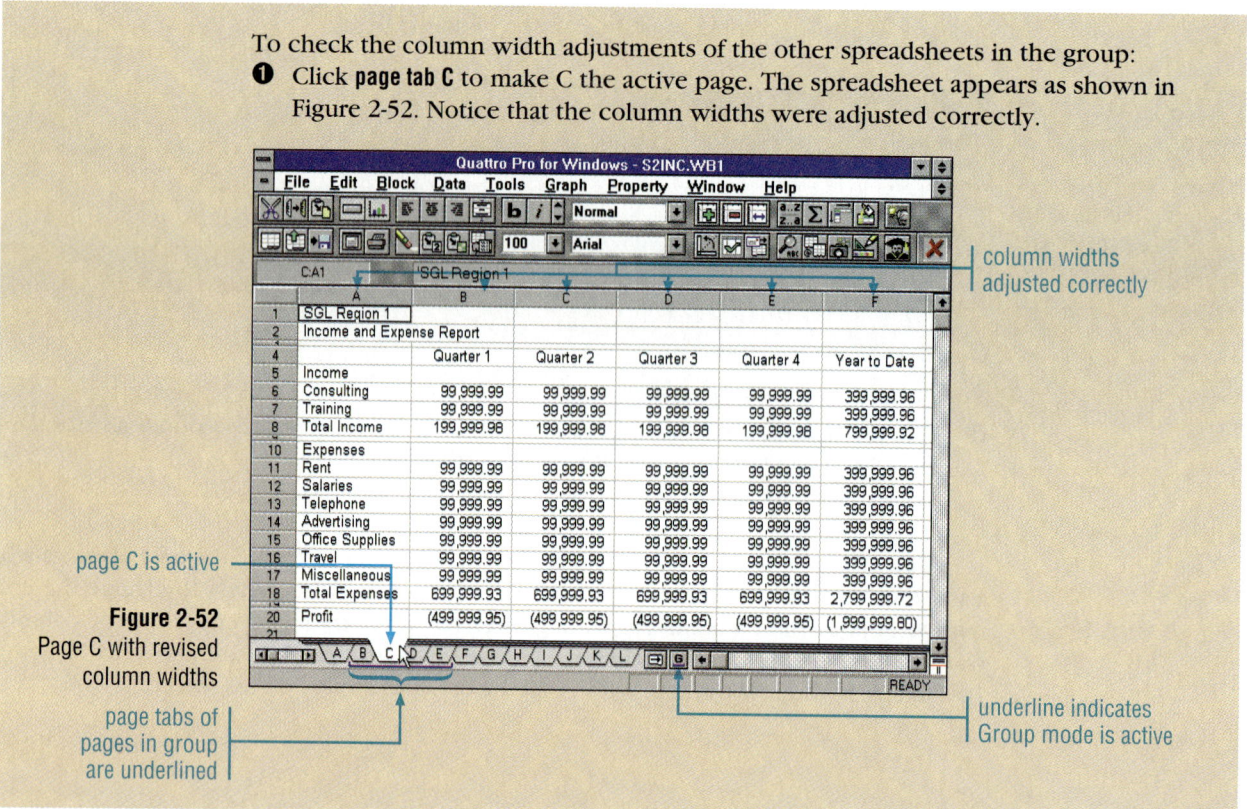

Figure 2-52
Page C with revised
column widths

page C is active

page tabs of
pages in group
are underlined

column widths
adjusted correctly

underline indicates
Group mode is active

❷ Click **page tab D** to make D the active page. Notice that the column widths were adjusted correctly.

❸ Click **page tab E** to make E the active page. Again, notice that the column widths were adjusted correctly.

❹ Click the **Group button** 🔲 to deactivate Group mode.

❺ Click **page tab A** to make A the active page.

❻ Click cell **A1** to make it the active cell.

Otis realizes that he hasn't saved his work recently, and he decides to save a copy of the revised notebook.

To save the S2INC.WB1 notebook with the same filename:
❶ Click the **Save Notebook button** 🔲 on the Productivity Tools SpeedBar (or click **File** then click **Save**).

If you want to take a break and resume the tutorial at a later time, you can exit Quattro Pro by double-clicking the Quattro Pro application Control menu box (or by clicking File then clicking Exit). When you want to resume the tutorial, launch Quattro Pro, maximize the Quattro Pro and NOTEBK1.WB1 windows, place your Student Disk in the disk drive, and open the file S2INC.WB1. You can then continue with the tutorial.

■   ■   ■

Now that the notebook template is nearly complete, Otis needs to remove the test values (99,999.99) in the regional spreadsheets to convert these to templates.

Clearing Test Values from the Spreadsheet

Otis decides to use Group mode to simplify the task of clearing the test values, but he realizes that he needs a group consisting of only spreadsheet pages C, D, and E. He will not include page B because clearing the cells on page B would remove the consolidation formula. Because a spreadsheet page can be in only one group at a time, Otis will have to delete the group named "Consolidation" and create a new group. He decides to name the new group "Regions."

To delete the Consolidation group and define the Regions group:
❶ Make sure that page C is the active page. This step is *not* necessary to define the group, but do it to be consistent with the steps.

❷ Click **Tools** then click **Define Group....** The Define/Modify Group dialog box appears.

❸ Click the group name **Consolidation** in the Defined Groups box. The group name, the first page, and the last page for Consolidation appear in the edit fields, and the Delete button becomes available for use. See Figure 2-53.

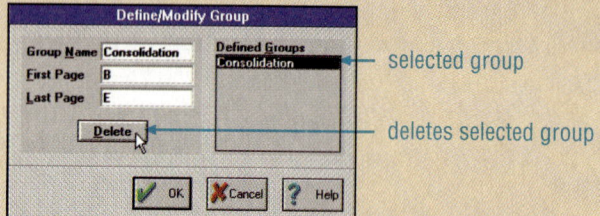

Figure 2-53
Deleting a
defined group

❹ Click the **Delete button**. The Consolidation group is deleted. Notice that the Define/Modify Group dialog box remains active.

❺ In the Group Name edit field, type **Regions** *but do not press [Enter]*.

❻ Click the **First Page edit field** (or press [Tab]) to move to the First Page edit field, then type **C** *but do not press [Enter]*.

❼ Click the **Last Page edit field** (or press [Tab]) to move to the Last Page edit field, then type **E**.

❽ Click **OK** or press [Enter].

Now Otis can clear the test values.

To clear the test values from the spreadsheet:
❶ Make sure page C is active.

❷ Click the **Group button** ⬛ to activate Group mode so you can work with the three region spreadsheets simultaneously. A line appears below the letter G on the group button and below the page tabs for pages C, D, and E.

❸ Highlight cells B6 through E7. *Do not drag to column F or into row 8.* Column F and row 8 contain formulas, and you don't want to clear them.
   TROUBLE? If you highlighted column F or row 8, drag the pointer from B6 to E7 again.

❹ Right-click anywhere in the highlighted block to open the SpeedMenu.

❺ Click **Clear Contents** to clear the test values from the selected cells.

❻ Highlight cells B11 through E17. *Do not drag to column F or row 18.* Column F and row 18 contain formulas, and you don't want to clear them.
   TROUBLE? If you highlighted column F or row 18, drag the pointer from B11 to E17 again.

❼ Right-click anywhere in the highlighted block to open the SpeedMenu.

❽ Click **Clear Contents** to clear the test values from the selected cells.

❾ Click any cell to remove the highlighting. Notice that the cells that contained the test values are now blank, and the cells containing formulas all show 0.00.

Otis wants to check the other spreadsheets in the group to make sure that the test values were deleted from them as well.

To check the other spreadsheets in the group:

❶ Click **page tab D** to inspect spreadsheet D. Notice that all the test values were deleted and the cells containing formulas show 0.00.

❷ Click **page tab E** to inspect spreadsheet E. Again, notice that all the test values were deleted and the cells containing formulas show 0.00.

❸ Click **page tab A** to return to spreadsheet A then press **[Home]** to make A1 the active cell.

❹ Click the **Group button** ▣ to deactivate Group mode.

Now the template notebook is complete and Otis is ready to save it, close the notebook, then exit Quattro Pro and Windows.

To save the S2INC.WB1 notebook with the same filename then close the notebook and exit Quattro Pro:

❶ Click the **Save Notebook button** ▣ on the Productivity Tools SpeedBar (or click **File** then click **Save**).

❷ Click **File** then click **Close** to close the notebook.

❸ Click **File** then click **Exit** to exit Quattro Pro.

■   ■   ■

Otis has finished his template notebook and is ready to circulate it to the regional managers.

Questions

1. What are the four activities required to create an effective spreadsheet?
2. Which command do you use to name a spreadsheet and save it?
3. According to the precedence of operations, calculate the results of the following formulas:

   2+3*6

   (4/2)*5

   2^2+5

   10+10/2
4. Why would you use a simple value such as 1 as a test value?
5. Describe the methods you can use to enter cell references in a formula.
6. When you copy a formula, what happens to the relative references?
7. Which Quattro Pro feature will automatically complete a series such as Jan, Feb, Mar?
8. All references in formulas are _____ unless you specify otherwise.
9. _____ references contain a dollar sign before the column letter and/or row number.
10. How do you clear the contents of a cell?
11. What is the difference between clearing a cell and clearing the contents of a cell?
12. Write the formula to go in cell A:B10 that will add the values in cell B10 in spreadsheets B, C, and D.
13. What is a group of spreadsheet pages, and how do you define one?
14. What is Group mode, and how does it affect your work in a notebook?
15. Why does Quattro Pro display asterisks in a cell?
16. How is a notebook template different from any other notebook?

Tutorial Assignments

Otis Nunley wants to test his notebook using realistic data. The test values he has used so far have shown him that the formulas appear to be working correctly, but he knows that a second check with another data set will help him be sure that he hasn't overlooked any problems. Otis knows that this is an extremely important template notebook. Regional managers will enter values into the spreadsheets, and they will assume the spreadsheets calculate the correct results. Otis is determined to test the notebook thoroughly before he distributes it to any regional offices.

You are the regional manager for Region 1 of SGL. Otis decides to send you a copy of the new quarterly income and expense report template notebook. Otis asks you to test the notebook by entering the information for the first two quarters of this year into the template for your region, and sending a printed copy of the spreadsheet back to him. Do the following:

1. Launch Quattro Pro, if necessary, and insert your Student Disk into the disk drive.
2. Open the template notebook T2INC.WB1.
3. Save the notebook as S2REG1.WB1 so that you do not change the original file.
4. Modify the documentation on page A to show the new filename of S2REG1.WB1.
5. Make page C, the page for Region 1, the active page. Enter the values for Quarter 1 and Quarter 2 as shown in Figure 2-54.
6. Compare your results with those in Figure 2-54 to verify that the formulas are correct.
7. Print the spreadsheet.
8. Save the notebook S2REG1.WB1, then close the notebook.

Figure 2-54

C	A	B	C	D	E	F
1	SGL Region 1					
2	Income and Expense Report					
3						
4		Quarter 1	Quarter 2	Quarter 3	Quarter 4	Year to Date
5	Income					
6	Consulting	37,920.00	32,550.00			70,470.00
7	Training	11,560.00	13,520.00			25,080.00
8	Total Income	49,480.00	46,070.00	0.00	0.00	95,550.00
9						
10	Expenses					
11	Rent	2,200.00	2,200.00			4,400.00
12	Salaries	7,200.00	7,200.00			14,400.00
13	Telephone	547.00	615.00			1,162.00
14	Advertising	1,215.00	692.00			1,907.00
15	Office Supplies	315.00	297.00			612.00
16	Travel	1,257.00	1,408.00			2,665.00
17	Miscellaneous	928.00	802.00			1,730.00
18	Total Expenses	13,662.00	13,214.00	0.00	0.00	26,876.00
19						
20	Profit	35,818.00	32,856.00	0.00	0.00	68,674.00

Otis shows the template to his boss, Joan LeValle. She suggests several additions to the template notebook. Joan mentions that some of the regions have started long-term education programs for their employees, so she wants you to add a separate expense category for education.

9. Open the template notebook T2INC.WB1.

10. Save the notebook as S2INC3.WB1 so that you do not change the original file.

11. Modify the documentation on page A to show the new filename of S2INC3.WB1.

12. In the spreadsheets on pages B, C, D, and E, insert a row where row 15 is currently located.

13. In the spreadsheets on pages B, C, D, and E, enter the row label "Education" in cell A15.

14. In the spreadsheets in the Regions group (pages C, D, and E), copy the formula from cell F14 to cell F15.

15. In the consolidation spreadsheet (page B), copy the formula from cells B14..F14 to cells B15..F15.

16. Change the page names on the page tabs. Name page A as "Documentation," page B as "SGL," page C as "Reg1," page D as "Reg2," and page E as "Reg3."

17. Save the notebook S2INC3.WB1, then close the notebook.

18. Open the template notebook S2INC3.WB1 and test it by entering 10 as the test value for each of the income and expense categories for each quarter in each regional spreadsheet. Make any revisions necessary to formulas or formats so that the notebook works according to Otis's plan.

19. Save the notebook with the test values as S2TEST.WB1.

20. Modify the documentation on the Documentation page to show the new filename of S2TEST.WB1.

21. Print a copy of each of the five pages in the notebook S2TEST.WB1.

22. Save the notebook S2TEST.WB1, then close the notebook.

SGL is expanding and has just added a fourth region. Otis asks you to revise the template notebook to include a template for Region 4 on page F.

23. Open the template notebook S2INC3.WB1.

24. Save the notebook as S2INC4.WB1 so that you do not change the original file.

25. Modify the documentation on the Documentation page to show the new filename of S2INC4.WB1.

26. Use the Block Copy command to copy the spreadsheet on page Reg3 to page F. (*Hint:* Remember to use the Model copy option.)

27. Rename page tab F to "Reg4."

28. Edit cell A1 on page Reg4 to read "SGL Region 4."

29. Modify the Regions group so that Reg4 is included. Check this by activating Group mode, then deactivate Group mode.

30. Modify the consolidation formulas on page SGL so that they add the numbers from all four regions.

31. Print a copy of page Reg4.

32. Save the notebook S2INC4.WB1, then close the notebook.

Case Problems

1. Tracking Ticket Sales for the Brookstone Dance Group

Robin Yeh is the ticket sales coordinator for the Brookstone Dance Group, a community dance company. Brookstone sells five types of tickets: season tickets, reserved seating, general admission, student tickets, and children's tickets.

Robin needs a way to track the sales of each of the five ticket types. She has done the initial planning for a Quattro Pro notebook that will track ticket sales. She has asked you to create the notebook, which will contain a documentation page and a spread page. Study Robin's spreadsheet plan in Figure 2-55 and her spreadsheet sketch in Figure 2-56, then build, test, and document a template into which Robin can enter ticket sales data.

Figure 2-55

Spreadsheet Plan for Brookstone Dance Group

Goal:
To create a spreadsheet to track monthly ticket sales

What results do I want to see?
Total ticket sales for each month
Total annual sales for each of the five ticket types
Total annual sales for all ticket types

What information do I need?
The monthly sales for each type of ticket

What calculations will I perform?
Total ticket sales = season tickets + reserved seating + geneeral admission + student tickets + children's tickets

Season tickets annual sales = sum of each month's sales of season tickets
Reserved seating annual sales = sum of each month's sales of reserved seating
General admission annual sales = sum of each month's sales of general admission
Student tickets annual sales = sum of each month's sales of student tickets
Children's ticket annual sales = sum of each month's sales of children's tickets

Figure 2-56

Brookstone Dance Group Ticket Sales

	Jan	Feb	Mar	April	YTD
Seasons tickets	:	:	:	:	{season ticket annual sales formula}
Reserved tickets	:	:	:	:	{reserved seating annual sales formula}
General admission	:	:	:	:	{general admission annual sales formula}
Student tickets	:	:	:	:	{student ticket annual sales formula}
Children's tickets	:	:	:	:	{children's ticket annual sales formula}
Total ticket sales	{total ticket sales formula}	{total ticket sales formula}	{total ticket sales formula}	{total ticket sales formula}	{total ticket sales formula}

1. Launch Quattro Pro and make sure you have a blank notebook on your screen. If the Quattro Pro window is open and you do not have a blank notebook, click File then click New.
2. Use page A for documentation. Model your documentation after Otis's documentation for SGL in the tutorial.

3. Save the template notebook as S2TCKTS.WB1.
4. Use page B to build your spreadsheet.
5. Center the labels for the months. Enter "Jan" then use SpeedFill to automatically fill in the rest of the month names.
6. Create the formulas to calculate total ticket sales and year-to-date sales for each ticket type.
7. Test the template using 100 as the test value, then make any changes necessary for the template to work correctly.
8. Clear the test values from the cells.
9. Save the notebook again.
10. Print both pages of the notebook.
11. Close the template notebook.
12. Open the notebook S2TCKTS.WB1 and enter some realistic data for January, February, and March. You can make up this data, keeping in mind that Brookstone typically has total ticket sales of about 500 per month.
13. Print page B with the realistic test data, then close the notebook without saving it.

2.   Tracking Customer Activity at Brownie's Sandwich Shop

Sherri McWilliams is the assistant manager at Brownie's Sandwich Shop. She is responsible for scheduling personnel. To plan an effective schedule, Sherri wants to know the busiest days of the week and the busiest hours of the day. She started to create a notebook to help track the customer activity in the shop, and she has asked if you could help her complete the spreadsheet. Open the notebook P2SNDWCH.WB1. Documentation is on page A and Sherri's spreadsheet is on page B.

1. Save the notebook as S2SNDWCH.WB1 so you will not modify the original file.
2. Complete the documentation of page A.
   For the spreadsheet on page B:
3. Use SpeedFill to complete the column titles for the days of the week.
4. Use SpeedFill to complete the labels showing open hours from 10:00AM to 9:00PM.
5. Use SpeedSum to create a formula to calculate the total number of customers in cell B15.
6. Copy the formula in cell B15 to cells C15 through H15.
7. Enter the column title "Hourly" in cell I1, and the title "Average" in cell I2. Sherri plans to use column I to display the average number of customers for each one-hour time period.
8. Enter the formula =@AVG(B3..H3) in cell I3, then copy it to cells I4 through I15.
9. Enter "Sandwich Shop Activity" in cell A1 as the spreadsheet title.
10. Save the notebook as S2SNDWCH.WB1.
11. Print both pages of the notebook.
12. On your printout, circle the busiest day of the week and the hour of the day with the highest average customer traffic.

3.   Activity Reports for Magazines Unlimited

Norm McGruder was just hired as a fulfillment driver for Magazines Unlimited. He is responsible for stocking magazines in supermarkets and bookstores in his territory. Each week Norm goes to each store in his territory, removes the outdated magazines, and delivers the current issues.

Plan, build, test, and document a template notebook that Norm can use to keep track of the number of magazines he removes and replaces from the Safeway supermarket during one week. Although Norm typically handles 100 to 150 different magazine titles at the Safeway store, for this Case Problem, create the template for only 12 of them: *Auto News*, *Bride*, *Fortune*, *Time*, *Newsweek*, *Ebony*, *PC Week*, *People*, *Forbes*, *Money*, *Business Week*, and *Sports Illustrated*.

You should document your notebook on page A, and your spreadsheet on page B should contain:
• a column that lists the magazine names
• a column that contains the number of magazines delivered

- a column that contains the number of magazines removed
- a column that contains a formula to calculate the number of magazines sold by subtracting the number of magazines removed from the number of magazines delivered
- a cell that displays the total number of magazines delivered
- a cell that displays the total number of magazines removed
- a cell that shows the total number of magazines sold during the week

To complete this Case Problem, do the following:

1. Create a notebook plan and a spreadsheet plan similar to those shown at the beginning of this tutorial. In the notebook plan, include a description of the notebook goal and how the spreadsheet pages will be used. In the spreadsheet plan, include a description of the spreadsheet goal, list the results you want to see, list the input information needed, and describe the calculations that must be performed.
2. Draw a spreadsheet sketch showing the layout for the template.
3. Create your documentation on page A.
4. Build the spreadsheet on page B by entering the title, the row labels, the column titles, and the formulas.
5. Test the spreadsheet using 100 as the test value. Make any changes necessary for the spreadsheet to function according to your plan.
6. Clear the test values from the spreadsheet.
7. Save the notebook as a template notebook called S2MAG.WB1.
8. Enter some realistic test data and print the spreadsheet.
9. Submit your notebook plan, your spreadsheet plan, your spreadsheet sketch, and the printout of the spreadsheet.

4.   Expanding the Activity Reports for Magazines Unlimited

Alice Sanders has just been hired as another fulfillment driver for Magazines Unlimited, and she and Norm McGruder now share the same territory. Norm decides to modify his notebook template by adding a page for Alice's work and a consolidation page for the territory. (*Note:* You must have completed Case Problem 3 before doing this Case Problem.)

1. Create a modified notebook plan for this notebook.
2. Open the S2MAG.WB1 notebook.
3. Save the notebook as S2MAG2.WB1.
4. Modify the documentation of page A.
5. Copy the spreadsheet on page B to pages C and D. Label the pages to indicate that page B reports territory totals, page C is Norm's page, and page D is Alice's page.
6. Modify page B so that it consolidates the data on pages C and D.
7. Test the spreadsheets using 100 as the test value. Make any changes necessary for the spreadsheets to function according to your plan.
8. Print all pages in the notebook.
9. Clear the test values from the spreadsheets.
10. Save the notebook template S2MAG2.WB1.
11. Enter some realistic test data and print the spreadsheet.
12. Submit your notebook plan, your spreadsheet plan, your spreadsheet sketch, and the printout of the spreadsheet.

Formatting and Printing

OBJECTIVES

In this tutorial you will:

- Change the Zoom Factor
- Change the font typeface, style, and point size
- Align cell contents
- Center text across columns
- Use formats for numbers, currency, and percentages
- Add color and line segments for emphasis
- Preview printouts
- Print in portrait and landscape orientation
- Center printouts on the page
- Print cell contents

Producing a Projected Sales Impact Report

CASE

Pronto Authentic Recipe Salsa Company

Anne Castelar is the owner of the Pronto Authentic Recipe Salsa Company, a successful business located in the heart of Tex-Mex country. She is working on a plan to add a new product, Salsa de Chile Guero Medium, to Pronto's line of gourmet salsas.

Anne wants to take out a bank loan to purchase additional food processing equipment to handle the increase in production required for the new salsa. She has an appointment with her bank loan officer at 2:00 this afternoon. In preparation for the meeting, Anne is creating a spreadsheet to show the projected sales of the new salsa and the expected effect on profitability.

Although the numbers and formulas are in place on the spreadsheet, Anne has not had time to change the visual appearance of the spreadsheet for the best impact. She was planning to do that now, but an unexpected problem with today's produce shipment requires her to leave the office for a few hours. Anne asks her office manager, Maria Stevens, to improve how the spreadsheet looks. Anne shows Maria a printout of the spreadsheet as it is now, and explains that she wants the finished spreadsheet to look very professional—like the examples you see in business magazines.

Anne also wants Maria to add a printed list of the spreadsheet cell contents to her notebook documentation. This printout will show the spreadsheet formulas, and will document exactly how each value was calculated.

After Anne leaves, Maria launches Quattro Pro and opens the notebook so that she can see Anne's spreadsheet and compare it to the printout. Let's launch Quattro Pro and follow Maria's steps as she improves the appearance of Anne's spreadsheet.

To launch Quattro Pro and organize your workspace:

❶ Launch Quattro Pro following your usual procedure.

❷ Make sure your Student Disk is in the disk drive.

❸ Make sure the Quattro Pro and NOTEBK1.WB1 windows are maximized.

Anne stored the spreadsheet as C3SALSA.WB1. Now Maria needs to open this file.

To open the C3SALSA.WB1 notebook:

❶ Click the **Open Notebook button** 📖 (or click **File** then click **Open...**) to display the Open File dialog box.

❷ If the A: drive name is not displayed in the Drives box, click the **Drives drop-down list arrow button**, then click **A:** in the list of drive names.

❸ Double-click **C3SALSA.WB1** in the File Name box to display the notebook shown in Figure 3-1.

TROUBLE? If you do not see C3SALSA.WB1 in the list, use the scroll bar to view additional filenames.

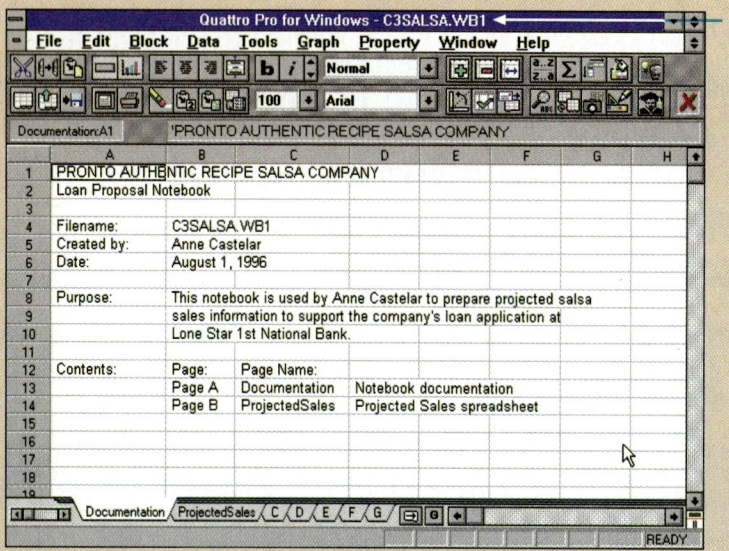

Figure 3-1
The C3SALSA.WB1
notebook

Before you begin to make changes to the notebook, let's save it using the filename S3SALSA1.WB1 so you can work on a copy of the spreadsheet. The original notebook, C3SALSA.WB1, will be left in its original state in case you want to do this tutorial again.

To save the spreadsheet as S3SALSA1.WB1:

❶ Click cell **B4** to make it the active cell.

❷ Type **S3SALSA1.WB1** then press **[Enter]**.

❸ Press **[Home]** to make cell A1 the active cell.

❹ Click **File** then click **Save As...** to display the Save File dialog box.

❺ Type **S3SALSA1** using either uppercase or lowercase *but don't press [Enter]* because you need to check some additional settings.

❻ Make sure the Drives box displays the name of the drive that contains your Student Disk.

❼ Click **OK** to save the notebook on your Student Disk. When the save is complete, you should see the new filename, S3SALSA1.WB1, displayed in the title bar.

TROUBLE? If a window appears with the message "File already exists: C3SALSA.WB1," click Cancel then repeat Steps 5 through 7. If you see the message "File already exists: S3SALSA1.WB1," click Replace to replace the old version with the current version.

Anne's projected sales spreadsheet is on the notebook page named ProjectedSales, so Maria switches to that page.

To make the ProjectedSales page the active spreadsheet:

❶ Click the **ProjectedSales page tab**. The projected sales spreadsheet appears as shown in Figure 3-2.

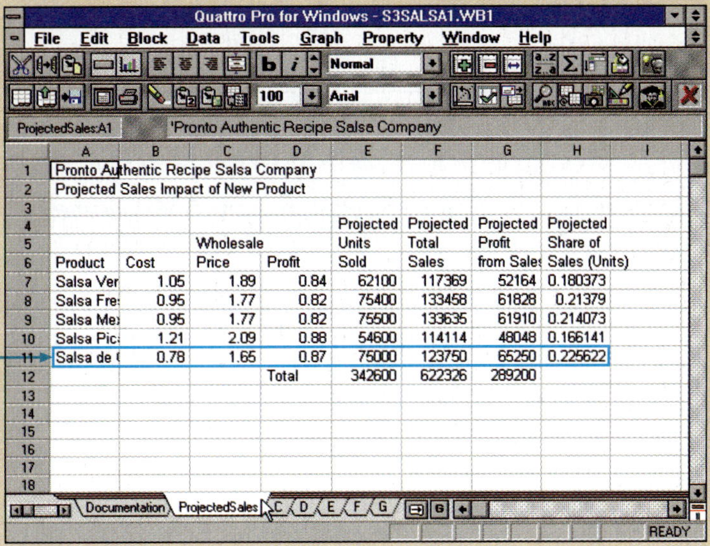

data for new salsa product

Figure 3-2
The projected sales spreadsheet

Looking at the spreadsheet on the screen, Maria thinks about how she wants the finished spreadsheet to look.

Changing the Appearance of the Spreadsheet

When you **format** a spreadsheet, you change how the spreadsheet appears on the screen and in printouts. Formatting can make your spreadsheets easier to understand and draw attention to important points.

Formatting changes only the appearance of the spreadsheet; it does not change the text or numbers stored in the cells. For example, if you format the number .123653 using a percentage format that displays only one decimal place, the number will appear on the spreadsheet as 12.4%, but the original number .123653 remains stored in the cell. When you save a notebook on disk, the formatting changes you've made are saved as part of the notebook file.

As an experienced Quattro Pro user, Maria can visualize the appearance of the formatted spreadsheet, which is shown in Figure 3-3. Comparing the unformatted spreadsheet in Figure 3-2 to the formatted spreadsheet in Figure 3-3 will give you a good idea of the differences in appearance that formatting can produce.

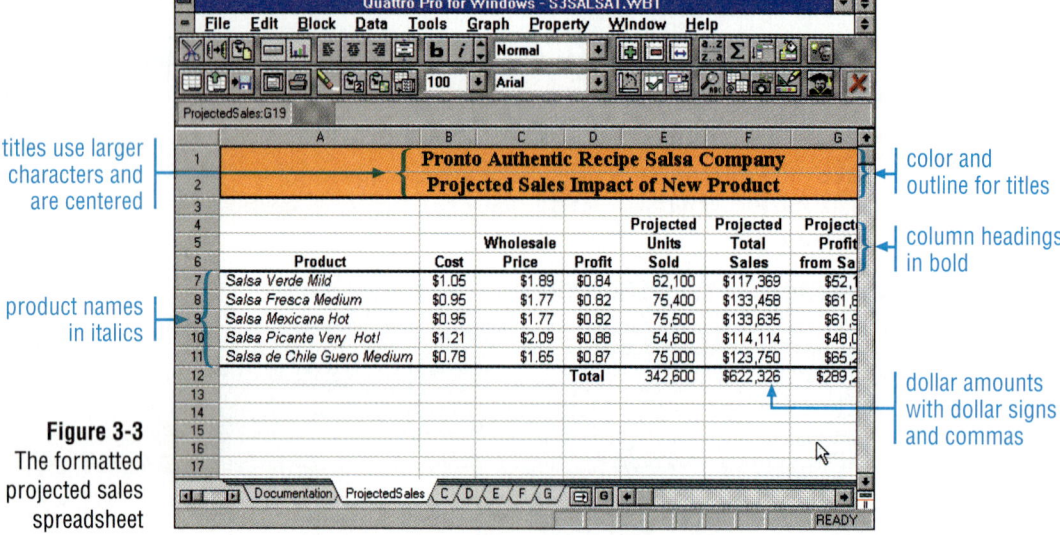

titles use larger characters and are centered

product names in italics

Figure 3-3
The formatted projected sales spreadsheet

color and outline for titles

column headings in bold

dollar amounts with dollar signs and commas

Based on her ideas, Maria sketches a format plan on the spreadsheet printout Anne gave her. Her spreadsheet format plan is shown in Figure 3-4.

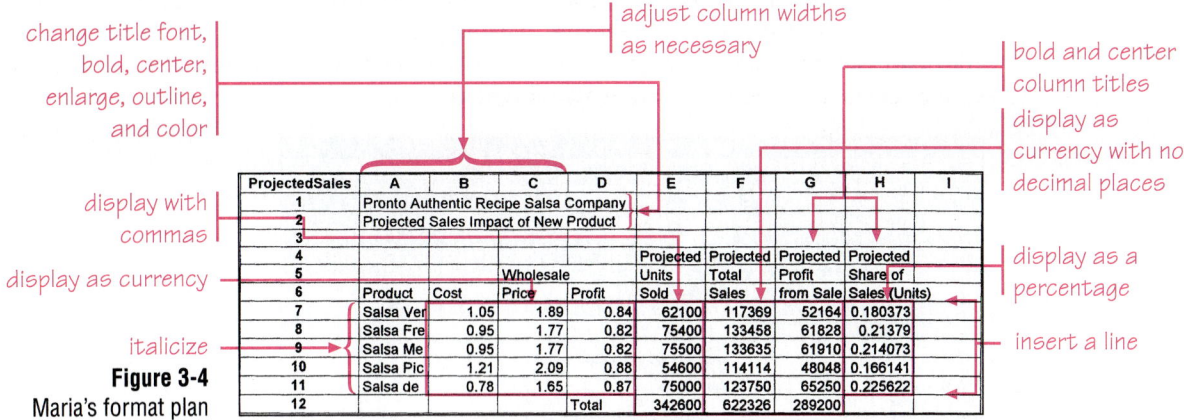

change title font,
bold, center,
enlarge, outline,
and color

adjust column widths
as necessary

bold and center
column titles

display as
currency with no
decimal places

display with
commas

display as currency

italicize

display as a
percentage

insert a line

Figure 3-4
Maria's format plan

Maria wants to start formatting the spreadsheet by making the full salsa names visible in column A. It will be easy to make column A wider, but Maria knows that if she widens this column, some of the spreadsheet will scroll off the screen. Maria remembers that Quattro Pro has a Zoom feature that allows her to adjust how much of the spreadsheet is seen on the screen.

Changing the Zoom Factor

Quattro Pro lets you shrink or enlarge the displayed spreadsheet so that you can see more or less of it by adjusting a notebook property called the **Zoom Factor**. Adjusting the Zoom Factor does not change the actual size of the spreadsheet—all column widths, row heights, and other property settings stay the same in memory on disk and when you print the notebook. The Zoom Factor just changes how much of the spreadsheet you can see. The Zoom Factor is normally set at 100%. Zoom Factor settings are displayed in the Zoom list, as shown in Figure 3-5.

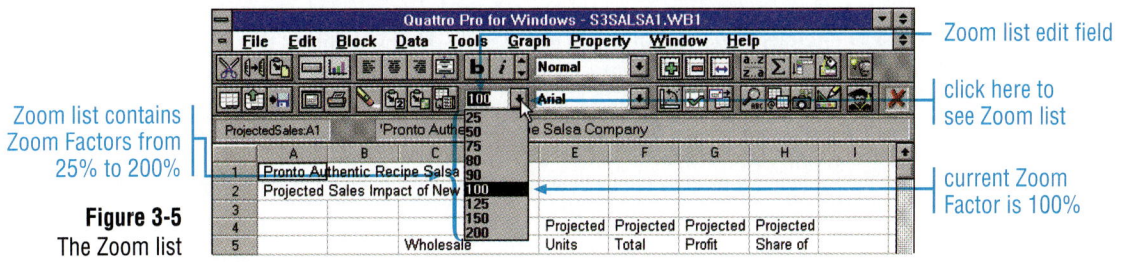

Zoom list edit field

click here to
see Zoom list

Zoom list contains
Zoom Factors from
25% to 200%

current Zoom
Factor is 100%

Figure 3-5
The Zoom list

A Zoom Factor greater than 100% magnifies the display, which means you see a smaller section of the spreadsheet, but with larger characters. A Zoom Factor less than 100% shrinks the display, letting you see a larger section of the spreadsheet, but with smaller characters. Figure 3-6 shows both types of display.

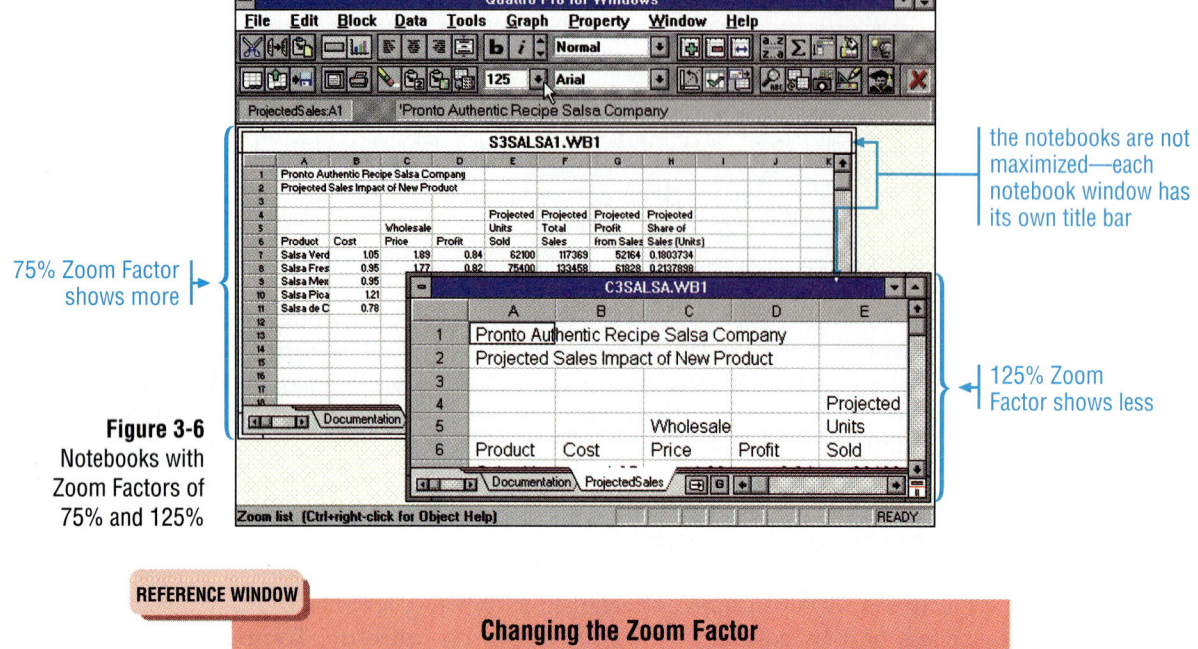

75% Zoom Factor shows more

the notebooks are not maximized—each notebook window has its own title bar

125% Zoom Factor shows less

Figure 3-6
Notebooks with Zoom Factors of 75% and 125%

Changing the Zoom Factor

- Click the Zoom drop-down list arrow button to display the list of Zoom Factors.
- Click the Zoom Factor you want.

Maria decides to use a Zoom Factor of 90%. This will allow her to see more of the spreadsheet so that she can adjust the width of column A and still view the rest of the columns.

To set the Zoom Factor to 90%:

❶ Click the **Zoom drop-down list arrow button** to display the list of Zoom Factors.

❷ Click **90**. The Zoom Factor of 90 appears in the Zoom edit field, and the display of the spreadsheet changes to show more of the page. Now you can see column J and rows 19 and 20.

TROUBLE? If your screen display is different, keep in mind that the amount of the spreadsheet you see depends on your computer and monitor.

Now Maria can extend the width of column A so that she can read the full names of all of the salsa products.

To change the width of column A:

❶ Position the pointer on the right edge of the A column border—the dividing line between column A and column B. Notice that the pointer changes to ↔.

❷ Click and drag the pointer to the right, between the *o* and *m* in *Company*.

❸ Release the mouse button. Column A adjusts to the new width and the full salsa titles are visible.

Now Maria is ready to format the spreadsheet.

Formatting a Spreadsheet

Quattro Pro automatically applies a format when you enter labels or data in cells. For example, when you enter a label, Quattro Pro left-aligns it in the cell using a character type called Arial with a type size of 10 points. When you enter a number, Quattro Pro applies a format referred to as the General numeric format. The **General numeric format** aligns numbers at the right side of the cell, and displays numbers just as you entered them. For example, if you enter 4, Quattro Pro displays a right-aligned 4, and if you enter 4.567, Quattro Pro displays a right-aligned 4.567.

You can use Quattro Pro's extensive array of formatting options to customize individual cells or blocks of cells. In Quattro Pro, a cell and its contents constitute an object, and you can change the property settings of any object by using the Active Block Object Inspector. Shortcuts for some of the changes are available in the formatting buttons on the SpeedBars.

REFERENCE WINDOW

Formatting Cells

- Click the cell or highlight the block of cells you want to format.

- Right-click the cell or anywhere in the block to display the SpeedMenu, then click Block Properties... to open the Active Block Object Inspector (or click Property then click Current Object...).

- Choose the properties you want to change from the Object Inspector menu, then make the changes.

- Click OK.

or

- Click the cell or highlight the block of cells you want to format.

- Click the formatting buttons on the SpeedBars to make the changes you want.

The Active Block Object Inspector, shown in Figure 3-7, gives you access to the property settings for all the cell properties you can change, and you use it to access Quattro Pro's formatting options. The Example box shows how the property settings will affect the cell or block of cells you are formatting.

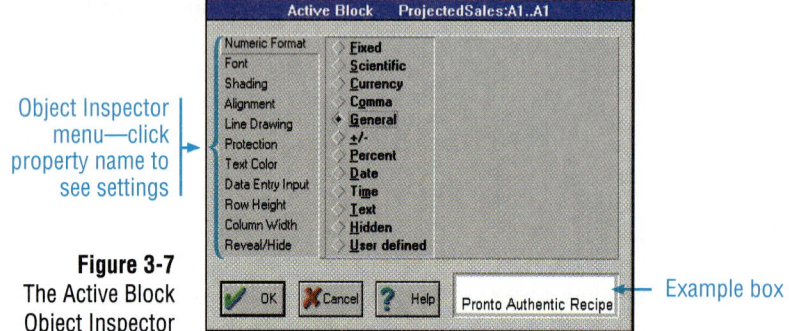

Object Inspector menu—click property name to see settings

Figure 3-7
The Active Block Object Inspector

Example box

The notebook SpeedBar and the Productivity Tools SpeedBar, shown in Figure 3-8, contain several formatting tools, including the Style list, the Font list, font style buttons, and alignment buttons.

Block Center button

Right Align button

Center button

Left Align button

notebook SpeedBar

Productivity Tools SpeedBar

Bold button

Italic button

Font Size arrows

Style list

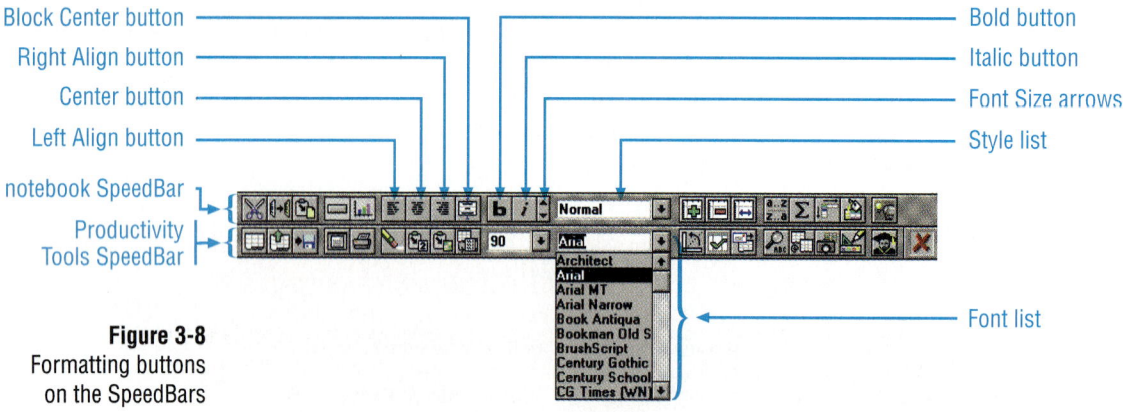

Font list

Figure 3-8
Formatting buttons on the SpeedBars

For most formatting tasks, Maria uses the Active Block Object Inspector, although she also uses the Bold button, the Italic button, the alignment buttons, and the Block Center button. She decides to use the Bold button to change the font style to boldface for some of the titles on the spreadsheet.

Changing the Font Typeface, Style, and Size

A **font** is defined as a set of letters, numbers, punctuation marks, and symbols with a specific design, size, and style. The specific design is called the **typeface**. Most fonts are available in many sizes. Font sizes are measured in **points** (a point is $\frac{1}{72}$ of an inch), and are also called **point sizes**. A font can have one or more of the following **styles**: regular, italic, bold, and bold italic. You can also select **font effects**, such as strikeout, underline, and color.

Although the term *font* actually means a combination of typeface, size, and style, it is commonly used to refer to just the typeface. Some examples of fonts are shown in Figure 3-9.

Typeface	Point Size	Style: Regular	Italic	Bold	Bold Italic
Times Roman	12	AaBbCc	AaBbCc	AaBbCc	AaBbCc
Times Roman	10	AaBbCc	AaBbCc	AaBbCc	AaBbCc
Times Roman	8	AaBbCc	AaBbCc	AaBbCc	AaBbCc
Courier	12	AaBbCc	AaBbCc	AaBbCc	AaBbCc
Courier	10	AaBbCc	AaBbCc	AaBbCc	AaBbCc
Courier	8	AaBbCc	AaBbCc	AaBbCc	AaBbCc
Helvetica	12	AaBbCc	AaBbCc	AaBbCc	AaBbCc
Helvetica	10	AaBbCc	AaBbCc	AaBbCc	AaBbCc
Helvetica	8	AaBbCc	AaBbCc	AaBbCc	AaBbCc

Figure 3-9
A selection of fonts

The notebook SpeedBar provides buttons for bold, italics, and increasing or decreasing font size. The Productivity Tools SpeedBar provides the Font list for changing the font typeface.

Maria begins by formatting the word "Total" in cell D12 in bold letters.

To change the style for cell D12 to bold:
❶ Click cell **D12**.
❷ Click the **Bold button** 🅱 to set the font style to bold. See Figure 3-8 for the location of the Bold button.

Maria also wants to display the spreadsheet titles and the column titles in bold letters. To do this she first highlights the block she wants to format, then she clicks the Bold button to apply the format.

To display the spreadsheet titles and column titles in bold:
❶ Highlight cells A1 through H6.
❷ Click the **Bold button** 🅱 to apply the bold style.
❸ Click any cell to remove the highlighting.

Next, Maria decides to display the names of the salsa products in italics.

To italicize the row labels:

❶ Highlight cells A7 through A11.

❷ Click the **Italic button** [i] to apply the italic style. See Figure 3-8 for the location of the Italic button.

❸ Click any cell to remove the highlighting and view the formatting you have done so far, as shown in Figure 3-10.

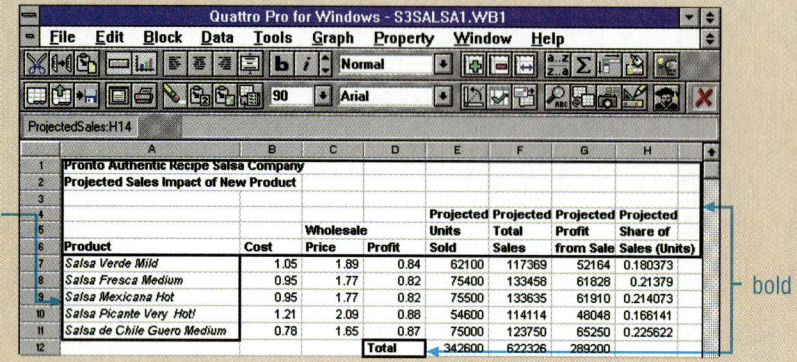

Figure 3-10
Bold and italic
styles applied

Maria wants to increase the size of the spreadsheet titles for emphasis. Typically, she would use the Font Size arrows to change the size, but she also wants to use a different font for the titles of this spreadsheet. She likes the Times New Roman typeface because it looks like the font used on the Pronto salsa jar labels. Maria decides to use the Active Block Object Inspector to change the typeface and the point size at the same time. To format the titles, Maria needs to highlight only cells A1 and A2—the cells containing the titles. Remember, even though the spreadsheet titles appear to be in columns A through C, they are just spilling over from column A.

To change the typeface and point size of the spreadsheet titles:

❶ Highlight cells A1 through A2.

❷ Right-click anywhere in the highlighted block to display the SpeedMenu.

❸ Click **Block Properties...** to open the Active Block Object Inspector.

❹ Click **Font** in the Object Inspector menu to display the font settings.

❺ Use the Typeface scroll bar to move through the typeface list, then click **Times New Roman,** as shown in Figure 3-11. Your list of typefaces might be different, depending on which ones you have installed on your computer.

❻ In Options, make sure that Bold is checked.

❼ Click the **Point Size drop-down list arrow button**, then click **14** to increase the font size to 14 points. See Figure 3-11.

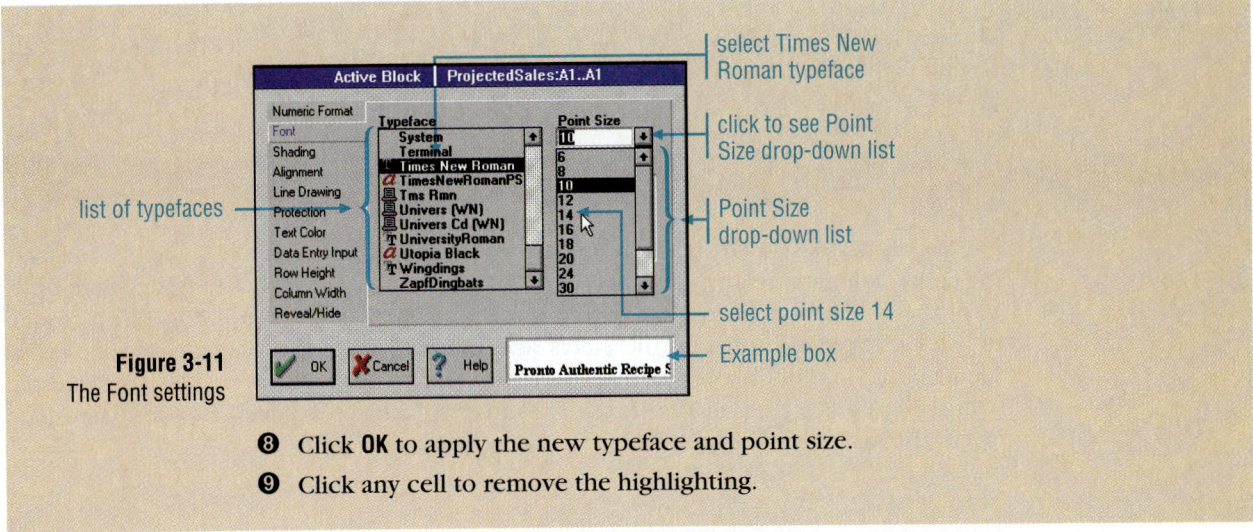

Figure 3-11
The Font settings

❽ Click **OK** to apply the new typeface and point size.

❾ Click any cell to remove the highlighting.

Looking at the spreadsheet, Maria realizes that she will have to adjust the height of rows 1 and 2 to accommodate the larger font size.

To increase the row height to fit the larger font of the spreadsheet titles:

❶ Drag the pointer across **row borders 1 and 2** to highlight rows 1 and 2.

❷ Right-click anywhere in the highlighted block to display the SpeedMenu, then click **Block Properties...** to open the Active Block Object Inspector.

❸ Click **Row Height** in the Object Inspector menu to display the row height settings.

❹ In Options, click **Reset Height** to have Quattro Pro automatically choose a height for the rows based on the font size.

❺ Click **OK**. Quattro Pro adjusts the row height.

❻ Click any cell to remove the highlighting.

Pleased with her progress so far, Maria continues with her formatting plan. Her next step is to adjust the alignment of the column titles.

Aligning Cell Contents

The **alignment** of data in a cell is the position of the data relative to the right and left edges of the cell. The contents of cells can be aligned on the left or right side of the cell, or centered in the cell. And, as you've already seen, when you enter numbers and formulas, Quattro Pro automatically aligns the numerical values on the right side of the cell. Quattro Pro automatically aligns text entries on the left side of the cell.

Quattro Pro's automatic alignment does not always create the most readable spreadsheet. As a general rule, you should center column titles, format columns of numbers so the decimal places are aligned, and leave columns of text aligned on the left.

The notebook SpeedBar provides four alignment buttons, as shown in Figure 3-8. You can also access alignment options by selecting the Alignment property in the Active Block Object Inspector.

Maria decides to center the column titles.

To center the column titles:

❶ Highlight cells A4 through H6.

❷ Click the **Center button** ▨ on the notebook SpeedBar to center the cell contents.

❸ Click any cell to remove the highlighting and view the centered titles.

Maria notices that she needs to change the width of columns C, G, and H to display the entire column title properly centered. She realizes that if she makes this change now, all of the columns might not fit on one screen, which would force her to scroll around the spreadsheet to format all the labels and values. Rather than using a smaller Zoom Factor, which would make the spreadsheet harder to read, Maria decides to make the width adjustments after she has finished formatting the spreadsheet. Her next step is to center the main spreadsheet titles.

Centering Text Across Columns

Sometimes you might want to center the contents of a cell across more than one column. This is particularly useful for centering the titles at the top of a spreadsheet.

Maria uses the Block Center button to center the spreadsheet titles in cells A1 and A2 across columns A through H.

To center the spreadsheet titles across columns A through H:

❶ Highlight cells A1 through H2.

❷ Click the **Block Center button** ▣ to center the titles across columns A through H. See Figure 3-8 for the location of the Block Center button.

TROUBLE? If the titles did not center in the area from column A to column H, you might have clicked the Center button ▨ instead of the Block Center button ▣. Repeat Steps 1 and 2.

❸ Click any cell to remove the highlighting. The spreadsheet now appears as shown in Figure 3-12.

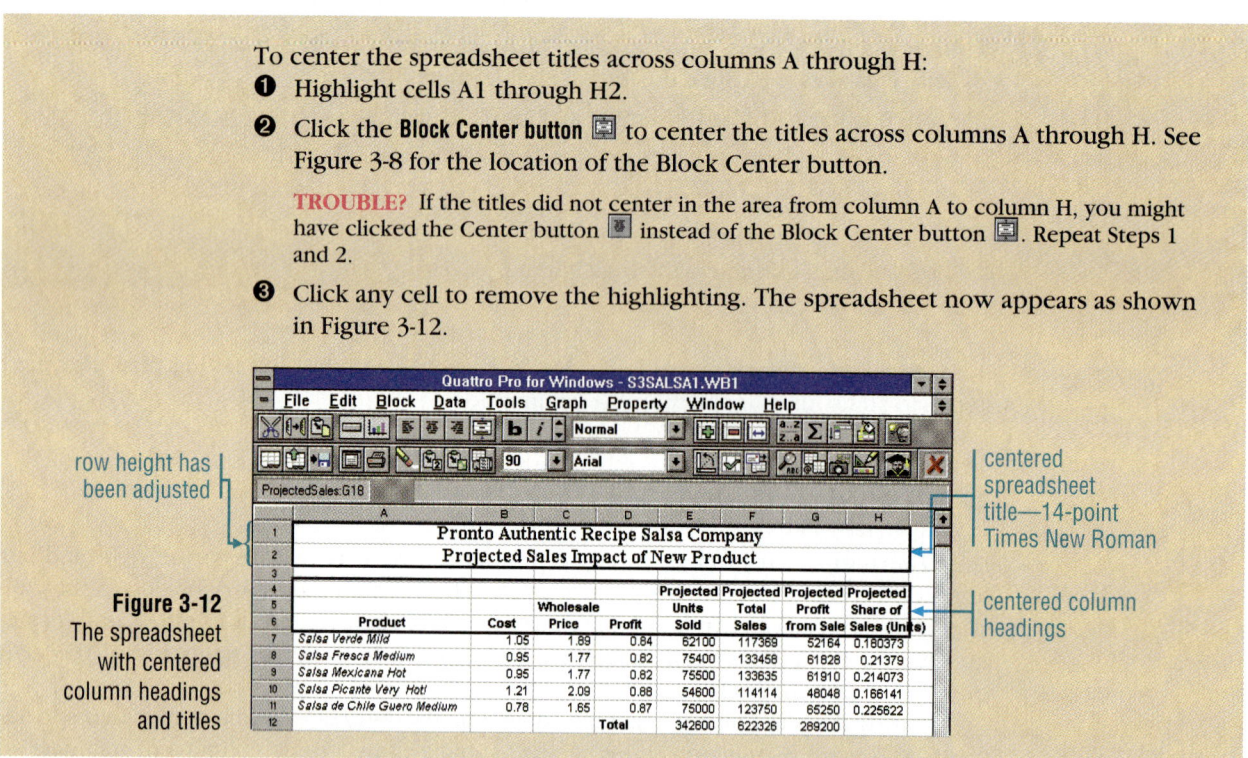

row height has been adjusted

Figure 3-12
The spreadsheet with centered column headings and titles

centered spreadsheet title—14-point Times New Roman

centered column headings

Maria looks at her plan and sees that she needs to format the numbers in the spreadsheet.

Numeric Formats

Quattro Pro provides several ways to format numbers, some of which are shown in Figure 3-13. You apply numeric formats using the Active Block Object Inspector.

Format	Description	Examples
Fixed	No commas to separate thousands, millions, and billions; displays a specified number of decimal places	23.2 0.05678 –3543
Scientific	Displays numbers in scientific notation with only one digit to the left of the decimal place	2.32E+1 5.678E-2 –3.542E+3
General	Displays numbers as entered; uses scientific notation if number is too wide for the cell	23.2 9.876E+11 –3543
Currency	Commas used to separate thousands, millions, and billions; displays numbers with a specified number of decimal places, a currency symbol, and negative numbers in parentheses	$23.20 $0.057 ($3,543)
Comma	Commas used to separate thousands, millions, and billions; displays a specified number of decimal places, and negative numbers in parentheses	126,783.29 0.057 (3,543)
Percent	Numbers displayed as percentages with a percent sign; displays a specific number of decimal places	5.67% 0.34% –67.77%
Date	Numbers displayed as dates in a format you select: DD-MMM-YY DD-MMM MMM-YY Long International Short International	 05-Aug-96 05-Aug Aug-96 08/05/96 08/05
Time	Numbers displayed as times in a format you select: HH:MM:SS AM/PM HH:MM AM/PM Long International Short International	 10:15:35 PM 10:35 PM 10:15:35 10:15
Text	Formulas displayed instead of results; numbers displayed in General format	+G7*$B$2
Hidden	Contents of cell are not shown, but still remain in cell	

Figure 3-13
Some Quattro Pro numeric formats

Formatting Numbers

- Click the cell or highlight the block of cells you want to format.

- Right-click the cell or block to display the SpeedMenu.

- Click Block Properties... to open the Active Block Object Inspector.

- Click Numeric Format in the Object Inspector menu.

- Click the format you want in the list of numeric formats.

- Adjust any settings associated with the format, for example the number of decimal places.

- Click OK.

Maria's plan shows that she will display the cost, wholesale price, profit, and total sales figures as currency.

Currency Format

The **Currency format**, as the name implies, is useful for indicating dollar figures in the spreadsheet. The Currency format specifies the following:
- a dollar sign prefix
- commas separating thousands, millions, and so on
- a decimal point separating dollars from cents (optional) with a selected number of digits shown after the decimal point
- negative numbers displayed in parentheses to match accounting standards

Maria wants to format the amounts in columns B, C, and D as currency with two decimal places.

To format columns B, C, and D as currency with two decimal places:

❶ Highlight cells B7 through D11.

❷ Right-click anywhere in the highlighted block to display the SpeedMenu, then click **Block Properties...** to open the Active Block Object Inspector. The Numeric Format settings are displayed when the Object Inspector is opened. Each setting has a *radio button* to its left, which you click to select the setting. You can select only one radio button at a time.

❸ Click the **Currency radio button** in the Numeric Format settings pane, as shown in Figure 3-14. A *spin box* (an edit field with up and down arrows for changing numbers quickly) appears for setting the number of decimal places.

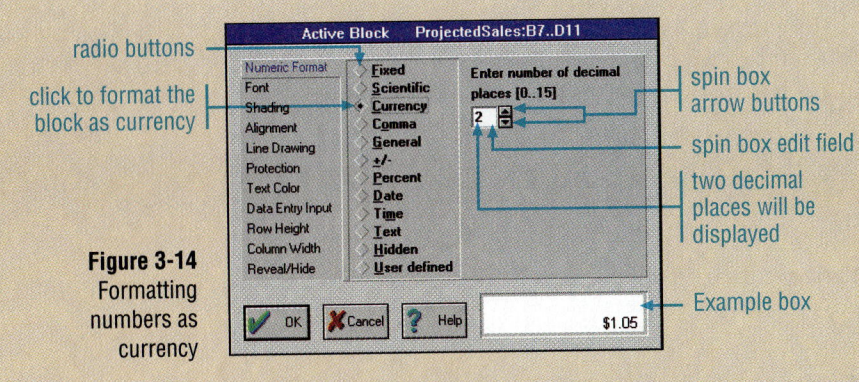

Figure 3-14
Formatting
numbers as
currency

❹ Make sure the number of decimal places is set to 2. If not, set the number of decimal places to 2 by clicking the spin box arrow buttons.

❺ Click **OK**. Quattro Pro reformats the numbers.

❻ Click any cell to remove the highlighting and view the new formatting. See Figure 3-15.

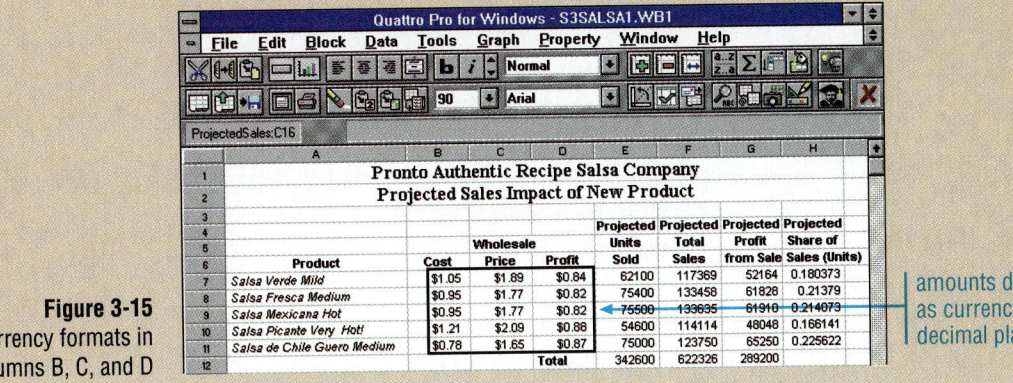

Figure 3-15
Currency formats in
Columns B, C, and D

When you have large dollar amounts on your spreadsheet, you might want to use the Currency format without displaying any decimal places. To do this you set the number of decimal places to 0 in the Currency settings. This format will round the amount to the nearest dollar. For example, 15,612.56 becomes $15,613, and $16,507.49 becomes $16,507.

Maria decides to format the Projected Total Sales column as currency rounded to the nearest dollar.

To format cells F7 through F12 as currency rounded to the nearest dollar:

❶ Highlight cells F7 through F12.

❷ Right-click anywhere in the highlighted block to display the SpeedMenu, then click **Block Properties...** to open the Active Block Object Inspector. The Numeric Format settings are displayed when the Object Inspector is opened.

❸ Click the **Currency radio button** in the Numeric Format settings pane. The spin box for setting the number of decimal places appears.

❹ Click the **spin box down arrow** until 0 appears in the edit field.

❺ Click **OK**. Quattro Pro reformats the numbers.

❻ Click any cell to remove the highlighting.

Next, Maria wants to apply formats to the numbers in columns E and H so they are easier to read.

Comma Format

The **Comma format** displays numbers in the same way as the Currency format, except the Comma format does not display dollar signs.

Maria wants to include a comma in the numbers for Projected Units Sold in column E, but she does not want to display any decimal places because unit sales must be in whole numbers. She will use the Comma format for these numbers.

To format the numbers in column E as comma with no decimal places:

❶ Highlight cells E7 through E12.

❷ Right-click anywhere in the highlighted block to display the SpeedMenu, then click **Block Properties...** to open the Active Block Object Inspector.

❸ Click the **Comma radio button** in the Numeric Format settings pane. The spin box for setting the number of decimal places appears.

❹ Click the **spin box down arrow** until 0 appears in the edit field.

❺ Click **OK**. Quattro Pro reformats the numbers.

❻ Click any cell to remove the highlighting and view the results.

Maria thinks the Projected Share of Sales numbers in column H are difficult to interpret, and she thinks it is not necessary to display so many decimal places. She decides to display these numbers as percentages.

Percent Format

The **Percent format** is useful when you want to show the relative size of a number compared to another number, or when you're dealing with numbers such as interest rates that are commonly expressed in percentage points. You initially enter percentages less than 100% as a decimal number less than 1.00. For example, if you want to enter 18.30%, you initially enter .183 in the cell. The Percent format displays numbers as percentages between 0% and 100%. For example, if the number 0.183 is in a cell formatted as percent with two decimal places, Quattro Pro would display the number as 18.30%. If you formatted the cell as percent without any decimal places, the number would be displayed as 18%.

The Percent format specifies the following:
- a percent sign (%) following the number
- the decimal point shifted two places to the right to convert the number to a percentage
- no commas separating thousands, millions, and so on
- a selected number of decimal places (optional)
- negative numbers displayed with a negative sign

Maria's format plan specifies percentages with no decimal places for the Projected Share of Sales values in column H.

To format the numbers in column H as percentages with no decimal places:

❶ Highlight cells H7 through H11.

❷ Right-click anywhere in the highlighted block to display the SpeedMenu, then click **Block Properties...** to open the Active Block Object Inspector.

❸ Click the **Percent radio button** in the Numeric Format settings pane. The spin box for setting the number of decimal places appears.

❹ Click the **spin box down arrow** until 0 appears in the edit field.

❺ Click **OK**. Quattro Pro reformats the numbers.

❻ Click any cell to remove the highlighting and view the results. See Figure 3-16.

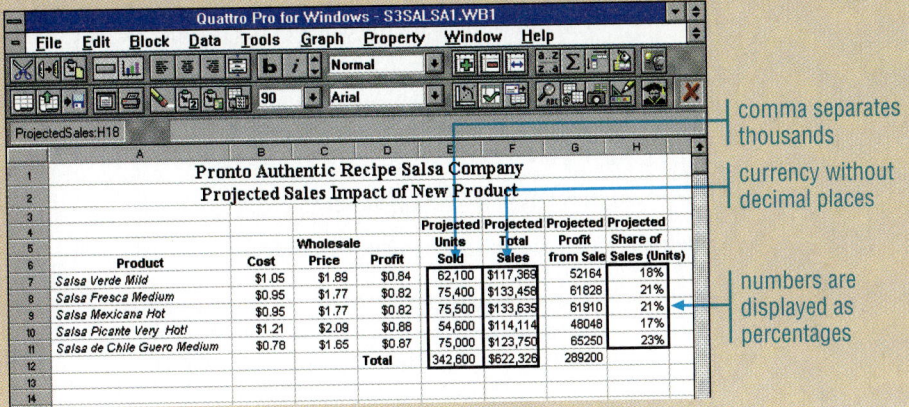

Figure 3-16
Percent format in column H

Maria realizes that she has not formatted column G, which contains the Projected Profit from Sales values. She decides that this column should be formatted as currency with no decimal places. Maria remembers that Quattro Pro has a Style list of predefined formats, and she decides to use the Style list if it contains the format she wants.

The Style List

The **Style list** on the notebook SpeedBar provides a group of predefined formats, or styles. You used the Style list in Tutorial 2 to format numbers using the Comma format with two decimal places. The definitions of the predefined styles available in the Style list are shown in Figure 3-17. To see these definitions, you can use Quattro Pro's Object Help to display a help screen with the definitions listed.

Style	Description	Examples
Comma	Comma numeric format with two decimal places	3,456,789.00 (5,678.00)
Comma0	Comma numeric format with no decimal places	3,456,789 (5,678)
Currency	Currency numeric format with two decimal places	$3,456,789.00 ($5,678.00)
Currency0	Currency numeric format with no decimal places	$3,456,789 ($5,678)
Date	Date format displays the name of the month, the date, and the year	January 4, 1996 December 15, 1996
Fixed	Fixed numeric format with two decimal places	12.00 0.56
Heading 1	Arial (or Helvetica) 18-point bold font	Report
Heading 2	Arial (or Helvetica) 12-point bold font	Report
Normal	General numeric format, Arial (or Helvetica) 10-point regular font, General alignment, white background with black text, no line drawing, cell protection on	Report 2.34
Percent	Percent numeric format with two decimal places	0.54% -7.78%
Total	Double line drawn at the top of the cell	═══════

Figure 3-17
Definitions of styles
in the Style list

Quattro Pro displays the contents of all cells in the Normal style unless you change the style or any of the properties (cell alignment, numeric format, text color, and others) that make up the style.

Maria wants to format the Projected Profit from Sales column as currency with no decimal places. She thinks that this is the Currency0 style, but she decides to check the Quattro Pro Help system to make sure.

To use the Quattro Pro Help system to see definitions of styles in the Style list:

❶ Move the pointer over the Style list edit field (where the word *Normal* is displayed on the notebook SpeedBar).

❷ Hold down [Ctrl] and right-click to open the Style list Object Help window.

❸ Click **Help** in the Object Help window to open the Quattro Pro Help system. The Quattro Pro Help window appears with the topic "Using Styles" displayed.

❹ Use the Quattro Pro Help window scroll bar to scroll through and read the information on Using Styles.

❺ Double-click the Quattro Pro Help window **Control menu box** to close the Help window (or click **File** on the Help window menu bar, then click **Exit**).

As Maria thought, the Currency0 style is the style she wants to use.

To format the numbers in column G with the Currency0 style:
❶ Highlight cells G7 through G12.
❷ Click the **Style list drop-down list arrow button**. The list of available styles appears, as shown in Figure 3-18.

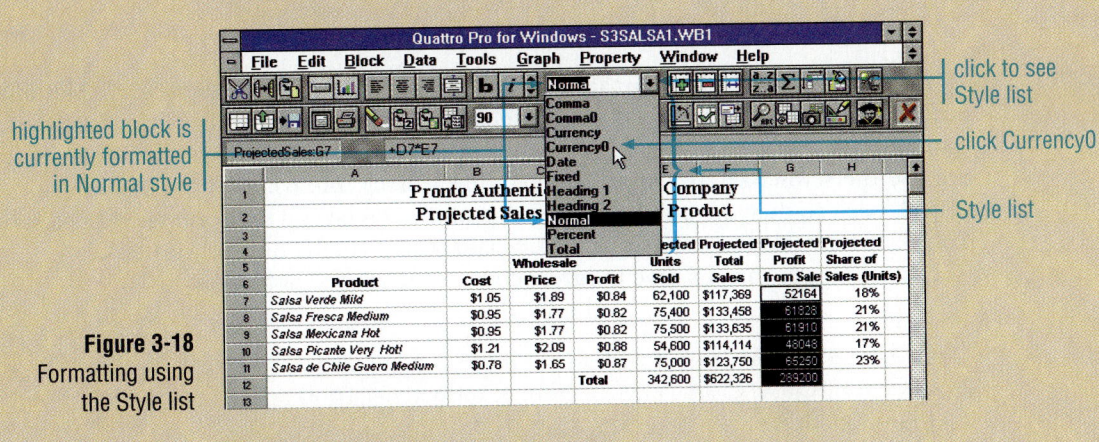

Figure 3-18
Formatting using
the Style list

❸ Click **Currency0** in the Style list.
❹ Click any cell to remove the highlighting.

Maria checks her plan once again and confirms that she has selected formats for all the cells on the spreadsheet. She delayed changing the width of columns C, G, and H because wider columns would have made the spreadsheet too wide to fit on one screen. Now that she has finished formatting the labels and values, she can change the column widths to best display the information in the columns.

To change the width of the columns using the Fit button:
❶ Highlight columns B through H.

TROUBLE? Check to make sure that only columns B through H are highlighted. The width of column A has already been adjusted. If column A is highlighted, repeat Step 1.

❷ Click the **Fit button** ⊞ on the notebook SpeedBar. Quattro Pro adjusts the widths of columns B through H.

❸ Click any cell to remove the highlighting, and view the changes in the column widths as shown in Figure 3-19.

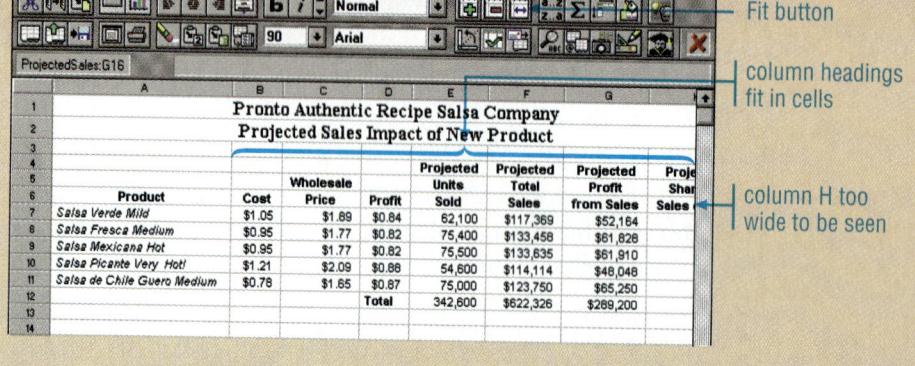

Figure 3-19
Results of the column width changes

As Maria expected, the spreadsheet is now too wide to fit on the screen. She might need to scroll to complete some additional formatting tasks. Remember from the previous tutorials that when you want to see a part of the spreadsheet that is not displayed, you can use the scroll bars. If you are highlighting a block, but some of the block is not displayed, you can drag the pointer to the edge of the screen and the spreadsheet will scroll. You'll see how this works when you add some borders in the next set of steps.

Maria decides that it's time to save a copy of the revised notebook.

To save the S3SALSA1.WB1 notebook with the same filename:
❶ Click the **Save Notebook button** 🖫 on the Productivity Tools SpeedBar (or click **File** then click **Save**).

If you want to take a break and resume the tutorial at a later time, you can exit Quattro Pro by double-clicking the Quattro Pro application Control menu box (or by clicking File then clicking Exit). When you want to resume the tutorial, launch Quattro Pro, maximize the Quattro Pro and NOTEBK1.WB1 windows, place your Student Disk in the disk drive, and open the file S3SALSA1.WB1. You can then continue with the tutorial.

Adding and Removing Lines and Outlines

A well-constructed spreadsheet is clearly divided into **zones** that visually group related information. Figure 3-20 shows the zones on Maria's spreadsheet. The Zoom Factor has been changed to 80% in Figure 3-20 so that you can see column H in the figure.

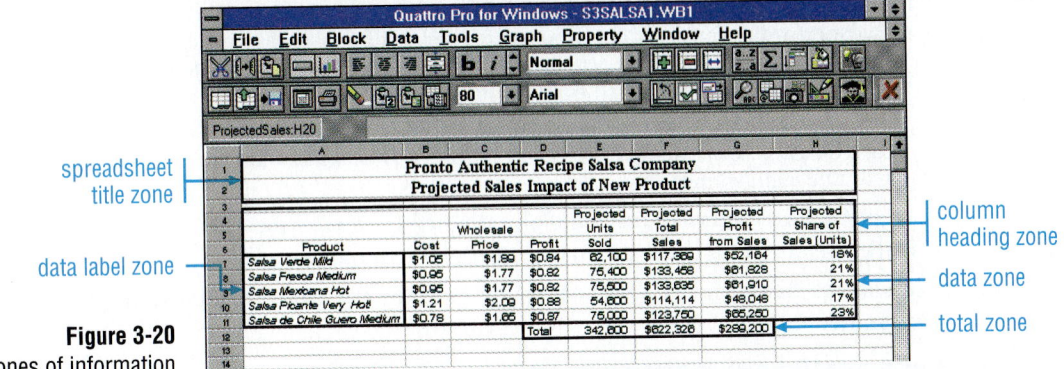

Figure 3-20
Zones of information

You can use **line segments** to help distinguish between different zones of the spreadsheet and add visual interest. You create line segments using the Line Drawing property in the Active Block Object Inspector. You can outline a single cell or a group of cells using the Outline button. You can add a horizontal line segment at the top or bottom of a cell or block of cells, or a vertical line segment on the right or left of a cell or block of cells. The Line Drawing settings also provide different line types, including different single line thicknesses and double lines.

REFERENCE WINDOW

Adding and Removing Line Segments

- Right-click the cell to which you want to add the line segment to select the cell and display the SpeedMenu.

  or

  Highlight the block of cells to which you want to add line segments, then right-click anywhere in the block to display the SpeedMenu.

- Click Block Properties... to open the Active Block Object Inspector.

- Click Line Drawing in the Object Inspector menu.

- Click the line type that you want to use in Line Types.

- In the sample block, click the line segments where you want the line to appear, then click OK.

  or

  Click a pattern button (All, Outline, or Inside) to draw the line segments, then click OK.

- To remove line segments from a cell or group of cells, you use the same procedure, but choose "No Line" as the line type.

Maria wants to put a thick line under all the column titles.

To put a line under the column titles:

❶ Highlight cells A6 through H6.

TROUBLE? If cell H6 is not displayed on your screen, drag the pointer from cell A6 to G6 then, without releasing the mouse button, continue moving the pointer to the right. The spreadsheet window will scroll so you can include cell H6 in the highlighted block. If the spreadsheet scrolls too fast and you highlight columns beyond H, move the mouse to the left—without releasing the mouse button—until H6 is the rightmost cell in the highlighted block.

TROUBLE? If you released the mouse button too soon, use the scroll bars to scroll column A back on the screen, then repeat Step 1, or hold down [Shift] and use the arrow keys to extend the highlighting.

❷ Right-click anywhere in the highlighted block to display the SpeedMenu, then click **Block Properties…** to open the Active Block Object Inspector.

❸ Click **Line Drawing** in the Object Inspector menu. The Line Drawing settings appear, as shown in Figure 3-21.

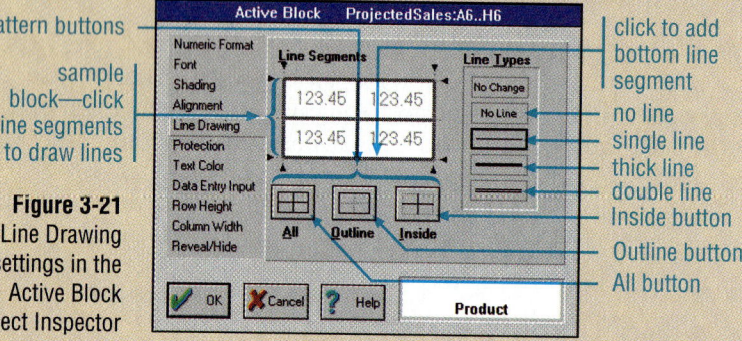

pattern buttons

sample block—click line segments to draw lines

Figure 3-21
The Line Drawing settings in the Active Block Object Inspector

click to add bottom line segment
no line
single line
thick line
double line
Inside button
Outline button
All button

❹ Click the **thick line** in Line Types. A dark box appears around the line type.

❺ Click the **bottom line segment** in the sample block *between the vertical line segments*, as shown in Figure 3-21. The bottom line segment is displayed with a thick line.

TROUBLE? If the thick line appeared on a vertical line segment, you clicked a line segment that Quattro Pro interpreted as a vertical line. Repeat Step 5, then click No Line in Line Types and click the vertical line segment with the thick line to remove the line.

❻ Click **OK**. Quattro Pro draws the line.

❼ Click any cell to remove the highlighting and view the line.

Maria also wants to add a line to separate the data from the totals in row 12. To accomplish this she highlights cells A12 through H12, then adds a thick line at the top of the block using the Line Drawing property. Why would she use a top line here, when she used a bottom line for the column titles? It is a good practice not to attach line segments to the cells in the data zone because when you copy cells, the cell formats are also copied. Maria knows from experience that if she attaches line segments to the wrong cells, lines could appear in every cell, or she could erase lines she wanted when she copies cell contents down a column.

To add a line separating the data and the totals:

❶ Highlight cells A12 through H12.

❷ Right-click anywhere in the highlighted block to display the SpeedMenu, then click **Block Properties...** to open the Active Block Object Inspector.

❸ Click **Line Drawing** in the Object Inspector menu. The Line Drawing settings appear.

❹ Click the **thick line** in Line Types. A dark box appears around the line type.

❺ Click the **top line** segment in the sample block *between the vertical line segments*. The top line segment is displayed with a thick line.

❻ Click **OK**. Quattro Pro draws the line.

❼ Click any cell to remove the highlighting and view the border.

Maria consults her format sketch and sees that she planned to put an outline around the title zone to add a professional touch. Let's add this outline now.

To place an outline around the title zone:

❶ Highlight cells A1 through H2.

❷ Right-click anywhere in the highlighted block to display the SpeedMenu, then click **Block Properties...** to open the Active Block Object Inspector.

❸ Click **Line Drawing** in the Object Inspector menu. The Line Drawing settings appear.

❹ Click the **thick line** in Line Types. A dark box appears around the line type.

❺ Click the **Outline button**. The top, bottom, and side line segments are displayed with a thick line.

❻ Click **OK**. Quattro Pro draws the outline.

❼ Click any cell to remove the highlighting and view the outline, as shown in Figure 3-22.

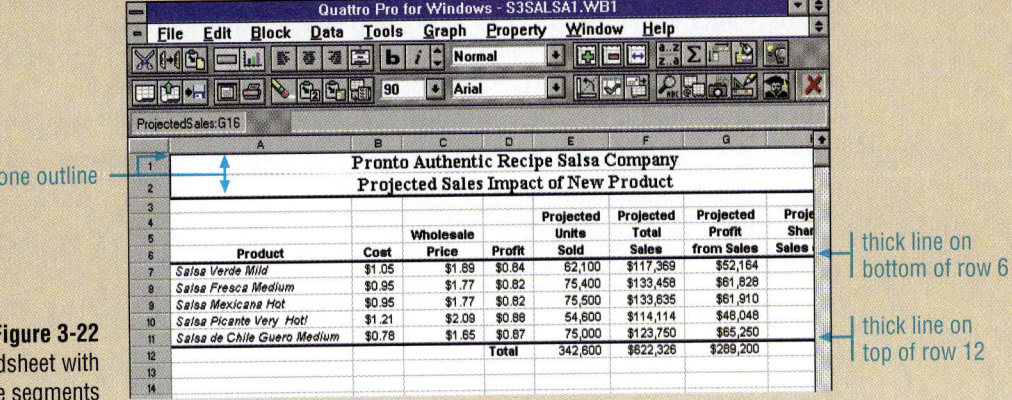

Figure 3-22
The spreadsheet with added line segments

In addition to the outline around the title zone, Maria wants to add color in the title zone.

Using Color for Emphasis

Colors can provide visual interest, emphasize zones of the spreadsheet, or indicate data entry areas. The use of colors should be based on the way you intend to use the spreadsheet. If you print the spreadsheet on a color printer and distribute it in hardcopy format, or if you are going to use a color projection device to display a screen image of your spreadsheet, you might want to take advantage of Quattro Pro's color formatting options. On the other hand, a printout you produce on a printer without color capability might look better if you use shades of gray, because it is difficult to predict how the colors you see on your screen will be translated into shades of gray on your printout.

You add color using the Shading property settings in the Active Block Object Inspector, as shown in Figure 3-23.

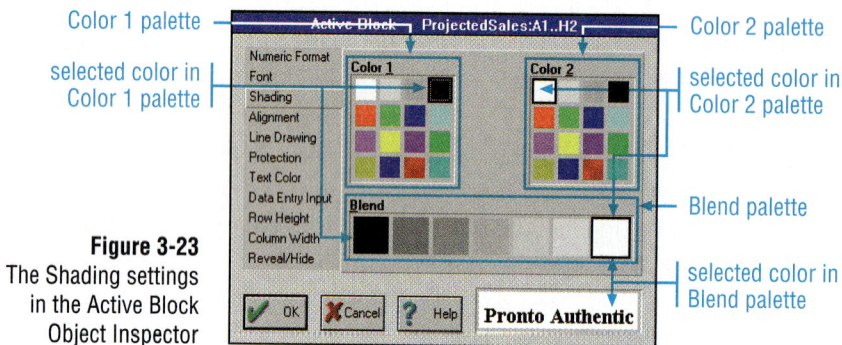

Color 1 palette

selected color in
Color 1 palette

Color 2 palette

selected color in
Color 2 palette

Blend palette

selected color in
Blend palette

Figure 3-23
The Shading settings
in the Active Block
Object Inspector

The Shading settings include two color palettes, labeled Color 1 and Color 2. You select colors from these palettes by clicking the color square you want. Below the color palettes is a Blend palette, which has seven color squares. These color squares are mixes of the two colors you select in the Color 1 and Color 2 palettes. The color square that you select in the Blend palette is the color that Quattro Pro will display in the spreadsheet.

Maria wants her spreadsheet to look good when it is printed in black and white on the office laser printer, but she also wants it to look good on the screen when she shows it to her boss. Maria decides to use a red-orange color similar to the color of one of the salsas. She knows from experience that this color looks good when it is printed and also looks good on the screen. She decides to apply this color shading to the title zone.

To apply a color to the title zone:

❶ Highlight cells A1 through H2.

❷ Right-click anywhere in the highlighted block to display the SpeedMenu, then click **Block Properties...** to open the Active Block Object Inspector.

❸ Click **Shading** in the Object Inspector menu. The Shading settings appear.

❹ In the Color 1 palette, click **red** (second row, first color).

TROUBLE? On a monochrome monitor, select black (first row, last color) instead of red.

❺ In the Color 2 palette, click **yellow** (third row, second color).

TROUBLE? On a monochrome monitor, select white (first row, first color) instead of yellow.

❻ In the Blend palette, click the shade of **orange** shown in Figure 3-24 (the third blend from the left).

TROUBLE? On a monochrome monitor, select the shade of gray in the middle square (the fourth blend from the left) instead of orange.

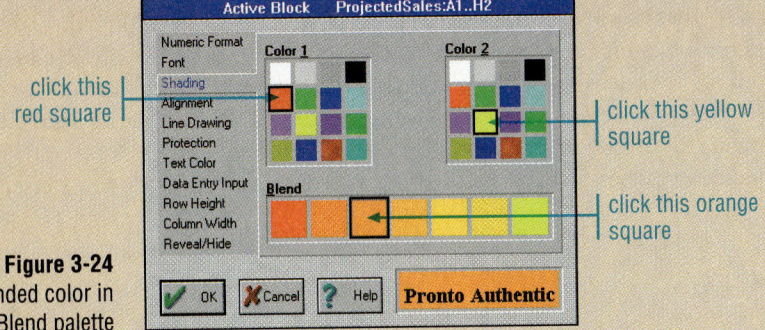

Figure 3-24
The blended color in
the Blend palette

❼ Click **OK**. Quattro Pro applies the color to the block.

❽ Click any cell to remove the highlighting and view the color in the title zone. See Figure 3-25.

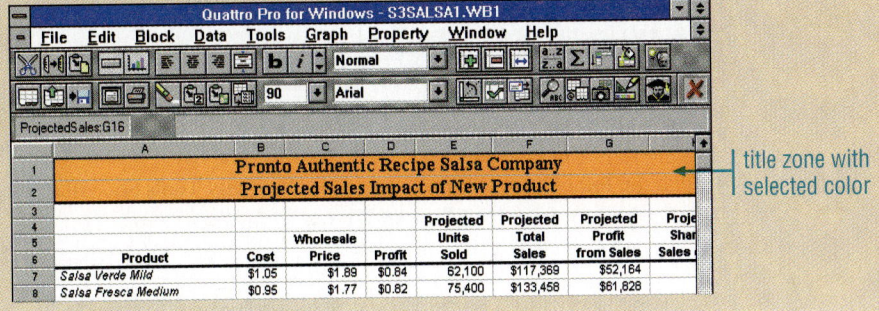

Figure 3-25
The color in
the title zone

Maria saves a copy of the revised notebook.

To save the S3SALSA1.WB1 notebook with the same filename:

❶ Click the **Save Notebook button** 📇 on the Productivity Tools SpeedBar (or click **File** then click **Save**).

If you want to take a break and resume the tutorial at a later time, you can exit Quattro Pro by double-clicking the Quattro Pro application Control menu box (or by clicking File then clicking Exit). When you want to resume the tutorial, launch Quattro Pro, maximize the Quattro Pro and NOTEBK1.WB1 windows, place your Student Disk in the disk drive, and open the file S3SALSA1.WB1. You can then continue with the tutorial.

Printing Spreadsheets

Now Maria is ready to print the spreadsheet. First, she must highlight the block of cells that she wants to print. Anytime you have a block (more than one cell) highlighted when you start printing, Quattro Pro assumes that you want to print the block.

You should always specify the print block. If you do not highlight a block of cells, Quattro Pro chooses a block for you. If you have printed before, usually Quattro Pro uses the block address of the last block you printed. For example, if the last block you printed was B6..H10 and you select the Print command without highlighting a new block, Quattro Pro will still use B6..H10 as the block to be printed.

Maria decides to use Quattro Pro's Print Preview feature to check her spreadsheet before she prints it.

Print Preview

Before you print a spreadsheet, you can see how the printout will look by using Quattro Pro's Print Preview feature. When you request a print preview, you can see the margins, page breaks, headers, and footers, which are not always visible on the screen. (Headers and footers are discussed later in this section.)

REFERENCE WINDOW

Using Print Preview

- Highlight the block of cells you want to print.

- Click the Print Preview button on the Productivity Tools SpeedBar (or click File then click Print Preview).

or

Click the Print button on the Productivity Tools SpeedBar (or click File then click Print) to open the Spreadsheet Print dialog box, then click the Preview button.

Maria wants to print the block of cells A1 through H12, so she selects and previews the block first.

To select and preview the block of cells to be printed:
❶ Highlight cells A1 through H12.
❷ Click the **Print Preview button** 🖻 on the Productivity Tools SpeedBar (or click **File** then click **Print Preview**) to see how the spreadsheet will look when printed. The Print Preview screen appears, containing the Print Preview SpeedBar and displaying the spreadsheet. See Figure 3-26.

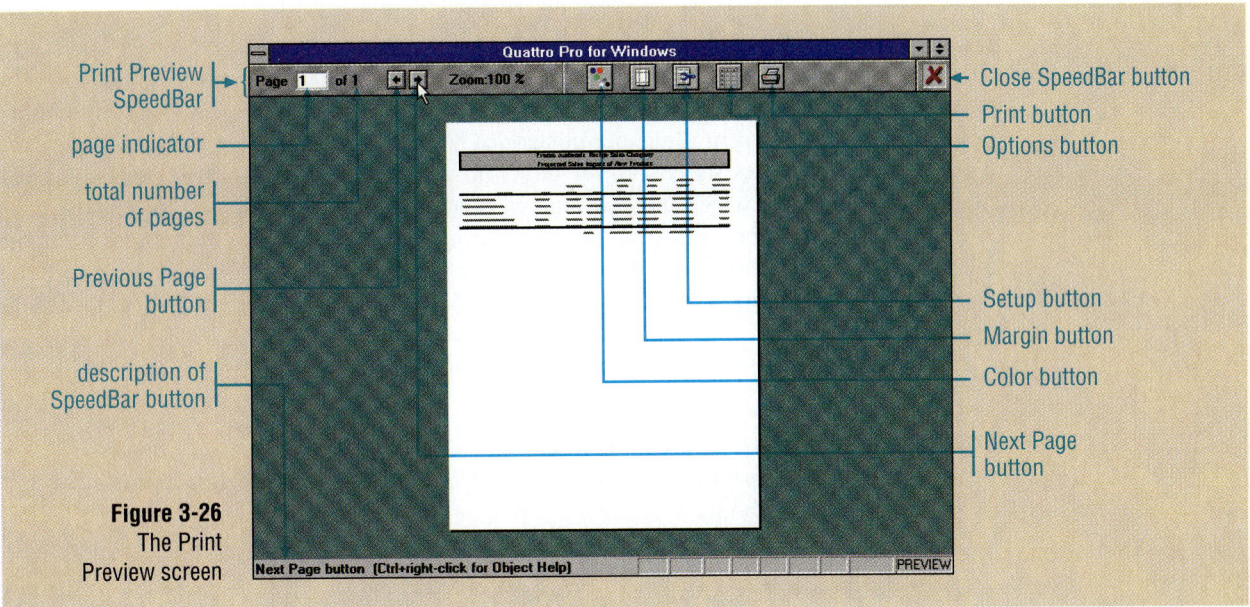

Figure 3-26
The Print
Preview screen

When Quattro Pro displays a full page on the Print Preview screen, it's usually difficult to see the text of the spreadsheet because it is so small. If you want to read the text, you can use the Print Preview Zoom feature (which is different from the Zoom Factor you used earlier with the notebook).

To display an enlarged section of the Print Preview spreadsheet:

❶ Position the pointer over the Print Preview spreadsheet. The pointer changes to 🔍.

❷ Click the portion of the Print Preview spreadsheet you want to enlarge (or press [+]).

❸ Right-click the Print Preview spreadsheet (or press [-]) to return the Print Preview spreadsheet to its original size.

The Print Preview SpeedBar contains several other buttons, as shown in Figure 3-26.

The Color button lets you switch between black-and-white and color printing. The Margin button allows you to adjust the margins on the Print Preview screen and immediately view the result of the change. The Setup button lets you change the way the page is set up by adjusting the margins, creating headers and footers (defined later), adding page numbers, changing the paper size, or centering the spreadsheet on the page. The Options button lets you choose whether or not to print spreadsheet gridlines and spreadsheet column letters and row numbers. The Print button prints the spreadsheet (it does not open the Spreadsheet Print dialog box, as does the Print button on the Productivity Tools SpeedBar). The Close SpeedBar button returns you to the spreadsheet window.

By looking at the print preview, Maria sees that the spreadsheet is too wide to fit on a single page. She decides to print the spreadsheet sideways so it will fit on a single sheet of paper.

Portrait and Landscape Orientations

Quattro Pro provides two print orientations, portrait and landscape. **Portrait** orientation prints the spreadsheet with the paper positioned so it is taller than it is wide. **Landscape** orientation prints the spreadsheet with the paper positioned so it is wider than it is tall. Because many spreadsheets are wider than they are tall, landscape orientation is used frequently.

You can specify the print orientation by using the Page Setup... command on the File menu or by using the Setup button on the Print Preview SpeedBar to open the Spreadsheet Page Setup dialog box. The print orientation setting is one of several settings that you can change in the Spreadsheet Page Setup dialog box.

Let's use landscape orientation for Maria's spreadsheet.

To change the print orientation to landscape:

❶ Click the **Setup button** ▦ on the Print Preview SpeedBar to display the Spreadsheet Page Setup dialog box.

❷ Click **Landscape** in the Print Orientation box, as shown in Figure 3-27.

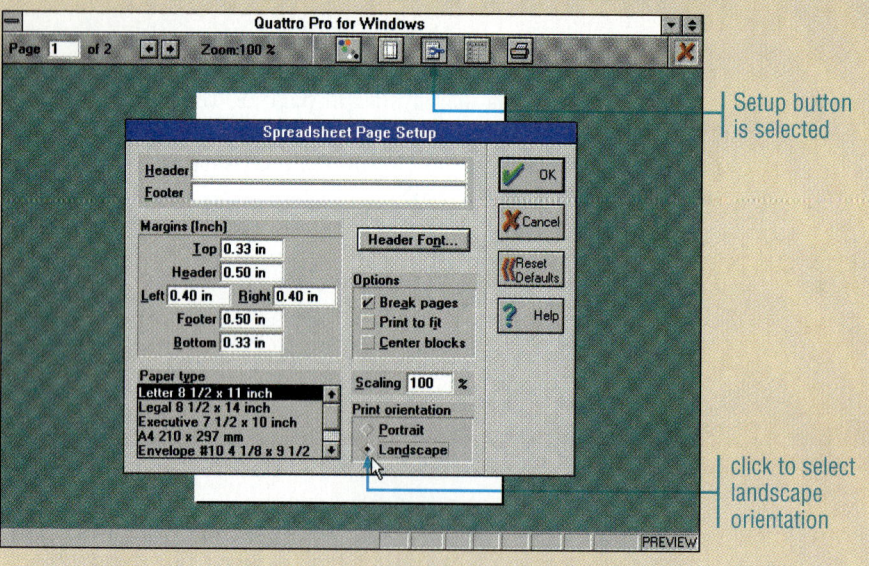

Figure 3-27
The Spreadsheet
Page Setup
dialog box

While the Spreadsheet Page Setup dialog box is open, Maria decides to add a header and footer to help document the spreadsheet.

Headers and Footers

A **header** is text that is printed in the top margin of every page. A **footer** is text that is printed in the bottom margin of every page. Headers and footers are not displayed as part of the notebook window. To see them, you must view the spreadsheet in the Print Preview window, or print the spreadsheet.

You can use a header or footer to provide basic documentation on your spreadsheet printout. A spreadsheet header could contain the name of the person who created the spreadsheet, the date the spreadsheet was created, and the filename of the spreadsheet.

Quattro Pro allows you to put header and footer information into three areas—a left-aligned area, a centered area, and a right-aligned area. The vertical bar character (|) is used to separate the information in each area, and up to two vertical bars can be used in each header and footer. Information entered before the first vertical bar is left-aligned. Information entered between the first vertical bar and the second vertical bar is centered. Information entered after the second vertical bar is right-aligned. The use of the vertical bar for controlling alignment is shown in Figure 3-28.

Text in Header or Footer Edit Field	Printed Header or Footer		
Income Statement	Income Statement		
|Income Statement		Income Statement	
||Income Statement			Income Statement
|Page #p		Page 1	
Income Statement||Page #p	Income Statement		Page 1
Income Statement|#p|#D	Income Statement	Page 1	9/15/96

Figure 3-28
Header and footer alignment

Quattro Pro uses special combinations of characters as formatting codes to insert dates, times, and filenames in a header or footer. You type these codes into the Header and Footer edit fields of the Spreadsheet Page Setup dialog box. Figure 3-29 shows some of the formatting codes that you can use.

Formatting Code	Description
#f	Notebook filename
#p	Current page number
#P	Total number of pages
#t	Current time in Short International Time format
#T	Current time in Long International Time format
#ts	Current time in Short Time format
#Ts	Current time in Long Time format
#d	Current date in Short International Date format
#D	Current date in Long International Date format
#ds	Current date in Short Date format
#Ds	Current date in Long Date format
#n	Rest of header or footer printed on a second line

Figure 3-29
Header and footer formatting codes

Maria wants to add a header containing the company name, the current date, and the filename; and she wants to add a footer containing the page number.

To add the header and footer to the spreadsheet:

❶ Make sure the Spreadsheet Page Setup dialog box is still open.

   TROUBLE? If you closed the Spreadsheet Page Setup dialog box, click the Setup button 🔲 to open it.

❷ Click the **Header edit field** to make it active.

❸ Type | (the vertical bar character). Any text you type now will be centered.

   TROUBLE? The vertical bar character is on the backslash key (\). On the keyboard the vertical bar appears broken into two parts (upper and lower). Hold down [Shift] and type [\] to display the vertical bar character.

❹ Type | (the vertical bar character) again. Any text you type now will be right-aligned.

❺ Type **Pronto Salsa Company** then press [Spacebar] to separate the company name from the next item in the header.

❻ Type **#D** to add the current date to the header, then press [Spacebar].

❼ Type **#f** to add the filename to the header.

❽ Click the **Footer edit field** to make it active.

❾ Type | (the vertical bar character). Any text you type now will be centered.

❿ Type **Page #p** to insert the word *Page* followed by a space and the page number. The Spreadsheet Page Setup dialog box now appears as shown in Figure 3-30.

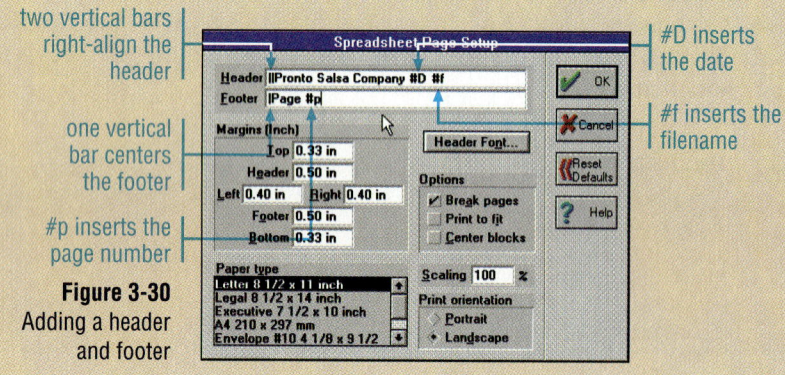

two vertical bars right-align the header

one vertical bar centers the footer

#p inserts the page number

Figure 3-30
Adding a header and footer

#D inserts the date

#f inserts the filename

Next, Maria decides to adjust the page margins to move the text away from the edges of the paper.

Setting Margins

The Spreadsheet Page Setup dialog box provides options for changing the page margins of your printed spreadsheet. Quattro Pro allows you to specify top, bottom, left, and right margins. In addition, you can specify the height of the area for the page header and footer. Figure 3-31 shows an example of an income statement printout that illustrates the margin locations.

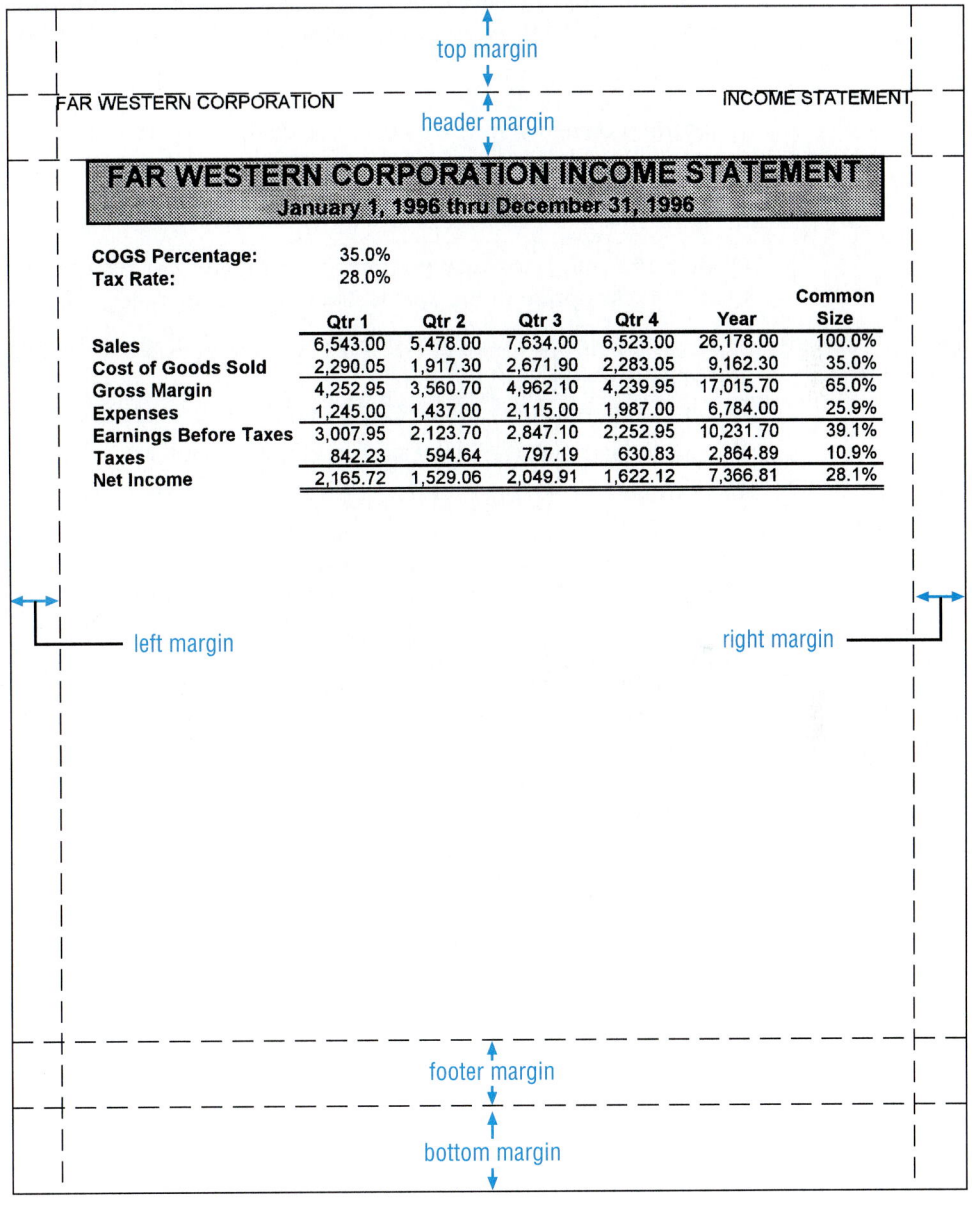

Figure 3-31
Page margins

Maria decides to use a 1.00-inch margin for the top, bottom, and sides of her printout. She will leave the header and footer margins at their default value of 0.50 inches.

To adjust the margins:

❶ Make sure the Spreadsheet Page Setup dialog box is still open.

❷ Click the **Top edit field** in the Margins section. Delete the current entry in the field, then type **1.00**.

❸ Click the **Left edit field**. Delete the current entry in the field, then type **1.00**.

❹ Click the **Right edit field**. Delete the current entry in the field, then type **1.00**.

❺ Click the **Bottom edit field**. Delete the current entry in the field, then type **1.00**. Your Spreadsheet Page Setup dialog box should now look like the one in Figure 3-32.

Maria prefers her spreadsheets to be centered on the printed page.

Centering the Printout

Quattro Pro will horizontally center the spreadsheet on the printout if you check the Center blocks option in the Spreadsheet Page Setup dialog box.

To center the printout:

❶ Make sure the Spreadsheet Page Setup dialog box is still open.

❷ In Options, click the **Center blocks check box** to select it.

❸ Compare the settings in your Spreadsheet Page Setup dialog box to those in Figure 3-32.

TROUBLE? If your Spreadsheet Page Setup dialog box does not match the one shown in Figure 3-32, make any necessary changes so that they are the same.

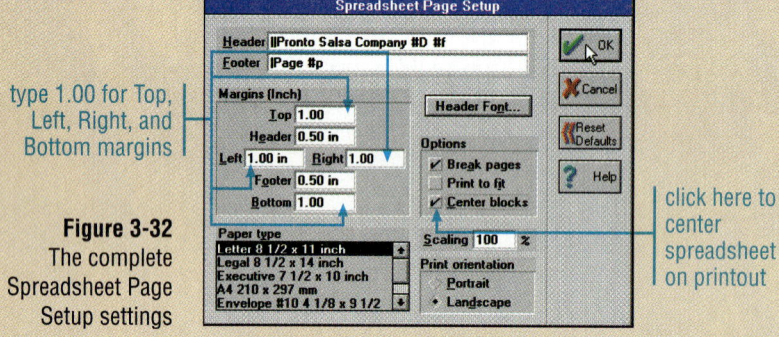

type 1.00 for Top, Left, Right, and Bottom margins

Figure 3-32
The complete Spreadsheet Page Setup settings

click here to center spreadsheet on printout

❹ Click **OK** to complete the Spreadsheet Page Setup changes and view the results of your changes in the Print Preview window. See Figure 3-33.

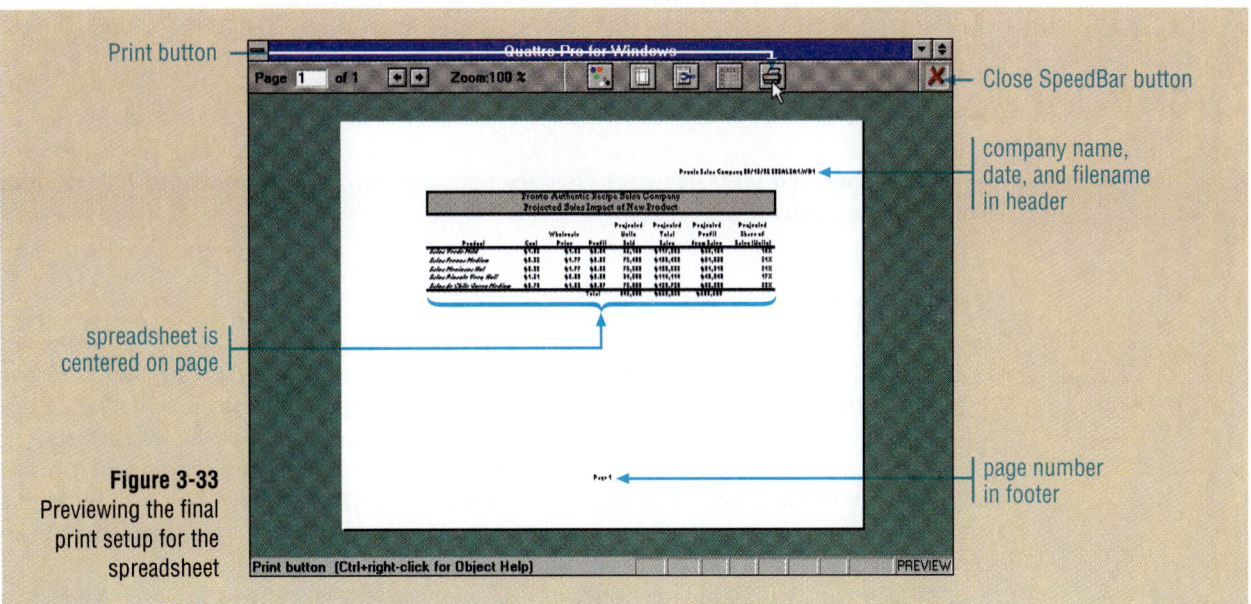

Figure 3-33
Previewing the final
print setup for the
spreadsheet

Maria is now ready to print the spreadsheet.

To print the spreadsheet and close the Print Preview window:

❶ Click the **Print button** 🖨 on the Print Preview SpeedBar. Figure 3-34 shows the printout.

❷ Click the **Close SpeedBar button** ❌ to exit Print Preview.

Pronto Salsa Company 08/15/96 S3SALSA1.WB1

Pronto Authentic Recipe Salsa Company Projected Sales Impact of New Product						
Product	**Cost**	**Wholesale Price**	**Profit**	**Projected Units Sold**	**Projected Total Sales**	**Projected Profit from Sales**	**Projected Share of Sales (Units)**
Salsa Verde Mild	$1.05	$1.89	$0.84	62,100	$117,369	$52,164	18%
Salsa Fresca Medium	$0.95	$1.77	$0.82	75,400	$133,458	$61,828	21%
Salsa Mexicana Hot	$0.95	$1.77	$0.82	75,500	$133,635	$61,910	21%
Salsa Picante Very Hot!	$1.21	$2.09	$0.88	54,600	$114,114	$48,048	17%
Salsa de Chile Guero Medium	$0.78	$1.65	$0.87	75,000	$123,750	$65,250	23%
			Total	342,600	$622,326	$289,200	

Page 1

Figure 3-34
The printed
spreadsheet

Maria saves her notebook to record the print settings on disk.

To save the notebook:
❶ Click the **Save Notebook button** 🖫 (or click **File** then click **Save**).

Maria is pleased with her work, but she still needs to print a list of the cell contents before Anne returns.

Printing Cell Contents

In Tutorial 2 you learned to incorporate documentation into your spreadsheet, and you learned that the spreadsheet plan and sketch are valuable paper-based documentation. In this tutorial, you will learn how to document the formulas you used to create the spreadsheet.

You can document the formulas you entered on a spreadsheet by printing a list of the cell contents of each cell. This list will contain every value, label, and formula in the spreadsheet. You do this by choosing the Cell formulas option in the Spreadsheet Print Options dialog box.

Maria wants a printout of the formulas, values, and labels in the spreadsheet for documentation.

To print the cell contents:
❶ Highlight cells A1 through H12.

❷ Click **File** then click **Page Setup...**. The Spreadsheet Page Setup dialog box appears.

❸ Because a printout of cell contents is in list form, click **Portrait** in Print orientation.

❹ Click **OK** in the Spreadsheet Page Setup dialog box.

❺ Click the **Print button** 🖨 (or click **File** then click **Print...**). The Spreadsheet Print dialog box appears.

❻ Click **Options...** to display the Spreadsheet Print Options dialog box.

❼ In Print options, click the **Cell formulas check box** to select it.

❽ Click **OK** in the Spreadsheet Print Options dialog box. The Spreadsheet Print dialog box reappears.

❾ Click **Print** in the Spreadsheet Print dialog box. A cell-by-cell list of the spreadsheet contents is printed, as shown in Figure 3-35. Note that the figure shows only the first page of the two-page printout. Also notice that the same header and footer appear on this printout.

Pronto Salsa Company 08/15/96 S3SALSA1.WB1

ProjectedSales:A1:   ^Pronto Authentic Recipe Salsa Company
ProjectedSales:A2:   ^Projected Sales Impact of New Product
ProjectedSales:E4:   ^Projected
ProjectedSales:F4:   ^Projected
ProjectedSales:G4:   ^Projected
ProjectedSales:H4:   ^Projected
ProjectedSales:C5:   ^Wholesale
ProjectedSales:E5:   ^Units
ProjectedSales:F5:   ^Total
ProjectedSales:G5:   ^Profit
ProjectedSales:H5:   ^Share of
ProjectedSales:A6:   ^Product
ProjectedSales:B6:   ^Cost
ProjectedSales:C6:   ^Price
ProjectedSales:D6:   ^Profit
ProjectedSales:E6:   ^Sold
ProjectedSales:F6:   ^Sales
ProjectedSales:G6:   ^from Sales
ProjectedSales:H6:   ^Sales (Units)
ProjectedSales:A7:   'Salsa Verde Mild
ProjectedSales:B7:   1.05
ProjectedSales:C7:   1.89
ProjectedSales:D7:   +C7-B7
ProjectedSales:E7:   62100
ProjectedSales:F7:   +C7*E7
ProjectedSales:G7:   +D7*E7
ProjectedSales:H7:   +G7/$ProjectedSales:$G$12
ProjectedSales:A8:   'Salsa Fresca Medium
ProjectedSales:B8:   0.95
ProjectedSales:C8:   1.77
ProjectedSales:D8:   +C8-B8
ProjectedSales:E8:   75400
ProjectedSales:F8:   +C8*E8
ProjectedSales:G8:   +D8*E8
ProjectedSales:H8:   +G8/$ProjectedSales:$G$12
ProjectedSales:A9:   'Salsa Mexicana Hot
ProjectedSales:B9:   0.95
ProjectedSales:C9:   1.77
ProjectedSales:D9:   +C9-B9
ProjectedSales:E9:   75500
ProjectedSales:F9:   +C9*E9
ProjectedSales:G9:   +D9*E9
ProjectedSales:H9:   +G9/$ProjectedSales:$G$12
ProjectedSales:A10:   'Salsa Picante Very Hot!
ProjectedSales:B10:   1.21
ProjectedSales:C10:   2.09
ProjectedSales:D10:   +C10-B10
ProjectedSales:E10:   54600
ProjectedSales:F10:   +C10*E10
ProjectedSales:G10:   +D10*E10

Figure 3-35
The cell contents of
the spreadsheet
(page 1 of 2)

Page 1

Because print settings are saved with the notebook, Maria returns the print setup back to the settings for printing the spreadsheet. This way she will be ready to print the spreadsheet the next time she uses the notebook.

To reset the print settings to print the spreadsheet:

❶ Click **File** then click **Page Setup**.... The Spreadsheet Page Setup dialog box appears.

❷ In Print orientation, click **Landscape**.

❸ Click **OK** in the Spreadsheet Page Setup dialog box.

❹ Click the **Print button** 🖫 (or click **File** then click **Print...**). The Spreadsheet Print dialog box appears.

❺ Click **Options...** to display the Spreadsheet Print Options dialog box.

❻ In Print options, click the **Cell formulas check box** to remove the checkmark from it.

❼ Click **OK** in the Spreadsheet Print Options dialog box. The Spreadsheet Print dialog box reappears.

❽ Click **Close** in the Spreadsheet Print dialog box.

Maria is ready to save and close the notebook.

To save and close the S3SALSA1.WB1 notebook:

❶ Click the **Save Notebook button** 🖫 on the Productivity Tools SpeedBar (or click **File** then click **Save**).

❷ Click **File** then click **Close** to close the notebook.

Maria exits Quattro Pro and Windows before turning off her computer. If you are not going to proceed to the Tutorial Assignments, you also need to exit Quattro Pro.

To exit Quattro Pro:

❶ Click **File** then click **Exit** to exit Quattro Pro.

■   ■   ■

As Maria looks over the printed spreadsheet and cell contents printout, Anne returns and asks to see the formatted spreadsheet. Anne examines the printouts and briefly checks the accuracy of the formulas shown on the cells contents printout. She thanks Maria for her excellent work before rushing off to her appointment with the loan officer.

Questions

1. Define the following terms using your own words:
   a. formatting
   b. font style
   c. headers
   d. footers
   e. spreadsheet titles
   f. column headings
2. If the number .128912 is in a cell, what will Quattro Pro display if you:
   a. format the number using the Percent format with no decimal places
   b. format the number using the Currency format with no decimal places
   c. format the number using the Currency format with two decimal places
3. Explain why Quattro Pro might display 1,045.39 in a cell, but when you look at the contents of the cell in the input line, it displays 1045.38672.
4. Explain the advantages and disadvantages of using the Style list to apply predefined formats to your spreadsheet.
5. List the ways you can access formatting options and settings.
6. List the formatting buttons that are available on the notebook SpeedBar.
7. Explain the options Quattro Pro provides for aligning data.
8. What is a potential problem with the way Quattro Pro automatically aligns data?
9. What is the general rule you should follow for aligning column headings, numbers, and text labels?
10. Why is it useful to include a comma to separate thousands, millions, and billions?
11. List three ways you can change column widths.
12. List the Quattro Pro formatting features you can use to draw attention to data or to provide visual interest.
13. Explain how you should position line segments so they are not disrupted when you copy cell contents.
14. Make a list of things you should look for when you use the Print Preview feature to ensure that your printed spreadsheets look professional.

Tutorial Assignments

Launch Windows and Quattro Pro, if necessary. Insert your Student Disk in the disk drive. Make sure the Quattro Pro and NOTEBK1.WB1 windows are maximized.

1. Open the notebook file T3SALSA2.WB1.
2. Save the notebook on your student disk as S3SALSA2.WB1 so that you will not modify the original file.
3. Revise the documentation on the Documentation page as follows.
   a. Change the filename in cell B4 to S3SALSA2.WB1.
   b. Put your name in cell B5.
   c. Put the current date in cell B6 (do not use an @function).
4. Save the notebook again to record the documentation changes on disk.

For the spreadsheet on the Documentation page:

5. Use the Style list and format the notebook title in cell A1 with the Heading 1 style. Adjust the row height if necessary.
6. Use the Style list and format the notebook subtitle in cell A2 with the Heading 2 style. Adjust the row height if necessary.
7. Bold the labels in cells A4, A5, A6, A8, A12, B12, and C12.

For the spreadsheet on the ProjectedSales page:

8. If you have a monochrome monitor, change the color in the title zone (A1..H2) to gray as described in the TROUBLE section *Using Color for Emphasis*.

9. Right-align the label "Total" in cell D12.

10. Center the percentages displayed in column H.

11. Bold the contents of cells A11 through H11 to emphasize the new product. Make any necessary column width adjustments.

12. Add color to cells A11 through H11 using the same color used for the titles.

 13. Use the Active Page Object Inspector to color the ProjectedSales page tab. Use a color similar to the color used for the titles.

14. Save the notebook again.

15. Highlight the block A1..H12, then preview the ProjectedSales spreadsheet printout.

16. Replace the company name in the header with your name so that it appears on the printout of the spreadsheet. Make sure the header also prints the date and spreadsheet filename.

17. Make sure the Spreadsheet Page Setup settings specify landscape orientation and that the spreadsheet is centered on the page.

18. Make sure the printout fits on one page.

19. Print the spreadsheet.

20. Print a list of the cell contents to document the cell formulas.

21. Reset the print settings and options for spreadsheet printing.

22. Save the notebook.

23. Turn in your spreadsheet printout and your printed list of cell contents.

Case Problems

1. Weatherby Sales Incentive Program

Carla Stambaugh is the assistant sales manager at Weatherby Inc., a manufacturer of outdoor and expedition clothing. Weatherby sales representatives contact retail chains and individual retail outlets to sell the Weatherby line of outdoor clothing products.

This year, to spur sales Carla has decided to run a sales incentive program for the sales representatives. Each sales representative has been assigned a sales goal 15% higher than his or her total sales for last year. All sales representatives who reach this new goal will be awarded an all-expenses-paid trip for two to Cozumel, Mexico.

Carla has been tracking the results of the sales incentive program with a Quattro Pro spreadsheet. She has asked you to format the spreadsheet so it will look professional. She also wants a printout before she presents the spreadsheet at the next sales meeting. Complete the following steps to format and print the spreadsheet:

1. Launch Windows and Quattro Pro as usual.

2. Open the spreadsheet P3SALES.WB1.

3. Save the notebook on your Student Disk as S3SALES.WB1 so that you will not modify the original file.

4. Revise the documentation on the Documentation page as follows.

   a. Change the filename in cell B4 to S3SALES.WB1.

   b. Put your name in cell B5.

   c. Put the current date in cell B6 (do not use an @function).

5. Save the notebook again to record the documentation changes on disk.

For the spreadsheet on the Documentation page:

6. Use the Style list and format the notebook title in cell A1 with the Heading 1 style. Adjust the row height if necessary.

7. Use the Style list and format the notebook subtitle in cell A2 with the Heading 2 style. Adjust the row height if necessary.

8. Bold the labels in cells A4, A5, A6, A8, A12, B12, and C12.

For the spreadsheet on the SalesIncentive page:

9. Make the formatting changes shown in Figure 3-36.

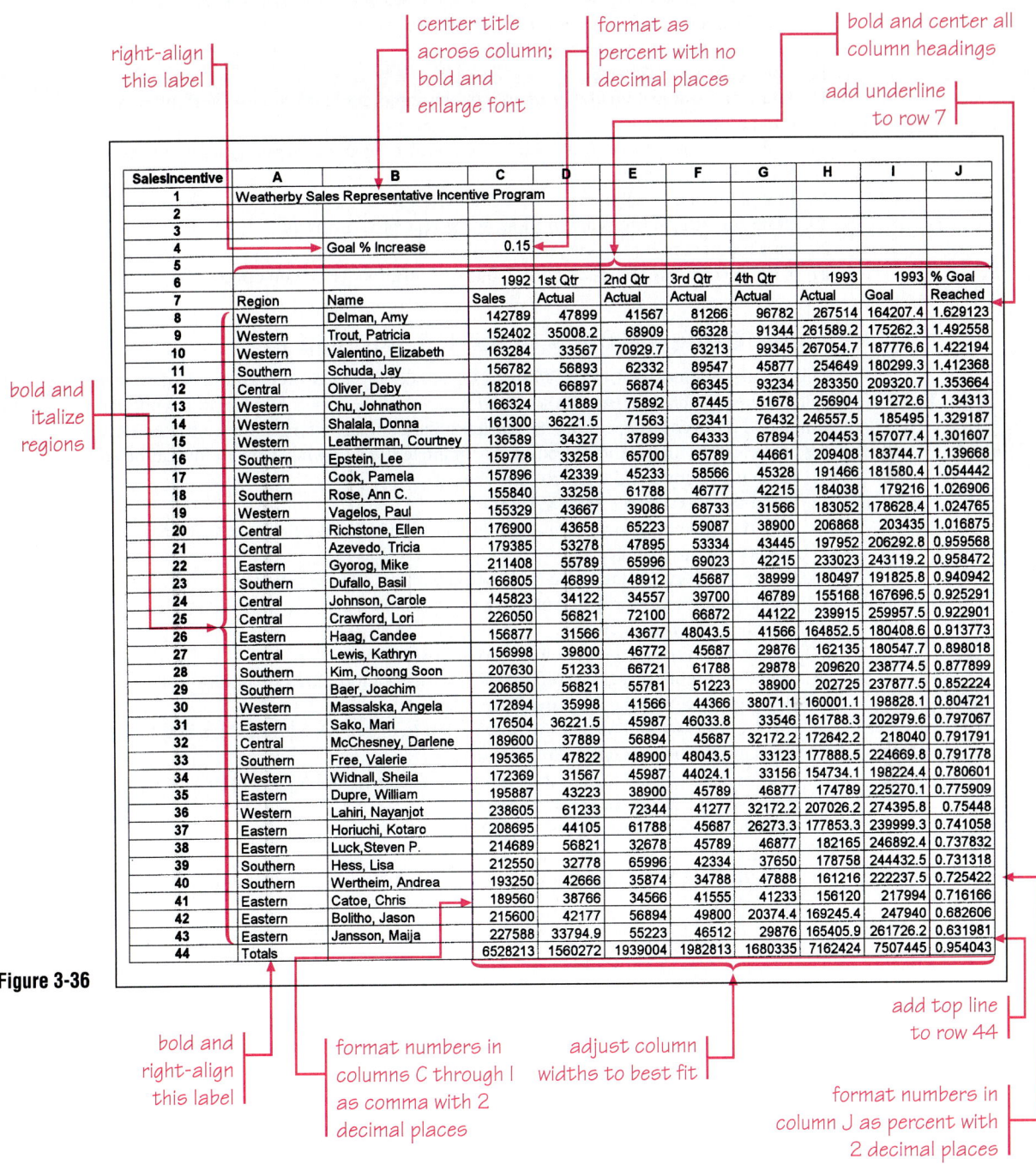

Figure 3-36

Annotations (pink handwriting):
- right-align this label
- center title across column; bold and enlarge font
- format as percent with no decimal places
- bold and center all column headings
- add underline to row 7
- bold and italize regions
- bold and right-align this label
- format numbers in columns C through I as comma with 2 decimal places
- adjust column widths to best fit
- add top line to row 44
- format numbers in column J as percent with 2 decimal places

SalesIncentive	A	B	C	D	E	F	G	H	I	J
1	Weatherby Sales Representative Incentive Program									
2										
3										
4		Goal % Increase	0.15							
5										
6			1992	1st Qtr	2nd Qtr	3rd Qtr	4th Qtr	1993	1993	% Goal
7	Region	Name	Sales	Actual	Actual	Actual	Actual	Actual	Goal	Reached
8	Western	Delman, Amy	142789	47899	41567	81266	96782	267514	164207.4	1.629123
9	Western	Trout, Patricia	152402	35008.2	68909	66328	91344	261589.2	175262.3	1.492558
10	Western	Valentino, Elizabeth	163284	33567	70929.7	63213	99345	267054.7	187776.6	1.422194
11	Southern	Schuda, Jay	156782	56893	62332	89547	45877	254649	180299.3	1.412368
12	Central	Oliver, Deby	182018	66897	56874	66345	93234	283350	209320.7	1.353664
13	Western	Chu, Johnathon	166324	41889	75892	87445	51678	256904	191272.6	1.34313
14	Western	Shalala, Donna	161300	36221.5	71563	62341	76432	246557.5	185495	1.329187
15	Western	Leatherman, Courtney	136589	34327	37899	64333	67894	204453	157077.4	1.301607
16	Southern	Epstein, Lee	159778	33258	65700	65789	44661	209408	183744.7	1.139668
17	Western	Cook, Pamela	157896	42339	45233	58566	45328	191466	181580.4	1.054442
18	Southern	Rose, Ann C.	155840	33258	61788	46777	42215	184038	179216	1.026906
19	Western	Vagelos, Paul	155329	43667	39086	68733	31566	183052	178628.4	1.024765
20	Central	Richstone, Ellen	176900	43658	65223	59087	38900	206868	203435	1.016875
21	Central	Azevedo, Tricia	179385	53278	47895	53334	43445	197952	206292.8	0.959568
22	Eastern	Gyorog, Mike	211408	55789	65996	69023	42215	233023	243119.2	0.958472
23	Southern	Dufallo, Basil	166805	46899	48912	45687	38999	180497	191825.8	0.940942
24	Central	Johnson, Carole	145823	34122	34557	39700	46789	155168	167696.5	0.925291
25	Central	Crawford, Lori	226050	56821	72100	66872	44122	239915	259957.5	0.922901
26	Eastern	Haag, Candee	156877	31566	43677	48043.5	41566	164852.5	180408.6	0.913773
27	Central	Lewis, Kathryn	156998	39800	46772	45687	29876	162135	180547.7	0.898018
28	Southern	Kim, Choong Soon	207630	51233	66721	61788	29878	209620	238774.5	0.877899
29	Southern	Baer, Joachim	206850	56821	55781	51223	38900	202725	237877.5	0.852224
30	Western	Massalska, Angela	172894	35998	41566	44366	38071.1	160001.1	198828.1	0.804721
31	Eastern	Sako, Mari	176504	36221.5	45987	46033.8	33546	161788.3	202979.6	0.797067
32	Central	McChesney, Darlene	189600	37889	56894	45687	32172.2	172642.2	218040	0.791791
33	Southern	Free, Valerie	195365	47822	48900	48043.5	33123	177888.5	224669.8	0.791778
34	Western	Widnall, Sheila	172369	31567	45987	44024.1	33156	154734.1	198224.4	0.780601
35	Eastern	Dupre, William	195887	43223	38900	45789	46877	174789	225270.1	0.775909
36	Western	Lahiri, Nayanjot	238605	61233	72344	41277	32172.2	207026.2	274395.8	0.75448
37	Eastern	Horiuchi, Kotaro	208695	44105	61788	45687	26273.3	177853.3	239999.3	0.741058
38	Eastern	Luck, Steven P.	214689	56821	32678	45789	46877	182165	246892.4	0.737832
39	Southern	Hess, Lisa	212550	32778	65996	42334	37650	178758	244432.5	0.731318
40	Southern	Wertheim, Andrea	193250	42666	35874	34788	47888	161216	222237.5	0.725422
41	Eastern	Catoe, Chris	189560	38766	34566	41555	41233	156120	217994	0.716166
42	Eastern	Bolitho, Jason	215600	42177	56894	49800	20374.4	169245.4	247940	0.682606
43	Eastern	Jansson, Maija	227588	33794.9	55223	46512	29876	165405.9	261726.2	0.631981
44	Totals		6528213	1560272	1939004	1982813	1680335	7162424	7507445	0.954043

10. Save this notebook.

E 11. Use the Quattro Pro Help system to read about the "Print to fit" print option.

12. Highlight the block A1..J44, then preview the SalesIncentive spreadsheet printout.

13. Use the Spreadsheet Page Setup dialog box to scale the spreadsheet to fit on one page printed in portrait orientation.

14. Center the spreadsheet.

15. Add a right-aligned header containing your name, the current date, and the notebook filename.

16. Add a centered footer containing the word *Page* and the current page number.

17. Print the spreadsheet.

18. Print a list of the cell contents to document the cell formulas.

19. Reset the print settings and options for spreadsheet printing.

20. Save the notebook.

21. Turn in your spreadsheet printout and your printed list of cell contents.

2. Age Group Changes in the U.S. Population

Rick Stephanopolous of United Western Insurance Group is preparing a report on changes in the United States population. Part of the report focuses on age group changes in the population from 1980 through 1990. Rick has created a spreadsheet that contains information from the U.S. Census reports, and he is ready to format the spreadsheet. Complete the following steps to format the spreadsheet:

1. Launch Windows and Quattro Pro as usual.

2. Open the spreadsheet P3CENSUS.WB1.

3. Save the notebook on your Student Disk as S3CENSUS.WB1 so that you will not modify the original file.

4. Revise the documentation on the Documentation page as follows:
   a. Change the filename in cell B4 to S3CENSUS.WB1.
   b. Put your name in cell B5.
   c. Put the current date in cell B6 (do not use an @function).

5. Save the notebook again to record the documentation changes on disk.

For the spreadsheet on the Documentation page:

6. Use the Style list and format the notebook title in cell A1 with the Heading 1 style. Adjust the row height if necessary.

7. Use the Style list and format the notebook subtitle in cell A2 with the Heading 2 style. Adjust the row height if necessary.

8. Bold the labels in cells A4, A5, A6, A8, A12, B12, and C12.

For the spreadsheet on the Analysis page:

9. Make the formatting changes shown in Figure 3-37, adjusting column widths as necessary.

center and
bold all labels
in row 5

center titles
across columns;
bold and enlarge
font; add an
outline and color

center across
columns B and
C; bold

center across
columns D and
E; bold

center across
columns F and
G; bold

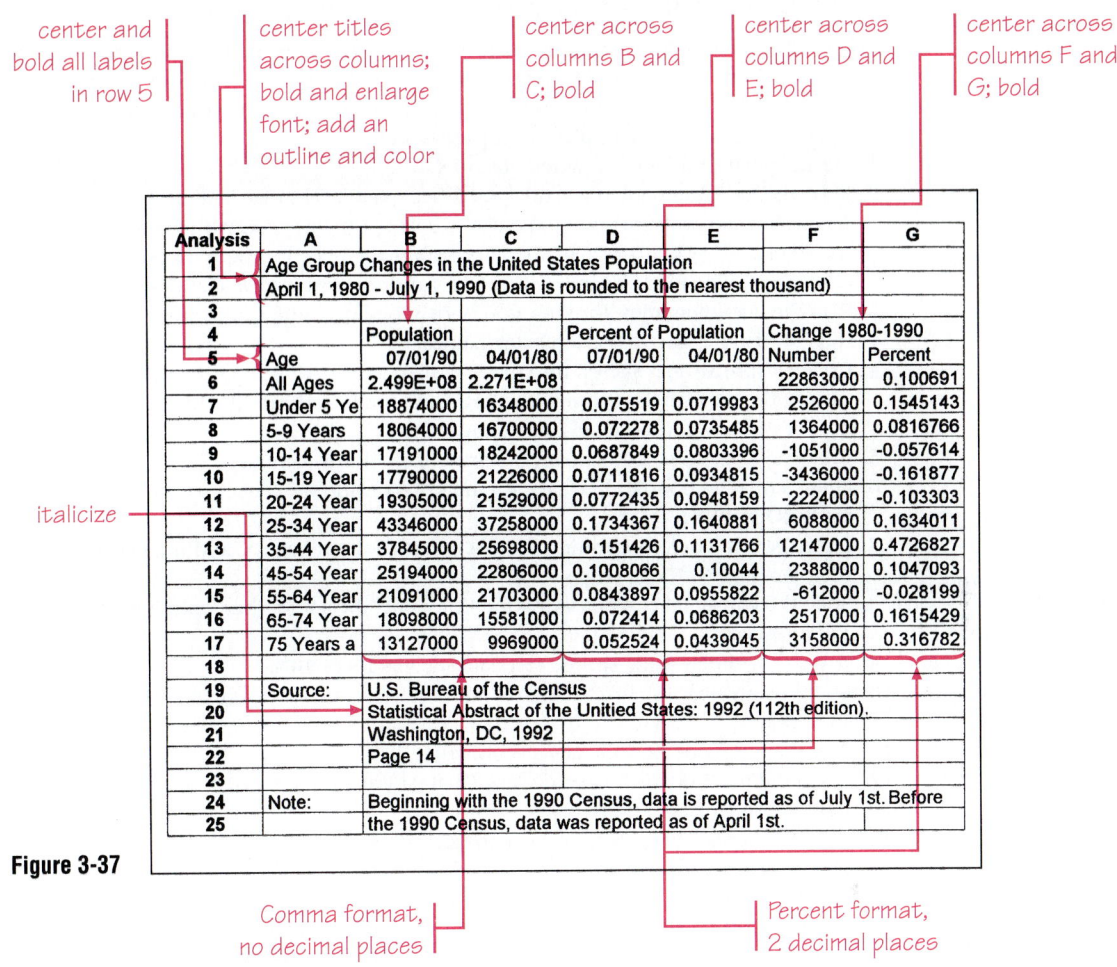

Analysis	A	B	C	D	E	F	G
1	Age Group Changes in the United States Population						
2	April 1, 1980 - July 1, 1990 (Data is rounded to the nearest thousand)						
3							
4		Population		Percent of Population		Change 1980-1990	
5	Age	07/01/90	04/01/80	07/01/90	04/01/80	Number	Percent
6	All Ages	2.499E+08	2.271E+08			22863000	0.100691
7	Under 5 Ye	18874000	16348000	0.075519	0.0719983	2526000	0.1545143
8	5-9 Years	18064000	16700000	0.072278	0.0735485	1364000	0.0816766
9	10-14 Year	17191000	18242000	0.0687849	0.0803396	-1051000	-0.057614
10	15-19 Year	17790000	21226000	0.0711816	0.0934815	-3436000	-0.161877
11	20-24 Year	19305000	21529000	0.0772435	0.0948159	-2224000	-0.103303
12	25-34 Year	43346000	37258000	0.1734367	0.1640881	6088000	0.1634011
13	35-44 Year	37845000	25698000	0.151426	0.1131766	12147000	0.4726827
14	45-54 Year	25194000	22806000	0.1008066	0.10044	2388000	0.1047093
15	55-64 Year	21091000	21703000	0.0843897	0.0955822	-612000	-0.028199
16	65-74 Year	18098000	15581000	0.072414	0.0686203	2517000	0.1615429
17	75 Years a	13127000	9969000	0.052524	0.0439045	3158000	0.316782
18							
19	Source:	U.S. Bureau of the Census					
20		Statistical Abstract of the Unitied States: 1992 (112th edition).					
21		Washington, DC, 1992					
22		Page 14					
23							
24	Note:	Beginning with the 1990 Census, data is reported as of July 1st. Before					
25		the 1990 Census, data was reported as of April 1st.					

italicize

Figure 3-37

Comma format,
no decimal places

Percent format,
2 decimal places

10. Save the notebook.
11. Highlight the block A1..G25, then preview the Analysis spreadsheet printout.
12. Use the Spreadsheet Page Setup dialog box to scale the spreadsheet to fit on one page printed in portrait orientation.
13. Center the spreadsheet.
14. Add a right-aligned header containing your name, the current date, and the notebook filename.
15. Add a centered footer containing the word *Page* and the current page number.
16. Print the spreadsheet.
17. Print a list of the cell contents to document the cell formulas.
18. Reset the print settings and options for spreadsheet printing.
19. Save the notebook.
20. Turn in your spreadsheet printout and your printed list of cell contents.

3.   Creating and Formatting Your Own Spreadsheet

Design a spreadsheet for a problem with which you are familiar. The problem might be a business problem from one of your other business courses, or it could be a numeric problem from a biology, education, or sociology course. Follow the steps below to plan your spreadsheet, prepare your planning documents, and complete the spreadsheet.

1. Decide what problem you would like to solve.
2. Refer to Otis's notebook plan and spreadsheet plan in Tutorial 2. Write similar documents for the problem you would like to solve. Write a statement of your goal, list the results you want to see, list the information you need for the spreadsheet cells, and describe the formulas you will need for the spreadsheet calculations.
3. Plan the documentation for your notebook based on Anne's documentation in this tutorial. Be sure to include page names.
4. Create a spreadsheet sketch for your spreadsheet showing the spreadsheet title(s), the data labels, column headings, and totals. Indicate the formats you will use for titles, headings, labels, data, and totals.
5. Create a formatting plan similar to Maria's plan in this tutorial.
6. Open a new notebook, then save the notebook using the name S3MYBOOK.WB1.
7. Build the notebook by creating the documentation on page A, and the spreadsheet on page B. Name pages A and B.
8. Build the spreadsheet by entering the titles and labels first, then entering the data and formulas.
9. Test the formulas using simple test data such as 1's or 10's.
10. After you are sure the formulas are correct, format the spreadsheet according to your plan.
11. Save the notebook periodically as you work.
12. When the notebook is formatted, use Quattro Pro's Print Preview feature to preview the spreadsheet on page B.
13. Make the Spreadsheet Page Setup settings needed to:
    a. center the spreadsheet
    b. print a right-aligned header containing your name, the date, and the filename
    c. print a centered footer containing the word *Page* and the page number
14. Print the cell contents for the spreadsheet page in your notebook.
15. Print the notebook documentation on page A.
16. Submit the following to your instructor:
    a. your planning sheet
    b. your planning sketch
    c. your planned documentation
    d. a printout of the pages in your notebook
    e. a printout of the cell contents in your spreadsheet page

Functions, Formulas, and Absolute References

Managing Loan Payments

Superior Sails Charter Company The Superior Sails Charter Company is based in Sault Ste. Marie, Michigan, on the shores of Lake Superior and close to the North Channel, one of the most pristine boating areas in the Northern Hemisphere. The company owns a large fleet of boats purchased with bank loans. Shabir Ahmad has spent the past two summers working for the charter company to help pay for his college education. This year the company finally has a computer. James LaSalle, the company owner, has asked Shabir to create some Quattro Pro notebooks so he will have better information to manage the business.

James asks Shabir to create a notebook to provide information about the monthly loan payments for each of the Superior Sails boats. He explains that he wants a notebook containing the following information about each loan:

- original amount of the loan
- interest rate of the loan
- number of payments needed to repay the loan
- payment amount per month

James also wants to see the monthly total amount that Superior Sails needs to pay for all of the loans, and he encourages Shabir to include any other information that might be useful for managing the boat loans.

Shabir thinks about the project then develops the notebook plan shown in Figure 4-1, and the documentation plan shown in Figure 4-2.

Figure 4-1
Shabir's notebook plan

Notebook Plan for Superior Sails Charter Company Loan Management Notebook

My Goal:
To develop a notebook to help management keep track of loan payments for boats in the Superior Sails fleet

What notebook pages will I use?
Page A   Notebook documentation
Page B   Loan Management spreadsheet

Figure 4-2
Shabir's documentation plan

Notebook Documentation Plan (Page A)

Superior Sails Charter Company
Loan Management Notebook

Filename: Notebook filename
Created by: Shabir Ahmad
Date: Date the notebook was created

Purpose: This notebook is used by Superior Sails Charter Company to track the
                 loan status of the company. It reports information on all bank loans
                 that the company has obtained to purchase sailboats for use in the
                 company's charter business.

Contents: Page: Name:
                 Page A   Documentation   Notebook documentation
                 Page B   Loans   Loan Management spreadsheet

Shabir then creates the spreadsheet plan shown in Figure 4-3, and the spreadsheet sketch shown in Figure 4-4. He decides that, in addition to the information James specified, the spreadsheet should show the total of the loans, the largest loan, the smallest loan, and the average amount of the loans. Shabir also decides to add a column that shows what percent each loan payment is of the total payment. This information might be useful if James decides to sell or replace any of his boats.

Spreadsheet Plan for Loan Management Spreadsheet (Page B)

My Goal:
To develop a spreadsheet to help management keep track of loan
payments for boats in the Superior Sails fleet

What results do I want to see?
Total payments due this month
The percent of total payment for each loan payment
The total amount of all loans
The amounts of the largest and smallest loans
The average loan amount

What information do I need?
A list of all boats in the Superior Sails fleet
The amount, interest rate, and number of monthly payments for each loan
The loan status (paid or due) for each boat

What calculations will I perform?
total loans = @SUM(all loans)
largest loan = @MAX(all loans)
smallest loan = @MIN(all loans)
average loan = @AVG(all loans)
monthly payment amount = @PAYMT(loan amount, interest rate, number of payments)
total payments due = @SUM(all payments for loans not paid off)
percent of total payment = loan payment/total payments due

Figure 4-3
Shabir's
spreadsheet plan

Superior Sails Charter Company – Loan Management Spreadsheet

Boat Type and Length	Loan Amount	Annual Interest Rate	Number of Monthly Payments	Monthly Payment Amount	Current Loan Status	Payments Due This Month	Percent of Total Payment
O'Day 34	$37,700	11.00%	60	${monthly payment amount formula}	xxx	${payment due this month formula}	{percentage of total formula}%

Total Loans: ${total loans formula}   Total Payments Due

Largest Loan: ${largest loan formula}

Smallest Loan: ${smallest loan formula}

Average Loan: ${average loan formula}

${total payments due formula}

Figure 4-4
Shabir's spreadsheet sketch

James approves of Shabir's plan then shows him where to find the information on the boat loans. Shabir begins to develop the notebook according to his plan.

In this tutorial you will work with Shabir to create a notebook to help James manage his boat loans. You will use several Quattro Pro functions to simplify the formulas you enter, and you will learn when to use absolute references in formulas. Let's get started by launching Quattro Pro and organizing the workspace.

To launch Quattro Pro and organize the workspace:

❶ Launch Windows and Quattro Pro following your usual procedure.

❷ Make sure your Student Disk is in the disk drive.

❸ Make sure the Quattro Pro for Windows and NOTEBK1.WB1 windows are maximized.

Shabir has already entered the documentation, the loan management spreadsheet labels, and the loan data provided by James. Let's open Shabir's notebook, named C4SAILS.WB1, and look at what he has done so far.

To open the C4SAILS.WB1 notebook:

❶ Click the **Open Notebook button** 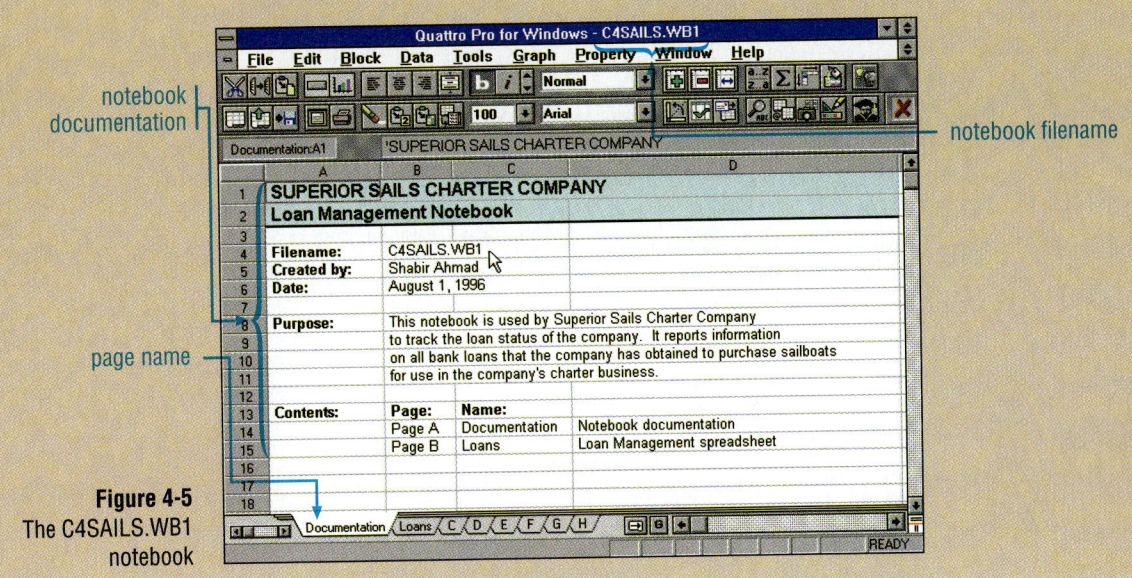 (or click **File** then click **Open...**) to display the Open File dialog box.

❷ If the A: drive name is not displayed in the Drives box, click the **Drives drop-down list arrow button** then click **A:** in the list of drive names.

❸ Double-click **C4SAILS.WB1** in the File Name box to display the notebook shown in Figure 4-5.

TROUBLE? If you do not see C4SAILS.WB1 in the list, use the scroll bar to view additional filenames.

Figure 4-5
The C4SAILS.WB1 notebook

The page named "Documentation" contains the notebook documentation, and Shabir has completed this page according to his documentation plan. Let's save the notebook using a different name, S4SAILS1.WB1, so that your changes will not alter the original file. The notebook C4SAILS.WB1 will be left in its original state in case you want to do this tutorial again.

To save the notebook as S4SAILS1.WB1:

❶ Make sure the Documentation page is the active page.

❷ Click cell **B4** to make it the active cell.

❸ Press **[F2]** for Edit mode, change the filename in cell B4 to **S4SAILS1.WB1**, then press **[Enter]**.

❹ Press **[Home]** to make cell A1 the active cell.

❺ Click **File** then click **Save As...** to display the Save File dialog box.

❻ Type **S4SAILS1** using either uppercase or lowercase *but don't press [Enter]* because you need to check some additional settings.

❼ Make sure the Drives box displays the name of the drive that contains your Student Disk.

❽ Click **OK** to save the notebook on your Student Disk. When the save is complete, you should see the new filename, S4SAILS1.WB1, displayed in the title bar.

TROUBLE? If a window appears with the message "File already exists: C4SAILS.WB1," click Cancel, then repeat Steps 4 through 7. If you see the message "File already exists: S4SAILS1.WB1," click Replace to replace the old version with the current version.

Now let's look at the Loans page, which contains Shabir's loan management spreadsheet.

To switch to the Loans page in the notebook:

❶ Click the **Loans page tab** to display Shabir's loan management spreadsheet, shown in Figure 4-6.

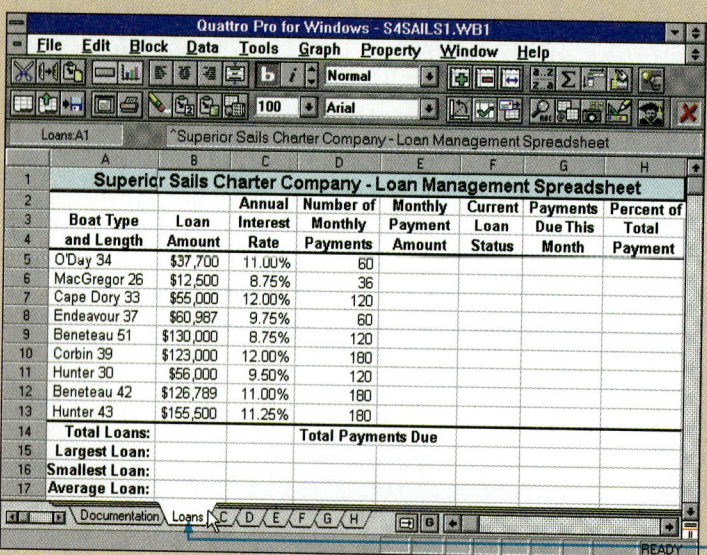

Figure 4-6
The loan management spreadsheet

Shabir listed the boats in column A and the loan amounts in column B; for example, the Beneteau 51-foot sailboat was purchased with a $130,000 loan. Shabir entered the annual interest rate for each loan in column C and formatted this column to display percentages with two decimal places. Column D contains the number of monthly payments required to pay off the loan. The loans are payable in 3 years (36 months), 5 years (60 months), 10 years (120 months), or 15 years (180 months). Although columns E through H do not contain data yet, Shabir typed the titles for these columns and selected appropriate formats (for example block E5..E13 has been formatted as currency).

Shabir plans to use several Quattro Pro @functions to simplify the formulas for the loan management spreadsheet.

Quattro Pro @Functions

Quattro Pro provides many functions, called @functions, that help you enter formulas for calculations and other specialized tasks, even if you don't know the mathematical details of the calculation. As you learned in Tutorial 1, an @function is a calculation tool that performs a predefined operation. You are already familiar with the @SUM function, which adds the values in a block of cells. Quattro Pro provides hundreds of @functions, organized into the categories shown in Figure 4-7.

@Function Category	Examples of @Functions in This Category
Mathematical	Round off numbers; generate random numbers; calculate factorial, sine, cosine, tangent
Statistical	Calculate sum, average, standard deviation; find minimum and maximum
Financial	Calculate loan payments, depreciation, net present value
Date and Time	Display today's date and/or time; calculate the number of days between two dates
Engineering	Calculate with binary and hexadecimal numbers; convert binary to decimal and decimal to binary; calculate with imaginary numbers
Logical	Evaluate conditional situations
Database	Calculate sum, average, standard deviation of data in a database
String	Find groups of text characters
Miscellaneous	Look up a value in a table; report the contents of a cell

Figure 4-7
Quattro Pro
@function categories

Each @function has a **syntax**, which tells you the order in which you must type the parts of the @function, and where to put commas, parentheses, and other punctuation. The general syntax of a Quattro Pro @function is:

$$@FUNCTION(argument1,argument2,...)$$

The syntax of most @functions requires you to type the @function name followed by one or more arguments in parentheses. The **arguments** specify the values, cell references, or formulas that Quattro Pro uses in the calculation. For example, the syntax of the @SUM function is:

$$@SUM(list)$$

In the @SUM function, the @function name is @SUM and the arguments are items in a list. A **list** is a set of numbers, cell references, or block references separated by commas.

For example, in the function @SUM(A1..A20) the list is the block reference A1..A20:

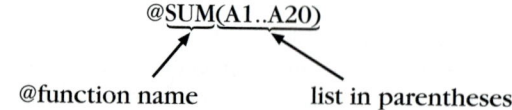

@function name   list in parentheses

You can use an @function in a simple formula such as =@SUM(A1..A20), or a more complex formula such as =@SUM(A1..A20)*(26-B1). As with all formulas, you enter the formula that contains an @function in the cell where you want to display the results. Although the @function name is always shown in uppercase, you can type it in either uppercase or lowercase. Also, even though the arguments are enclosed in parentheses, you do not have to type the closing parenthesis if the @function is at the end of the formula because Quattro Pro supplies it automatically when you press [Enter]. On a color monitor, Quattro Pro shows unmatched parentheses in red and matched parentheses in green, which helps you check to make sure you've entered all necessary parentheses.

REFERENCE WINDOW

Typing an @Function in a Formula

- Click the cell where you want to display the result of the formula.
- Type = to begin the formula.
- Type the @function name in either uppercase or lowercase.
- Type an opening parenthesis, (.
- Enter the appropriate arguments using the keyboard or mouse.
- Type a closing parenthesis,).
- When the formula is complete, press [Enter] (or click the check mark button on the input line) to display the results.

Shabir needs to calculate the total value of all the loans. He types a formula using the @SUM function into cell B14 to add the values of the individual loans. Let's do this with him.

To use the @SUM function to find the total of the loan amounts:
1. Make sure the Loans page is the active page.
2. Click cell **B14** to move to the cell where you want to enter the formula.
3. Type **=@SUM(** to begin the formula. Notice that the opening parenthesis is shown in red (on a color monitor only).
4. Type the block address **B5..B13**.

❺ Type **)** and notice that the matching parentheses are green (on a color monitor only), as shown in Figure 4-8.

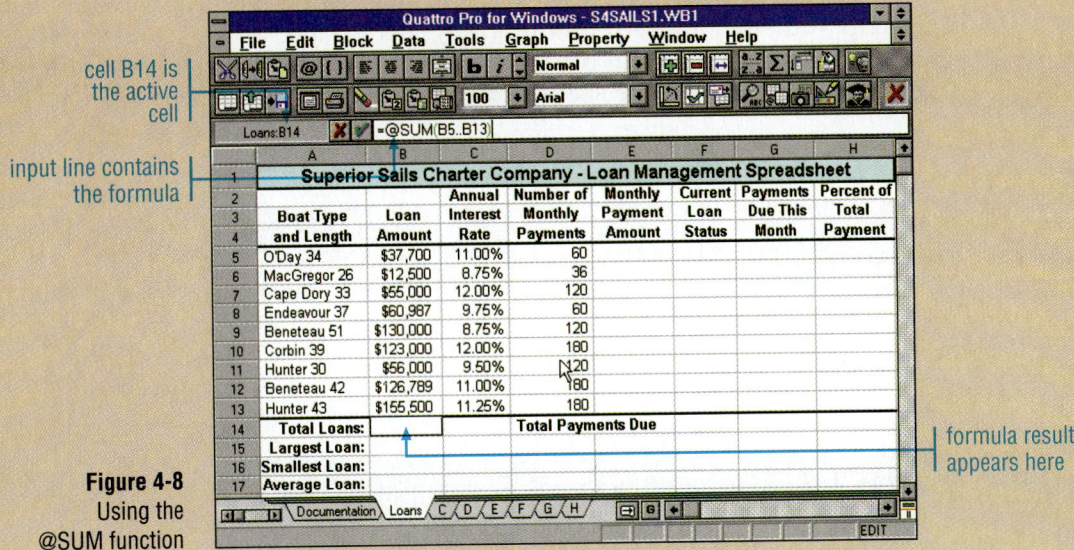

cell B14 is the active cell

input line contains the formula

formula result appears here

Figure 4-8
Using the @SUM function

❻ Press **[Enter]**. Cell B14 displays $757,476 as the total of the loan amounts, as shown in Figure 4-9.

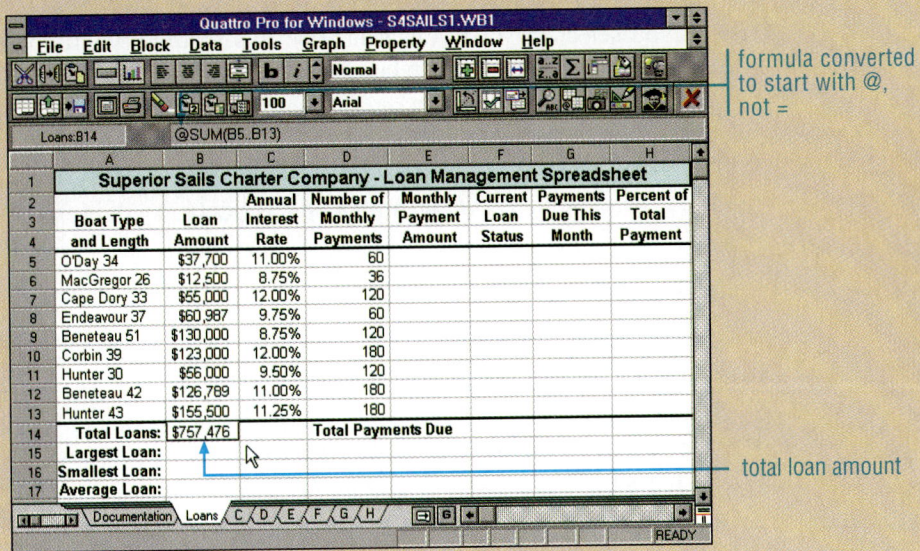

formula converted to start with @, not =

total loan amount

Figure 4-9
The total of the loan amounts

Notice that the formula in the input line in Figure 4-9 reads @SUM(B5..B13) instead of =@SUM(B5..B13). Remember from Tutorial 2 that Quattro Pro converts the equal sign (=) you type to start formulas.

As an alternative to typing the name of the @function, you can use the @Functions button to select the @function you want. When you begin entering a formula with an equal sign, Quattro Pro replaces two of the buttons on the SpeedBar with new buttons that help you enter formulas more easily: the @Functions button replaces the SpeedButton tool, and the Macros button (which you won't use in this book) replaces the Graph tool. The changes in the SpeedBar are shown in Figures 4-10 and 4-11.

notebook SpeedBar

Figure 4-10
The notebook SpeedBar as it usually appears

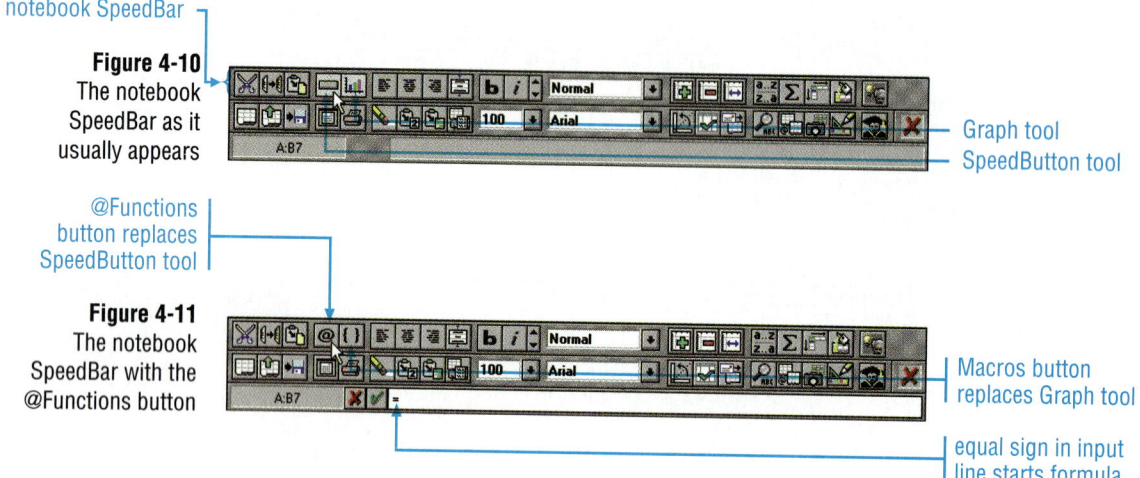

Graph tool
SpeedButton tool

@Functions button replaces SpeedButton tool

Figure 4-11
The notebook SpeedBar with the @Functions button

Macros button replaces Graph tool

equal sign in input line starts formula

When you click the @Functions button, Quattro Pro opens a list of @functions from which you select the one you want. Use this method when you are not certain which @function you want to use or when you want to check the @function's syntax.

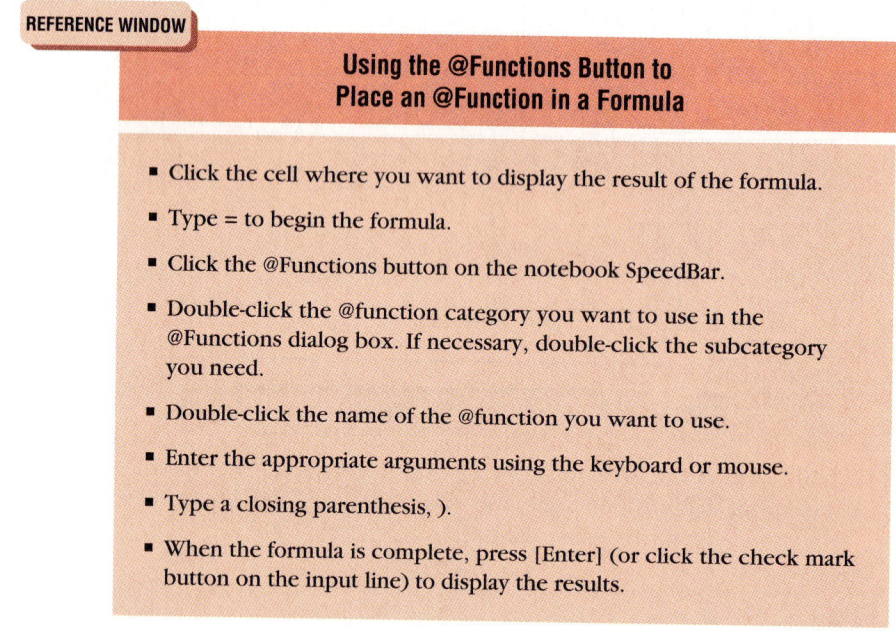

REFERENCE WINDOW

Using the @Functions Button to Place an @Function in a Formula

- Click the cell where you want to display the result of the formula.

- Type = to begin the formula.

- Click the @Functions button on the notebook SpeedBar.

- Double-click the @function category you want to use in the @Functions dialog box. If necessary, double-click the subcategory you need.

- Double-click the name of the @function you want to use.

- Enter the appropriate arguments using the keyboard or mouse.

- Type a closing parenthesis,).

- When the formula is complete, press [Enter] (or click the check mark button on the input line) to display the results.

Shabir also needs a formula in G14 that calculates the total value of the loan payments due this month. He'll enter this formula using the @Functions button. Because he has not completed the other calculations in the spreadsheet, a value of $0.00 will appear in cell G14.

To use the @Functions button to place the @SUM function in the formula:

❶ Click cell **G14** to move to the cell where you want to type the formula.

❷ Type **=** to begin the formula. Notice that the @Functions button appears on the notebook SpeedBar.

❸ Click the **@Functions button** 🔳 to display the @Functions dialog box, as shown in Figure 4-12.

@function categories

Figure 4-12
The @Functions dialog box

double-click here

❹ Double-click **All @Functions** to open the All @Functions dialog box. Use the scroll bar to scroll through the list of @functions until the function name SUM appears, as shown in Figure 4-13.

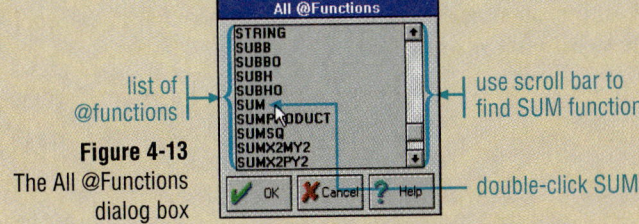

list of @functions

Figure 4-13
The All @Functions dialog box

use scroll bar to find SUM function

double-click SUM

❺ Double-click **SUM**. Quattro Pro places "@SUM(" in the formula in the input line and displays the @function syntax in the status line. Notice that the opening parenthesis is shown in red (on a color monitor only).

❻ Highlight cells G5 through G13.

❼ Type **)** and notice that the matching parentheses are now shown in green (on a color monitor only).

❽ Press **[Enter]**. Because cells G5 through G13 are currently empty, cell G14 displays $0.00 as the total of the loan payments due this month, as shown in Figure 4-14.

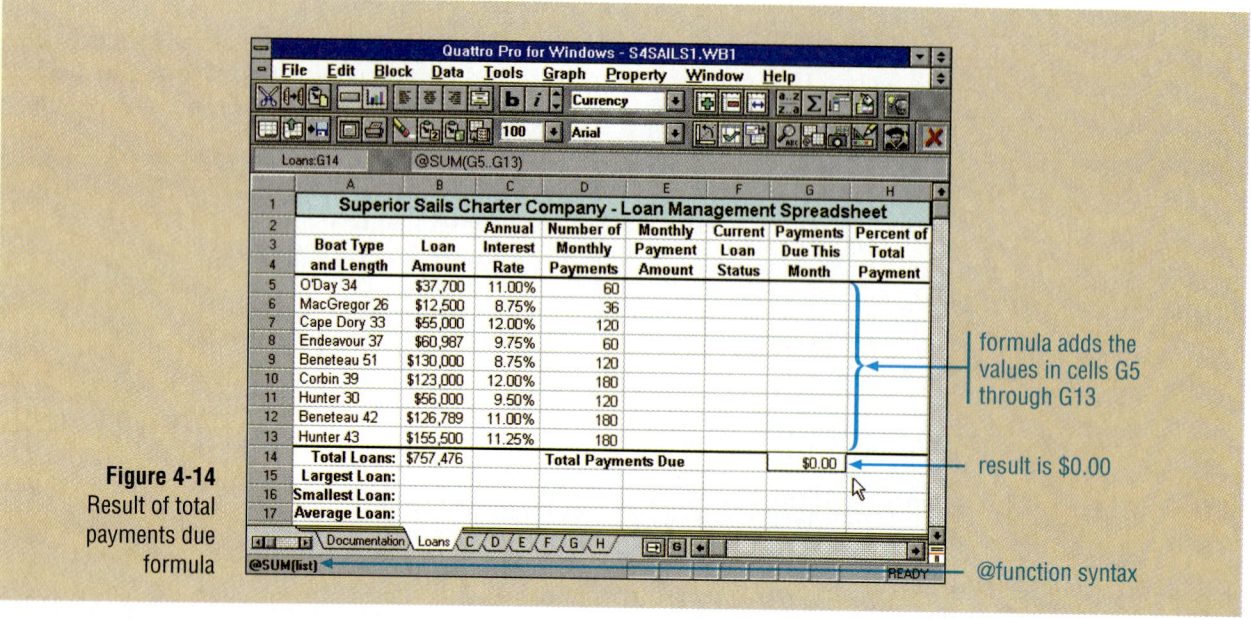

Figure 4-14
Result of total
payments due
formula

Shabir consults his plan and sees that he next needs to enter a formula to find the largest loan amount. He can do this by using an @function that finds the maximum value in a block. To find the syntax of the @function he needs, he uses the Quattro Pro Help system (he could also use Appendix B of the *Quattro Pro for Windows User's Guide*). Quattro Pro's @functions use common names or abbreviations, so Shabir expects the maximum @function to use the word *maximum*.

To use the Help system to find information on the @function that calculates the maximum value:

❶ Press [F1] to open the Quattro Pro Help window.

❷ Click the phrase **@Functions**, which is underlined and displayed in green on a color monitor, as shown in Figure 4-15.

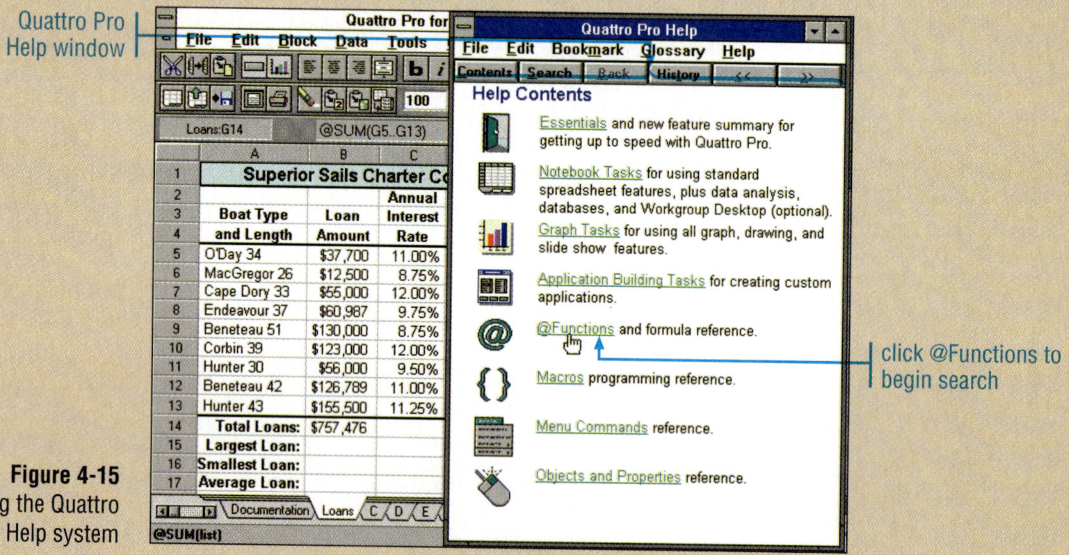

Figure 4-15
Using the Quattro
Pro Help system

❸ Click **Function Index** to open the @Function Index.

❹ Scroll down the @Function Index to find the @MAX topic, then click **@MAX**. As Shabir expected, the @function for finding the maximum value used part of the word *maximum*.

❺ Double-click the **Help window Control menu box** when you are done reading the @MAX information.

The @MAX Function

The **@MAX** function is a statistical @function that finds the largest number in a set of numbers. The syntax of the @MAX function is:

$$@MAX(list)$$

As in the @SUM function, in the @MAX function the list is a set of numbers, cell references, or block references separated by commas. You can mix the items in the list. For example, you could use @MAX(16, 18, A24, A26, B5..B10) in a formula. When you enter large numbers, do not use commas, because Quattro Pro uses commas to separate the items in the list. For example, if you want to include the number 12,345, enter it as 12345 (without the comma) in the list.

You can use the @MAX function to display the largest number in a set of numbers or to include the largest number in a set in a calculation.

Shabir wants to find the largest loan amount in the block of cells from B5 through B13 in the loan management spreadsheet on page B of his notebook. He wants to display the largest amount in cell B15 next to the label "Largest Loan:"

To use the @MAX function to find the largest loan amount:

❶ Click cell **B15** to move to the cell where you want to type the formula.

❷ Type **=@MAX(** to begin the formula.

❸ Highlight cells B5 through B13. See Figure 4-16.

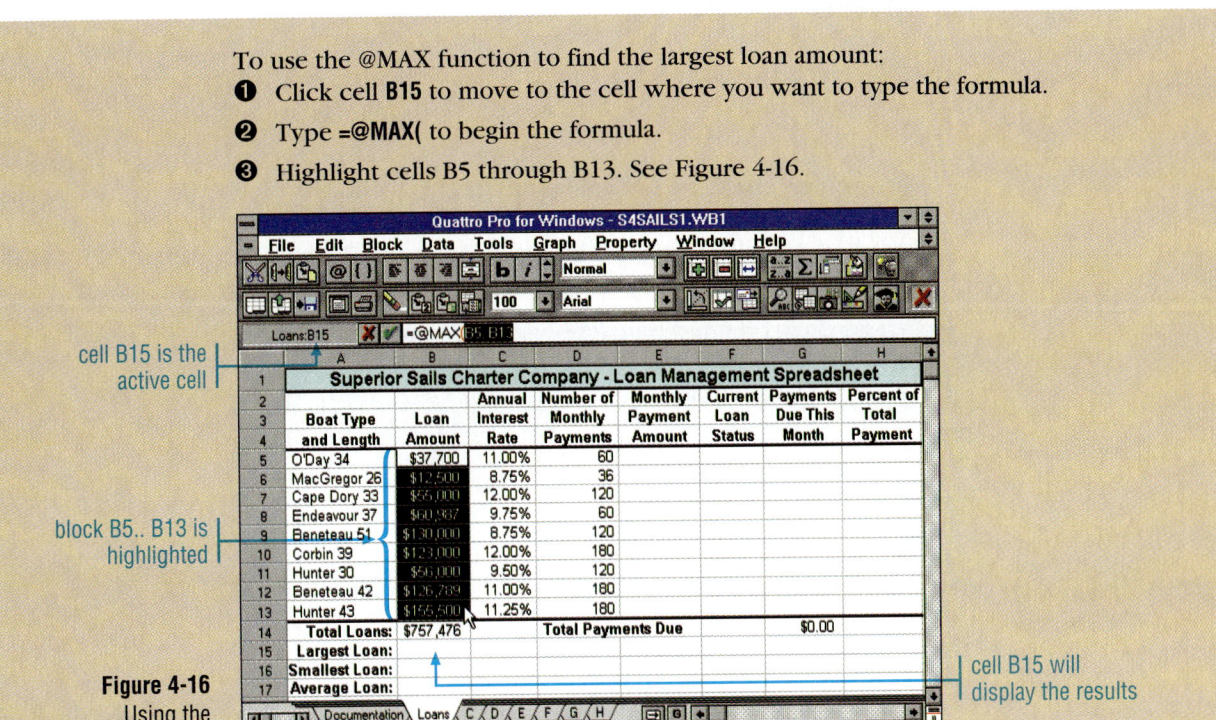

Figure 4-16
Using the
@MAX function

❹ Press **[Enter]**. Cell B15 displays $155,500 as the largest loan amount.

Next, Shabir wants to find the smallest loan amount.

The @MIN Function

The **@MIN** function is a statistical @function that finds the smallest number in a set of numbers. The syntax of the @MIN function is:

@MIN(list)

You can use the @MIN function to display the smallest number in a set of numbers or to use the smallest number of a set in a calculation.

Shabir wants to find the smallest loan amount and display it in cell B16.

To use the @MIN function to find the smallest loan amount:

❶ Click cell **B16** to move to the cell where you want to type the formula.

❷ Type **=@MIN(** to begin the formula.

❸ Highlight cells B5 through B13.

❹ Press **[Enter]**. Cell B16 displays $12,500 as the smallest loan amount.

Shabir consults his plan again and decides that his next step is to calculate the average loan amount.

The @AVG Function

The **@AVG** function is a statistical @function that calculates the average, or the arithmetic mean, of a set of numbers. The syntax for the @AVG function is:

@AVG(list)

When you use the @AVG function, the "list" is typically a block of cells. To calculate the average of a block of cells, Quattro Pro adds the values in the block then divides by the number of non-blank cells in the block. Figure 4-17 shows the results of using the @AVG function on three blocks.

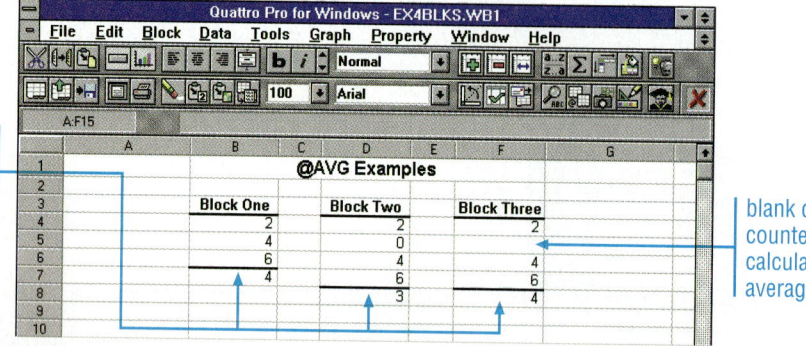

these cells contain formulas that calculate averages using @AVG

blank cell is not counted when calculating the average

Figure 4-17
How @AVG handles zeros and blank cells

The first block has no blank cells or cells that contain zeros, so the sum of the numbers, 12, is divided by 3 to find the average of 4. In the second block, the cell with zero is counted, so the sum, 12, is divided by 4 to find the average of 3. In the third block, the blank cell is not counted, so the sum, 12, is divided by 3 to find the average of 4. Keep this in mind when using the @AVG function, or your results might not be what you expected.

Shabir wants to calculate the average of the boat loans listed in cells B5 through B13, and display the result in cell B17. Shabir is not certain whether the correct spelling of the @function name is @AVE or @AVG. Therefore, he decides to use the @Functions button instead of typing the function name.

To use the @Functions button to place @AVG in the formula in cell B17:

❶ Click cell **B17**.

❷ Type **=** to begin the formula.

❸ Click the **@Functions button** 🔲 on the notebook SpeedBar. The @Functions dialog box appears.

❹ Double-click **Statistical** in the @Function dialog box category list. The Statistical dialog box appears.

❺ An average is a "descriptive statistic" because it describes a set of numbers, so double-click **Descriptive** in the Statistical dialog box category list. The Descriptive dialog box appears, as shown in Figure 4-18. Shabir sees that the correct name is AVG, not AVE.

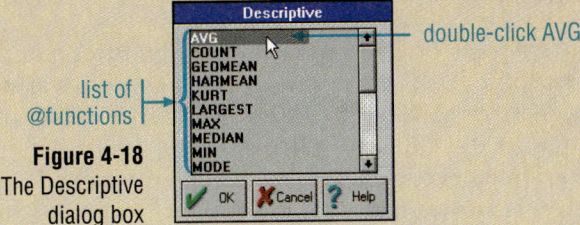

list of @functions

double-click AVG

Figure 4-18
The Descriptive dialog box

❻ Double-click **AVG**. Quattro Pro places "@AVG(" in the formula in the input line, as shown in Figure 4-19.

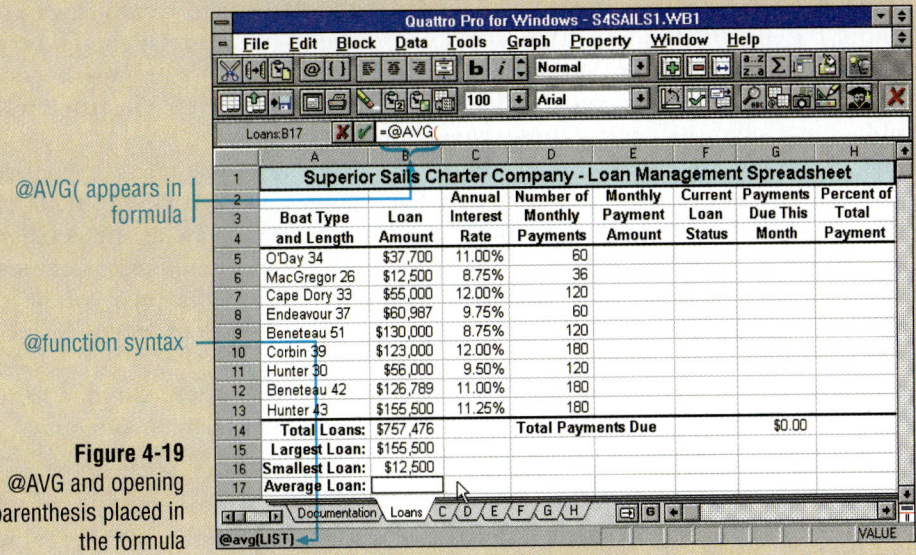

@AVG(appears in formula

@function syntax

Figure 4-19
@AVG and opening parenthesis placed in the formula

❼ Highlight cells B5 through B13.

❽ Press [Enter]. Cell B17 displays $84,164 as the average loan amount.

Next, Shabir checks his plan and decides to create the formula to calculate the monthly payment for each loan.

The @PAYMT Function

The **@PAYMT** function is a financial @function that calculates the periodic payment needed to repay a loan. For example, if you want to borrow $5,000 at 11% interest and pay it back over 5 years, you can use the @PAYMT function to find out that your monthly payment would be $108.71.

The syntax of the @PAYMT Function is:

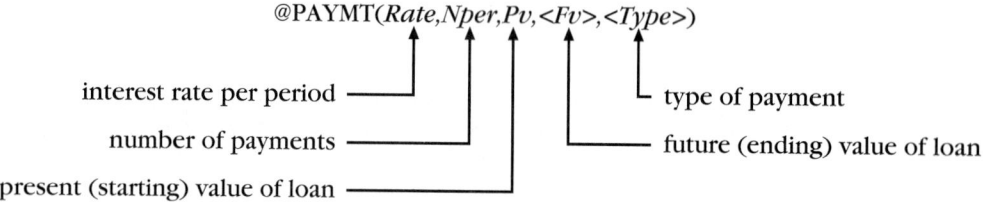

The *Rate* argument is the interest rate per period. Usually, interest rates are expressed as annual rates. For example, a 10% interest rate with a single payment at the end of the year means that if you borrow $1,000 for a year, you must pay back the $1,000 plus $100 interest—that's 10% of $1,000—at the end of the year.

The *Nper* argument is the total number of payments required to pay back the loan.

The *Pv* argument is the present, or starting, value of the loan, which is the total amount borrowed.

The last two arguments, *<Fv>* and *<Type>*, are optional. Generally, the ending value of a loan will be $0.00, so there is usually no need to use the *<Fv>* argument. The *<Type>* arguments indicate whether the payment is made at the start of the month (Type=1) or the end of the month (Type=0). Typically, loan payments are made at the end of the month, so 0 is the default type. Shabir will not need to include either of these options in his formula for the loan management spreadsheet. You can refer to the Quattro Pro Help system for more information about these two optional arguments.

When you enter the arguments for the @PAYMT function, you must be consistent about the units you use for *Rate* and *Nper*. For example, if you use the number of monthly payments for *Nper*, then you must express the interest rate as the percentage per month. Usually, the loan payment period is monthly, but the interest is expressed as an annual rate. If you are repaying the loan in monthly installments, you need to divide the annual interest rate by 12 when you enter the rate as an argument for the @PAYMT function.

To illustrate the @PAYMT function, suppose you wanted to know the monthly payment for a $5,000 loan at 11% annual interest that you must pay back in 36 months. You would use the @PAYMT function in the formula:

=@PAYMT(11%/12,36,5000)

In this formula the interest rate is entered as a percentage including the percent sign. An alternative is to enter percentages as their decimal equivalents. For example, you could enter the formula as:

=@PAYMT(.11/12,36,5000)

Also notice that the amount of the loan, $5,000, was entered without the comma (or the dollar sign). Quattro Pro uses commas to separate arguments, so you always enter large numbers without commas in @functions.

As another example, suppose you wanted to know the monthly payment for a $95,000 30-year loan at 9% (.09) interest. You would use the @PAYMT function in the formula:

=@PAYMT(.09/12,30*12,95000)

Notice that the number of years, 30, is multiplied by 12 months per year to get the number of monthly payments (*Nper*).

Quattro Pro displays the @PAYMT result as a negative number because you must pay the money out to someone else. Think of this as money that you subtract from your checkbook. In Tutorial 3 you learned that numbers formatted as currency are placed in parentheses to show negative amounts. This is an accounting convention used in financial statements. If you prefer to display the payment amount as a positive number, place a minus sign in front of the @PAYMT function.

REFERENCE WINDOW

Using @PAYMT to Calculate a Monthly Payment

- Click the cell where you want to display the monthly payment amount.

- Type = to begin the formula.

- If you want to display the result as a positive number, type – (minus sign).

- Type @PAYMT(.

  or

  Click the @Functions button, double-click Financial, double-click Annuity, then double-click PAYMT.

- Type the annual interest rate followed by % (or enter the address of the cell containing the annual interest rate) then type /12 to divide by 12 months per year.

- Type a comma to separate the arguments.

- Type the number of monthly payments required to repay the loan (or enter the address of the cell containing the number of payments).

- Type a comma to separate the arguments.

- Type the amount of the loan (without commas).

- Press [Enter] (or click the check mark button on the input line) to complete the formula.

Shabir wants to display the monthly payment for the O'Day 34 loan in cell E5. The annual interest rate is in cell C5, but it must be divided by 12 to obtain the monthly interest rate. The number of payments is in cell D5, and the loan amount is in cell B5. Let's enter the =@PAYMT(C5/12,D5,B5) formula for the O'Day 34 loan.

To calculate the monthly payment for the O'Day 34 loan:

❶ Click cell **E5** to move to the cell where you want to enter the formula. Notice that Shabir has formatted cell E5 as currency.

❷ Type **=@PAYMT(** to begin the formula.

❸ Click cell **C5** to specify the location of the annual interest rate.

❹ Type **/12** to convert the annual interest rate to a monthly interest rate.

❺ Type a comma to separate the first argument from the second argument.

❻ Click cell **D5** to specify the location of the number of payments.

❼ Type a comma to separate the second argument from the third argument.

❽ Click cell **B5** to specify the location of the loan amount. See Figure 4-20.

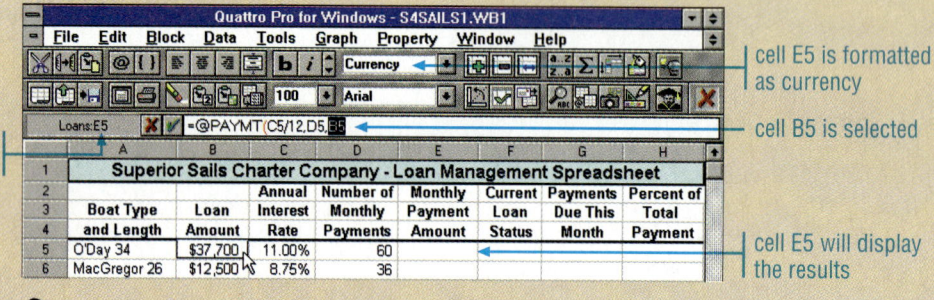

cell E5 is formatted as currency

cell B5 is selected

cell E5 is the active cell

Figure 4-20
Entering the formula using @PAYMT

cell E5 will display the results

❾ Press **[Enter]** to complete the formula and display ($819.69) in cell E5.

As expected, the @PAYMT function displays the payment in parentheses to indicate a negative number. Because many people find it confusing to see loan payments as negative numbers, Shabir decides to change the formula to display the payment as a positive number. He uses [F2] to edit the contents of cell E5.

To display the payment as a positive number:

❶ Make sure cell E5 is the active cell.

❷ Press **[F2]** to edit the formula in cell E5. Notice that Quattro Pro has dropped the equal sign from the formula so that it now starts with @PAYMT.

❸ Press **[Home]** to position the insertion point at the beginning of the formula.

❹ Type **–** (minus sign). The formula is now –@PAYMT(C5/12,D5,B5).

❺ Press **[Enter]** to complete the edit. Cell E5 now displays the value $819.69 without the parentheses.

Shabir tests this formula by comparing the result to a table of loan payment amounts. He finds that the amount in cell E5 on his spreadsheet is correct. Now that he is confident he has used the @PAYMT function correctly, he can copy the formula in cell E5 to calculate the payments for the rest of the loans.

To copy the @PAYMT formula to cells E6 through E13:

❶ Make sure cell E5 is the active cell.

❷ Click the **Copy button** 🔲 on the notebook SpeedBar.

❸ Highlight cells E6 through E13.

❹ Click the **Paste button** 🔲 on the notebook SpeedBar. The formula is copied to cells E6 through E13.

❺ Click any cell to remove the highlighting and view the payment amounts displayed in cells E5 through E13, as shown in Figure 4-21.

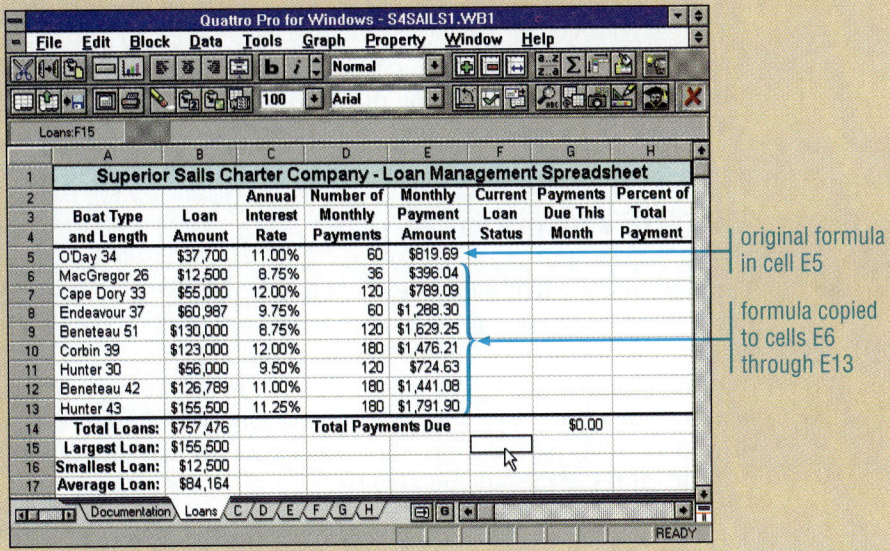

Figure 4-21
The payment formula copied from cell E5 to cells E6 through E13

Before Shabir continues to build the spreadsheet, he decides to save his notebook.

To save the notebook:

❶ Click the **Save Notebook button** 🔲 (or click **File** then click **Save**).

If you want to take a break and resume the tutorial at a later time, you can exit Quattro Pro by double-clicking the Control menu box in the upper-left corner of the screen. When you resume the tutorial, launch Quattro Pro, maximize the Quattro Pro and NOTEBK1.WB1 windows, place your Student Disk in the disk drive, and then open the S4SAILS1.WB1 notebook file. You can then continue with the tutorial.

■   ■   ■

Shabir considers his plan again. James wants a list of all the boat loans, but he wants a sum of only those payments that he must make this month. The sum of all payments in column E would include loans that James has already paid off. Shabir needs a way to tell which loans are paid off so he can add only the ones that haven't been paid off. Shabir looks at the loan information and finds that the O'Day 34, the Endeavour 37, and the Beneteau 51 loans have been paid in full. Shabir's plan is to type the word *Paid* in column F if a boat loan has been paid off.

To enter the current loan status for the loans that have been paid in full:

❶ Click cell **F5** because this is where you want to enter the status of the O'Day 34 loan.

❷ Type **Paid** then press **[Enter]**.

❸ Click cell **F8** to enter the status of the Endeavour 37 loan.

❹ Type **Paid** then press **[Enter]**.

❺ Click cell **F9** to enter the status of the Beneteau 51 loan.

❻ Type **Paid** then press **[Enter]**.

Next, Shabir wants to use column G to display the payment amounts for the loans that are not paid. To do this he needs to use the @IF function, which displays different results based on a logical choice.

The @IF Function

There are times when the value you store or display in a cell depends on certain conditions. The **@IF** function lets you specify the if-then-else logic required to calculate or display information based on one or more conditions.

One example of an if-then-else condition in Shabir's spreadsheet is: *if* the loan status is "Paid," *then* place a zero in the Payments Due This Month column, otherwise (*else*) display the monthly payment amount in the Payments Due This Month column.

The syntax of the @IF function is:

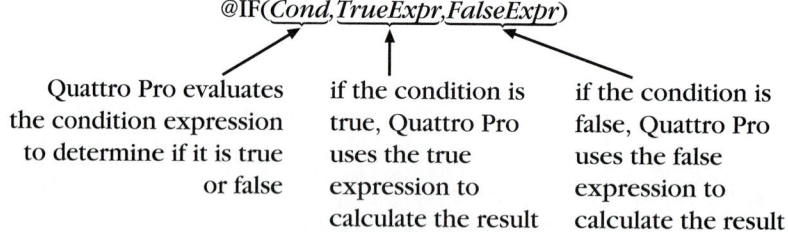

@IF(*Cond,TrueExpr,FalseExpr*)

| Quattro Pro evaluates the condition expression to determine if it is true or false | if the condition is true, Quattro Pro uses the true expression to calculate the result | if the condition is false, Quattro Pro uses the false expression to calculate the result |

The *Cond*ition is any value or expression that Quattro Pro can evaluate as true or false. For example, Quattro Pro evaluates the expression 2=2 as true when you use it as a *Cond*ition. Similarly, Quattro Pro evaluates the expression 2=1 as false. Most expressions you use for *Cond*itions will contain numbers or cell references separated by one of the comparison operators shown in Figure 4-22. Some examples of expressions are 2>3, B5=C3, and B8<=0. An expression can also include text, but you must put quotation marks around any text that you use in the @IF function.

Operator	Description
=	equal to
<>	not equal to
<	less than
>	greater than
<=	less than or equal to
>=	greater than or equal to

Figure 4-22
Comparison operators

The *TrueExpression* argument specifies what to display in the cell if the *Condition* is true.

The *FalseExpression* argument specifies what to display in the cell if the *Condition* is false.

REFERENCE WINDOW

Using @IF to Display Results Based on Specified Conditions

- Click the cell where you want to display the result of the formula that contains the IF function.

- Type = to begin the formula.

- Type @IF(.

  or

  Click the @Functions button, double-click Logical, then double-click IF.

- Type the *Condition*, type a comma, type the *TrueExpression*, type a comma, then type the *FalseExpression*.

- Press [Enter] (or click the check mark button on the input line) to complete the formula.

For example, suppose you want Quattro Pro to display a warning message if the loan amount in cell B5 is greater than $150,000. You can use the formula:

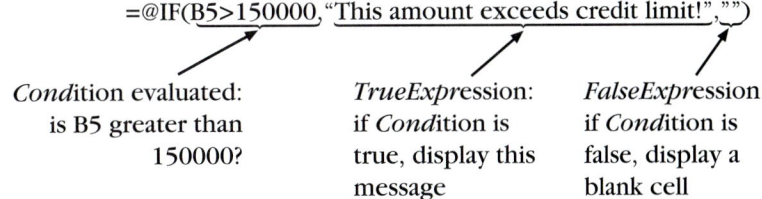

=@IF(B5>150000, "This amount exceeds credit limit!", "")

*Cond*ition evaluated: is B5 greater than 150000?

*TrueExpr*ession: if *Cond*ition is true, display this message

*FalseExpr*ession: if *Cond*ition is false, display a blank cell

Notice the quotation marks around the text that contains the credit limit message, and the quotation marks without any text (which will leave the cell blank). When you use text as an argument for the @IF function, you must enclose the text in quotation marks.

As another example, suppose you want to add a $1,000 bonus to the salary of any salesperson who sells more than $10,000 of merchandise. This example is illustrated in the spreadsheet shown in Figure 4-23. Cell B7 contains the amount of merchandise sold by Sergio Amanti, $13,789.00. Sergio's base salary of $3,000.00 is in cell C7. Notice that cell C3 contains the comparison amount of $10,000, and that cell C4 contains the bonus amount of $1,000.

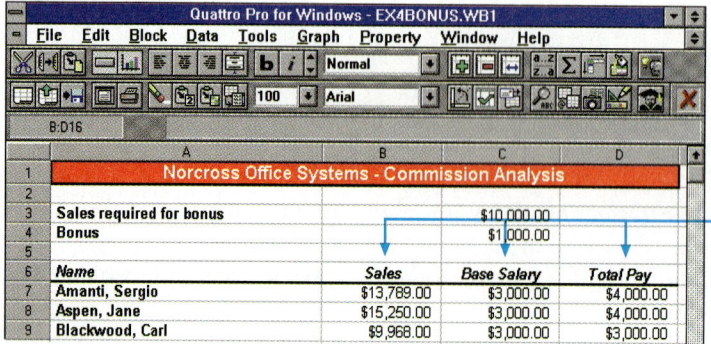

Figure 4-23
The conditions for awarding a bonus to Sergio Amanti

if sales in B7 ≥ $10,000, then add $1,000 to base salary in C7 and display result in D7; else display only value in C7 in cell D7

To calculate Sergio's total pay, including the bonus if he earned it, you would enter the formula =@IF(B7>=C3,C7+C4,C7) in cell D7. In this case if the amount sold in cell B7 is at least $10,000 (the amount in cell C3), Quattro Pro would add $1,000 (the amount in cell C4) to the base salary in cell C7 and display the total pay in cell D7. If the amount sold in cell B7 is less than $10,000, Quattro Pro will display only the base salary as the total pay in cell D7.

The use of the cell references to cells C3 and C4 in the formula is important. You should always put input values, such as the sales required for a bonus and the bonus in this example, in separate cells with appropriate labels. This allows you to change the conditions by simply replacing the input values with new numbers, rather than having to edit your formulas.

Now let's consider the formula Shabir needs to use. In cell G5 he wants to display the amount of the payment that is due. The logic for this situation is: *if* the current loan status is "Paid," *then* put a zero in the Payments Due This Month column, otherwise (*else*) put the monthly payment amount from column E in the Payments Due This Month column. Shabir's formula for cell G5 will be:

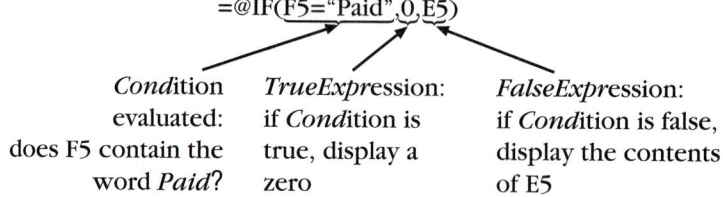

*Cond*ition evaluated: does F5 contain the word *Paid*?	*TrueExpre*ssion: if *Cond*ition is true, display a zero	*FalseExpre*ssion: if *Cond*ition is false, display the contents of E5

If this formula works, Shabir expects to see a zero in cell G5 because the O'Day 34 loan is paid off. Let's see if the formula produces the results he expects.

To enter the formula containing the @IF function:

❶ Click cell **G5** to move to the cell where you want to type the formula.

❷ Type **=@IF(** to begin the formula.

❸ Type **F5="Paid"**. Make sure you include the quotation marks.

❹ Type a comma to separate the first and second arguments.

❺ Type **0**. Make sure you type the number zero, not the capital letter "**O.**"

❻ Type a comma to separate the second and third arguments.

❼ Type **E5** then press **[Enter]** to complete the formula. Cell G5 displays the value $0.00.

TROUBLE? If you see the error message ERR in cell G5, look carefully at the formula displayed in the formula bar to make sure that you included quotation marks around "Paid" and that you typed the number zero and not the capital letter *O*. Use [F2] to edit the formula.

TROUBLE? If you see a dialog box with the error message "Unterminated string," you left out the ending quotation mark around "Paid." Click OK in the dialog box, and edit the formula.

The formula produced the expected results, so Shabir decides to copy the formula to cells G6 through G13.

To copy the @IF formula to cells G6 through G13:

❶ Make sure cell **G5** is the active cell.

❷ Click the **Copy button** 🖺 on the notebook SpeedBar.

❸ Highlight cells G6 through G13.

❹ Click the **Paste button** 🖺 on the notebook SpeedBar. The formula is copied to cells G6 through G13.

❺ Click any cell to remove the highlighting and view the payment amounts displayed in cells G5 through G13 as shown in Figure 4-24. Note also that cell G14 now displays the total amount of the payments due.

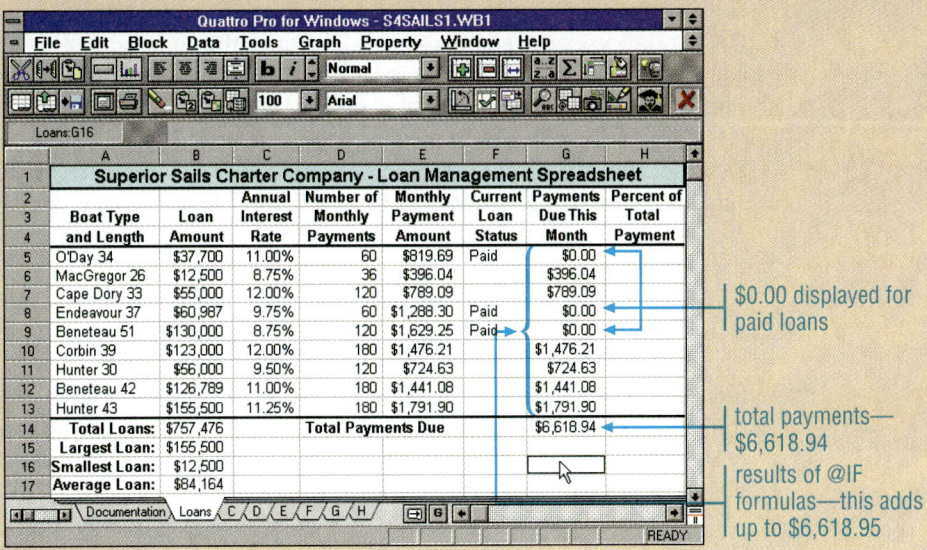

Figure 4-24
The @IF formula
copied from cell
G5 to cells G6
through G13

$0.00 displayed for
paid loans

total payments—
$6,618.94

results of @IF
formulas—this adds
up to $6,618.95

Shabir carefully checks the results of the @IF formulas in cells G5 through G13. He sees that the formulas produced zeros in cells G5, G8, and G9 because the loans for those boats are paid. In the other cells, the @IF formulas correctly placed the same value as that displayed in column E. Shabir is satisfied that the formulas in column G are correct.

The formula that Shabir put in cell G14 earlier to calculate the total payments due this month now shows that Superior Sails will pay $6,618.94. He double-checks the calculation of cells G5 through G13 on his calculator, and is surprised to find that the correct total of the values shown in column G is $6,618.95. Somehow, the value in cell G14 is off by one cent. Shabir realizes that he has encountered an apparent error caused by rounding.

Apparent Errors Caused by Rounding

Apparent errors caused by rounding are discrepancies that occur when cell formatting causes the displayed numbers to be rounded off to fewer digits than are actually stored in the cells. When these discrepancies happen, your spreadsheet can tell you that 2 + 2 = 5, as shown in Figure 4-25.

correct sum appears when cells are formatted to show all digits

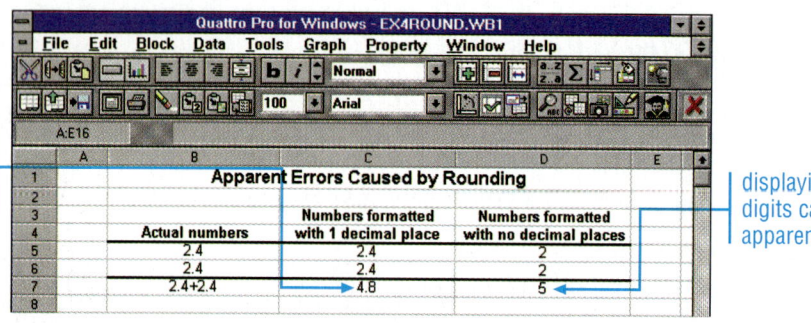

displaying fewer digits can cause apparent errors

Figure 4-25
Apparent errors caused by rounding

Notice that in Figure 4-25, the actual number stored in cells C5, C6, D5 and D6 is 2.4. When you add 2.4 and 2.4 you get 4.8, which is correctly displayed in cell C7. But the numbers in cells D5 through D7 are formatted so that no decimal places are displayed, and Quattro Pro must round off the numbers to fit the reduced number of decimal places. Quattro Pro uses the standard rounding rules that numbers 0, 1, 2, 3, and 4 round down, and numbers 5, 6, 7, 8, and 9 round up. Therefore, 2.4 is rounded down to 2, but 4.8 is rounded up to 5. The result is the apparent error 2 + 2 = 5.

These apparent errors are likely to occur in calculations that include any values that are displayed with fewer decimal places than are actually stored in the cell. Operations such as division, multiplication by a fraction or percentage, squaring, taking the square root, and the use of @functions can result in values that contain more decimal places than the cells show.

Apparent errors caused by rounding are very common, but often go undetected. You should always check for this type of error in your spreadsheets.

Shabir realizes that when he used the @PAYMT function to calculate the loan payments in column E, he inadvertently created a situation where fewer decimal places are displayed than are stored in the spreadsheet. For example, the monthly payment for the O'Day 34 in cell E5 is actually $819.6893498386529, which is rounded to two decimal places for display, appearing on screen as $819.69.

The @IF function in column G repeated these roundings, resulting in the discrepancy between the displayed sum of $6,618.94 in cell G14 and the actual sum of $6,618.95. Shabir knows that he can eliminate this problem by using the @ROUND function to make the values stored in the spreadsheet match the values displayed.

The @ROUND Function and Nesting @Functions

The **@ROUND** function is a mathematical function that stores a number or the result of a calculation rounded to a specified number of decimal places. If you specify the number or result in further calculations, Quattro Pro uses the rounded value. The syntax of the @ROUND function is:

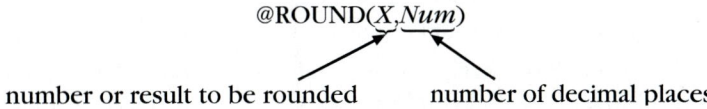

@ROUND(*X,Num*)

number or result to be rounded   number of decimal places

The *X* can be a number, such as 7.8365112, or the result of a formula, such as (345*2)/15 or @PAYMT(B5/12,B6,B7). When you are rounding the result of a formula that uses an @function, then you are using one @function as part of an argument of another @function. This is known as **nesting @functions**.

The *Num* is the number of decimal places that you want to round the number or result to. Generally, you will round to the same number of decimal places that you used when you formatted the cell containing the formula.

Shabir needs to round the results of the monthly payment amounts in column E to two decimal places. For example, cell E5 contains the formula -@PAYMT(C5/12,D5,B5). This formula is the *X* for the @ROUND function. Shabir will edit the formula in cell E5 to include the @ROUND function, and the final result will be the formula:

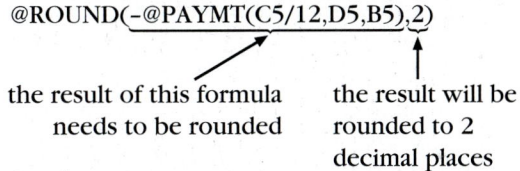

@ROUND(-@PAYMT(C5/12,D5,B5),2)

the result of this formula   the result will be
needs to be rounded   rounded to 2
decimal places

REFERENCE WINDOW

Using @ROUND to Round the Stored Results of a Formula

- Click the cell that contains the formula you want to round.

- Press [F2] to start editing then press [Home] to move the insertion point to the beginning of the formula.

- Type @ROUND(in front of the current formula.

  or

  Click the @Functions button then double-click Mathematical in the @Functions dialog box, then double-click ROUND.

- Press [End] to move the insertion point to the end of the formula.

- Type a comma to separate the arguments.

- Type the number of decimal places to which Quattro Pro should round the result.

- Press [Enter] (or click the check mark button on the input line) to complete the formula.

Shabir edits the formula is cell E5 to include the @ROUND function.

To add the @ROUND function to the formula in cell E5:

❶ Click cell **E5** to make it the active cell.

❷ Press **[F2]** to edit the formula in cell E5.

❸ Press **[Home]** to position the insertion point at the beginning of the formula.

❹ Type **@ROUND(** in front of the current formula.

❺ Press **[End]** to move the insertion point to the end of the formula.

❻ Type **,2)** then compare your formula with the edited formula shown in Figure 4-26.

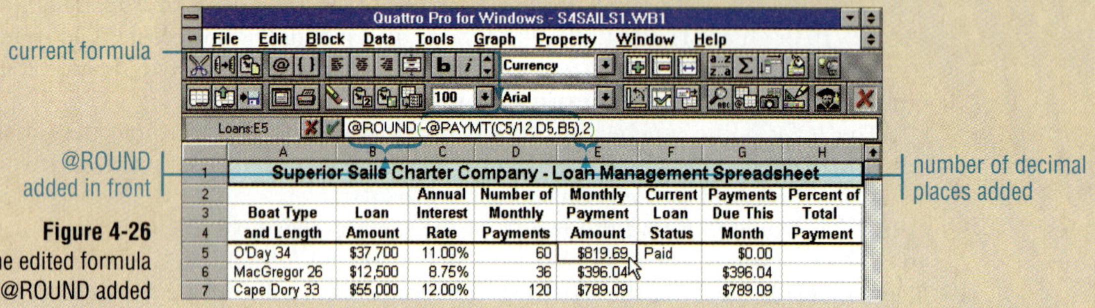

current formula

@ROUND
added in front

Figure 4-26
The edited formula
with @ROUND added

number of decimal
places added

❼ Press **[Enter]** to accept the edit. Cell E5 displays the positive value $819.69. Quattro Pro will now use $819.69 in calculations instead of $819.6893498386529.

Now he copies the formula with @ROUND in cell E5 to cells E6 through E13.

To copy the @PAYMT formula to cells E6 through E13:

❶ Make sure cell E5 is the active cell.

❷ Click the **Copy button** 🔲 on the notebook SpeedBar.

❸ Highlight cells E6 through E13.

❹ Click the **Paste button** 🔲 on the notebook SpeedBar. Quattro Pro copies the formula to cells E6 through E13.

❺ Click any cell to remove the highlighting.

Shabir sees that the Total Payments Due figure is now $6,618.95 instead of $6,618.94. Using @ROUND solved the problem of the discrepancy.

Now Shabir wants to add a label in cell F14 to indicate the month and year for which the Total Payments Due amount is calculated. Quattro Pro's @TODAY function can display the date.

The @TODAY Function

The **@TODAY** function reads the computer system clock and displays the current date in the cell that contains the @TODAY function. The syntax of the @TODAY function is:

@TODAY

No arguments are required for this function. Shabir wants the date displayed in cell F14.

To enter the @TODAY function in cell F14:

❶ Click cell **F14**.

❷ Type **=@TODAY**.

❸ Press **[Enter]**. A five-digit number appears in cell F14, representing today's date.

Quattro Pro uses serial numbers to represent dates. The numbers begin with 0, which represents December 30, 1899. The number 1 represents December 31, 1899, 2 represents January 1, 1900, and so on. The serial numbers can range from –109,571 (which is January 1, 1600) to 474,816 (which is December 31, 3199). For example, the serial number 34,949 represents September 7, 1995. The serial number that you will see when you use the @TODAY function depends on the current date according to your computer's internal clock.

To display the date in a date format rather than as a serial number, you must format the cell accordingly. Shabir wants to display only the month and the year, so he formats cell F14 using the Active Block Object Inspector.

To format today's date to show only the month and year:

❶ Right-click cell **F14** to open the SpeedMenu, then click **Block Properties...** to display the Active Block Object Inspector.

❷ Click the **Date radio button** in the Numeric Format settings pane. The Date Format settings appear.

❸ In the Date Format settings, click the **radio button** for the setting MMM-YY.

❹ Click **OK**. Quattro Pro reformats the date.

The date doesn't look quite right. Shabir thinks it should be bold and aligned on the left side of the cell.

To bold and left-align the date:

❶ Make sure cell F14 is the active cell.

❷ Click the **Bold button** 🅱 on the notebook SpeedBar.

❸ Click the **Left Align button** ⬚ on the notebook SpeedBar. The date now appears as shown in Figure 4-27.

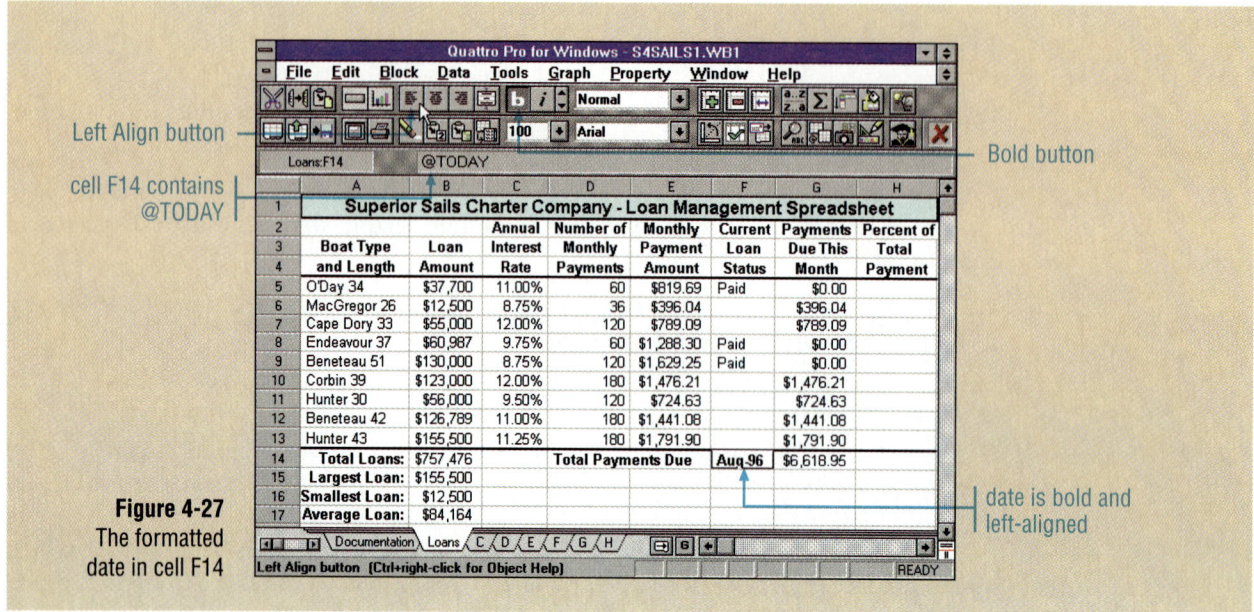

Left Align button

cell F14 contains @TODAY

Bold button

Figure 4-27
The formatted
date in cell F14

date is bold and
left-aligned

Now Shabir consults his spreadsheet plan and sees that he has only one column left to complete the spreadsheet. He wants column H to display the percent of the total payment that each individual loan payment represents. For example, if the total of all the loan payments is $10,000 and the O'Day 34 payment is $1,000, the O'Day 34 payment is 10% of the total payment. To do this calculation Shabir needs to divide each payment by the total payment, as shown in the equation:

percent of total payment = payment due this month/ total payments due

Shabir needs to enter the formula =G5/G14 in cell H5.

To enter the formula to calculate the percent of total payment in cell H5:

❶ Click cell **H5** to move to the cell where you want to enter the formula.

❷ Type **=G5/G14** then press **[Enter]** to complete the formula and display 0.00% in cell H5.

Cell H5 seems to display the correct result. James is paying $0 for the O'Day 34 loan, which is 0% of the $6,618.95 total. Next, Shabir copies the formula to cells H6 through H13.

To copy the percent formula to cells H6 through H13:

❶ Make sure cell H5 is the active cell.

❷ Click the **Copy button** 🖼 on the notebook SpeedBar.

❸ Highlight cells H6 through H13.

❹ Click the **Paste button** 🖼 on the notebook SpeedBar. Quattro Pro copies the formula to cells H6 through H13.

❺ Click any cell to remove the highlighting and view the results as shown in Figure 4-28.

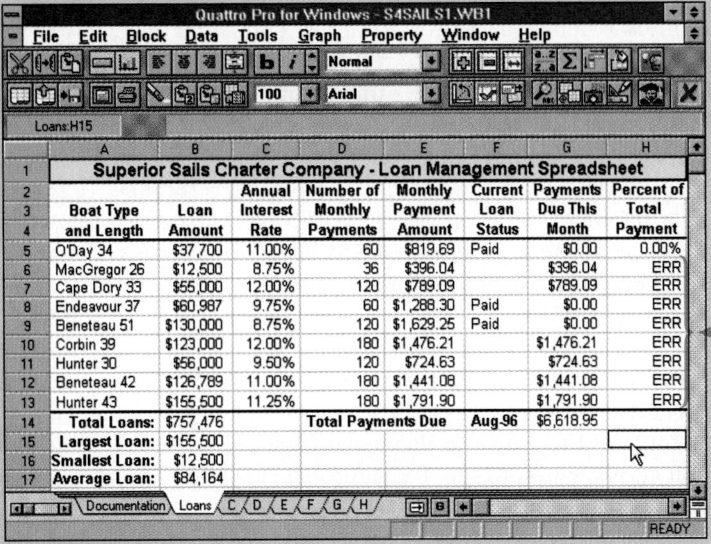

Figure 4-28
Error messages
produced by copying
the formula

		Quattro Pro for Windows - S4SAILS1.WB1						
	A	**B**	**C**	**D**	**E**	**F**	**G**	**H**
1	Superior Sails Charter Company - Loan Management Spreadsheet							
2			Annual	Number of	Monthly	Current	Payments	Percent of
3	Boat Type	Loan	Interest	Monthly	Payment	Loan	Due This	Total
4	and Length	Amount	Rate	Payments	Amount	Status	Month	Payment
5	O'Day 34	$37,700	11.00%	60	$819.69	Paid	$0.00	0.00%
6	MacGregor 26	$12,500	8.75%	36	$396.04		$396.04	ERR
7	Cape Dory 33	$55,000	12.00%	120	$789.09		$789.09	ERR
8	Endeavour 37	$60,987	9.75%	60	$1,288.30	Paid	$0.00	ERR
9	Beneteau 51	$130,000	8.75%	120	$1,629.25	Paid	$0.00	ERR
10	Corbin 39	$123,000	12.00%	180	$1,476.21		$1,476.21	ERR
11	Hunter 30	$56,000	9.50%	120	$724.63		$724.63	ERR
12	Beneteau 42	$126,789	11.00%	180	$1,441.08		$1,441.08	ERR
13	Hunter 43	$155,500	11.25%	180	$1,791.90		$1,791.90	ERR
14	Total Loans:	$757,476		Total Payments Due		Aug-96	$6,618.95	
15	Largest Loan:	$155,500						
16	Smallest Loan:	$12,500						
17	Average Loan:	$84,164						

ERR indicates a
formula error

Shabir knows something is wrong. Cells H6 through H13 display ERR, a message that means Quattro Pro detected an error in the formulas. Shabir examines the formulas he copied into cells H6 through H13.

To examine the formulas in cells H6 through H13:

❶ Click cell **H6** and look at the formula +G6/G15 displayed in the input line. The formula uses relative references, which were discussed in Tutorial 2. The first relative reference changed from G5 in the original formula to G6 in the copied formula. That's correct because the loan amount for row 6 is in cell G6. The second relative reference changed from G14 in the original formula to G15, which is not correct. This formula should still refer to cell G14 because that cell contains the total of the payments, and the correct formula is +G6/G14. There is no number in cell G15, so when Quattro Pro calculated the formula +G6/G15 it used zero as the value in cell G15. The calculation was $273.34/0, which couldn't be done because division by zero is impossible. This resulted in the error message.

❷ Look at the formulas in cells H7 through H13 and see how the relative references changed in each.

Shabir realizes that he should have used an absolute reference instead of a relative reference for cell G14.

Absolute References

Sometimes when you copy a formula, you don't want Quattro Pro to automatically change all the cell references to reflect their new position in the spreadsheet. If you want a cell reference to point to the same location in the spreadsheet even when you copy it, you must use an absolute reference. An **absolute reference** is a cell reference that must not change if the formula containing the reference is copied to other cells.

The dollar sign ($) indicates an absolute reference. A reference like $G$14 is an absolute reference, whereas one to G14 is a relative reference. If you copy a formula that contains the absolute reference $G$14, the reference will stay the same. On the other hand, if you copy a formula containing the relative reference G14, the reference to G14 could change to G15, G16, G17, G18 and so forth as you copy it to other cells.

To include an absolute reference in a formula, you can type the dollar sign when you type the cell reference, or you can use [F4] to change the cell reference type. You can always edit a formula that contains the wrong cell reference type.

In Quattro Pro, you can also make page references absolute if you need references to cells on certain pages to stay the same. The absolute reference $B:$G$15 will always refer to cell G15 on page B.

Now Shabir must change the reference G14 to $G$14, using an absolute reference to indicate the location of the Total Payments Due amount.

To change the formula in cell H5 from +G5/G14 to +G5/$G$14:

❶ Click cell **H5** to move to the cell containing the formula.

❷ Press [**F2**] to edit the formula in the input line.

❸ Make sure the insertion point is just to the right of the reference G14, as shown in Figure 4-29.

Figure 4-29
Changing G14 to an
absolute reference

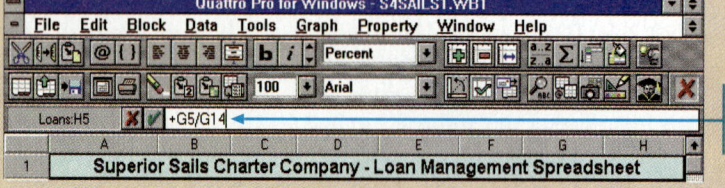

make sure insertion
point is here, then
press [F4]

❹ Press [**F4**]. The reference changes to $Loans:$G$14.

❺ Shabir does not need an absolute page reference. Press [**F4**] four times to change the reference to $G$14.

> TROUBLE? If you pressed [F4] too many times and went past the correct reference, don't worry. [F4] cycles through the eight possible reference combinations as you press it. Press [F4] until the correct reference is displayed.

❻ Press [**Enter**] to complete the edit and display 0.00% in cell H5.

Cell H5 still displays 0.00% as the result of the formula, which is correct. The problem in Shabir's original formula did not surface until he copied it to cells H6 through H13. He copies the revised formula and checks to see if it produces the correct results.

To copy the revised percent formula from cell H5 to cells H6 through H13:

❶ Make sure cell H5 is the active cell.

❷ Click the **Copy button** 🖼 on the notebook SpeedBar.

❸ Highlight cells H6 through H13.

❹ Click the **Paste button** 🖼 on the notebook SpeedBar. Quattro Pro copies the formula to cells H6 through H13.

❺ Click any cell to remove the highlighting and view the results as shown in Figure 4-30.

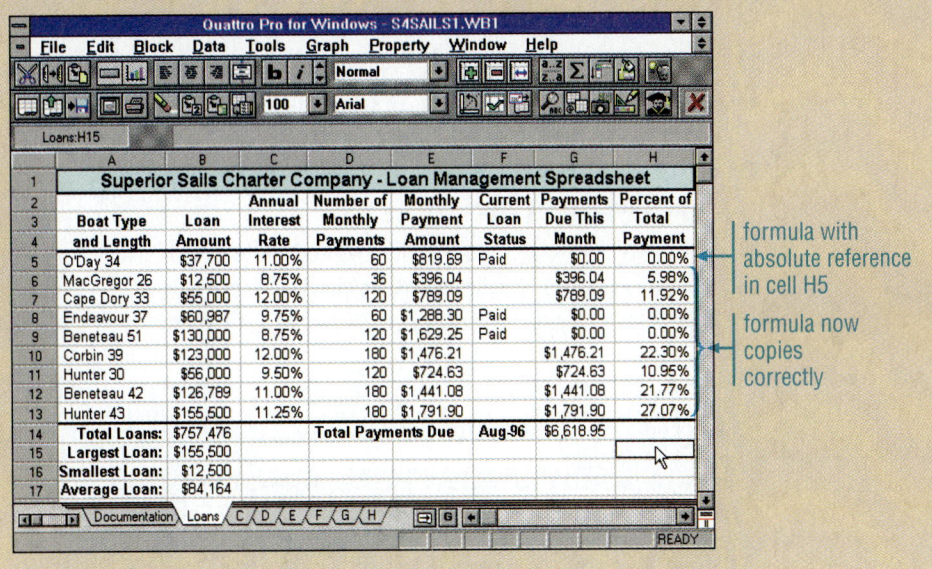

Figure 4-30
The results of copying the formula with an absolute reference

The revised formula works correctly and Shabir is pleased. The spreadsheet is now complete.

Shabir is just about to close the notebook when James stops in the office. Shabir shows him the notebook. James thinks the spreadsheet looks great, but notices that the MacGregor 26 loan in row 6 should be marked "Paid" because he just made the last payment a month ago. Shabir says it is easy to make the change and explains that the spreadsheet will recalculate the amount for the total payments due this month.

To change the loan status of the MacGregor 26:

❶ Click cell **F6** to make it the active cell.

❷ Type **Paid** and watch cell G14 as you press **[Enter]**.

As a result of changing the loan status, the amount in cell G6 changed to $0.00, the total payments due in cell G14 changed to $6,222.91, and Quattro Pro recalculated the percentages in column H. James is impressed. Now Shabir can save the notebook then print the spreadsheet.

To save the notebook:

❶ Click the **Save Notebook button** 🔲 (or click **File** then click **Save**).

Shabir is ready to print the notebook. He wants to print it in landscape orientation and center it from left to right on the page.

To print the spreadsheet in landscape orientation:

❶ Make sure your printer is ready to print.

❷ Highlight cells A1 through H17, the block of cells you want to print.

❸ Click the **Print Preview button** 🔲 (or click **File** then click **Print Preview**) to see how the spreadsheet will look when it is printed.

❹ Click the **Setup button** 🔲 on the Print Preview SpeedBar to display the Spreadsheet Page Setup dialog box.

❺ In Print orientation, click the **Landscape radio button**.

❻ In Options, click the **Center blocks check box** to place a check mark in it. The Spreadsheet Page Setup dialog box now appears as shown in Figure 4-31.

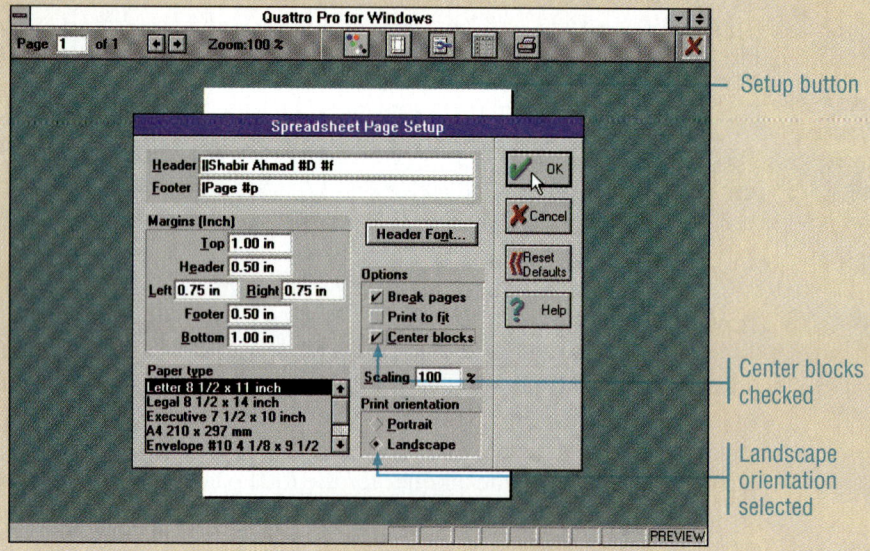

Figure 4-31
The Spreadsheet Page
Setup settings

❼ Click **OK** to return to the Print Preview window.

❽ Click the **Print button** 🔲 on the Print Preview SpeedBar to print the spreadsheet. Figure 4-32 shows the printout of the loan management spreadsheet.

❾ Click the **Close SpeedBar button** ❌ to exit Print Preview.

❿ Click the **Save Notebook button** 🔲 to save your file once again, so that it includes the print formatting options you specified.

Shabir Ahmad 08/01/96 S4SAILS1.WB1

Superior Sails Charter Company—Loan Management Spreadsheet

Boat Type and Length	Loan Amount	Annual Interest Rate	Number of Monthly Payments	Monthly Payment Amount	Current Loan Status	Payments Due This Month	Percent of Total Payment
O'Day 34	$37,700	11.00%	60	$819.69	Paid	$0.00	0.00%
MacGregor 26	$12,500	8.75%	36	$396.04	Paid	$0.00	0.00%
Cape Dory 33	$55,000	12.00%	120	$789.09		$789.09	12.68%
Endeavour 37	$60,987	9.75%	60	$1,288.30	Paid	$0.00	0.00%
Beneteau 51	$130,000	8.75%	120	$1,629.25	Paid	$0.00	0.00%
Corbin 39	$123,000	12.00%	180	$1,476.21		$1,476.21	23.72%
Hunter 30	$56,000	9.50%	120	$724.63		$724.63	11.64%
Beneteau 42	$126,789	11.00%	180	$1,441.08		$1,441.08	23.16%
Hunter 43	$155,500	11.25%	180	$1,791.90		$1,791.90	28.80%

Total Loans:	$757,476
Largest Loan:	$155,500
Smallest Loan:	$12,500
Average Loan:	$84,164

Total Payments Due   Aug-96 $6,222.91

Figure 4-32
Printout of the loan management spreadsheet

If you want to take a break and resume the tutorial at a later time, you can exit Quattro Pro by double-clicking the Control menu box in the upper-left corner of the screen. When you resume the tutorial, launch Quattro Pro, maximize the Quattro Pro and NOTEBK1.WB1 windows, place your Student Disk in the disk drive, and open the file S4SAILS1.WB1. You can then continue with the tutorial.

Using the Spreadsheet for What-If Analysis

Next, James wonders how much less his monthly payment would be if he refinanced some of the loans, so that instead of paying 12% interest he would pay 11%. Shabir shows him that this sort of what-if analysis is easy to do.

To change the interest rates and look at the effect on the total payment:
❶ Click cell **C7**, which contains one of the 12% interest rates.
❷ Type **11%** then press **[Enter]**. The total loan payment in cell G14 changes from $6,222.91 to $6,191.45.
❸ Click cell **C10**, which also contains a 12% interest rate.
❹ Type **11%** then press **[Enter]**. The total loan payment in cell G14 changes to $6,113.25.

James uses a calculator to find the difference between $6,222.91 and $6,113.25. The result is $109.66, and James sees that he could save about $110 each month by refinancing the two loans that are at 12% interest. Now he wonders "what if" he bought a West Wight Potter 19-foot sailboat for $9,000 at 11% interest.

To add another boat to the list, Shabir must insert a row at the current location of row 14. Then he must copy the formulas to calculate the monthly payment amount, the payments due this month, and the percent of total payment to the new row.

To insert a row for the new boat, enter the data, and copy the necessary formulas:
❶ Right-click the **row border** for row 14 to highlight the row and open the SpeedMenu.
❷ Click **Insert...** to insert a blank row.
❸ Highlight block A13..H13, which contains the data and formulas for the Hunter 43.
❹ Click the **Copy button** 🔳 on the notebook SpeedBar.
❺ Highlight cells A14 through H14.
❻ Click the **Paste button** 🔳 on the notebook SpeedBar. Quattro Pro copies the data and formulas for the Hunter 43 to cells A14 through H14.

Shabir now needs to edit the data in cells A14 through D14 for the Hunter 43.

To edit the data for the Hunter 43:
❶ Click cell **A14** to make it the active cell.
❷ Type **W W Potter 19** then press [→] to enter the label and move the pointer to cell B14.

❸ Type **9000** as the loan amount then press [→] to enter the number and move the pointer to cell C14.

❹ Type **11%** as the interest rate then press [→] to enter the number and move the pointer to cell D14.

❺ Type **60** as the number of payments then press [Enter] to enter the number. The monthly payment of $195.68 is displayed in cell E14.

Shabir and James look at the total payments due in cell G15, and they notice that something is wrong. The amount in this cell did not change to reflect the addition of the West Wight Potter. They look at the formulas in cells G15, B15, B16, B17, and B18 to find out what happened.

To view the contents of cells G15, B15, B16, B17, and B18:

❶ Click cell **G15** to make it the active cell. The formula for this cell appears in the input line as @SUM(G5..G13). The formula was not updated to include cell G14 in the new row.

❷ Click cell **B15** and look at the formula that appears in the input line, and then do the same for cells B16, B17, and B18. The block address in all the formulas stayed as B5..B13. Quattro Pro did not update them to include cell B14.

It is obvious that these formulas need to be updated to include row 14. Shabir realizes what happened, and explains to James that if you add a row located within the current rows in a formula, the formula will update. However, if you add a row that is *outside the rows included in a formula*, you must *manually update the formulas* to include the new row.

The original blocks in these formulas were B5..B13 and G5..G13. Shabir could have inserted a row in the current location of row 10, for example, and the block in the total payment formula would have "stretched" to include cells G5 through G14. Because Shabir inserted a row in the current location of row 14, which was not within the original blocks, he needs to manually update the formulas in cells G15, B15, B16, B17, and B18.

To update the formulas in cells G15, B15, B16, B17, and B18:

❶ Click cell **G15**, which contains the first formula you need to change.

❷ Press [F2] to display the formula in the input line in Edit mode.

❸ Press [←] then press [Backspace] to delete the 3.

❹ Type **4** then press [Enter].

❺ Repeat Steps 2 through 4 for cells B15, B16, B17, and B18, so that the formulas in these cells contain the argument B5..B14. Figure 4-33 shows the final results of the revised spreadsheet.

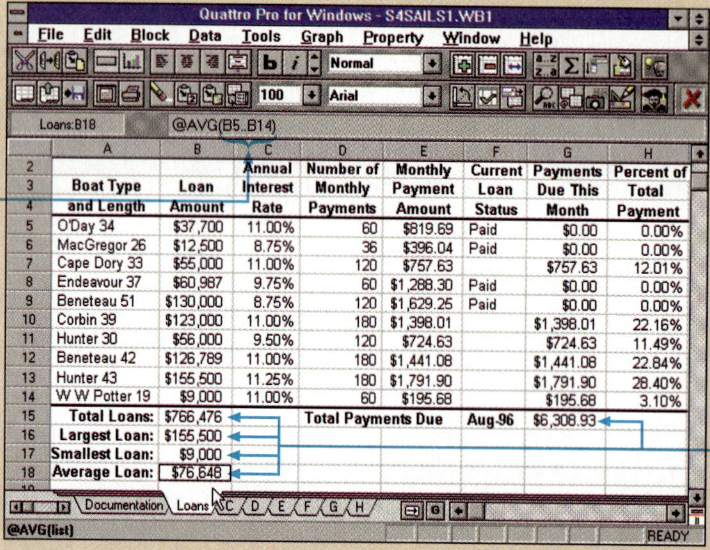

formula in cell
B18 now uses
correct block

Figure 4-33
The spreadsheet
with manually
updated formulas

updated formulas
give correct results

Now Shabir and James can see that the total loan payment would be $6,308.93 with the loan payment for a new West Wight Potter 19. The total amount of loans taken by the company, shown in cell B15, would be $766,476. The amount of the largest loan, shown in cell B16, did not change. The smallest loan, shown in cell B17, is now $9,000. The amount shown in cell B18 for the average loan changed from $84,164 to $76,648.

James now understands how important it is to check each formula to make sure it works. Shabir agrees and explains that there are many ways to test a spreadsheet to verify the accuracy of the results. For example, he can use test data or compare results with known values, such as those in loan payment tables.

James does not want a printout of the what-if analysis, so Shabir closes the notebook without saving it. The version he has saved is the notebook before he changed the interest rates from 12% to 11% and added the West Wight Potter.

To close the notebook without saving the what-if analysis:

❶ Double-click the document window **Control menu box**.

❷ Click **No** when you see the message "Save changes in A:\S4SAILS1.WB1?"

❸ Exit Quattro Pro if you are not going to do the Tutorial Assignments now.

To complete his loan management notebook, Shabir used many Quattro Pro @functions to simplify the formulas he entered. He was able to troubleshoot the problem he encountered when he copied the percent of total payment formula, which resulted in a column of ERR error messages, because he remembered that absolute references don't change when copied to other cells. Shabir is pleased that James was impressed by the capabilities of the notebook to do what-if analyses.

Questions

1. Write the definition of an @function then refer to Tutorial 1 and write the definition of a formula. Explain the relationship between @functions and formulas.
2. List the Quattro Pro @functions you used in Tutorial 4.
   a. Briefly explain what each @function does.
   b. Write the syntax for each @function.
   c. Write a sample @function in which you use cell references or constant numbers for the arguments.

3. Use the *Borland Quattro Pro for Windows User's Guide* or the Quattro Pro Help system to find one @function for each category listed in Figure 4-7.
   a. List the @function name.
   b. Indicate the category to which this @function belongs.
   c. Write a short description of what this @function does.
4. Explain the advantage of using the @MAX and @MIN functions on large lists that change frequently.
5. Explain the difference between the way the @AVG function handles zeros and the way it handles blank cells that are included in the block of cells to be averaged.
6. When would you use the @Functions button instead of typing a function directly into a cell?
7. Write the formula you would use to calculate the monthly payment for a $10,000 loan at 8% annual interest that you must pay back in 48 months.
8. Write the formula you would use to calculate the monthly payment for a $150,000 30-year home loan at 8.75% annual interest.
9. What is an apparent error due to rounding? How do you prevent these errors?
10. Write the formula you would use in cell C5 to display the message "Over budget" whenever the amount in cell B5 is greater than or equal to $800,000, but to display the message "Budget OK" if the amount in cell B5 is less than $800,000.
11. Cell A9 either contains the word *Bonus* or is blank. Cell B9 is formatted to display numbers as currency with no decimal places. Write the formula you would use in cell B9 to display the value $100 if cell A9 contains the word *Bonus,* but to display $0 if cell A9 is empty.
12. Explain the meaning of the serial numbers that Quattro Pro displays for dates when you use the @TODAY function.
13. Explain the meaning of the message ERR that sometimes appears in cells.
14. Which function key can you use to change the cell reference type from relative to absolute?
15. Explain the difference between absolute and relative references.

Tutorial Assignments

Launch Windows and Quattro Pro, if necessary, then complete the Tutorial Assignments.
1. Open the file T4SAILS2.WB1.
2. Save the notebook on your Student Disk as S4SAILS2.WB1 so that you will not modify the original file.
3. Revise the documentation on the Documentation page as follows:
   a. Change the filename in cell B4 to S4SAILS2.WB1.
   b. Put your name in cell B5.
   c. Put the current date in cell B6 (do not use an @function).
4. Save the notebook again to record the documentation changes.
For the spreadsheet on the Loans page:

5. Shabir did not have the paperwork for the CSY Gulfstar 42 loan, so it was not included in the spreadsheet. The CSY Gulfstar 42 was purchased with a $165,000 loan at 9.5% (.095) interest for 20 years.

   a. Insert a blank row at row 12. The blank row will appear between the Hunter 30 and the Beneteau 42. (*Hint:* Because you are adding the row in the middle of the block specified for the function arguments, you will not need to adjust the @SUM, @MAX, @MIN, and @AVG formulas.)

   b. Enter the name of the boat, CSY Gulfstar 42, in column A.

   c. Enter the loan amount in cell B12, the interest rate in cell C12, and the number of monthly payments in cell D12.

   d. In cell E12, enter a formula using the @PAYMT function to calculate the monthly payment.

   e. In cell G12, enter a formula using the @IF function to display $0.00 if the loan is paid, or display the loan payment if the loan is not paid.

   f. Copy the formula in cell H11 to cell H12 to calculate the percent of total payment.

6. Save the revised notebook.

7. The percent of total payment values in column H are subject to apparent errors due to rounding because they are calculated using division. The @ROUND function is needed to control the possible apparent errors. Remember that percentages are stored in the spreadsheet as decimal numbers, but are displayed as percentages when formatted as percents. For example, 12.34% is stored in the spreadsheet as .1234. This means that if you want the percentages to be displayed with two decimal places, then you round the decimal numbers in the spreadsheet to four decimal places.

   a. Edit the formula in cell H5 to add the @ROUND function to the formula.

   b. Copy the formula from cell H5 to cells H6 through H14.

8. Save the revised notebook.

9. Use Print Preview to prepare the spreadsheet for printing.

   a. Highlight block A1..H18 then start Print Preview.

   b. Set the Spreadsheet Page Setup settings so that the spreadsheet prints in landscape orientation, is horizontally centered, and the header contains your name instead of Shabir's.

10. Print the spreadsheet then exit Print Preview.

11. Use a felt marker or pen to indicate on your printout which cells display different results after the addition of the CSY Gulfstar 42.

12. Shabir needs to display some more information on the spreadsheet.

   a. Enter the label "Largest Payment:" in cell A19. In cell B19 enter the formula to find the largest loan payment in column G.

   b. Enter the label "Smallest Payment:" in cell A20. In cell B20 enter the formula to find the smallest loan payment in column G.

   c. Enter the label "Average Interest Rate:" in cell A21. In cell B21 enter the formula to calculate the average of the interest rates in column C.

13. Format the text in cells A19 through A21 as bold and right-aligned in the cell. Adjust the column width of column A, if necessary. Use the Style list to format B19 and B20 as Currency0. Format cell B21 as Percent.

14. Save the revised notebook.

15. Print a copy of the revised spreadsheet, including rows 19 through 21. (*Hint:* Make sure you highlight the new print block before you start to print.)

16. Print the spreadsheet cell contents for the spreadsheet on the Loans page. Use portrait orientation, but use the same header and footer you used for the spreadsheet.

17. Print a copy of the notebook documentation on the Documentation page. Use portrait orientation, but keep the printout centered and use the same header and footer you used for the spreadsheet.

18. Submit copies of all printouts, including the annotated printout from Tutorial Assignment 11.

Case Problems

1. Compiling Data on the U.S. Airline Industry

The editor of *Aviation Week and Space Technology* has asked Muriel Guzzetti's research consulting firm to research the current status of the U.S. airline industry for use in an upcoming article. Muriel collects information on the revenue miles and passenger miles for each of the major U.S. airlines. She wants to calculate the following summary information:

- total revenue miles for the U.S. airline industry
- total passenger miles for the U.S. airline industry
- each airline's share of the total revenue miles
- each airline's share of the total passenger miles
- the average revenue miles for U.S. airlines
- the average passenger miles for U.S. airlines

Complete the following steps:

1. Open the notebook P4AIR.WB1.
2. Save the notebook on your Student Disk as S4AIR.WB1 so that you will not modify the original file.
3. Revise the documentation on page A as follows:
   a. Change the filename in cell B4 to S4AIR.WB1.
   b. Put your name in cell B5.
   c. Put the current date in cell B6 (do not use an @function).
   d. Use cells B9, B10, and B11 as needed to complete the statement of purpose for the notebook.

For the spreadsheet on page A:

4. Put the page name "Documentation" on the A page tab.

For the spreadsheet on page B:

5. Put the page name "Analysis" on the B page tab.
6. Use the @SUM function to calculate the industry total revenue miles in cell B12.
7. Use the @SUM function to calculate the industry total passenger miles in cell D12.
8. In cell C5, enter the formula to calculate American Airlines' share of the total industry revenue miles using the following equation:

   American's share of total industry revenue miles =
   American's revenue miles/industry total revenue miles

   (*Hint:* You are going to use this formula for the rest of the airlines, so consider which cell reference should be absolute.)
9. Copy the formula from cell C5 to calculate each airline's share of the total industry revenue miles.
10. In cell E5, enter the formula to calculate American Airlines' share of the total industry passenger miles then copy this formula for the other airlines.
11. In cell B13, use the @AVG function to calculate the average revenue miles for the U.S. airline industry.
12. In cell D13 use the @AVG function to calculate the average passenger miles for the U.S. airline industry.
13. Format the spreadsheet so it is easier to read:
    a. Bold the titles and column headings.
    b. Center the title across the entire spreadsheet and center the column headings over each column.
    c. Add a line at the bottom of cells A4 through E4, and add a line at the top of cells A12 through E12.
    d. Format column B and column D to display numbers with commas.
    e. Format columns C and E as percentages with two decimal places.
    f. Add an outline around the spreadsheet title, and add color to the outlined area.
14. Save the spreadsheet.

15. Produce three printouts:
    a. Print the notebook documentation in portrait orientation and centered on the page. Use a right-aligned header that contains your name, the current date, and the filename, and a centered footer containing the page number.
    b. Print the Analysis spreadsheet in portrait orientation and centered on the page. Use a right-aligned header that contains your name, the current date and the filename, and a centered footer containing the page number.
    c. Print the cell contents for the Analysis spreadsheet in portrait orientation. Use a right-aligned header that contains your name, the current date, and the filename, and a centered footer containing the page number.

2. Commission Analysis at Norcross Office Systems

Maija Jansson is the sales manager for Norcross Office Systems, an office supply store. Maija is thinking of changing the commission structure to motivate the sales representatives to increase sales. Currently, sales representatives earn a monthly base salary of $500.00. In addition to the base salary, sales representatives earn a 5% (.05) commission on their total sales when their monthly sales volume is $5,000.00 or more.

To look at some options for changing the commission structure, Maija collected past payroll information for one of the employees, Jim Marley. Jim's monthly sales are typical of most Norcross sales representatives. Maija wants to design a notebook that will help her determine how much money Jim would have earned in the past 12 months had the commission structure been different. Maija has completed some of the notebook and has asked you to help her finish it.

To complete the notebook:
1. Open the notebook named P4BONUS.WB1.
2. Save the notebook on your Student Disk as S4BONUS.WB1 so that you will not modify the original file.
3. Revise and complete the documentation of page A as follows:
    a. Change the filename in cell B4 to S4BONUS.WB1.
    b. Put your name in cell B5.
    c. Put the current date in cell B6 (do not use an @function).
    d. Use cells B9, B10, and B11 as needed to complete the statement of purpose for the notebook.

For the spreadsheet on page A:
4. Put the page name "Documentation" on the A page tab.

For the spreadsheet on page B:
5. Put the page name "ComAnalysis" on the B page tab.
6. Enter the names of the months January through December in column A. (*Hint:* Use SpeedFill to automatically fill cells A7 through A18 with the names of the months.)
7. In cell C7, enter the formula that uses the @IF function to calculate Jim's bonus for January.
    a. For the *Cond*ition argument, enter the expression to check if Jim's sales are greater than or equal to the sales required for the commission in cell C3.
    b. For the *TrueExpr*ession argument, multiply Jim's sales by the commission percent in cell C4.
    c. For the *FalseExpr*ession argument, enter a zero.
8. Copy the formula in cell C7 to cells C8 through C18. (*Hint:* If your formulas produced zeros for every month, something is wrong. Examine the formula in cell C7 and determine which references need to be absolute. Edit the formula then copy it again. Your formulas are correct if cell C18 shows that Jim earned a $278.10 commission.)
9. In cell E7, enter the formula to calculate Jim's total pay for January. Calculate Jim's total pay by adding his commission to his base salary.

10. Copy the formula in cell E7 to cells E8 through E18.
11. In cell E19, use the @SUM function to calculate Jim's total pay for the year.
12. Format the spreadsheet as follows:
    a. Center the title across the entire spreadsheet.
    b. Add an outline around the spreadsheet title, and add color to the outlined area.
    c. Format cell C4 as a percentage with two decimal places.
    d. Format any other cell or block of cells that you think needs a different appearance.
13. Save the notebook.
14. Write your answers to the following questions:
    a. How much did Jim earn in the last 12 months under the current commission structure?
    b. How much would Jim have earned last year had the commission been 8%?
    c. How much would Jim have earned in the last 12 months had the commission rate been 6%, but he had to make at least $5,500 in sales each month before he could earn a commission?
15. Print the notebook documentation in portrait orientation and centered on the page. Use a right-aligned header that contains your name, the current date, and the filename, and a centered footer containing the page number.
16. Print two versions of your ComAnalysis spreadsheet:
    a. Print the spreadsheet showing what Jim would have earned if he had to sell $5,000 each month to earn a commission, with a 5% commission. Print the spreadsheet in portrait orientation and centered on the page. Use a right-aligned header that contains your name, the current date, and the filename, and a centered footer containing the page number.
    b. Print the spreadsheet showing what Jim would have earned if he had to sell $5,500 each month to earn a commission, with a 6% commission. Print the spreadsheet in portrait orientation and centered on the page. Use a right-aligned header that contains your name, the current date, and the filename, and a centered footer containing the page number.
17. Print the cell contents for the ComAnalysis spreadsheet using portrait orientation and centered on the page. Use a right-aligned header that contains your name, the current date, and the filename, and a centered footer containing the page number.

3. Calculating Car Loans at First Federal Bank

Paul Vagelos is a loan officer in the Consumer Loan Department of the First Federal Bank. Paul evaluates customer applications for car loans, and he wants to create a notebook that will calculate the monthly payments, total payments, and total interest paid on a loan. Paul has finished most of the notebook but needs to complete a few more sections. To complete the notebook:

1. Open the notebook P4CAR1.WB1 then save it as S4CAR1.WB1 on your Student Disk.
2. Revise and complete the documentation of page A as follows:
    a. Change the filename in cell B4 to S4CAR1.WB1.
    b. Put your name in cell B5.
    c. Put the current date in cell B6 (do not use an @function).
    d. Use cells B9, B10, and B11 as needed to complete the statement of purpose for the notebook.

For the spreadsheet on page A:

3. Put the page name "Documentation" on the A page tab.

For the spreadsheet on page B:

4. Put the page name "CarLoans" on the B page tab.

5. Enter the formula in cell B8 that uses the @PAYMT function to calculate the monthly payment for the loan amount in cell B3, at the interest rate in cell B4, for the term in cell A8. Display the monthly payment as a positive amount.
6. Edit the formula in cell B8 to contain absolute references for any cell references that should not change when you copy the formula.
7. Copy the formula in cell B8 to cells B9 through B12.
8. Enter the formula in cell D8 to calculate the total interest using the following equation:

total interest = total payments – loan amount

9. Edit the formula in cell D8 to contain absolute references for any cell references that should not change when you copy the formula.
10. Copy the formula in cell D8 to cells D9 through D12.
11. Make any formatting changes you think are appropriate to have a professional-looking spreadsheet.
12. Save the notebook with formatting changes.
13. Preview the printed spreadsheet. Make any page setup settings necessary to produce a professional-looking printout, then print the CarLoans spreadsheet.
14. Print the notebook documentation on the Documentation page.
15. Print the cell contents for the CarLoans spreadsheet.

Graphs and Graphing

Graphing Sales Information

O B J E C T I V E S

In this tutorial you will:

- Plan and construct graphs
- Identify the elements of a Quattro Pro graph
- Create a line graph and a bar graph
- Move a graph and change its size
- Create, edit, and format graph elements and graph text
- Add color to a graph
- Insert manual page breaks
- Learn which graph type represents data most effectively

CASE

Cast Iron Concepts   Carl O'Brien is the assistant marketing director at Cast Iron Concepts, a distributor of traditional cast iron stoves. Carl is working on a new product catalog and his main concern is how much space to allocate for each product. In previous catalogs the Box Windsor stove was allocated one full page. The Star Windsor and the West Windsor stoves were each allocated a half page.

Cast Iron Concepts has two sales regions—the western region and the eastern region. Carl has collected sales information from both regions for each of the three stove models, and has combined the data in a consolidated sales spreadsheet. He has discovered that Box Windsor stove sales have steadily decreased since 1992. Although the Box Windsor stove was the best-selling model during the 1980s, sales of Star Windsor stoves and West Windsor stoves have increased steadily and overtaken the Box Windsor sales. Carl believes that the space allocated to the Box Windsor stove should be reduced to a half page, while the Star Windsor stove and the West Windsor stove should each have a full page.

Carl needs to convince the marketing director to change the space allocation in the new catalog, so he is preparing a presentation for the next department meeting. At the presentation Carl plans to show two graphs that illustrate the sales pattern of the Box Windsor, Star Windsor, and West Windsor stoves. Carl has stored the sales figures in a Quattro Pro notebook named C5WINDSR.WB1. He will generate the graphs from the data in the notebook.

To launch Quattro Pro, organize the workspace, and open the C5WINDSR.WB1 notebook:

❶ Launch Quattro Pro following your usual procedure.

❷ Make sure your Student Disk is in the disk drive.

❸ Click the **Open Notebook button** 🖼 (or click **File** then click **Open...**) to display the Open File dialog box.

❹ Make sure the Drives box displays the A: drive name.

❺ Double-click **C5WINDSR.WB1** in the File Name box to display the notebook, as shown in Figure 5-1.

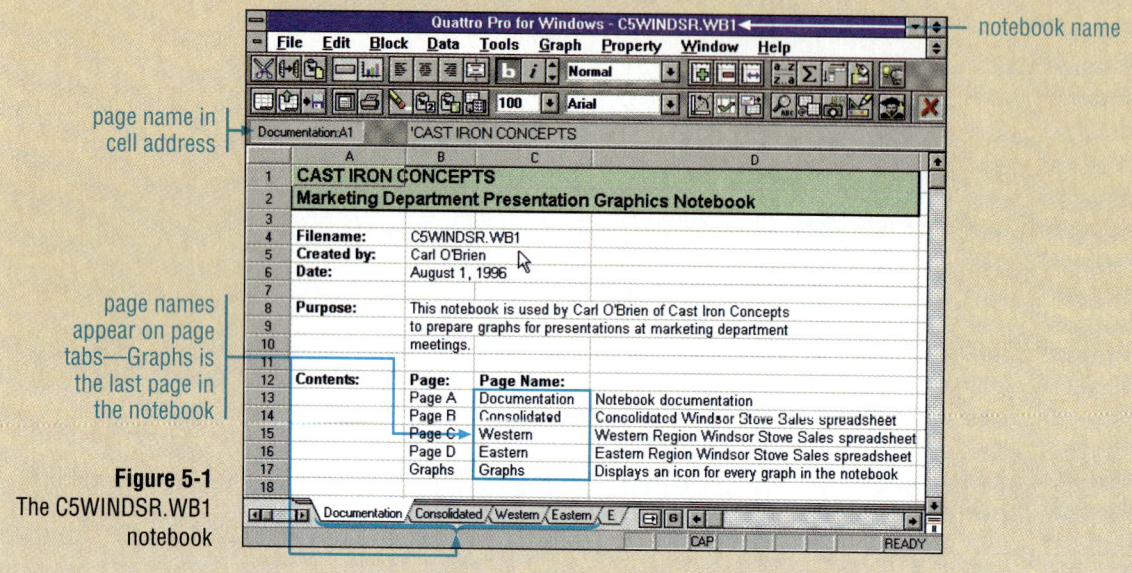

page name in cell address

page names appear on page tabs—Graphs is the last page in the notebook

Figure 5-1
The C5WINDSR.WB1 notebook

Carl has entered his notebook documentation on page A. Notice that Carl has named each of the first four pages: page A, Documentation, documents the notebook; page B, Consolidated, is the consolidated sales spreadsheet containing figures for both regions; page C, Western, is the western region sales spreadsheet; and page D, Eastern, is the eastern region sales spreadsheet.

Let's save the notebook with the name S5WINDSR.WB1. The original notebook, C5WINDSR.WB1, will be left in its original state in case you want to do this tutorial again.

To save the notebook as S5WINDSR.WB1:

❶ Make sure page A is the active page.

❷ Click cell **B4** to make it the active cell.

❸ Change the filename in cell B4 to **S5WINDSR.WB1**, then press **[Enter]** .

❹ Press **[Home]** to make cell A1 the active cell.

❺ Click **File** then click **Save As...** to display the Save File dialog box.

❻ Type **S5WINDSR** using either uppercase or lowercase *but don't press [Enter]* because you need to check some additional settings.

❻ Make sure the Drives box displays the name of the drive that contains your Student Disk.

❼ Click **OK** to save the notebook on your Student Disk. When the save is complete, you should see the new filename, S5WINDSR.WB1, displayed in the title bar.

TROUBLE? If a window appears with the message "File already exists: C5WINDSR.WB1," click Cancel then repeat Steps 4 through 7. If you see the message "File already exists: S5WINDSR.WB1," click Replace to replace the old version with the current version.

Let's look at the three pages containing the spreadsheets Eastern, Western, and Consolidated.

To switch to the Eastern page in the notebook:

❶ Click the **Eastern page tab** to display the Windsor stove sales spreadsheet for the eastern region, shown in Figure 5-2.

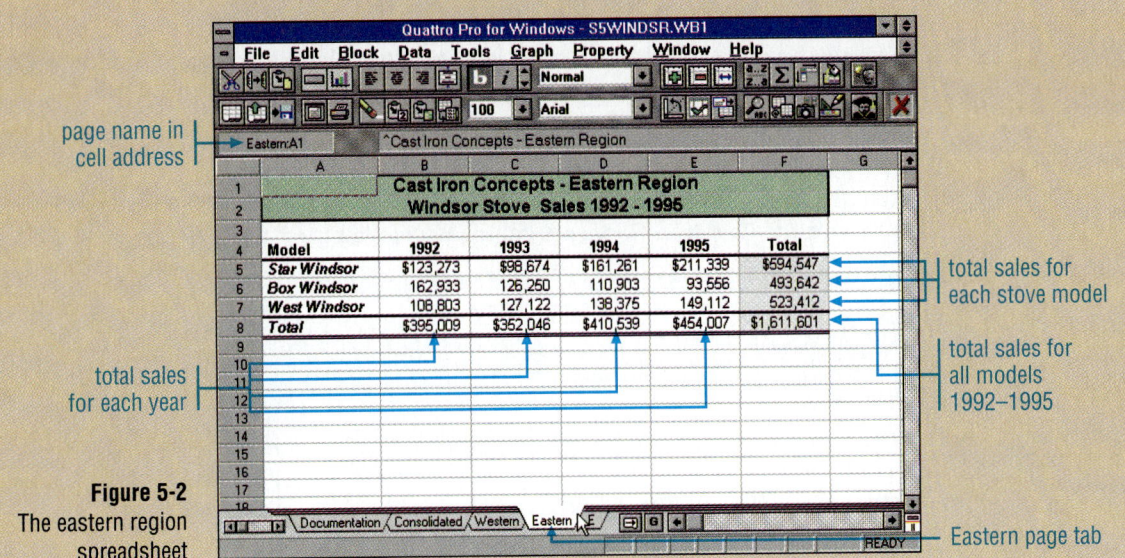

Figure 5-2
The eastern region spreadsheet

The spreadsheet shows the sales generated by each of the three Windsor stove models for the period 1992 through 1995. Column F shows the total sales in dollars during the four-year period for each model, while row 8 contains the total sales in dollars for each year as well as the total sales for all four years.

Next, switch to the Western page in the notebook:

❷ Click the **Western page tab** to display the sales spreadsheet for the western region, shown in Figure 5-3.

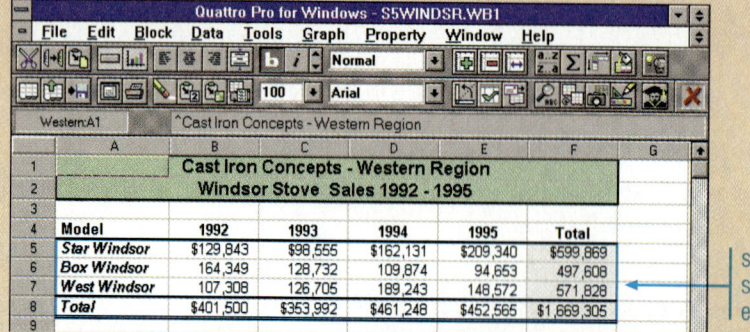

Figure 5-3
The western region spreadsheet

> same spreadsheet structure used for eastern region

The spreadsheet uses the same structure as that of the eastern region: the sales generated by each of the three Windsor stove models for the period 1992 through 1995, the total sales during the four-year period for each model, and the total sales for each year as well as the total sales for all four years.

Now, switch to the Consolidated page, which contains the spreadsheet that combines the sales information from both the eastern and western regions:

❸ Click the **Consolidated page tab** to display the spreadsheet with consolidated sales figures for the Cast Iron Concepts company. See Figure 5-4.

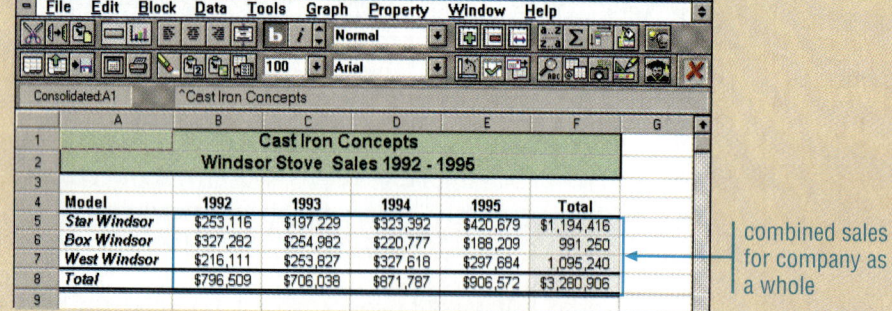

Figure 5-4
The consolidated spreadsheet

> combined sales for company as a whole

The consolidated sales spreadsheet also uses the same structure, but the sales figures show the sum of the sales from the two regions. You learned how to do this type of calculation in Tutorial 2.

Carl wants to produce several graphs that will help him convince the marketing director to change the catalog space allocated to each Windsor stove model. In this tutorial, you will work with Carl as he plans and creates graphs for his presentation.

Quattro Pro Graphs and the Graphs Page

Quattro Pro can create **floating graphs** that "float" above the spreadsheet, blocking from view but not replacing the cells beneath them. Floating graphs are useful when you want to see a graph next to its data on a spreadsheet. However, Quattro Pro graphs do *not* have to be floating graphs, and you can create graphs that do not appear on a spreadsheet page.

For every graph that you create, both floating and nonfloating, Quattro Pro creates a **graph icon** that appears on the Graphs page at the end of the notebook. You access the Graphs page by clicking the **SpeedTab button** at the bottom of the notebook window. Figure 5-5 shows the location of the SpeedTab button.

Figure 5-5
The SpeedTab
button

SpeedTab
button—
arrow points
right toward
Graphs page

Carl has already created one graph, which Quattro Pro named Graph1. Let's switch to the Graphs page to see the icon for Graph1.

To switch to the Graphs page in the notebook:

❶ Click the **SpeedTab button** ▣ to display the Graphs page of Carl's notebook, as shown in Figure 5-6.

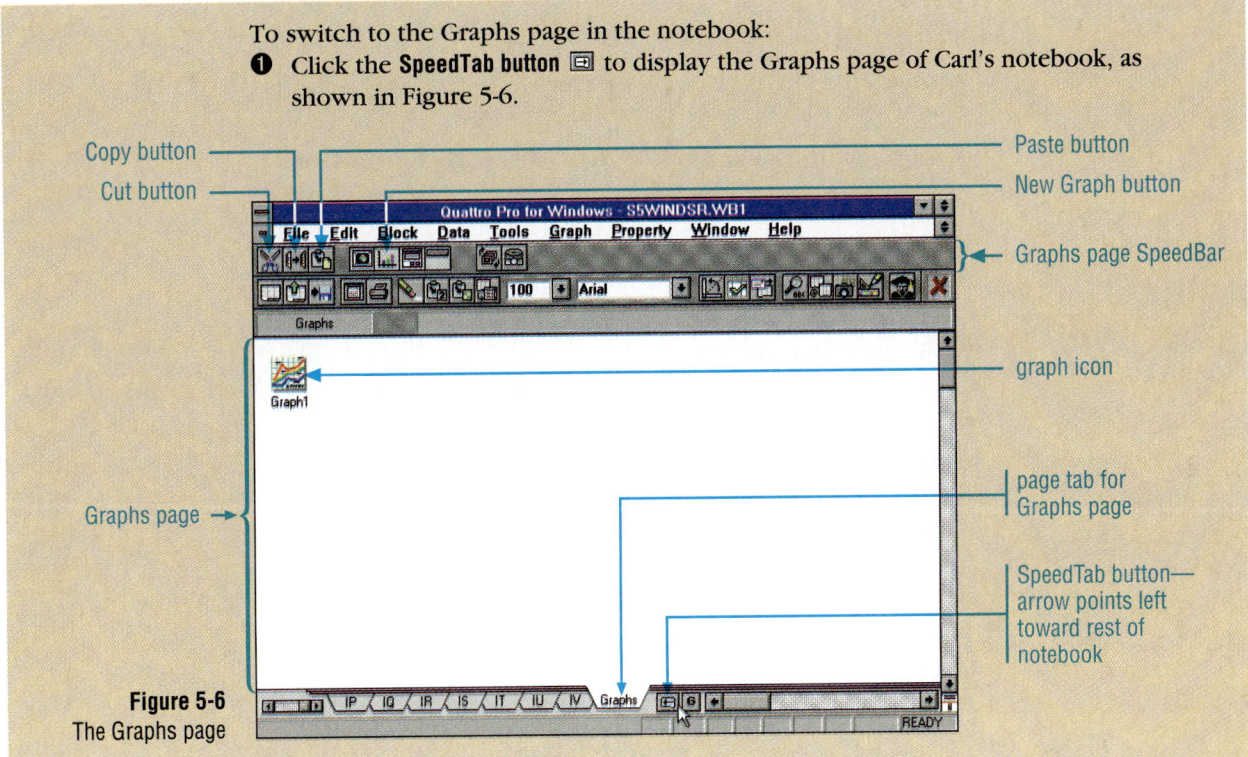

Copy button

Cut button

Paste button

New Graph button

Graphs page SpeedBar

graph icon

page tab for
Graphs page

Graphs page →

SpeedTab button—
arrow points left
toward rest of
notebook

Figure 5-6
The Graphs page

The Graphs page contains the graph icon for Graph1. Notice that in Figure 5-6 the arrow on the SpeedTab button now points left (back toward the rest of the notebook). If you click the SpeedTab button now, Quattro Pro will return you to the spreadsheet page that you were on.

The Graphs page has its own SpeedBar, which replaces the notebook SpeedBar. The New Graph button creates a graph in a graph window, which will be discussed later in this tutorial. The Cut, Copy, and Paste buttons work the same as their equivalents on the notebook SpeedBar.

Let's take a look at the graph that Carl has already prepared.

Viewing Graphs

You can view graphs at any time in Quattro Pro using the Graph View command. You don't have to be on the Graphs page.

REFERENCE WINDOW

Viewing a Graph

- Press [F11] (or click Graph then click View).

- In the Select Graph list, double-click the name of the graph you want to view (or click the graph name, then click OK).

- When you are done viewing the graph, press [Enter] (or [Esc], or [Spacebar]).

Let's look at the graph named Graph1.

To view the graph named Graph1:

❶ Press [**F11**] (or click **Graph** then click **View**). The Graph View dialog box appears.

❷ In the Select Graph list, double-click **Graph1**. The graph named Graph1 appears, as shown in Figure 5-7.

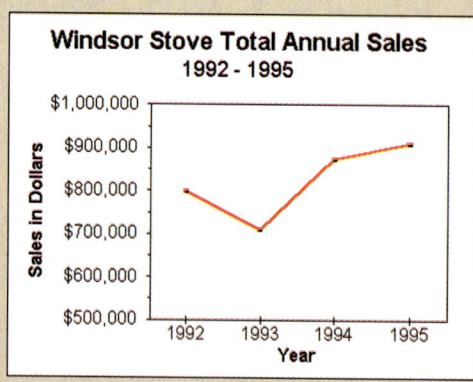

Figure 5-7
Graph1

Carl's graph is a line graph of the total annual sales of all the Windsor stove products from 1992 to 1995. Each year's sales are represented as a point on the graph, and the points are connected by line segments. Looking at the graph, you can see a dip in sales in 1993 (down to about $700,000), and climbing sales in 1994 and 1995 (up to about $900,000).

Quattro Pro Graph Elements

Let's use Carl's graph to define the elements of a graph, shown in Figure 5-8. It is important that you understand the Quattro Pro graph terminology so you can successfully construct and edit graphs.

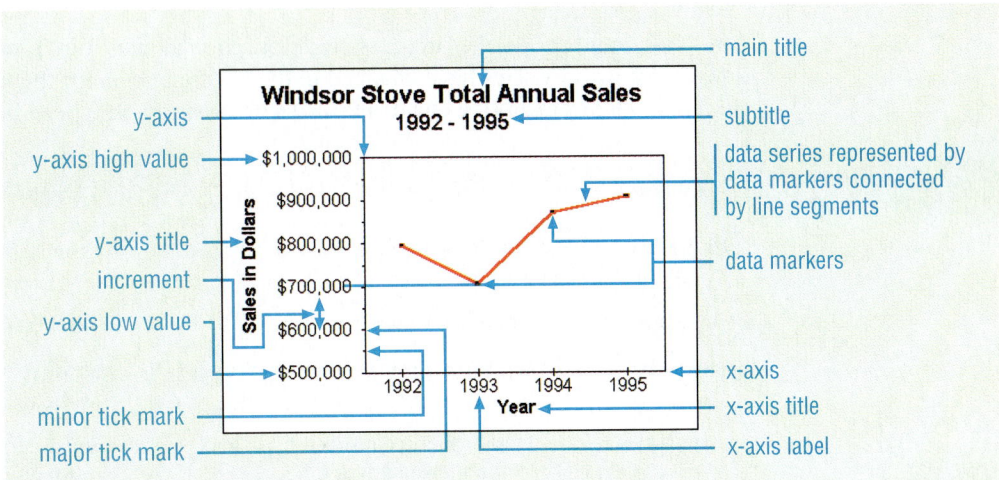

Figure 5-8
Elements of a
Quattro Pro graph

The **main title** and **subtitle** identify the graph. The horizontal axis of the graph is referred to as the **x-axis**, and the vertical axis is called the **y-axis**. Each axis on a graph can have a **title** that identifies the scale, or categories, of the graph data. In Figure 5-8 the x-axis title is "Year" and the y-axis title is "Sales in Dollars."

The **y-axis values** show the scale for the y-axis, which ranges from the low value, $500,000, to the high value, $1,000,000. Quattro Pro automatically generates this scale based on the values selected for the graph, but you can edit it, if necessary. Value labels are shown on the y-axis by tick marks. **Major tick marks** have a value label; **minor tick marks** fall between major tick marks, and don't have a value label. The difference between consecutive y-axis values is called the **increment**.

The x-axis has an **x-axis title** to identify the axis and **x-axis labels** to show the categories of the data.

A **data point** is a single value in a cell in the spreadsheet. A **data marker** is a symbol, bar, area, or slice that represents a single data point on a graph. For example, the 1995 sales of the Windsor stoves in cell Consolidated:E8 of the consolidated sales spreadsheet is a data point. The small square on the graph line in Figure 5-8 that shows the 1995 sales of Windsor stoves is a data marker.

A **data series** is a group of related data points, such as the Windsor stove sales shown in cells Consolidated:B8..E8 on the consolidated sales spreadsheet. On a line graph such as the one in Figure 5-8, a data series is shown as a set of data markers connected by **line segments**.

Now let's return to Carl's consolidated sales spreadsheet.

To close the graph and return to the Consolidated page:

❶ Press [Enter].

❷ Click the **SpeedTab button** 🔳.

   TROUBLE? If you didn't return to the Consolidated page, you might have clicked the left
   scroll arrow rather than 🔳. Check Figure 5-6 for the location of 🔳 then try again.

Quattro Pro returns to the Consolidated page. Notice that the Consolidated page tab, not the Documentation page tab, is the first tab shown at the bottom of the screen.

Quattro Pro Graph Types

Carl's first graph shows the progression of total annual sales, but now he needs to break that down to show how sales have changed in the last four years for the individual stove models. He can choose from among Quattro Pro's 13 different graph types, shown in Figure 5-9.

Graph Type	Uses	Example
Bar graphs	Compare values in categories or values over time	Compare regional sales
Line graphs	Track values over time	Track annual sales
Stacked bar graphs	Show the contribution of each series to the total	Show each region's contribution to the total sales
Area graphs	Show the contribution of each series to the total over time	Show each region's contribution to total sales over time
100% Stacked bar graphs	Show percentage contribution of each series to the total	Show each region's percentage contribution to total sales
Comparison graphs	Use connecting lines to help viewer follow changes	Show each region's contribution to total sales over time
Pie graphs	Compare individual values to the whole	Show regional percentage of sales
Doughnut graphs	Compare individual values to the whole	Show regional percentage of sales
Column graphs	Compare individual values to the whole	Show regional percentage of sales
XY graphs	Show relationships by plotting values of one series against the values of another series	Show relationship between sales and commission rates
High-low graphs	Show the difference in values of two to four series	Track stock performance (high-low-open-close)
Surface graphs	Show relationships of values of three variables as a 3-D surface	Plot mathematical functions
Radar graphs	Show x-axis values as distance from a center point	Compare sales performance of salespersons

Figure 5-9
Quattro Pro
graph types

Quattro Pro also provides variations that you can apply to many of the graph types. These include 2-D (two-dimensional) and 3-D (three-dimensional) graphs, rotated (x-axis appearing on the vertical axis and y-axis on the horizontal axis), multiple (two graphs of the same type on different axes), and combined (two graphs of different types on the same axis). You can find more information on graph types and variations in the *Borland Quattro Pro User's Guide* and in the Quattro Pro Help system.

Quattro Pro also gives you the ability to create a text graph that contains only text, such as an outline of important points, for use in slide shows and graphics presentations.

Carl wants to show the change in total dollar sales for each model during the period 1992 through 1995. He decides to create a line graph to illustrate this change.

Creating a Line Graph

As you saw in Graph1, a **line graph** represents a data series by connecting each data point with a line segment. The primary use of a line graph is to show trends or changes over time. Generally, the x-axis labels are categories reflecting the time periods for the data, such as days, months, or years. If you are plotting more than one data series, Quattro Pro represents each with one line on the graph. Make sure you include a block of labels to be used as a legend. A **legend** indicates which data series is represented by each line.

Carl begins by making a sketch of the line graph he wants to create, as shown in Figure 5-10. He uses the years 1992, 1993, 1994, and 1995 for the x-axis labels (contained in row 4 of the spreadsheet).

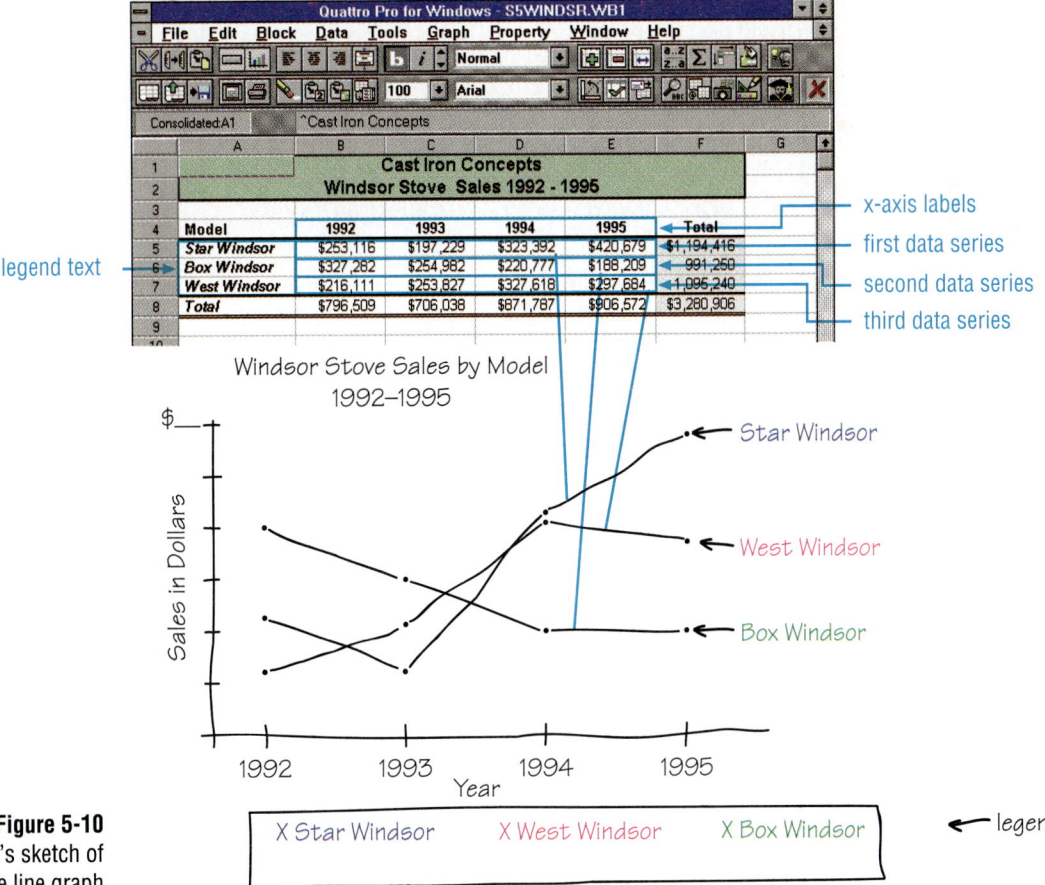

Figure 5-10
Carl's sketch of
the line graph

The first graph line will show the Star Windsor sales for the four-year period (contained in row 5); the second will show the Box Windsor sales (contained in row 6); and the third will show the West Windsor sales (contained in row 7).

Carl does not include any of the total sales figures from column F or row 8 in the graph, because he knows it would be confusing to show yearly sales and total sales on the same graph.

Carl decides to use the Graph Expert to create a floating graph that will appear on the Consolidated page just below the data.

Using the Graph Expert to Create a Floating Graph

The **Graph Expert** is a Quattro Pro feature that helps you create a graph. To use the Graph Expert, you first highlight the block of data you want to graph, and then you start the Graph Expert, which leads you through four steps to help you create the graph. After you create a graph using the Graph Expert, you can move it to a new location and make other modifications.

REFERENCE WINDOW

Creating a Graph with the Graph Expert

- Position the pointer in the upper-left corner of the data area you want to graph.

- Click and drag the pointer to select all the cells you want to graph, which might include row and column labels.

- Click the Experts button on the notebook SpeedBar, then click the Graph Expert button to start the Graph Expert (or click Help, click Experts, then click Graph...).

- Follow the Graph Expert instructions to create the graph.

- To move the graph position the pointer anywhere in the graph. Click and hold the left mouse button until the pointer changes to ✋, then drag the graph to a new location.

- Resize the graph until it's the shape and size you want.

Carl starts by highlighting the block of cells he needs. This block includes the row containing the x-axis labels, and the three rows containing the stove model labels and the three data series. Quattro Pro will use the stove model labels for the legend.

To highlight the graph block and start the Graph Expert:

❶ Highlight cells A4 through E7. Make sure you have not highlighted any cells in column F or in row 8.

❷ Click the **Experts button** 🖼 on the notebook SpeedBar. The Experts in Quattro Pro for Windows dialog box appears.

❸ Click **Graph Expert**.

❹ When the Graph Expert – Step 1 of 4 dialog box appears, make sure the Graph data edit field shows the block Consolidated:A4..E7. See Figure 5-11.

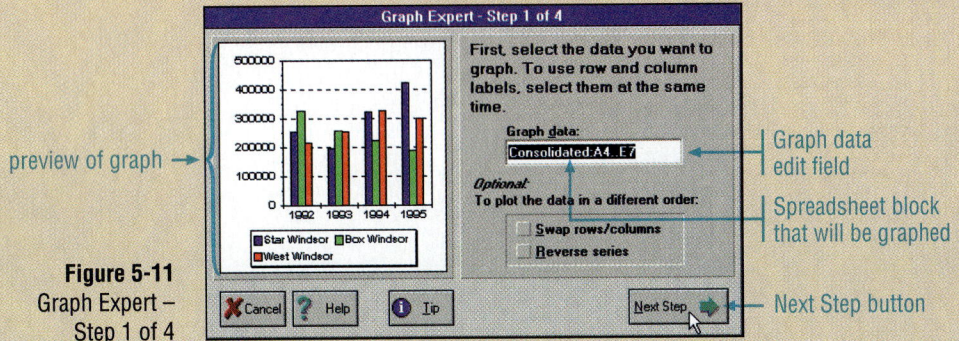

preview of graph →

Figure 5-11
Graph Expert –
Step 1 of 4

Graph data
edit field

Spreadsheet block
that will be graphed

Next Step button

TROUBLE? If the Graph data box does not display Consolidated:A4..E7, you highlighted the wrong cells to use for the graph. Notice that the *complete* block address *including the spreadsheet page name* must appear in the Graph data edit field. You can either enter Consolidated:A4..E7 in the Graph data edit field, or you can click Cancel in the Graph Expert – Step 1 of 4 box (or press [Esc]), click Cancel in the Experts in Quattro Pro box (or press [Esc]), then repeat Steps 1 through 4.

Once Carl has the correct data selected, he can create his graph.

To create the line graph:

❶ Click **Next Step** to display Graph Expert – Step 2 of 4.

❷ Click **Line or Area** to choose the general graph type, then click **Next Step** to display Graph Expert – Step 3 of 4.

❸ Make sure that the leftmost Regular button is selected and that the example graph in the graph window displays a two-dimensional graph, as shown in Figure 5-12.

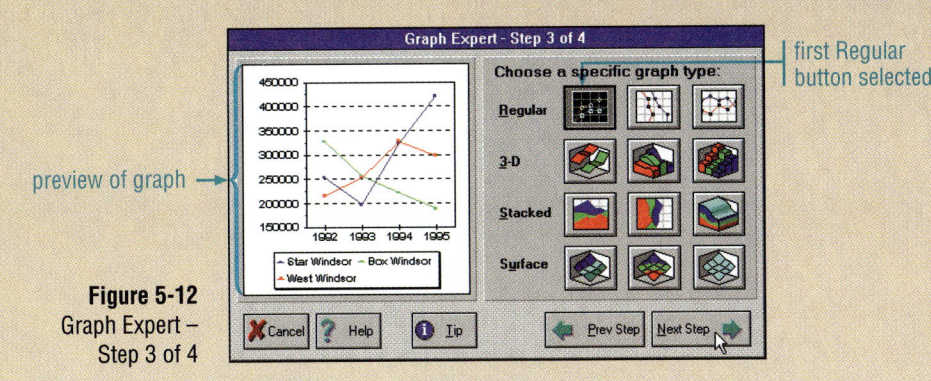

first Regular
button selected

preview of graph →

Figure 5-12
Graph Expert –
Step 3 of 4

❹ Click **Next Step** to display Graph Expert – Step 4 of 4.

❺ In the Title edit field, type **Windsor Stove Sales by Model** as the graph title.

❻ Press **[Tab]** to move to the Subtitle edit field, then type **1992–1995** as the subtitle.

❼ Press **[Tab]** to move to the X-Axis edit field, then type **Year** as the x-axis title.

❽ Press **[Tab]** to move to the Y-Axis edit field, then type **Sales in Dollars** as the y-axis title.

❾ Make sure that Notebook Page is selected as the Destination setting. The Graph Expert – Step 4 of 4 dialog box should appear as shown in Figure 5-13.

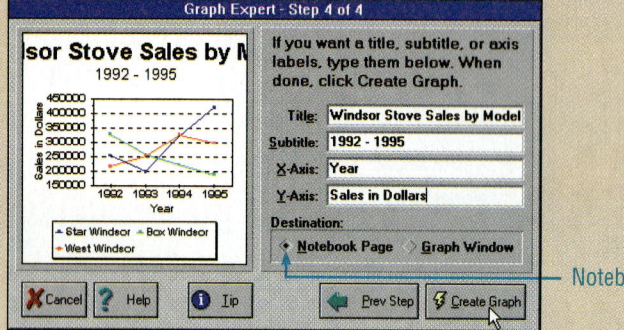

Figure 5-13
Graph Expert –
Step 4 of 4

❿ Click **Create Graph**. Quattro Pro creates the graph and places it on top of the high-lighted data block in the spreadsheet.

Carl wants to move the graph below the data on the spreadsheet.

To place the graph between rows 11 and 28:

❶ Place the pointer anywhere in the graph. Click and hold the left mouse button until the pointer shape changes to 🖑 .

❷ Drag the graph down the spreadsheet until the upper-left corner of the graph border is in cell A11. Release the mouse button. The graph moves to the new location.

❸ Use the black square handles on the graph border to adjust the size of the graph. Place the pointer over a black square handle, click and hold the left mouse button until the pointer changes to ✛ , then drag the black square handle to adjust the graph size until it fills the block A11..F28, as shown in Figure 5-14. Scroll your screen so that you can see all of the graph.

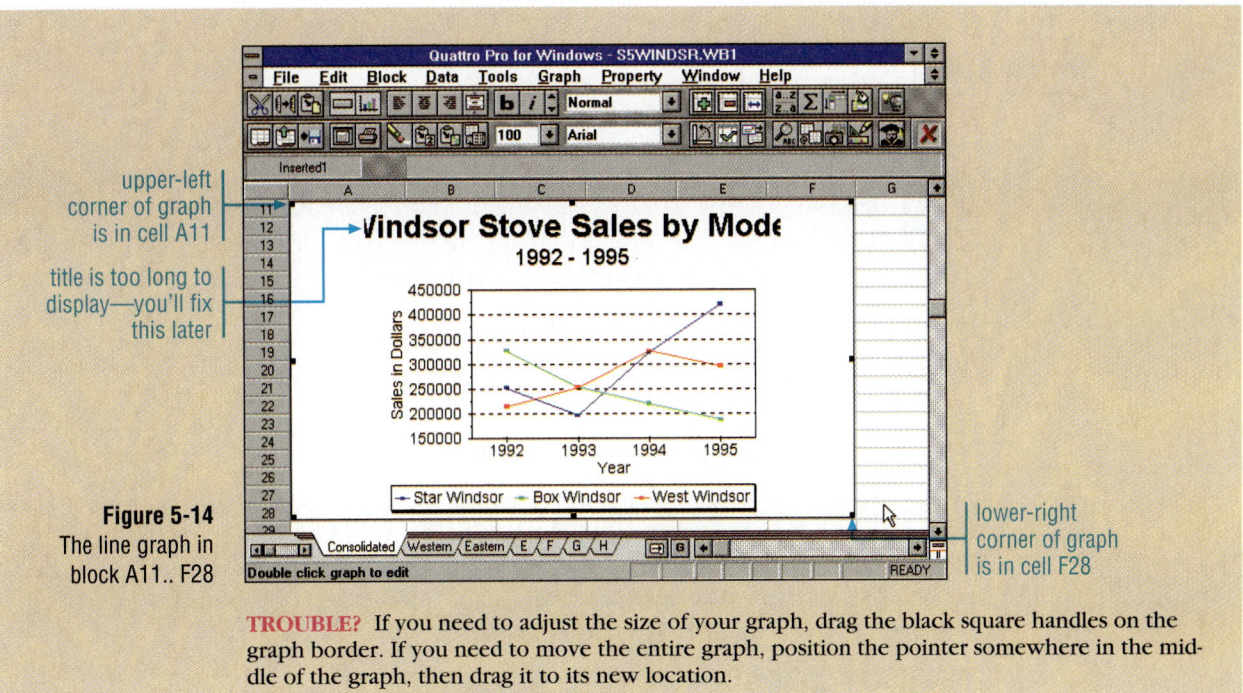

upper-left
corner of graph
is in cell A11

title is too long to
display—you'll fix
this later

Figure 5-14
The line graph in
block A11.. F28

lower-right
corner of graph
is in cell F28

TROUBLE? If you need to adjust the size of your graph, drag the black square handles on the graph border. If you need to move the entire graph, position the pointer somewhere in the middle of the graph, then drag it to its new location.

Quattro Pro automatically assigns a name to a new graph, as with Graph1, but Carl prefers to choose more descriptive names for his graphs.

Graph Names

When you create a graph, Quattro Pro gives the graph a name consisting of the word "Graph" followed by a number, as in "Graph1." You can see the assigned name by looking at the graph's icon on the Graphs page.

To see the icon on the Graphs page for the new graph:
❶ Click the **SpeedTab button** ⊞ to switch to the Graphs page. Notice that there is now an icon for Graph2. This is the new graph.

TROUBLE? If your new icon has a different name, such as Graph3 or Graph4, that's OK. Just continue with the tutorial and substitute your icon's name for Graph2 in this section.

The name that Quattro Pro assigns depends on the names of the graphs already in the notebook and any graphs created in your current Quattro Pro session. This makes it difficult to predict exactly what name Quattro Pro will use. You can, however, rename a graph with the name of your choice.

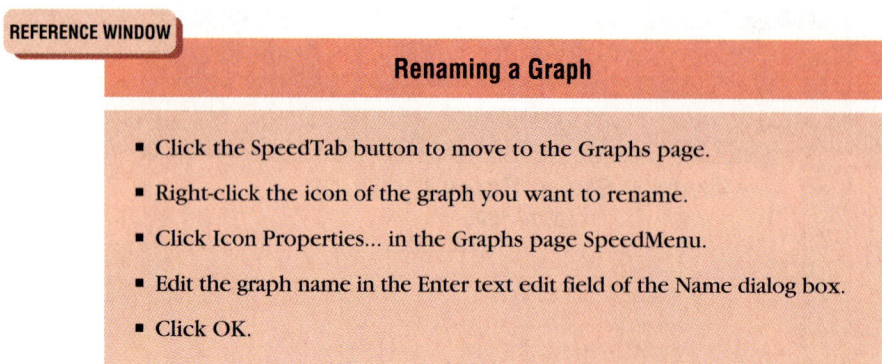

Renaming a Graph

- Click the SpeedTab button to move to the Graphs page.
- Right-click the icon of the graph you want to rename.
- Click Icon Properties... in the Graphs page SpeedMenu.
- Edit the graph name in the Enter text edit field of the Name dialog box.
- Click OK.

Carl decides to name the graph "SalesByModel."

To name the new graph "SalesByModel":

❶ Right-click the **Graph2 icon** to display the Graphs page SpeedMenu, as shown in Figure 5-15. Notice that this SpeedMenu has a different set of commands from the SpeedMenu you see in a spreadsheet page.

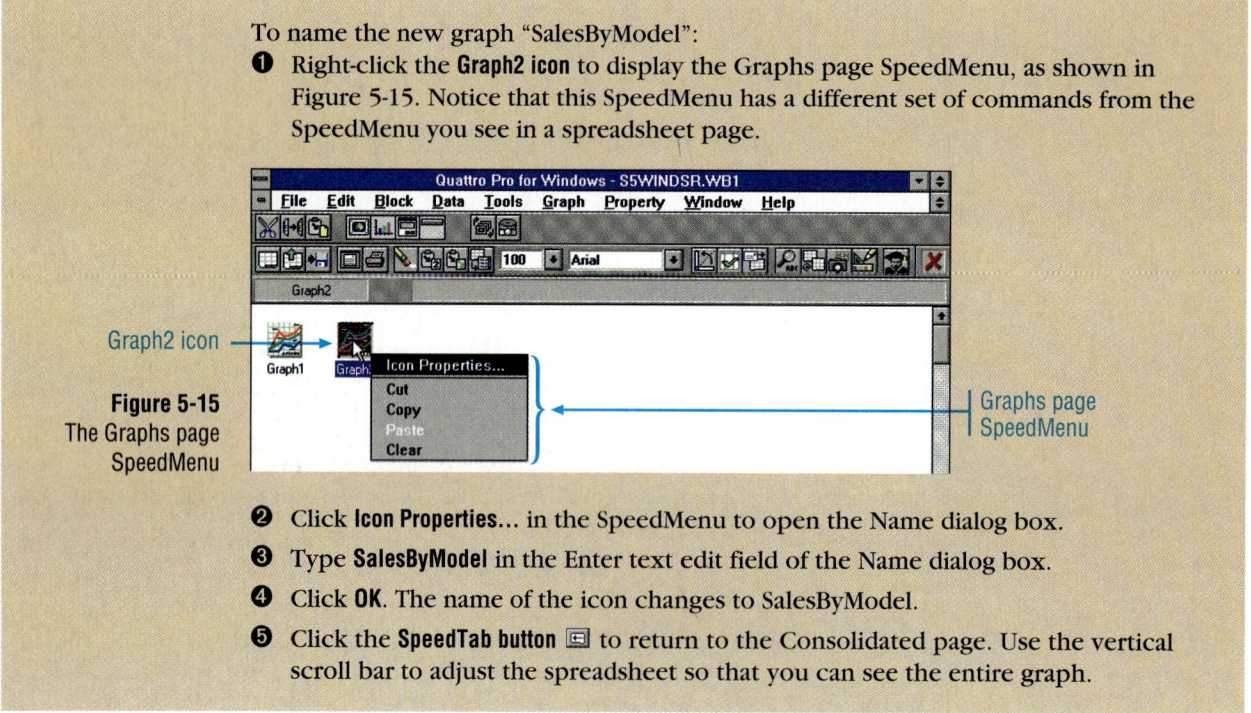

Graph2 icon

Figure 5-15
The Graphs page
SpeedMenu

Graphs page
SpeedMenu

❷ Click **Icon Properties...** in the SpeedMenu to open the Name dialog box.

❸ Type **SalesByModel** in the Enter text edit field of the Name dialog box.

❹ Click **OK**. The name of the icon changes to SalesByModel.

❺ Click the **SpeedTab button** to return to the Consolidated page. Use the vertical scroll bar to adjust the spreadsheet so that you can see the entire graph.

Carl notices that there are some problems with the graph. The title "Windsor Stove Sales by Model" is too large to fit the graph, and the numbers on the y-axis are not formatted as currency. Carl also decides that he wants to bold the y-axis and x-axis titles so they'll stand out more. To edit the graph, Carl will use the graph window.

The Graph Window

The **graph window** is used for editing and annotating graphs. To open the graph window for a floating graph, you double-click anywhere on the floating graph. To open the graph window for a nonfloating (or a floating) graph, you switch to the Graphs page then double-click the icon for the graph. You can also use the Edit... command on the Graph menu to select the graph from the list of graphs in the notebook.

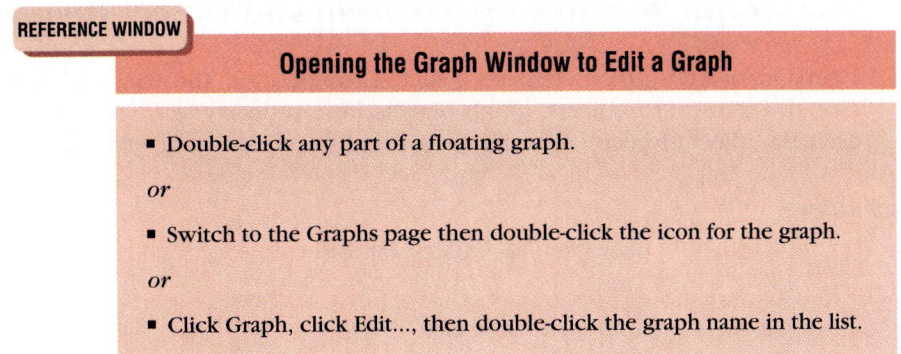

REFERENCE WINDOW

Opening the Graph Window to Edit a Graph

- Double-click any part of a floating graph.

or

- Switch to the Graphs page then double-click the icon for the graph.

or

- Click Graph, click Edit..., then double-click the graph name in the list.

Now Carl opens the graph window so that he can edit his line graph.

To open the graph window for the line graph:
❶ Double-click anywhere on the line graph. The graph appears in the S5WINDSR.WB1:SalesByModel graph window, as shown in Figure 5-16.

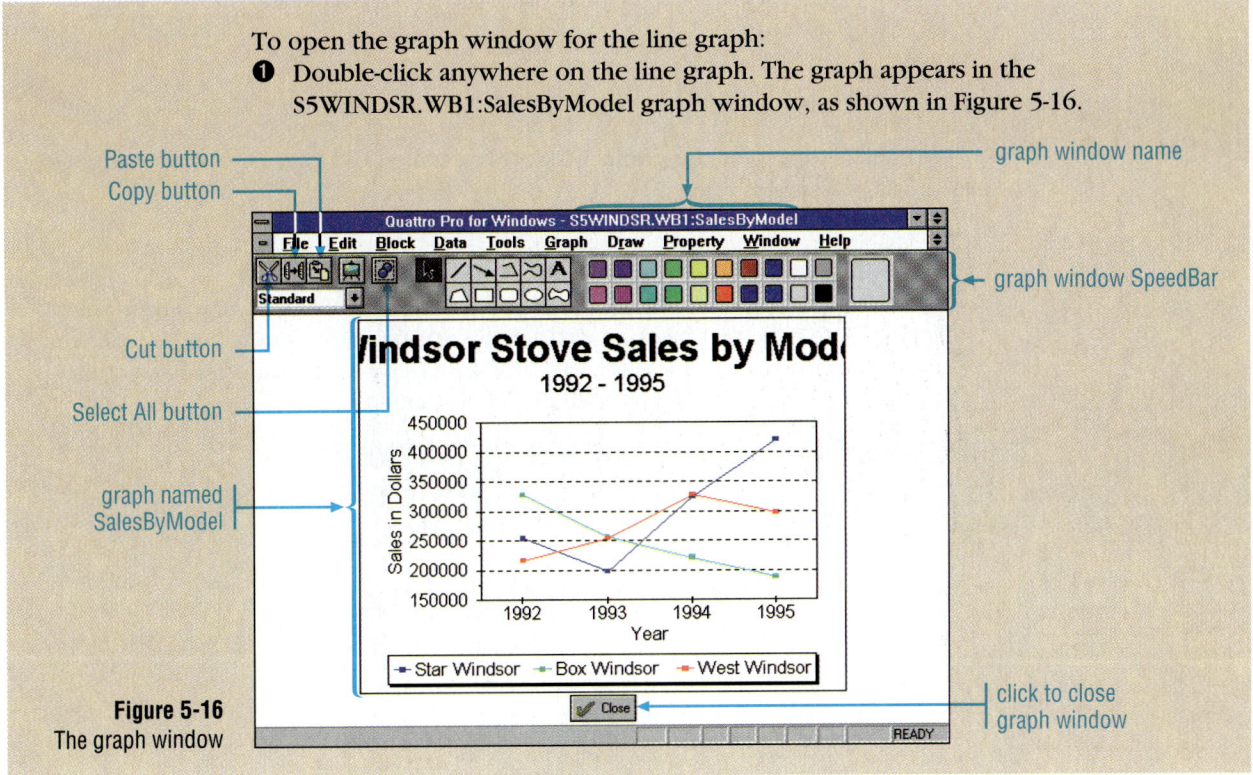

Figure 5-16
The graph window

The Close button in the graph window closes the graph window and returns you to the notebook window. The graph window has its own SpeedBar, as shown in Figure 5-16.

The graph window SpeedBar includes Cut, Copy, and Paste buttons that copy and move graph elements between graphs. The Select All button makes most of the elements in the graph active at the same time so that you can apply formatting changes to all of them at once. The only elements Quattro Pro doesn't include are data series (for example, the lines in a line graph).

To change the font size of the graph title so that it fits on the graph, Carl will have to change the graph title property setting by using an Object Inspector.

The Graph Window SpeedMenu and Object Inspectors

Many Quattro Pro graph elements—such as titles, axes, and lines—are **graph objects**. Like all Quattro Pro objects, graph objects have property settings that you can change using an Object Inspector available from the graph window SpeedMenu.

REFERENCE WINDOW

Using the Graph Object Inspector

- Right-click the graph object you want to change.

- Click Properties... on the SpeedMenu.

- To modify a property, click the property name in the Object Inspector menu. Adjust any settings you want in the settings pane to the right of the menu.

- Click OK.

Carl needs to display the graph window SpeedMenu so that he can open the Object Inspector for the graph title.

To display the graph window SpeedMenu:

❶ Right-click the graph title. The graph window SpeedMenu appears, as shown in Figure 5-17. Notice that black square handles appear above and below the title and subtitle. When you select a graph object, Quattro Pro places these handles on or around the object to indicate which object is selected.

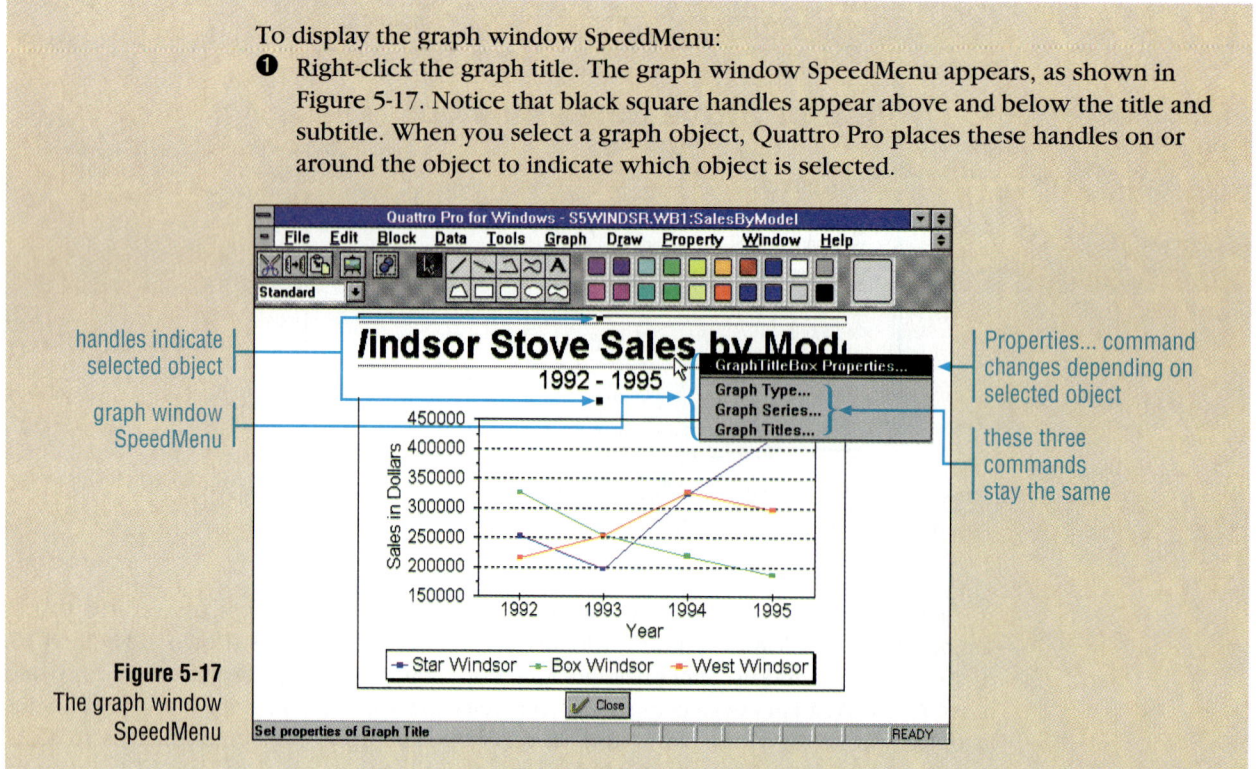

handles indicate selected object

graph window SpeedMenu

Properties... command changes depending on selected object

these three commands stay the same

Figure 5-17
The graph window SpeedMenu

The SpeedMenu you see in the graph window is different from the SpeedMenu you see in the notebook window. The graph window SpeedMenu always contains the three commands Graph Type..., Graph Series..., and Graph Titles.... The Properties... command at the top of the SpeedMenu varies according to the graph object you selected. The SpeedMenu for the title, shown in Figure 5-16, contains Graph TitleBox Properties... as its first command. This opens the Object Inspector for the graph title. The Properties... command always opens the appropriate Object Inspector.

Changing the Title Font Size

Carl will use the Graph Title Object Inspector to change the font size of the title text.

To change the title text font size:

❶ Make sure the SpeedMenu is still open. If it isn't, right-click the graph title to open the SpeedMenu. The first command on the SpeedMenu should be Graph TitleBox Properties....

❷ Click **Graph TitleBox Properties...** in the SpeedMenu. The Graph Title Object Inspector appears.

   TROUBLE?   If the Graph Subtitle Object Inspector appears, you right-clicked the subtitle instead of the title. Click Cancel then repeat Steps 1 and 2.

❸ Click **Text Font** in the Object Inspector menu to display the title font settings pane, as shown in Figure 5-18. (Your list of typefaces and point sizes may be different depending upon the fonts installed on your system.)

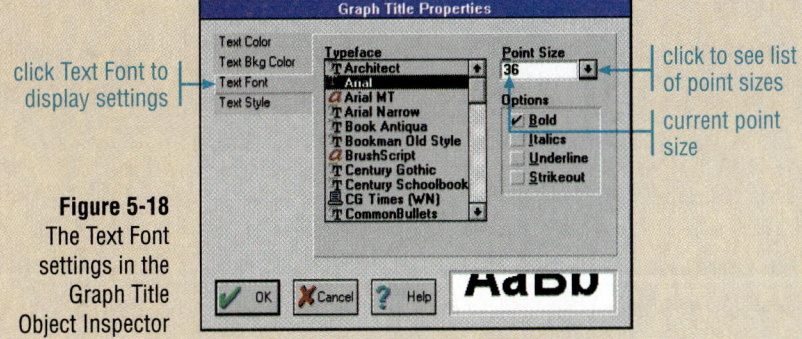

Figure 5-18
The Text Font
settings in the
Graph Title
Object Inspector

❹ Click the **Point Size drop-down list arrow** to display the list of font sizes.

❺ Click **30** in the list of font sizes.

❻ Click **OK**. The entire title is now visible in your graph.

Now Carl wants to change the format of the numbers on the y-axis to currency.

Formatting of the Y-Axis Values

Quattro Pro considers all elements of the y-axis, except for the y-axis title, to be the same object, called the primary or **y1-axis**. The term "y1-axis" is used because some Quattro Pro graphs add a secondary y-axis on the right side of a graph, called the **y2-axis**. The y1-axis object includes the values, the vertical line segment representing the axis, and the tick marks on the line segment.

Carl uses the Y-Axis Object Inspector to format the values on the y-axis.

To format the values on the y-axis as currency with no decimal places:
❶ Right-click any y-axis value to open the SpeedMenu.
❷ Click **Y-Axis Properties…** in the SpeedMenu. The Y-Axis Object Inspector appears.
❸ Click **Numeric Format** in the Object Inspector menu to display the numeric format settings pane.
❹ Click the **Currency radio button**. The spin box for setting the number of decimal places appears.
❺ Click the **spin box down arrow** until 0 appears in the edit field.
❻ Click **OK**. The y-axis values now appear as currency with no decimal places.

Now Carl wants to make the axis titles appear in bold.

Changing the Font Style of the Axis Titles

The y-axis and x-axis titles are both graph objects. The axis title settings are controlled by the Axis Title Object Inspector, which Carl uses to change the font style of the y-axis and x-axis titles.

To bold the y-axis and x-axis titles:
❶ Right-click the y-axis title, **Sales in Dollars**, to open the SpeedMenu.
❷ Click **Axis Title Properties…** in the SpeedMenu. The Axis Title Object Inspector appears.
❸ Click **Text Font** in the Object Inspector menu to display the title font settings.
❹ In the Options settings, click **Bold**.
❺ Click **OK**.
Now Carl changes the font style of the x-axis title.
❻ Right-click the x-axis title, **Year**, to open the SpeedMenu.
❼ Click **Axis Title Properties…** in the SpeedMenu. The Axis Title Object Inspector appears.
❽ Repeat Steps 3 through 5 to change the font style of the x-axis title.

Carl has completed making his planned changes. As he views the graph, however, he decides to use a heavy black line to represent the Star Windsor sales to draw attention to this stove. He also decides to use different shapes for the data markers for the three lines.

Formatting Lines in a Line Graph

You can change the appearance of the lines and data markers on a graph. Quattro Pro provides a variety of line colors, styles (such as dashed lines and dotted lines), and weights, or thicknesses. You can also customize data marker colors and shapes.

Each graph line is an object with its own Object Inspector, which you use to apply the formats you want. Carl wants to make the graph line for Star Windsor sales a thick, black line. He also decides to use different data markers for each of the stoves: a solid square for the Star Windsor, a solid circle for the Box Windsor, and a solid triangle for the West Windsor. The different-shaped data markers help to distinguish the different data series, which is especially useful if you have a monochrome monitor or if you print your graphs on a printer without color capability.

To format the Star Windsor line:

❶ Right-click the blue line that represents the sales trend for the Star Windsor stove. The SpeedMenu appears.

   TROUBLE? If you are using a monochrome monitor, refer to Figure 5-23 for the location of the line representing Star Windsor sales.

❷ Click **Line Series Properties...** in the SpeedMenu. The Line Series Object Inspector appears.

❸ Click **Line Color** in the Object Inspector menu to open the Line Color settings pane, shown in Figure 5-19.

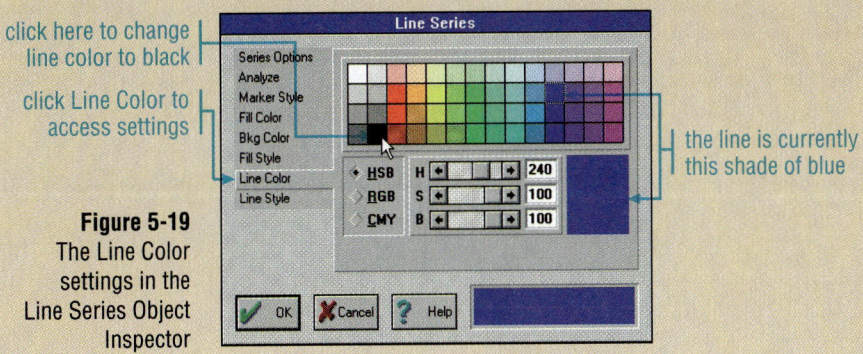

click here to change line color to black

click Line Color to access settings

Figure 5-19
The Line Color settings in the Line Series Object Inspector

the line is currently this shade of blue

❹ In the color palette, click the black square shown in Figure 5-19 to change the line color to black.

❺ Click **Line Style** in the Object Inspector menu to open the Line Style settings pane.

❻ Click the black line shown in Figure 5-20 to change the line thickness.

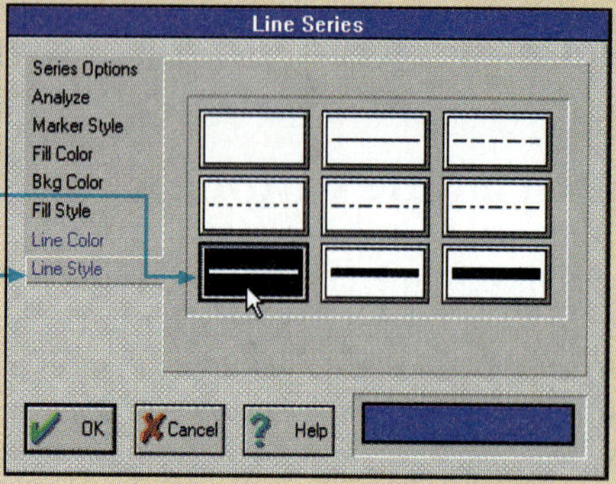

click Line Style to
access settings

click here to change
to thicker line style

Figure 5-20
The Line Style
settings in the
Line Series
Object Inspector

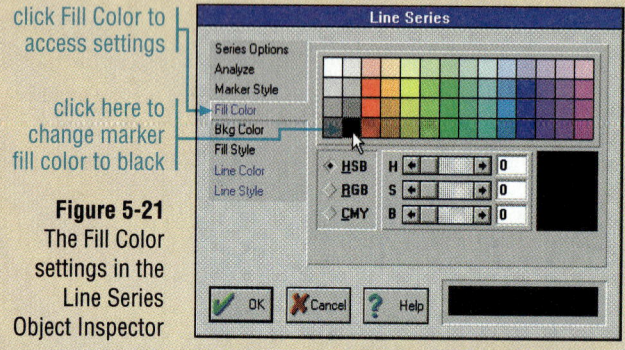

The Star Windsor data series already uses a solid square as the data marker, but the color needs to be changed to black.

❼ Click **Fill Color** in the Object Inspector menu. The Fill Color settings pane appears.

❽ In the color palette, click the black square shown in Figure 5-21 to change the marker fill color to black.

click Fill Color to
access settings

click here to
change marker
fill color to black

Figure 5-21
The Fill Color
settings in the
Line Series
Object Inspector

❾ Click **OK**. The line for Star Windsor sales now appears with the formatting changes.

Next, Carl needs to change the marker styles of the data series for the Box Windsor and West Windsor sales.

To format the Box Windsor and West Windsor lines:

❶ Right-click the green line that represents the sales trend for the Box Windsor stove. The SpeedMenu appears.

TROUBLE?   If you are using a monochrome monitor, refer to Figure 5-23 for the location of the line representing Box Windsor sales.

❷ Click **Line Series Properties…** in the SpeedMenu. The Line Series Object Inspector appears.

❸ Click **Marker Style** in the Object Inspector menu to open the Marker Style settings pane.

❹ Click the solid circle shown in Figure 5-22 to change the marker style to a solid circle.

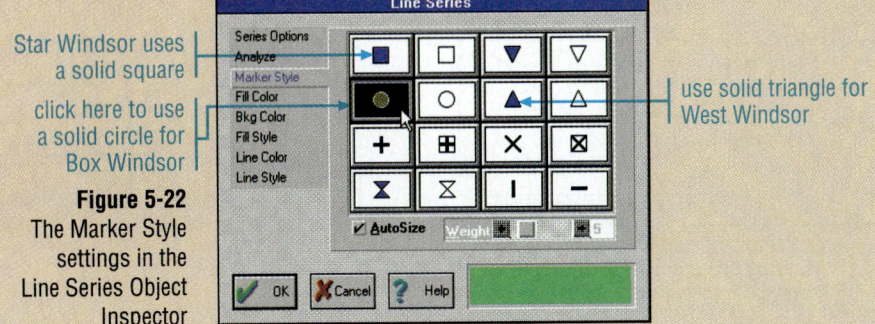

Star Windsor uses a solid square

click here to use a solid circle for Box Windsor

use solid triangle for West Windsor

Figure 5-22
The Marker Style settings in the Line Series Object Inspector

❺ Click **OK**.

❻ Right-click the red line that represents the sales trend for the West Windsor stove. The SpeedMenu appears.

TROUBLE?   If you are using a monochrome monitor, refer to Figure 5-23 for the location of the line representing West Windsor sales.

❼ Click **Line Series Properties…** in the SpeedMenu to open the Line Series Object Inspector.

❽ Click **Marker Style** in the Object Inspector menu to open the Marker Style settings pane.

❾ Click the solid triangle shown in Figure 5-22 to change the marker style to a solid triangle.

❿ Click **OK**. The graph now shows the different marker styles for the three lines.

Carl has completed changing and formatting the graph. He is ready to close the graph window and save the notebook.

To close the SalesByModel graph window and save the changes made to the notebook:

❶ Click **Close** at the bottom of the graph window. Quattro Pro closes the graph window, and the notebook window reappears. The floating graph in the spreadsheet now looks like Figure 5-23.

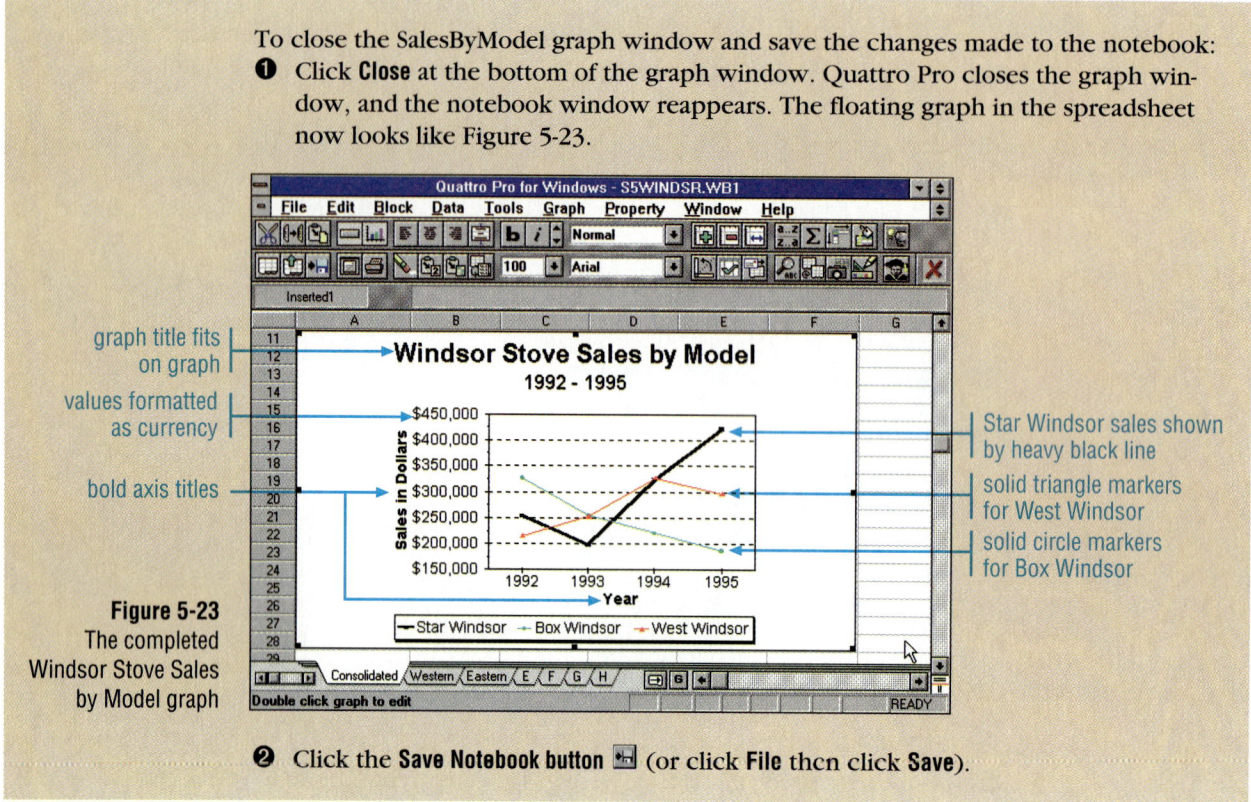

graph title fits
on graph

values formatted
as currency

bold axis titles

Figure 5-23
The completed
Windsor Stove Sales
by Model graph

Star Windsor sales shown
by heavy black line

solid triangle markers
for West Windsor

solid circle markers
for Box Windsor

❷ Click the **Save Notebook button** 🔲 (or click **File** then click **Save**).

Carl decides to print a copy of the graph.

Printing a Graph

You can print floating graphs as part of the spreadsheet page, or you can print just the graph.

To print the line graph:

❶ Click the Windsor Stove Sales by Model graph to select it.

❷ Click the **Print button** 🔲 on the Productivity Tools SpeedBar to display the Graph Print dialog box.

❸ Click **Print** in the Graph Print dialog box to print the graph, shown in Figure 5-24.

❹ Click the **Save Notebook button** 🔲 (or click **File** then click **Save**) to update the print settings in the notebook file.

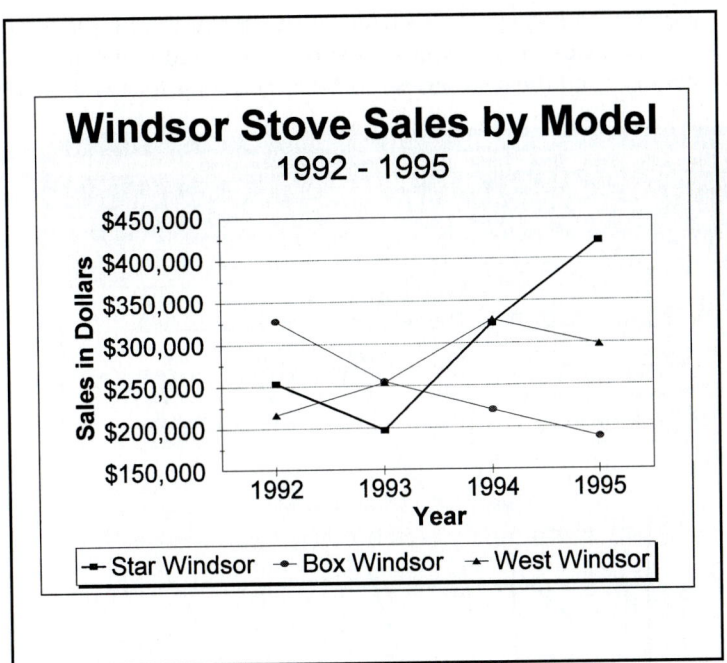

Figure 5-24
The printed graph

Carl's line graph illustrates the sales of the three stove models over the past four years. He is pleased with how this graph looks, but he also wants graphs that focus on the sales of the three stove models in the most recent year, 1995, so he will work on those next.

If you want to take a break and resume the tutorial at a later time, you can exit Quattro Pro by double-clicking the Control menu box in the upper-left corner of the screen. When you resume the tutorial, launch Quattro Pro, maximize the Quattro Pro and NOTEBK1.WB1 windows, place your Student Disk in the disk drive, and then open the S5WINDSR.WB1 notebook file. You can then continue with the tutorial.

■   ■   ■

Carl wants to show that the West Windsor and Star Windsor stove models currently generate more of the total Windsor stove sales than the Box Windsor model. Because a bar graph is an effective way to compare values, Carl decides to create a bar graph to show the sales for each model in 1995.

Creating a Bar Graph

Quattro Pro's **bar graph** type uses vertical bars to represent data values. Quattro Pro can also rotate a bar graph so that the bars are horizontal, which is useful when you have long x-axis labels. Both the bar graph and the rotated bar graph are excellent choices if you want to show comparisons.

Figure 5-25 shows Carl's sketch of the bar graph he plans to make comparing 1995 stove model sales. He examines his spreadsheet and notes that the data labels are located in column A, and the data series for the bar graph is located in column E.

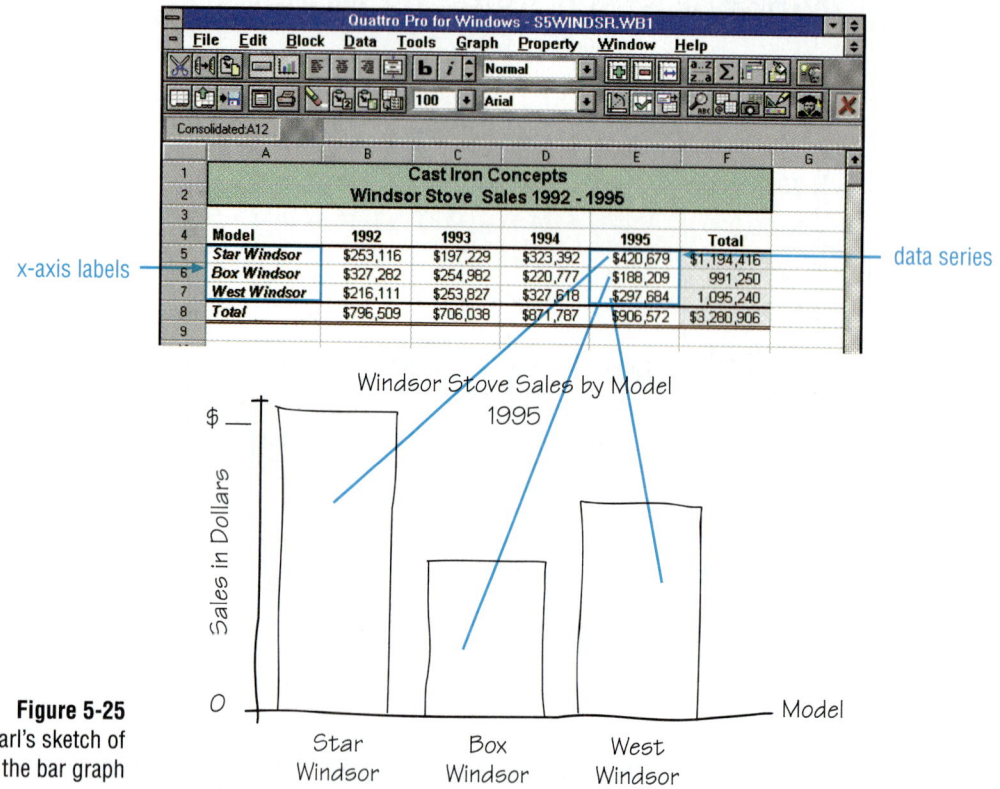

Figure 5-25
Carl's sketch of the bar graph

Instead of using the Graph Expert, Carl will create the bar graph using Quattro Pro's Graph New command, which gives more flexibility for defining graph elements.

Using the Graph New Command to Create a Graph

You can create graphs by using the New command on the Graph menu (this command is also available as New Graph... on the spreadsheet SpeedMenu). When you create a graph using the Graph New command, you enter the block addresses of the x-axis series, the legend series, and the data series using the Graph New dialog box, shown in Figure 5-26. This gives you more control over the selection of the blocks that Quattro Pro uses in the graph.

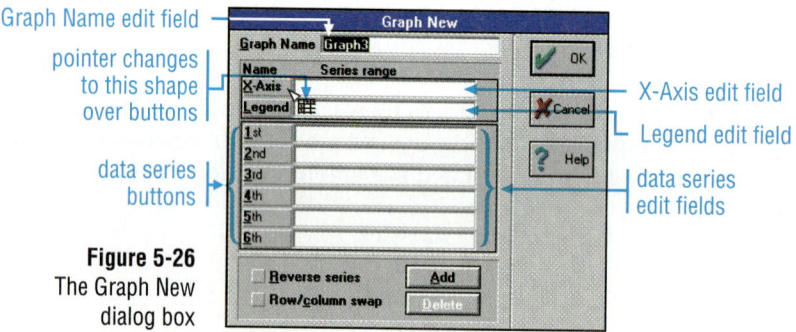

Figure 5-26
The Graph New dialog box

As shown in Figure 5-26, the pointer changes to ⛏ when it is over the X-Axis button, the Legend button, or one of the data series buttons. Whenever the pointer changes to ⛏ over a button, clicking that button reduces the dialog box to a title bar above the input line. You can then highlight the block on the spreadsheet that you want for the corresponding edit field. When you press [Enter], Quattro Pro inserts the block address into the edit field, and the dialog box reappears.

REFERENCE WINDOW

Creating a Graph Using the Graph New Command

- Click Graph then click New....

- If you want to change the suggested graph name, edit the name in the Graph Name edit field.

- To enter the block addresses for the x-axis series, the legend series, and the data series, click the series button, use the pointer to highlight the block in the spreadsheet, then press [Enter].

  or

  Type the block address in the series edit field.

- When you have entered the block addresses of all the series you want to use in the graph, click OK.

Carl is ready to create his bar graph, which he decides to name "Sales1995."

To create the bar graph using the Graph New command:
❶ Make sure that the Consolidated page is the active page.
❷ Make sure the Windsor Stove Sales by Model floating graph is *not* selected. If it is, click any cell outside the graph to deselect it.
❸ Press [**Home**] to move to cell A1.
❹ Click **Graph** then click **New...**. The Graph New dialog box appears, and the Graph Name edit field is active. Press [**Backspace**] to delete Quattro Pro's suggested name, then type **Sales1995**.
❺ Click the **X-Axis button**, then highlight cells A5 through A7. When you click the X-Axis button, the Graph New dialog box shrinks to a title bar to facilitate your highlighting the cells, as shown in Figure 5-27.

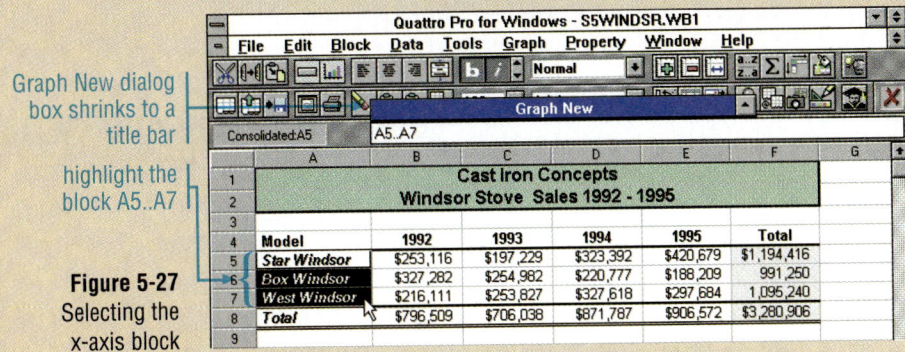

Graph New dialog box shrinks to a title bar

highlight the block A5..A7

Figure 5-27
Selecting the x-axis block

❻ Press [Enter]. The Graph New dialog box reappears with the block A5..A7 entered as the x-axis series, as shown in Figure 5-28.

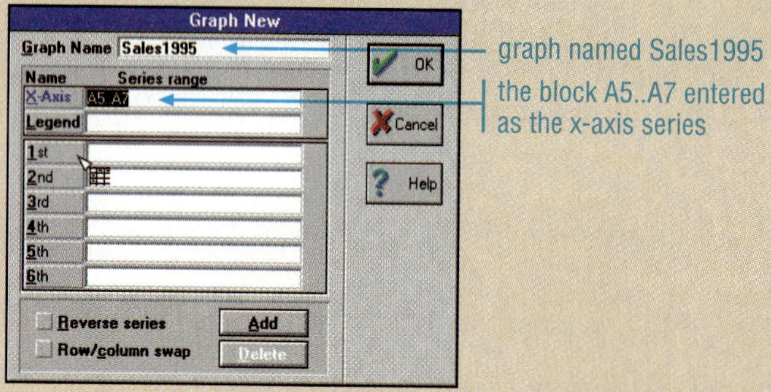

Figure 5-28
The x-axis series entered in the Graph New dialog box

❼ Click the **1st button**, then highlight cells E5 through E7. Because there is only one data series in this graph, you don't need a legend.

❽ Press [Enter]. The Graph New dialog box reappears with the block E5..E7 entered as the 1st data series.

❾ Click **OK**. Quattro Pro creates the graph in the Sales1995 graph window, as shown in Figure 5-29.

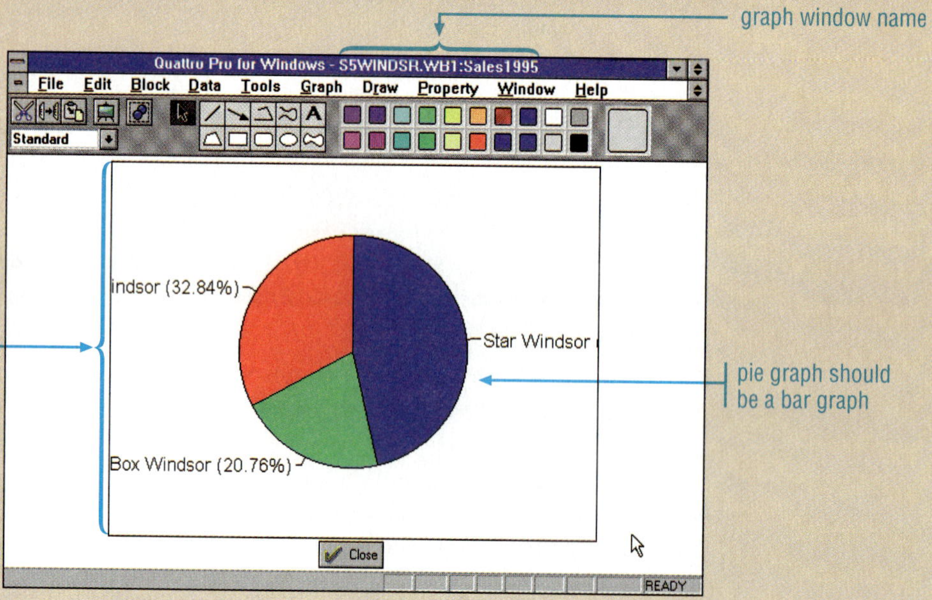

Figure 5-29
The Sales1995 graph

Carl immediately sees a problem with the graph. He wants a bar graph, but Quattro Pro created a pie graph. He needs to change the graph type to a bar graph.

Selecting Graph Types

When you create a graph, Quattro Pro chooses a graph type based on the number of data series and the number of values in each series. You can change the graph type by using the Graph Types dialog box, available through either the Type... command on the Graph Menu or the Graph Type... command on the graph window SpeedMenu.

REFERENCE WINDOW

Selecting a Graph Type

- Right-click anywhere on the graph to open the graph window SpeedMenu, then click Graph Type... (or click Graph then click Type...).
- Select the graph type (line graph, bar graph, etc.) you want to use.
- Select the variation (2-D, 3-D, Rotated, Combination) you want to use.
- Click OK.

Carl changes the graph to a two-dimensional bar graph.

To change the graph to a two-dimensional bar graph:
❶ Right-click anywhere within the graph borders to open the graph window SpeedMenu.
❷ Click **Graph Type...**. The Graph Types dialog box appears, as shown in Figure 5-30.

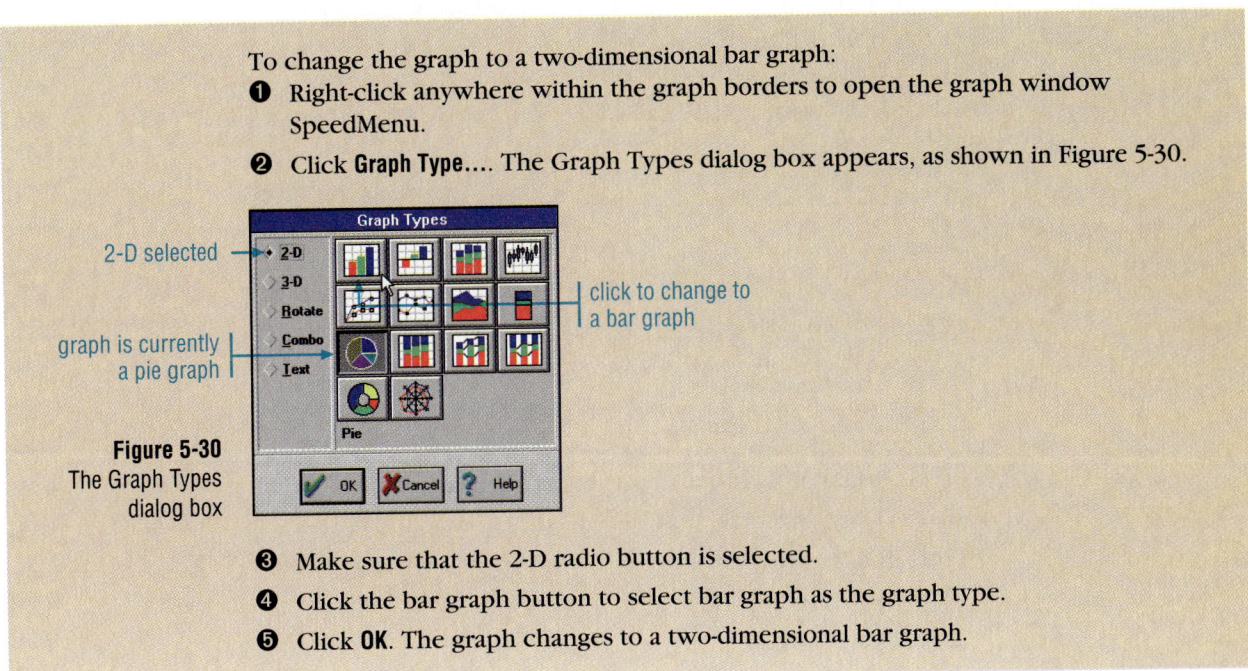

2-D selected

click to change to a bar graph

graph is currently a pie graph

Figure 5-30
The Graph Types dialog box

❸ Make sure that the 2-D radio button is selected.
❹ Click the bar graph button to select bar graph as the graph type.
❺ Click **OK**. The graph changes to a two-dimensional bar graph.

Carl now has a bar graph, but the graph doesn't have any titles. Carl needs to add the main title, the subtitle, and the axis titles.

Adding Graph Titles

You can add or edit graph titles by using the Graph Titles dialog box, available through either the Titles... command on the Graph Menu or the Graph Titles... command on the graph window SpeedMenu.

Adding or Editing Graph Titles

- Right-click anywhere on the graph to open the graph window SpeedMenu, then click Graph Titles... (or click Graph then click Titles...). The Graph Titles dialog box appears.

- For each title you want to add or edit, click the edit field for that title, then type or edit the title.

- When the titles are complete, click OK.

Carl wants to use "Windsor Stove Sales by Model" as the main title, "1995" as the subtitle, "Model" as the x-axis title, and "Sales in Dollars" as the y-axis title.

To add the titles to the bar graph:

❶ Right-click anywhere on the graph to open the graph window SpeedMenu.

❷ Click **Graph Titles...**. The Graph Titles dialog box appears, as shown in Figure 5-31.

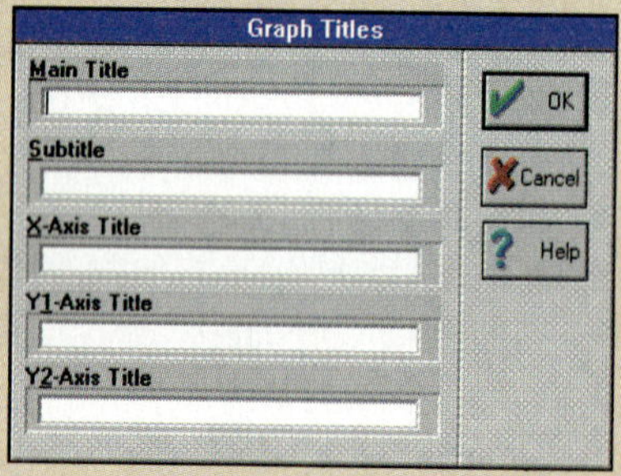

Figure 5-31
The Graph Titles dialog box

❸ Type **Windsor Stove Sales by Model** in the Main Title edit field.

❹ Press **[Tab]** to select the Subtitle edit field, then type **1995**.

❺ Press **[Tab]** to select the X-Axis Title edit field, then type **Model**.

❻ Press **[Tab]** to select the Y1-Axis Title edit field, then type **Sales in Dollars**.

❼ Click **OK**. The graph appears, as shown in Figure 5-32.

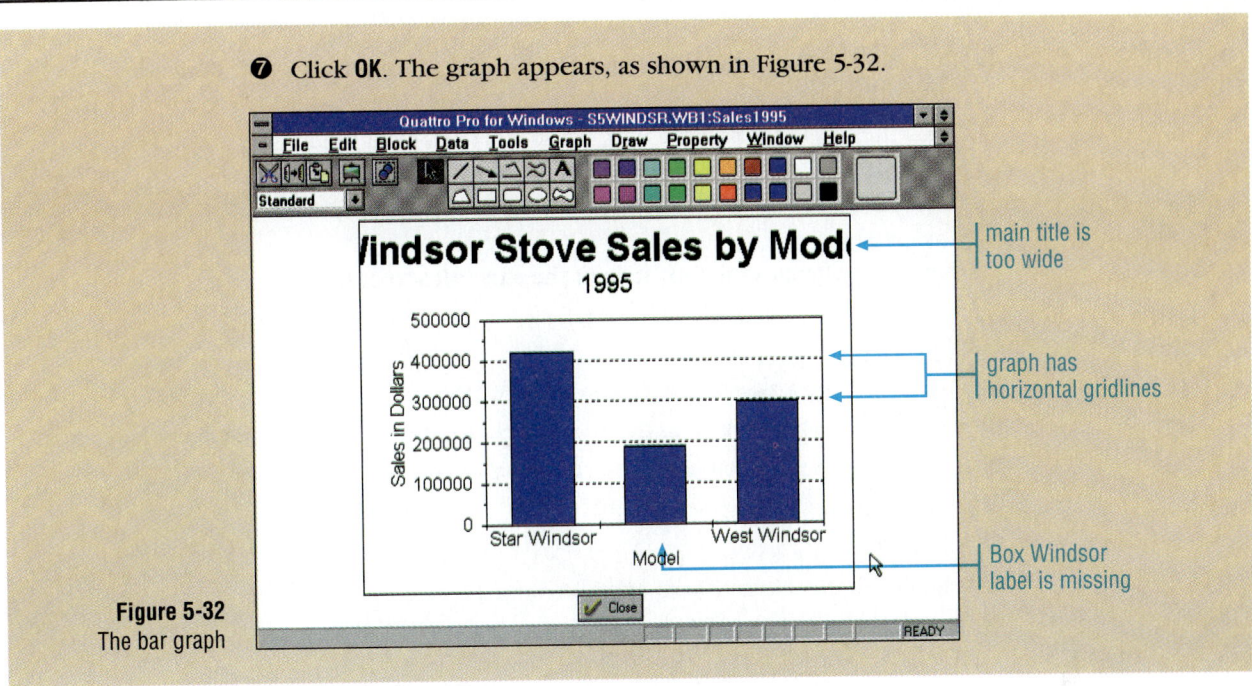

Figure 5-32
The bar graph

Carl notices that he needs to make some corrections. The main title is too wide, and the Box Windsor label doesn't appear on the x-axis. Carl also wants to format this graph to match the appearance of his line graph by bolding the axis titles and formatting the y-axis labels as currency. He also decides that he doesn't want to use the horizontal grid lines currently on the graph, and that the x-axis labels should also be bold.

First, Carl changes the title font size.

To change the title font size:
❶ Right-click the graph title to open the SpeedMenu.
❷ Click **Graph TitleBox Properties...** in the SpeedMenu. The Graph Title Object Inspector appears.
❸ Click **Text Font** in the Object Inspector menu to display the title font settings.
❹ Click the **Point Size drop-down list arrow** to display the list of font sizes.
❺ Click **30** in the list of font sizes.
❻ Click **OK**.

Next, Carl formats the values on the y-axis.

To format the values on the y-axis:
❶ Right-click any y-axis values to open the SpeedMenu.
❷ Click **Y-Axis Properties...** in the SpeedMenu to open the Y-Axis Object Inspector.
❸ Click **Numeric Format** in the Object Inspector menu to display the numeric format settings.

❹ Click the **Currency radio button**. The spin box for setting the number of decimal places appears.

❺ Click the **spin box down arrow** until 0 appears in the edit field.

❻ Click **OK**.

Now Carl changes the font style of the axis titles to bold.

To bold the axis titles:

❶ Right-click the y-axis title to open the SpeedMenu.

❷ Click **Axis Title Properties...** in the SpeedMenu to open the Axis Title Object Inspector.

❸ Click **Text Font** in the Object Inspector menu to display the title font settings.

❹ In the Options settings, click **Bold**.

❺ Click **OK**.

❻ Right-click the x-axis title to open the SpeedMenu.

❼ Repeat Steps 2 through 5 above.

Carl needs to fix the problem of the missing Box Windsor label on the x-axis. He also wants the x-axis labels to be bold so that they will stand out.

Formatting the X-Axis Labels

The Box Windsor label is missing because the label font size is too large. When x-axis labels overlap each other, Quattro Pro displays only as many labels as it can fit. You can change the font size and other properties of the x-axis elements by using the X-Axis Object Inspector. The x-axis object includes the axis labels, the horizontal line segment representing the axis, and the tick marks on the line segment.

Carl uses the X-Axis Object Inspector to format the x-axis labels.

To format the labels on the x-axis:

❶ Right-click the x-axis just below the horizontal line representing the axis. The SpeedMenu appears.

TROUBLE? If all three labels already appear on your graph, you should still complete these steps, but you might want to use a different point size from the size specified in Step 5.

TROUBLE? If the first SpeedMenu command is "Graph Pane Properties..." or "Bar Series Properties...," you clicked *above* the x-axis. If the first SpeedMenu command is "Axis Title Properties..." or "Graph Setup and Background Properties...," you clicked *below* the x-axis. In either case, press [Esc] then repeat Step 1.

❷ Click **X-Axis Properties...** in the SpeedMenu to open the X-Axis Object Inspector.

❸ Click **Text Font** in the Object Inspector menu to display the font settings.

❹ Click the **Point Size drop-down list arrow** to display the list of font sizes.

❺ Click **14** in the list of font sizes.

TROUBLE? Your monitor might require a different font size. Experiment until the x-axis labels look like those in Figure 5-33.

❻ In Options, click **Bold**.

❼ Click **OK**.

❽ Click the lower-left corner of the graph to deselect the x-axis. The graph now appears as shown in Figure 5-33.

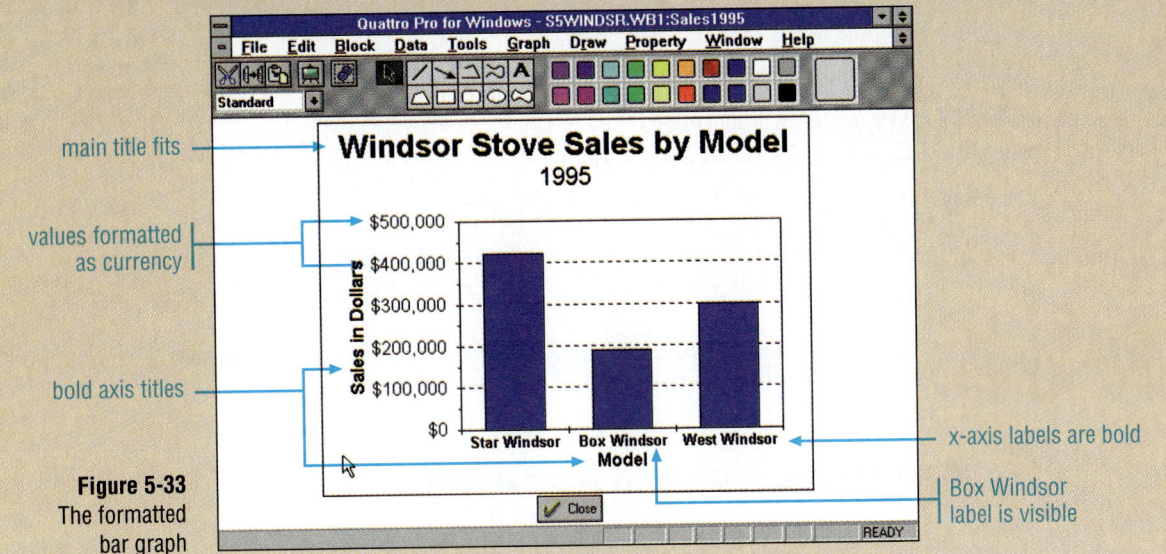

main title fits

values formatted as currency

bold axis titles

Figure 5-33
The formatted bar graph

x-axis labels are bold

Box Windsor label is visible

Carl is now ready to remove the horizontal grid lines from the graph.

Formatting Horizontal Grid Lines

Horizontal grid lines are the horizontal lines that start at the tick marks on the y-axis and extend across the graph. They are useful for determining the value of a data marker on a line graph, or the bar height on a bar graph. Sometimes you'll want to include grid lines in a graph, but other times you'll decide that they only add visual clutter.

Grid lines can start at both major tick marks (tick marks next to axis labels) and minor tick marks (tick marks without axis labels). You control the display of horizontal grid lines by using the Major Grid Style and Minor Grid Style settings in the Y-Axis Object Inspector.

Carl removes the horizontal grid lines from the bar graph.

To remove the horizontal grid lines from the bar graph:

❶ Right-click any y-axis values to open the SpeedMenu.

❷ Click **Y-Axis Properties...** in the SpeedMenu. The Y-Axis Object Inspector appears.

❸ Click **Major Grid Style** in the Object Inspector menu to display the settings for the major tick mark grid lines.

❹ Click the **Line style check box**, as shown in Figure 5-34, to display the grid line examples.

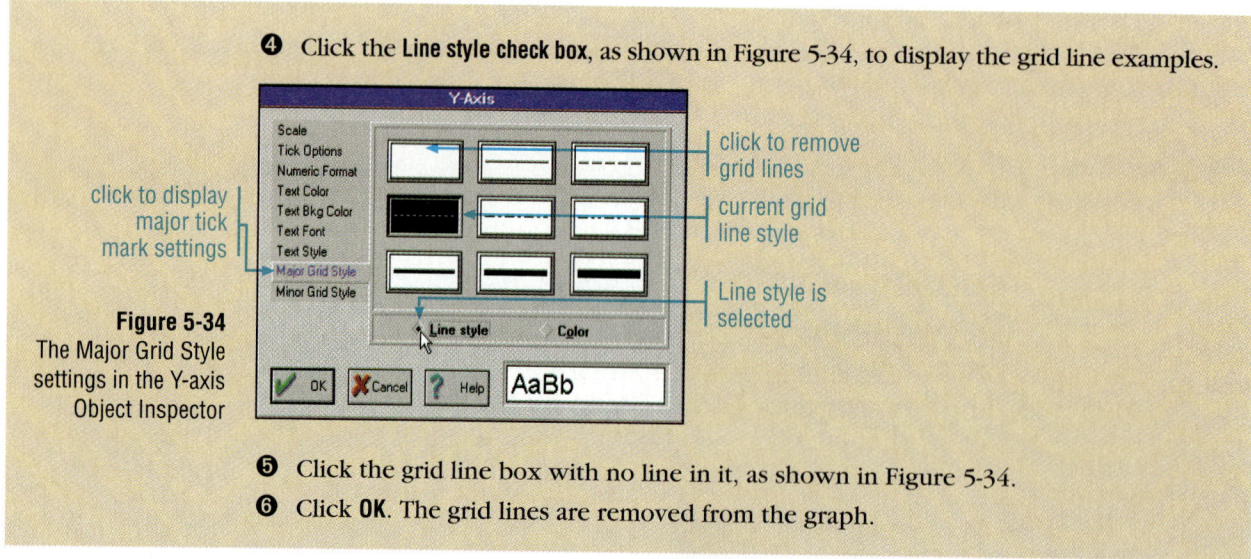

Figure 5-34
The Major Grid Style
settings in the Y-axis
Object Inspector

❺ Click the grid line box with no line in it, as shown in Figure 5-34.

❻ Click **OK**. The grid lines are removed from the graph.

Looking at the graph, Carl decides that it would be more effective if he changed the color of the bars and the background area behind them.

Formatting Bars in a Bar Graph

You can format the appearance of bars in a bar graph using the Bar Series Object Inspector. For example, you can change bar width, the amount of space between bars, bar color, and the shading pattern that is used in the bars.

Carl decides to use a shade of green as the bar color.

To change the bar color to green:

❶ Right-click any bar to open the SpeedMenu.

❷ Click **Bar Series Properties...** in the SpeedMenu to open the Bar Series Object Inspector.

❸ Click **Fill Color** in the Object Inspector menu to display the color palette for the bar fill color, as shown in Figure 5-35.

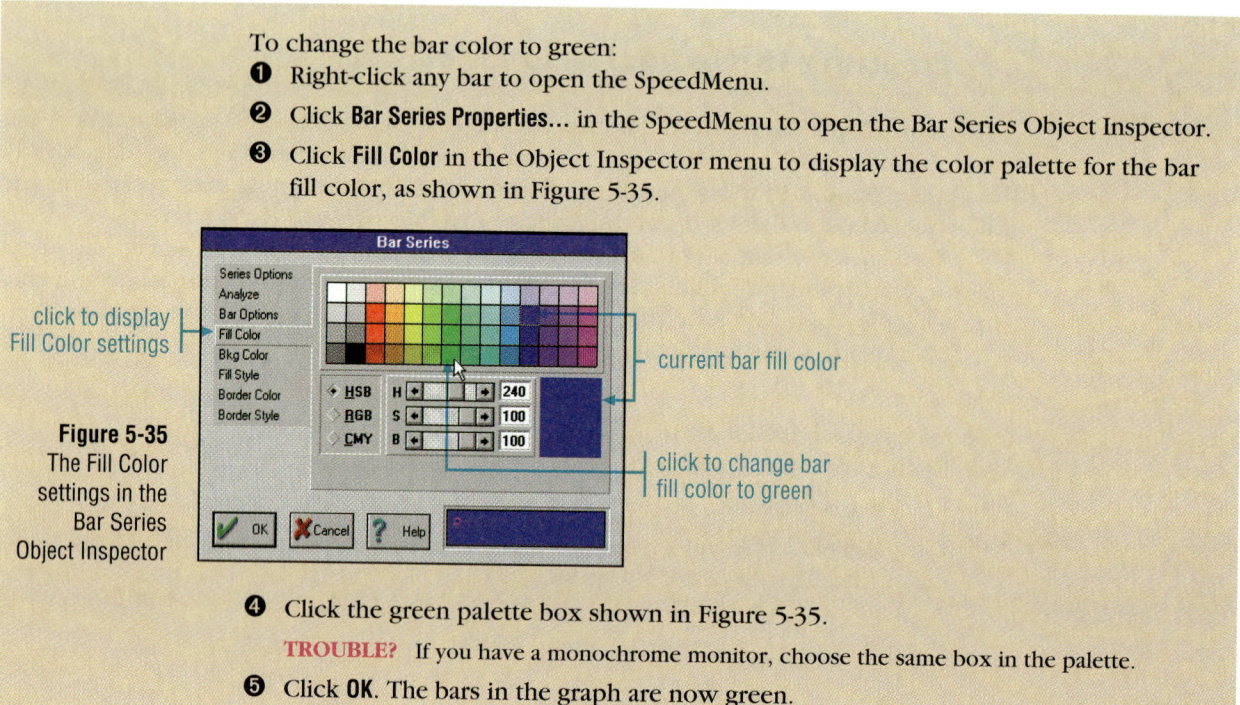

Figure 5-35
The Fill Color
settings in the
Bar Series
Object Inspector

❹ Click the green palette box shown in Figure 5-35.

TROUBLE?   If you have a monochrome monitor, choose the same box in the palette.

❺ Click **OK**. The bars in the graph are now green.

Now Carl wants to change the background color.

Formatting the Graph Pane

The rectangular area that contains the graph is called the **graph pane**. Using the Graph Pane Object Inspector, you can format the appearance of the graph pane by changing the pane color, the shading pattern used in the pane, and the type of line border around the pane.

Carl decides to use a light shade of yellow as the background color in the graph pane.

To change the background color to light yellow:
- ❶ Right-click anywhere in the graph pane *except* on a bar. The SpeedMenu appears.
- ❷ Click **Graph Pane Properties…** in the SpeedMenu. The Graph Pane Object Inspector appears.
- ❸ Click **Fill Style** in the Object Inspector menu to display the fill style settings.
- ❹ Click the **Solid radio button**.
- ❺ Click **Fill Color** in the Object Inspector menu to display the color palette for the fill color, as shown in Figure 5-36. Make sure you've selected Fill Color, not Bkg Color.

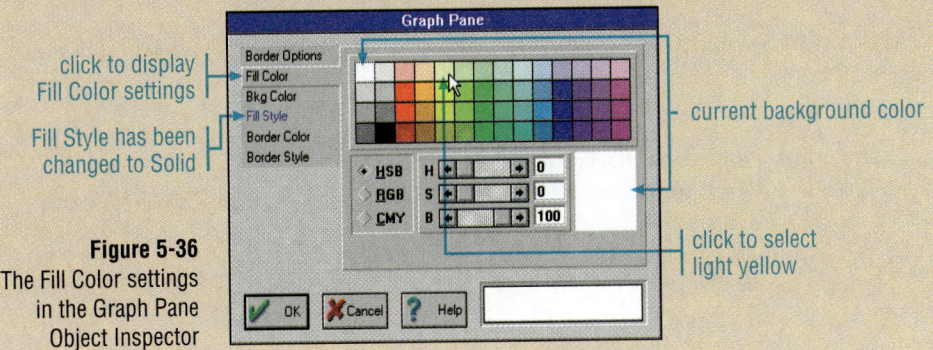

click to display
Fill Color settings

Fill Style has been
changed to Solid

current background color

click to select
light yellow

Figure 5-36
The Fill Color settings
in the Graph Pane
Object Inspector

- ❻ Click the light yellow palette box shown in Figure 5-36.

    TROUBLE? If you have a monochrome monitor, choose the same box in the palette.
- ❼ Click **OK**.

❽ Click the lower-left corner of the graph to deselect the x-axis. The graph pane background color is now light yellow, as shown in Figure 5-37.

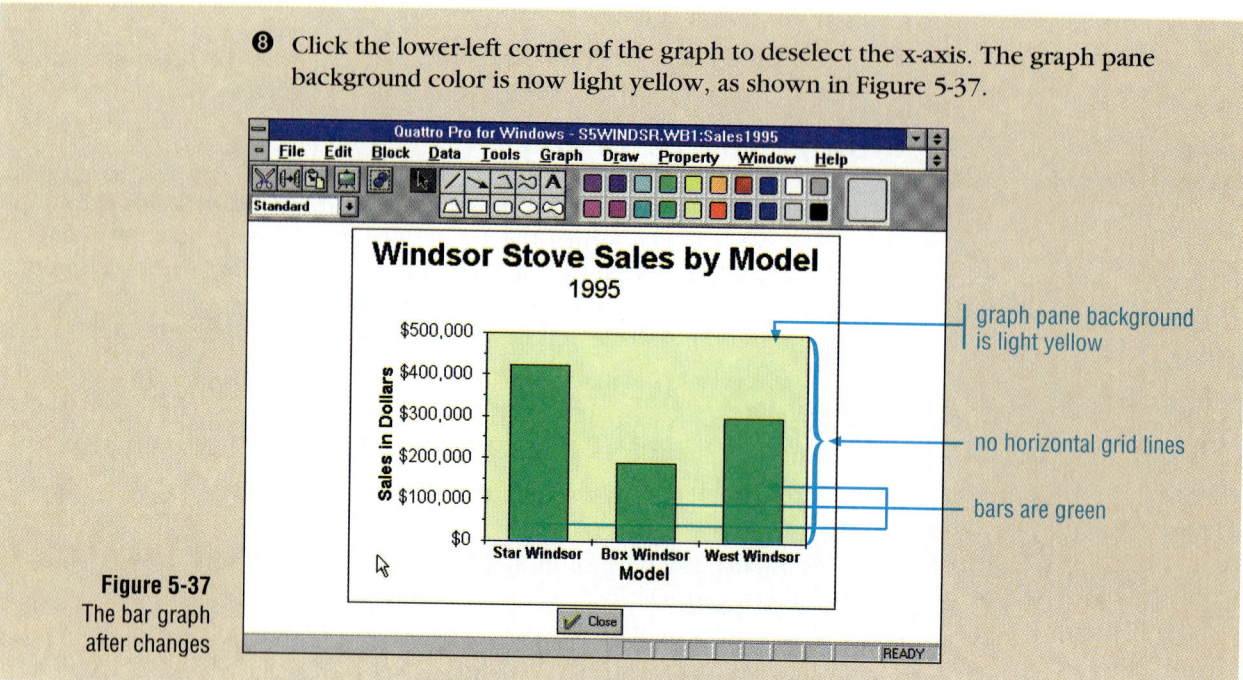

Figure 5-37
The bar graph
after changes

Carl is satisfied with his bar graph. He closes the graph window, and then decides to save the notebook.

To close the graph window and save the notebook:
❶ Click **Close** at the bottom of the graph window. Quattro Pro closes the graph window, and the notebook window reappears.
❷ Click the **Save Notebook button** ⊞ (or click **File** then click **Save**).

Because Carl created his bar graph using Graph New rather than the Graph Expert, it is *not* a floating graph, so it appears as a graph icon on the Graphs page. To see his graph, Carl would use the Graph View command or the graph window. Carl decides that he wants to display the graph on the Consolidated page next to the data it represents.

Inserting a Previously Created Graph on a Spreadsheet

If you create a graph using the Graph New command, you can insert a copy of the graph as a floating graph on a spreadsheet. The original graph remains available through its icon on the Graphs page.

REFERENCE WINDOW

Inserting a Graph on a Spreadsheet

- Select the notebook page where you want to insert the graph.
- Click Graph then click Insert.
- In the Select Graph list, double-click the name of the graph you want to insert (or click the graph name, then click OK).
- Using the pointer, outline the area for the graph in the spreadsheet.

Carl inserts the bar graph on the Consolidated spreadsheet in cells A31 through F48.

To insert the bar graph:
 ❶ Make sure the Consolidated page is active.

 ❷ Scroll the spreadsheet until cell A31 is visible in the upper-left corner of the notebook window, then click cell **A31** to make it the active cell.

 ❸ Click **Graph** then click **Insert**. The Graph Insert dialog box appears, as shown in Figure 5-38.

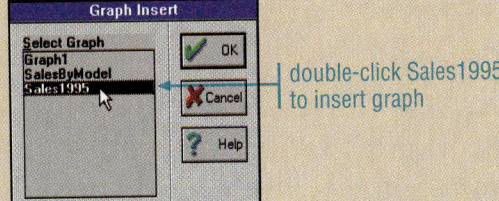

Figure 5-38
The Graph Insert
dialog box

double-click Sales1995
to insert graph

 ❹ In the Select Graph list, double-click **Sales1995**. The pointer changes to ▟▙.

 ❺ Drag the pointer to outline the block in the spreadsheet from A31 through F48. Release the mouse button. The floating graph appears over block A31..F48, as shown in Figure 5-39.

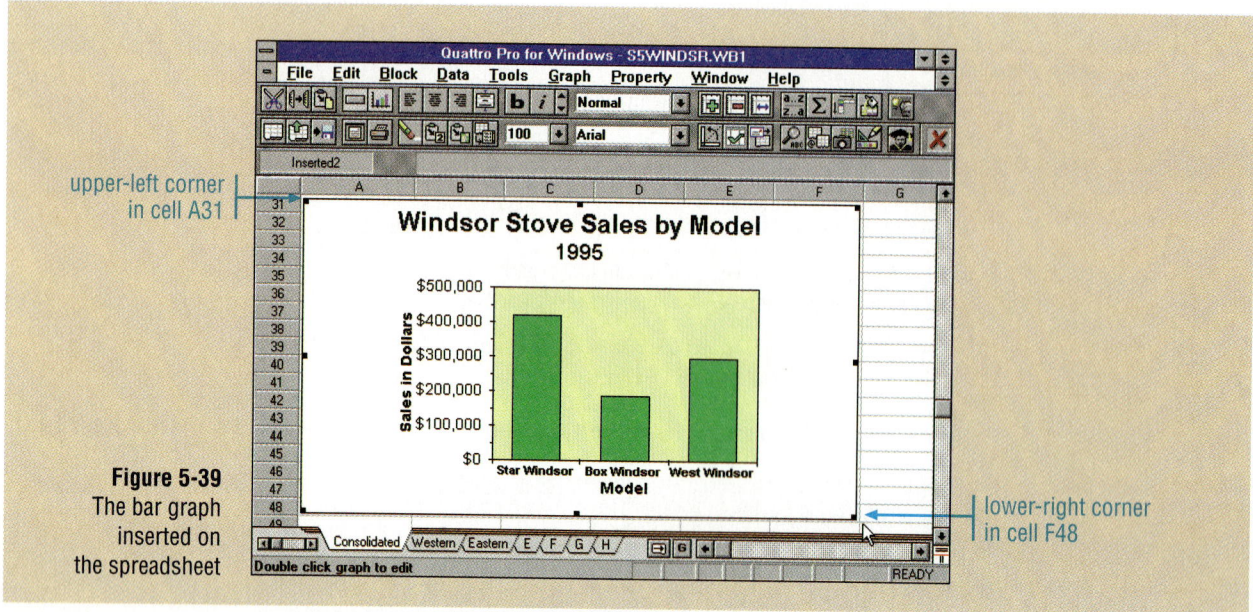

upper-left corner in cell A31

lower-right corner in cell F48

Figure 5-39
The bar graph inserted on the spreadsheet

Carl is pleased with the appearance of the floating graph, so he saves the notebook with the inserted bar graph.

To save the notebook:

❶ Deselect the graph by clicking any cell outside the graph to remove the black square handles and make a spreadsheet cell active.

❷ Press [Home] to make cell A1 the active cell.

❸ Click the **Save Notebook button** 📇 (or click **File** then click **Save**).

If you want to take a break and resume the tutorial at a later time, you can exit Quattro Pro by double-clicking the Control menu box in the upper-left corner of the screen. When you resume the tutorial, launch Quattro Pro, maximize the Quattro Pro and NOTEBK1.WB1 windows, place your Student Disk in the disk drive, and then open the S5WINDSR.WB1 notebook file. You can then continue with the tutorial.

Now that he has completed the graphs, Carl considers the overall layout of the Consolidated spreadsheet and his printing requirements. He has two graphs arranged vertically, and he wants to print the spreadsheet with the two graphs. Carl highlights the block containing the spreadsheet and the two graphs, and then previews the printout.

To preview the printout of the spreadsheet and the graphs:

❶ Make sure the Consolidated page is active.

❷ Highlight cells A1 through F50, which include the spreadsheet and the two graphs.

❸ Click the **Print Preview button** ▣ on the Productivity Tools SpeedBar. The preview of the printout appears, as shown in Figure 5-40. Notice that only part of the bar graph appears on the first page.

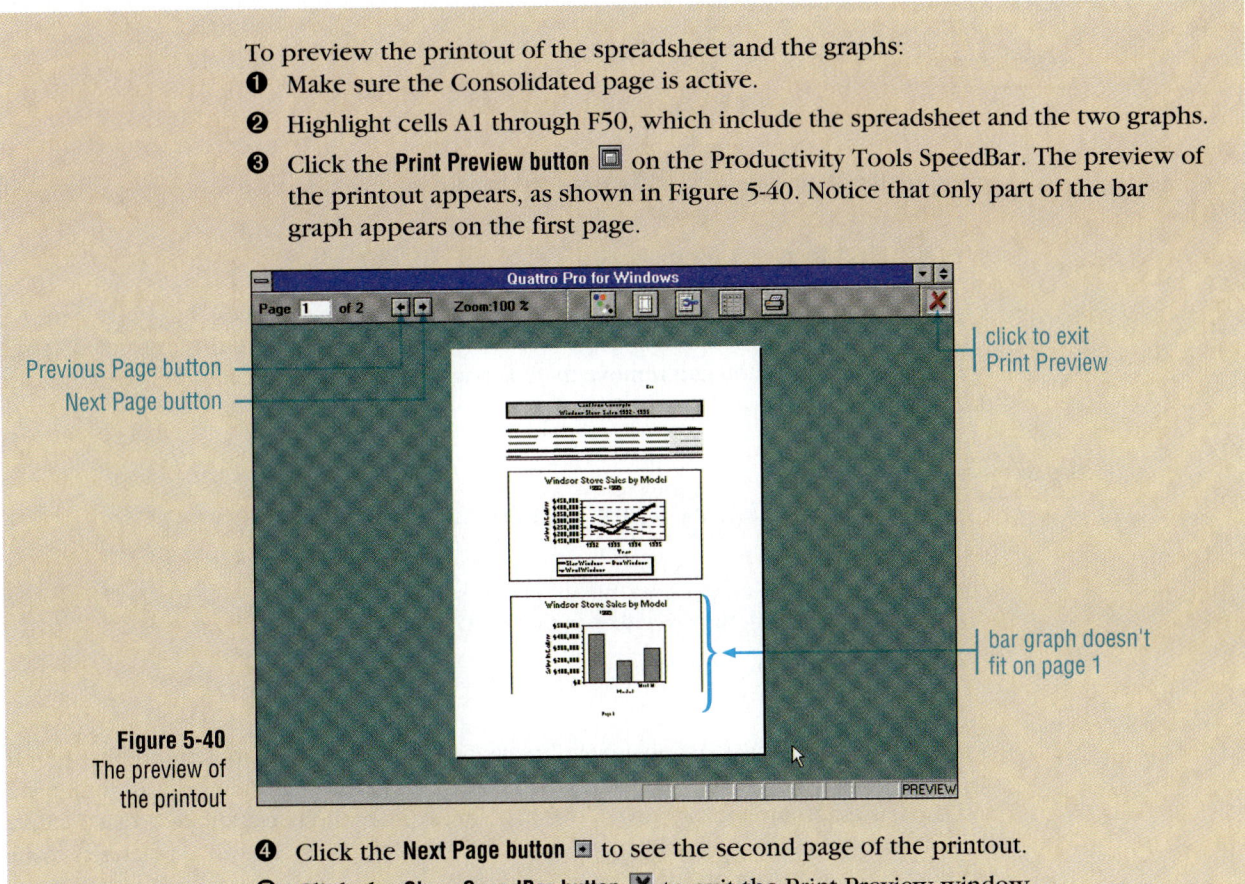

Previous Page button

Next Page button

click to exit Print Preview

bar graph doesn't fit on page 1

Figure 5-40
The preview of the printout

❹ Click the **Next Page button** ▣ to see the second page of the printout.

❺ Click the **Close SpeedBar button** ✖ to exit the Print Preview window.

Because the bar graph is split between two pages, Carl decides to insert manual page breaks in the spreadsheet.

Inserting Manual Page Breaks

A large Quattro Pro spreadsheet might contain hundreds of rows and columns. When it is printed, it must be split up to fit onto individual pages of paper using **page breaks** to mark where pages begin and end. Quattro Pro automatically inserts page breaks in the spreadsheet based on the paper size and margin settings.

You can specify **manual page breaks**, which are different from the automatic page breaks Quattro Pro inserts, using the Insert Break command on the Block menu. When you insert a manual page break, Quattro Pro adds a row containing the page break character to the spreadsheet. Each manual page break appears on the spreadsheet as a pair of colons (::). This new row is never printed, and you should not enter any labels, data, or formulas in a row containing a page break character.

Inserting Manual Page Breaks

- Click the cell in column A of the row where you want to insert a page break.
- Click Block then click Insert Break.

When you insert a manual page break, Quattro Pro adjusts the automatic page breaks as necessary. You can remove manual page breaks, but you can't remove automatic page breaks.

Deleting Manual Page Breaks

- Right-click the row border (row number) of the row containing the page break to select the row and open the SpeedMenu.
- Click Delete... in the SpeedMenu.

Carl decides to insert manual page breaks between the line graph and the bar graph, and after the bar graph. The spreadsheet and the line graph will then print on one page, and the bar graph on another page. The page break after the bar graph is a visual indication on the spreadsheet of where the page ends. If Carl ever adds more material to his spreadsheet, it will start on a new page.

To add manual page breaks:
❶ Scroll the spreadsheet until you can see row 30.
❷ Click cell **A30** to make it the active cell.

❸ Click **Block** then click **Insert Break** to add the first page break. A new row 30 is inserted in the spreadsheet with a page break character (::) in cell A30, as shown in Figure 5-41.

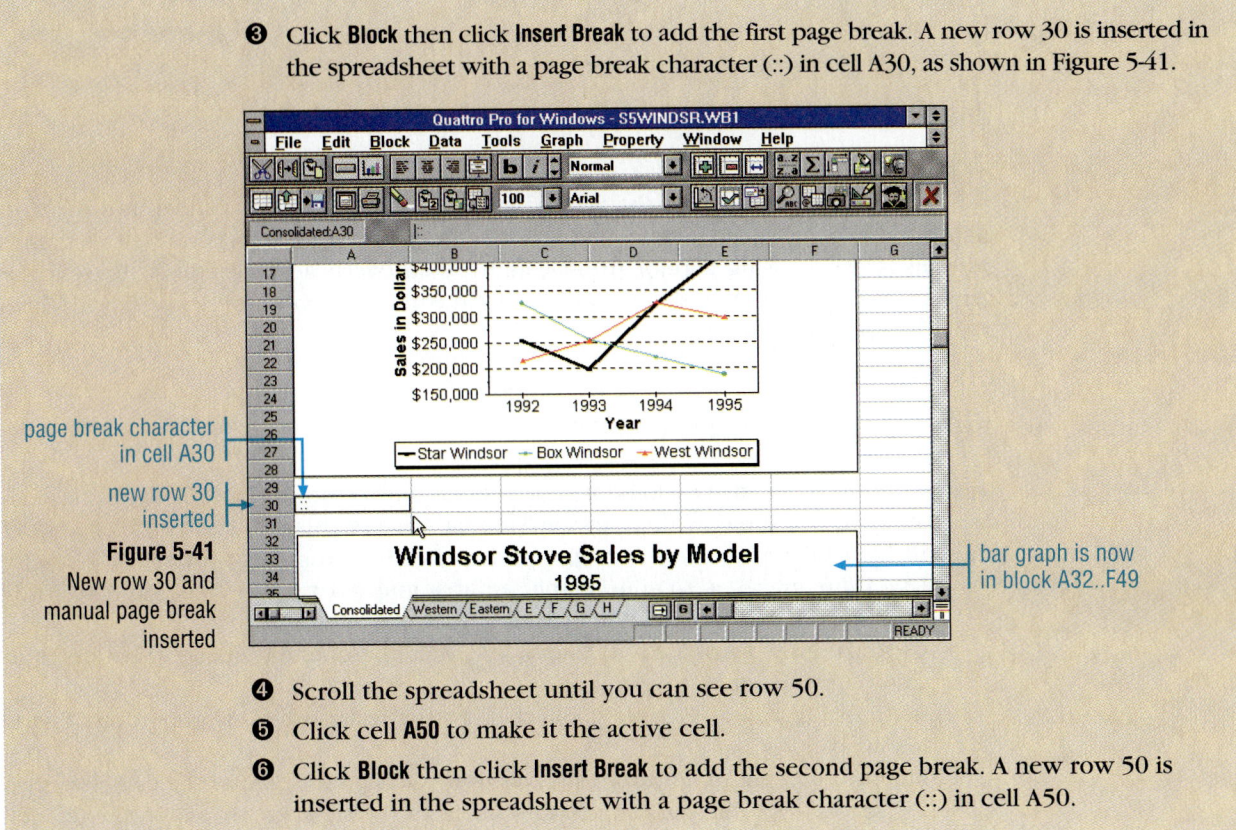

page break character in cell A30

new row 30 inserted

Figure 5-41
New row 30 and manual page break inserted

bar graph is now in block A32..F49

❹ Scroll the spreadsheet until you can see row 50.

❺ Click cell **A50** to make it the active cell.

❻ Click **Block** then click **Insert Break** to add the second page break. A new row 50 is inserted in the spreadsheet with a page break character (::) in cell A50.

Now Carl looks at the print preview again to make sure that the first page will contain the spreadsheet and the line graph, and the second page will contain the bar graph.

To preview the printout:

❶ Highlight the block A1..F50. Notice that this block includes row 50 with the manual page break.

❷ Click the **Print Preview button** 🔲 on the Productivity Tools SpeedBar. The Print Preview screen appears displaying the first page of the spreadsheet. Notice that only the spreadsheet and the line graph are on the page.

❸ Click the **Next Page button** 🔳 on the Print Preview SpeedBar to view the second page of the spreadsheet. Notice that this page contains the bar graph.

❹ Click the **Close SpeedBar button** ✖ to close the Print Preview screen.

Carl saves the notebook with the new print block settings and the manual page breaks.

To save the notebook:
❶ Click cell **A1** to make it the active cell.
❷ Click the **Save Notebook button** 🖫 (or click **File** then click **Save**).

Carl will print copies of the two pages containing the spreadsheet and the two graphs to hand out at the meeting. He will also print individual copies of the two graphs on transparencies using a color printer, and use an overhead projector to present the graphs at the meeting. You don't need to print the graphs now because you'll print them in the Tutorial Assignments.

Tips for Creating Graphs

Quattro Pro includes many additional graph types and graph options. You will have an opportunity to use some of these in the Tutorial Assignments and Case Problems. Here are some hints to help you construct graphs that effectively represent your data.

- Use a line graph, a 3-D line graph, an area graph, or a 3-D area graph to show trends or changes over a period of time.
- Use a bar graph, a rotated bar graph, a 3-D bar graph, or a rotated 3-D bar graph to show comparisons.
- Use a pie graph or a 3-D pie graph to show the relationship or proportion of parts to a whole.
- Before you begin to construct a graph using Quattro Pro, locate the cell blocks on the spreadsheet that contain the data series you want to graph, and locate the cell block that contains the x-axis labels. Then draw a sketch showing the x-axis, x-axis title, x-axis category labels, y-axis, y-axis labels, and data series.
- Design the graph so that viewers can understand the main point at first glance. Too much detail can make a graph difficult to interpret.
- Plot consistent categories of data. For example, if you want to plot monthly income, do not include the year-to-date income as one of the data points.
- Every graph should have a descriptive title, a title for the x-axis, a title for the y-axis, and x-axis labels.

In this tutorial Carl created a line graph and a bar graph. He modified the graphs by formatting text, adding titles, removing grid lines, formatting graph lines, and selecting graph colors. Finally, he manually inserted page breaks to position each graph appropriately on the spreadsheet printout.

Questions

1. Identify each of the numbered elements in Figure 5-42.

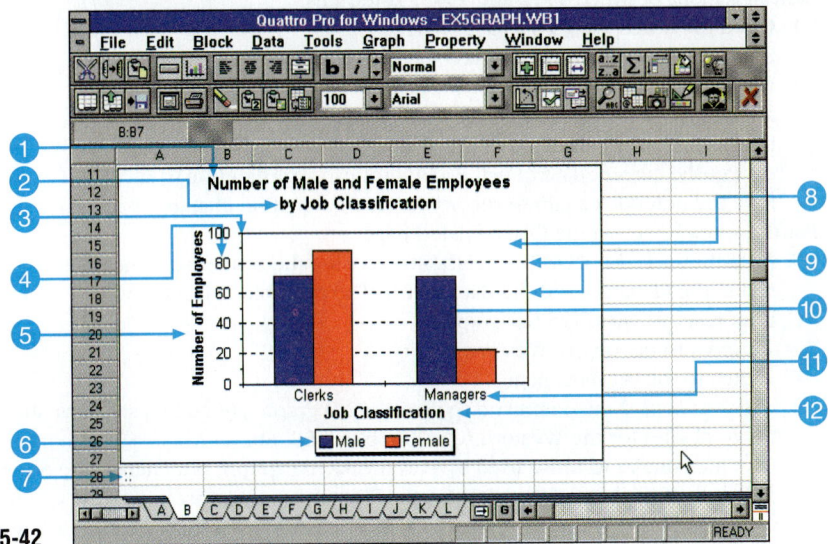

Figure 5-42

2. Write a one-sentence definition for each of the following terms:
   - data point
   - data marker
   - data series
   - floating graph
   - Graphs page
   - graph icon
   - graph window
3. List the graph types that are effective for showing change over time.
4. List the graph types that are effective for showing comparisons.
5. When do you need to open the graph window?
6. How many data series can you show using a pie graph?
7. Suppose you wanted to use the data from Figure 5-4 to graph the sales trend for the Star Windsor stove.
   a. How many data series would you graph?
   b. Which block contains the data series?
   c. Which block contains the x-axis labels?
   d. Would you include cell F5 in the data block? Why or why not?
8. Describe the advantage of using a 3-D graph rather than a 2-D graph.
9. Describe how to use manual page breaks.
10. Look for examples of graphs in magazines, books, or the textbooks you use for other courses. Select one graph and photocopy it.
    a. Label each of the graph components.
    b. Write a one-page evaluation of the effectiveness of the graph.
11. Use your library resources to research the topic of graphing. Compile a one- to two-page list of tips for creating effective graphs. Make sure you include a bibliography.

Tutorial Assignments

Carl wants to create two line graphs that show the change in total stove sales in the Western and Eastern regions between 1992 and 1995. To do this:

1. Open the notebook T5WINDSR.WB1.
2. Save the notebook using the new name S5GRAPHS.WB1.
3. Revise the documentation on the Documentation page as follows:
   a. Change the filename in cell B4 to S5GRAPHS.WB1.
   b. Put your name in cell B5.
   c. Put the current date in cell B6 (do not use an @function).
4. Save the notebook again to record the documentation changes.

For the spreadsheet on the Consolidated page:

5. Print the spreadsheet with the graphs, revising the header so it includes your name, the filename, and the date. (*Hint:* The print block is A1..F50.)
6. Print just the Sales1995 bar graph.

For the spreadsheet on the Western page:

7. Switch to the Western page.
8. Use the Graph New command to create a 2-D graph named "West1" that shows the total sales for the Western region in block B8..E8.
9. Use titles similar to those used by Carl for his line graph, but change the title to reflect the fact that this graph is for the Western region only.
10. Create a floating graph by inserting West1 on the Western page between rows 11 and 28.
11. Use the graph window to make the graph line thick with triangular data markers.
12. Insert a manual page break between the West1 graph and the spreadsheet for the Western region sales above it.
13. Print the Western region sales spreadsheet with the graph.
14. Print just the West1 graph.

For the spreadsheet on the Eastern page:

15. Switch to the Eastern page.
16. Use the Graph New command to create a line graph named "East1" that shows the total sales for the Eastern region in block B8..E8.
E 17. Make East1 a 3-D line graph. (*Hint:* Quattro Pro calls a 3-D line graph a ribbon graph.)
18. Use titles similar to those used by Carl for his line graph, but change the title to reflect the fact that this graph is for the Eastern region only.
19. Create a floating graph by inserting East1 on the Eastern page between rows 11 and 28.
20. Insert a manual page break between the East1 graph and the spreadsheet for the Eastern region sales above it.
21. Print the Eastern region sales spreadsheet with the graph.
22. Print just the East1 graph.
23. Save the notebook.
24. Submit copies of your printouts.

Case Problems

1. Graphing Production Data at TekStar Electronics

Julia Backes is the executive assistant to the president of TekStar Electronics, a manufacturer of consumer electronics. Julia is compiling the yearly manufacturing reports. She has collected the production totals for each of TekStar's four manufacturing plants and has created a notebook containing the production totals. Julia has asked you to help her create a 3-D pie graph and a bar graph to accompany the report.

1. Open the notebook P5PROD.WB1, then save it as S5PROD.WB1 on your Student Disk.
2. Revise and complete the documentation on the Documentation page as follows:
   a. Change the filename in cell B4 to S5PROD.WB1.
   b. Put your name in cell B5.
   c. Put the current date in cell B6 (do not use an @function).
   d. Use cells B9, B10, and B11 as needed to complete the statement of purpose for the notebook.

   For the spreadsheet on the Production page:
   To help Julia, create a 3-D pie graph showing the relative percentage of VCRs produced at the four plants:

E 3. Use Graph New to create the 3-D pie graph. Show the plant name and the percentage of VCRs produced at that plant. (*Hint:* Use block A4..A7 as the x-axis block, and B4..B7 as the first data series.)
4. Enter "Total VCR Production" as the graph title.
5. Adjust the graph so that all the labels are displayed correctly.

E 6. Explode the slice representing VCR production at the Atlanta plant. (*Hint:* Use the Pie Graph Object Inspector. Right-click the pie slice representing VCR production at the Atlanta plant, click Pie Graph Properties..., then use the Explode Slice settings.)

E 7. Select colors for the slices of the pie graph to give it visual impact.
8. Insert a floating graph in the block A10..F27.
   To help Julia, create a bar graph showing production totals for all four plants:
9. Use the Graph Expert to create the bar graph. Show the production totals of VCRs, stereos, and TVs for each plant.
10. Enter "Total Production Quantities" as the graph title.
11. Place the floating graph in block A30..F47.
12. Adjust the graph so that all labels are displayed correctly.
13. Select colors to enhance the visual impact of the graph.
14. Save the notebook.
15. Preview the spreadsheet, then insert a manual page break so that the spreadsheet prints on one page and the graphs on another. Adjust the size and position of the graphs, if necessary, so that the printout is centered. Modify the header to include your name.
16. Print the spreadsheet and both graphs.
17. Print each graph individually.
18. Save the notebook.
19. Submit your printouts.

2. Showing Sales Trends at Bentley Twig Furniture

You are a marketing assistant at Bentley Twig Furniture, a small manufacturer of rustic furniture. Bentley's major products are rustic twig chairs, rockers, and tables. Your boss, Jack Armstrong, has asked you to create a line graph showing the sales of the three best-selling products during the period 1991 through 1994.

You have collected the necessary sales figures, entered them into a notebook, and are ready to prepare the line graph.

1. Open the notebook P5TWIG.WB1, then save it as S5TWIG.WB1 on your Student Disk.
2. Revise and complete the documentation on the Documentation page as follows:
   a. Change the filename in cell B4 to S5TWIG.WB1.
   b. Put your name in cell B5.
   c. Put the current date in cell B6 (do not use an @function).
   d. Use cells B9, B10, and B11 as needed to complete the statement of purpose for the notebook.

For the spreadsheet on the SalesComp page:

3. Use the Graph Expert to prepare a line graph that shows the change in sales for the three best-selling items over the period 1991 through 1994. Enter "Total Unit Sales" as the graph title and "1991–1994" as the graph subtitle.
4. Place the graph in block A10..F27.
5. Switch to the Graphs page and rename the graph as "TotalSales."
6. Adjust the graph as necessary so that all the labels are displayed correctly.
7. Bold the x-axis and y-axis labels.
8. Change all the lines to a heavier line weight and assign each line a different data marker.
9. Save the notebook.
10. Preview the spreadsheet and make any changes necessary so that the printed spreadsheet and graph are positioned on the page for the best visual impact. Modify the header to include your name.
11. Print the spreadsheet and graph.
12. Print just the graph.
13. Submit your printouts.

3.   Sales Comparisons at WestWind Outfitters

You are working in the Marketing Department of WestWind Outfitters, a manufacturer of camping equipment. WestWind management is considering an expansion of its Canadian marketing efforts. You have been asked to prepare a graph showing the relative sales of major camping equipment items in the U.S. and Canada. You have prepared a simple notebook containing the latest figures for WestWind sales of camp stoves, sleeping bags, and tents in the U.S. and Canadian markets. You now want to prepare a 3-D bar graph to illustrate the relative sales in each market.

1. Open the notebook P5CAMP.WB1, then save it as S5CAMP.WB1 on your Student Disk.
2. Revise and complete the documentation on the Documentation page as follows:
   a. Change the filename in cell B4 to S5CAMP.WB1.
   b. Put your name in cell B5.
   c. Put the current date in cell B6 (do not use an @function).
   d. Use cells B9, B10, and B11 as needed to complete the statement of purpose for the notebook.

For the spreadsheet on the SalesComp page:

E 3. Use the Graph Expert to create a 3-D bar graph showing the relative sales in each market. Enter "U.S. and Canadian Unit Sales" as the graph title.
4. Place the graph in block A10..D27.
5. Adjust the graph so the labels are displayed correctly.
E 6. Bold the axis labels.
7. Save the notebook.
8. Preview the graph. Adjust the print settings so that the printout is centered on the page, and adjust the header to include your name. Adjust the size of the graph, if necessary, to fit the spreadsheet and graph on a single page.
9. Print the spreadsheet and graph.
10. Print just the graph.
11. Submit your printouts.

E 4. Duplicating a Printed Graph

Look through books, business magazines, or textbooks for your other courses to find an attractive graph, then photocopy it. Create a notebook that contains the data displayed on the graph. You can estimate the data values that are plotted on the graph. Do your best to duplicate the graph you found. You might not be able to duplicate the graph fonts or colors exactly, but choose the closest available substitutes. When your graph is complete, save it, preview it, then print it. Submit the photocopy of the original graph as well as the printout of the graph you created.

Managing Data with Quattro Pro

Analyzing Personnel Data

CASE

Northwest State University

Sarah Magnussan is an administrative assistant to Ralph Long, the dean of the College of Business at Northwest State University. The dean frequently asks Sarah to look up and summarize data about the College of Business faculty. To fulfill these requests more efficiently and accurately, Sarah has created a Quattro Pro notebook that contains the name, academic rank, department, date hired, salary, and gender of each faculty member in the College of Business.

The College of Business is divided into two academic departments: the Management department and the Accounting department. Each faculty member holds an academic rank, such as professor or associate professor. Most faculty members are hired at the rank of instructor or assistant professor. After a period of time, a faculty member might be promoted to associate professor and then to full professor. Faculty salaries usually reflect the faculty member's rank and length of service in the department.

Sarah has become quite proficient using Quattro Pro to manage the data in her faculty notebook. **Data management** refers to the tasks required to maintain and manipulate a collection of data. Data management tasks typically include: entering data, updating data to keep it current, sorting data, searching for data, and creating reports.

In previous tutorials, you learned how to use Quattro Pro to perform calculations using the numeric data or values you entered into spreadsheet cells. In this tutorial, you will learn how to use Quattro Pro to manage both numeric and non-numeric data. You will discover how easy it is to sort the data in a spreadsheet, and how Quattro Pro can help you search for data that matches the criteria you specify. Let's work along with Sarah as she uses Quattro Pro to manage the data in her faculty notebook.

To launch Quattro Pro and organize the workspace:
❶ Launch Windows and Quattro Pro.
❷ Make sure your Student Disk is in the disk drive.
❸ Make sure the Quattro Pro and NOTEBK1.WB1 windows are maximized.

Sarah's file of faculty data is stored on your Student Disk as C6FACUL.WB1. Let's open the file then save it with a different filename.

To open the C6FACUL.WB1 Notebook:
❶ Click the **Open Notebook button** 🖻 (or click **File** then click **Open...**) to display the Open File dialog box.
❷ Make sure the Drives box displays the name of the drive that contains your Student Disk.
❸ Double-click **C6FACUL.WB1** in the File Name box to display the notebook, shown in Figure 6-1.

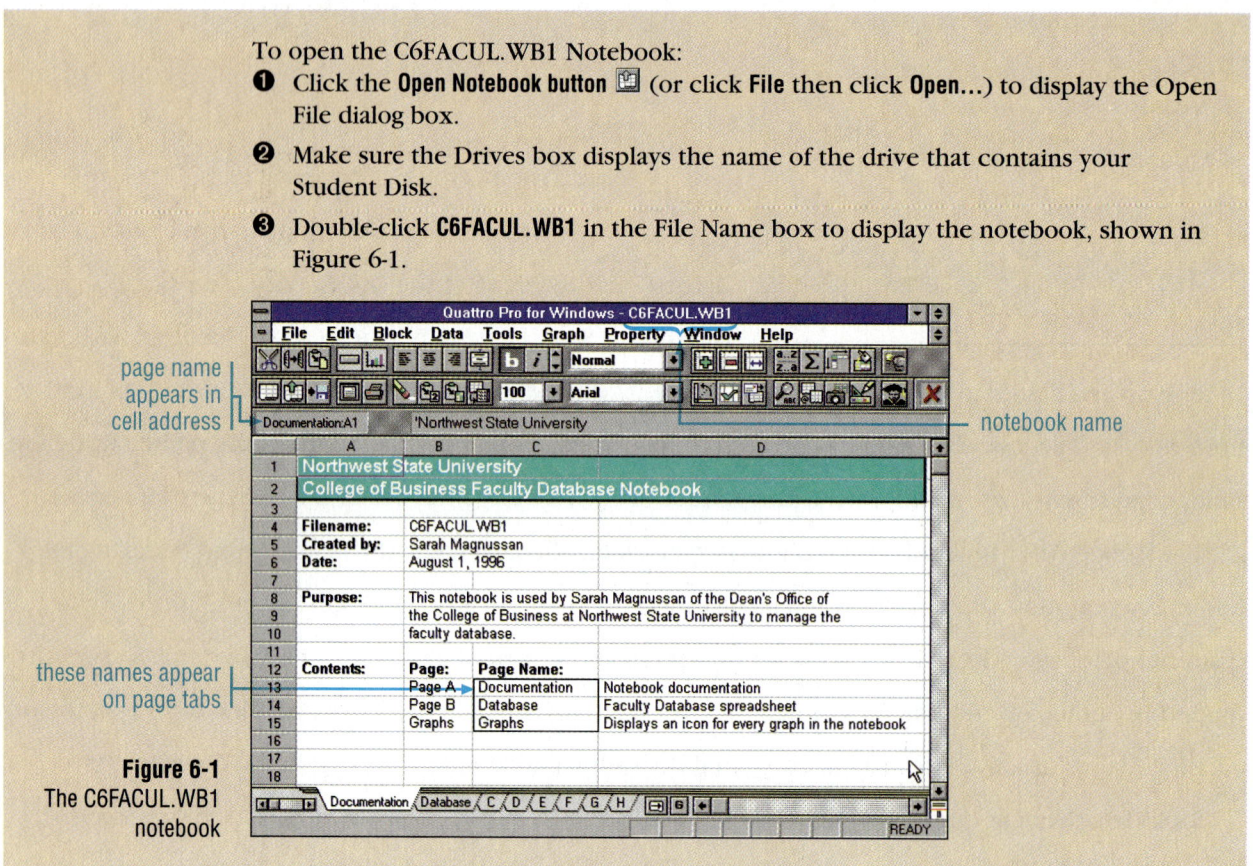

page name appears in cell address

notebook name

these names appear on page tabs

Figure 6-1
The C6FACUL.WB1 notebook

Sarah has entered her notebook documentation on page A. She has listed page A, Documentation; page B, Database, which contains the faculty database spreadsheet; and the Graphs page, which is at the end of the notebook. The page names appear on the page tabs.

Let's save the notebook as S6FACUL1.WB1 so that your changes will not alter the original file.

To save the notebook as S6FACUL1.WB1:

❶ Make sure Documentation is the active page.

❷ Click cell **B4** to make it the active cell.

❸ Change the filename in B4 to **S6FACUL1.WB1**, then press **[Enter]**.

❹ Press **[Home]** to make cell A1 the active cell.

❺ Click **File** then click **Save As...** to display the Save File dialog box.

❻ Type **S6FACUL1** using either uppercase or lowercase letters *but don't press [Enter]* because you need to check an additional setting.

❼ Make sure the Drives box displays the name of the drive that contains your Student Disk.

❽ Click **OK** to save the notebook on your Student Disk. When the save is complete, you should see the new filename, S6FACUL1.WB1, displayed in the title bar.

Let's look at the Database page, which contains Sarah's faculty database spreadsheet.

To switch to the Database page in the notebook:

❶ Click the **Database page tab**. The spreadsheet is shown in Figure 6-2.

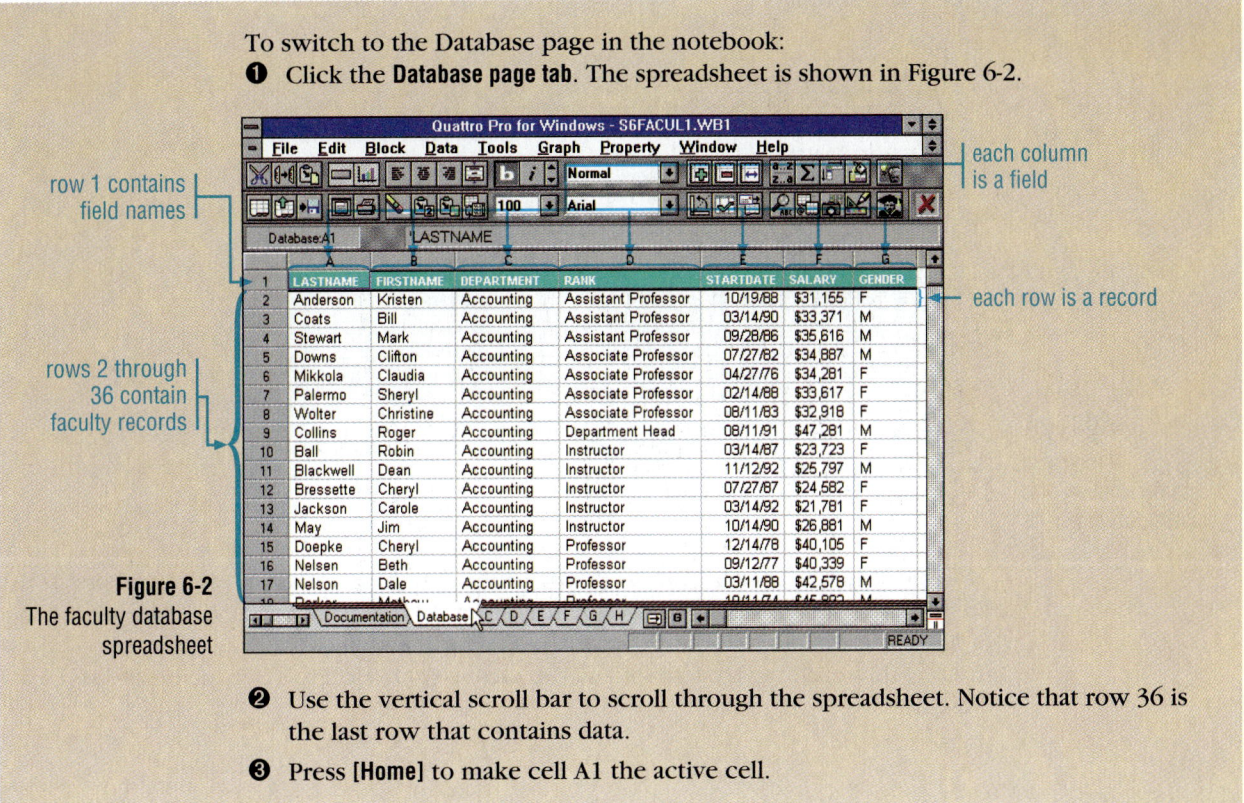

row 1 contains field names

rows 2 through 36 contain faculty records

each column is a field

each row is a record

Figure 6-2
The faculty database spreadsheet

❷ Use the vertical scroll bar to scroll through the spreadsheet. Notice that row 36 is the last row that contains data.

❸ Press **[Home]** to make cell A1 the active cell.

Rows 2 through 36 of Sarah's spreadsheet contain the data about individual faculty members in the College of Business. The data include last name, first name, department, rank, date hired (in the column labeled STARTDATE), salary, and gender. The column titles in row 1 identify the data in each column.

Sarah refers to this spreadsheet as her "faculty database." She refers to each row in the spreadsheet as a "record," and she refers to each column as a "field." Let's see why Sarah uses these terms.

Quattro Pro Databases

A **Quattro Pro database** is a spreadsheet or a section of a spreadsheet in which each row contains the data about one person, place, or object. As you can see in Figure 6-2, each row in Sarah's spreadsheet contains data about one faculty member. Each row in a Quattro Pro database is called a **record**.

The Quattro Pro spreadsheet shows you the data arranged in a table format. Each column in a Quattro Pro database is called a **field** and contains the data about one characteristic related to each record. For example, a characteristic of faculty members is their salaries, so Sarah's database includes a column of salaries. A field is identified by a **field name** positioned at the top of the column that holds the data for that field. In Figure 6-2 the field names are LASTNAME, FIRSTNAME, DEPARTMENT, RANK, STARTDATE, SALARY, and GENDER.

Another way to envision a Quattro Pro database is as a set of cards or forms, like those shown in Figure 6-3. Here each card is a record that corresponds to a row of the Quattro Pro database. Each entry line on a card is a field. In Quattro Pro you can view your data either in rows and columns on the spreadsheet, or in a database form that is similar to a card file.

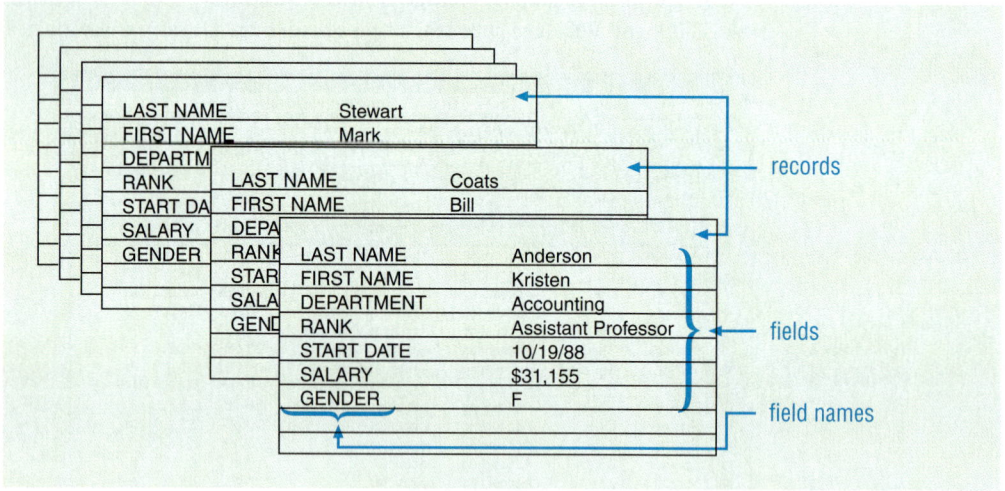

Figure 6-3
A card file representation of a Quattro Pro database

The dean has asked Sarah to provide him with a list of all faculty members in the College of Business, sorted in alphabetical order by last name. He also wants another list of all faculty members by rank with the faculty members sorted alphabetically by last name within each rank. Sarah knows she can use Quattro Pro's Sort command to create these lists.

Sorting Data

You can sort the records in a Quattro Pro database according to the contents of one or more fields. For example, in Sarah's spreadsheet you can sort the faculty records according to last name, department, rank, or any other field.

The field that determines the order for the sort is called the **sort key.** For example, to sort a list of names alphabetically by last name, the sort key would be the name of the field containing the last names, in this case LASTNAME. You can specify up to five sort keys to create a sort within a sort. If the first sort key is LASTNAME, the second might be FIRSTNAME. In this way, if four records contain the last name "Smith," Quattro Pro will use FIRSTNAME to sort within the Smiths, so that Anna Smith precedes Zachary Smith.

Figure 6-4 shows an example of the faculty database sorted using three sort keys: DEPARTMENT, RANK, and LASTNAME. Quattro Pro first sorted all the records alphabetically by department: Accounting then Management. Then within each department Quattro Pro sorted the records alphabetically by rank. For example, within the Accounting department all the records with Assistant Professor in the RANK field are listed before the records with Associate Professor in the RANK field. Finally, Quattro Pro sorted the records within each rank alphabetically by last name. The accounting instructor Robin Ball appears before Dean Blackwell.

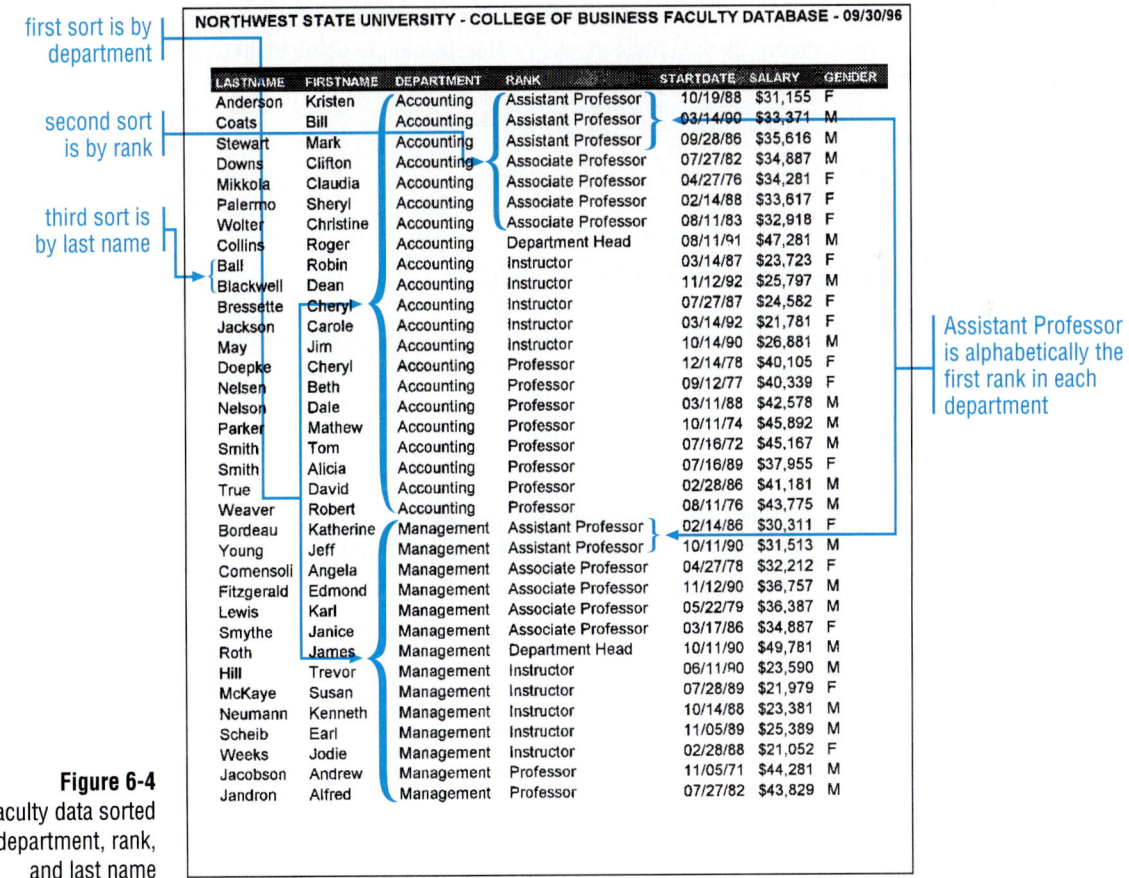

first sort is by department

second sort is by rank

third sort is by last name

Assistant Professor is alphabetically the first rank in each department

Figure 6-4
Faculty data sorted by department, rank, and last name

To sort the data in a Quattro Pro database, you first select the cells that you want to include in the sort, and then you use the Sort command on the Data menu to specify the sort keys and to sort the data. When you select the data, don't include the row containing the field names in the database. If you do, Quattro Pro will sort this row along with the rows containing the records.

When you are selecting cells in a database to be sorted, you must be sure to include the entire row of data that corresponds to a record. If you do not, you will sort only some of the fields for each record and your database will be scrambled. If a sort doesn't work properly, use the Undo command to return the database to its condition before the sort.

REFERENCE WINDOW

Sorting a Block of Cells

- Highlight the block of cells you want to sort. Do not include the field names in the sort block.

- Click Data then click Sort....

- Click the 1st Sort Key edit field, then click the column border of the column that you want to use as the first sort key.

- If you want to select a second sort key, click the 2nd Sort Key edit field, then click the column border of the column that you want to use as the second sort key.

- Select up to a total of five sort keys in the same way.

- Click OK.

Sorting Data Using One Sort Key

The dean wants a list of faculty members sorted alphabetically by last name. To prepare this list, Sarah highlights cells A2 through G36, which contain the records she wants to sort. She then uses the Data Sort dialog box to instruct Quattro Pro to sort by the contents of the LASTNAME field in column A.

To sort the records alphabetically by last name:

❶ Make sure that the Database page is the active page.

❷ Highlight cells A2 through G36.

❸ Click **Data** then click **Sort...** to open the Data Sort dialog box. The block address Database:A2..G36 is displayed in the Block edit field. Notice that row 1 is *not* in the block because it contains the field names. See Figure 6-5.

❹ In the Sort Keys settings, click the **1st Column edit field** to make it active.

❺ In the spreadsheet, click **column border A** to select column A as the first sort key. Database:A appears in the 1st Column edit field, as shown in Figure 6-5.

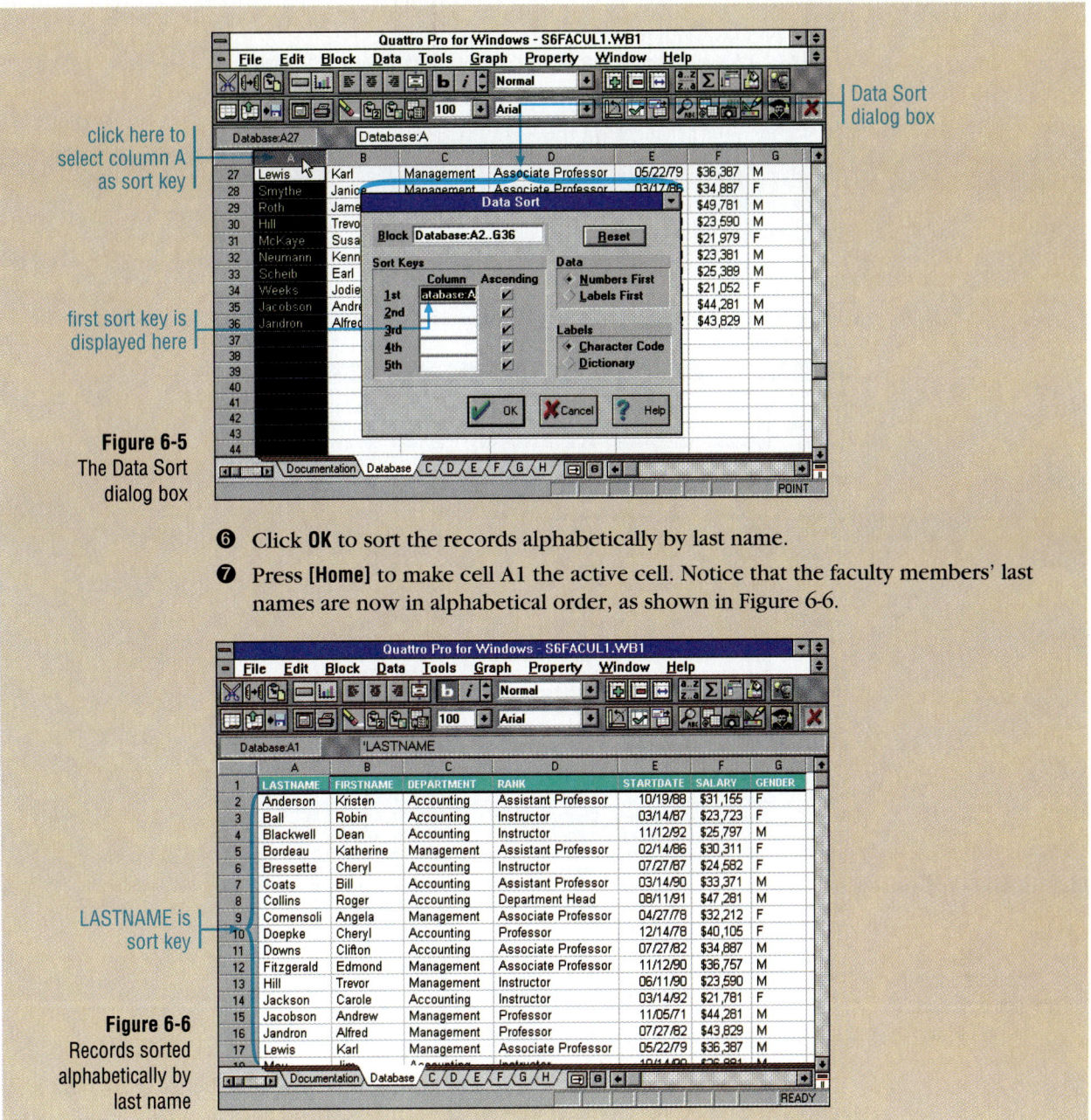

Figure 6-5
The Data Sort
dialog box

❻ Click **OK** to sort the records alphabetically by last name.

❼ Press **[Home]** to make cell A1 the active cell. Notice that the faculty members' last names are now in alphabetical order, as shown in Figure 6-6.

Figure 6-6
Records sorted
alphabetically by
last name

Sarah saves the notebook with the sorted database file, then previews the Database spreadsheet and prints it for the dean.

To save, preview, and print the spreadsheet:

❶ Click the **Save Notebook button** 🖫 (or click **File** then click **Save**).

❷ Highlight block A1..G36, then click the **Print Preview button** ▣.

❸ Click the **Print button** 🖨 on the Print Preview SpeedBar.

❹ Click the **Close SpeedBar button** ✖ on the Print Preview SpeedBar.

❺ Press [**Home**] to make cell A1 the active cell. Figure 6-7 shows Sarah's printed spreadsheet.

NORTHWEST STATE UNIVERSITY - COLLEGE OF BUSINESS FACULTY DATABASE - 09/30/96

LASTNAME	FIRSTNAME	DEPARTMENT	RANK	STARTDATE	SALARY	GENDER
Anderson	Kristen	Accounting	Assistant Professor	10/19/88	$31,155	F
Ball	Robin	Accounting	Instructor	03/14/87	$23,723	F
Blackwell	Dean	Accounting	Instructor	11/12/92	$25,797	M
Bordeau	Katherine	Management	Assistant Professor	02/14/86	$30,311	F
Bressette	Cheryl	Accounting	Instructor	07/27/87	$24,582	F
Coats	Bill	Accounting	Assistant Professor	03/14/90	$33,371	M
Collins	Roger	Accounting	Department Head	08/11/91	$47,281	M
Cornensoli	Angela	Management	Associate Professor	04/27/78	$32,212	F
Doepke	Cheryl	Accounting	Professor	12/14/78	$40,105	F
Downs	Clifton	Accounting	Associate Professor	07/27/82	$34,887	M
Fitzgerald	Edmond	Management	Associate Professor	11/12/90	$36,757	M
Hill	Trevor	Management	Instructor	06/11/90	$23,590	M
Jackson	Carole	Accounting	Instructor	03/14/92	$21,781	F
Jacobson	Andrew	Management	Professor	11/05/71	$44,281	M
Jandron	Alfred	Management	Professor	07/27/82	$43,829	M
Lewis	Karl	Management	Associate Professor	05/22/79	$36,387	M
May	Jim	Accounting	Instructor	10/14/90	$26,881	M
McKaye	Susan	Management	Instructor	07/28/89	$21,979	F
Mikkola	Claudia	Accounting	Associate Professor	04/27/76	$34,281	F
Nelsen	Beth	Accounting	Professor	09/12/77	$40,339	F
Nelson	Dale	Accounting	Professor	03/11/88	$42,578	M
Neumann	Kenneth	Management	Instructor	10/14/88	$23,381	M
Palermo	Sheryl	Accounting	Associate Professor	02/14/88	$33,617	F
Parker	Mathew	Accounting	Professor	10/11/74	$45,892	M
Roth	James	Management	Department Head	10/11/90	$49,781	M
Scheib	Earl	Management	Instructor	11/05/89	$25,389	M
Smith	Alicia	Accounting	Professor	07/16/89	$37,955	F
Smith	Tom	Accounting	Professor	07/16/72	$45.167	M
Smythe	Janice	Management	Associate Professor	03/17/86	$34,887	F
Stewart	Mark	Accounting	Assistant Professor	09/28/86	$35,616	M
True	David	Accounting	Professor	02/28/86	$41,181	M
Weaver	Robert	Accounting	Professor	08/11/76	$43,775	M
Weeks	Jodie	Management	Instructor	02/28/88	$21,052	F
Wolter	Christine	Accounting	Associate Professor	08/11/83	$32,918	F
Young	Jeff	Management	Assistant Professor	10/11/90	$31,513	M

Figure 6-7
Database printout
with records sorted
by last name

The dean also requested a list of faculty records sorted alphabetically by rank and, within each rank, sorted alphabetically by last name. Sarah decides to create and use block names to help her identify the elements of her database when she completes this sort.

Creating Block Names

Quattro Pro allows you to create a **block name** of up to 15 characters for a cell or a block of cells. Block names are easier to remember and use than block addresses. Anytime you are entering a cell or block address, you can press [F3] to select a named block from the list of block names you have created. Quattro Pro displays block names in formulas whenever possible, which makes formulas easier to read. For example, if you name cell B10 as REVENUE and cell B20 as EXPENSES, Quattro Pro will display the formula +B10-B20 as +REVENUE-EXPENSES.

Block names are very useful for printing. Often you will have several blocks in your spreadsheet that you want to print. By creating a block name for each of the print blocks, you can tell Quattro Pro what block to print by name instead of by address.

Block names are also useful when working with databases. For example, you can specify sort keys using block names rather than column letters.

To create a block name, you use the Names command on the Block menu or the Create Name... command on the SpeedMenu. Use combinations of letters and numbers when you create block names, but don't use only numbers. Use the underscore character (_) instead of a space between words. You can use lowercase or uppercase letters when you create a block name, but Quattro Pro always displays block names in uppercase.

REFERENCE WINDOW

Creating a Block Name

- Right-click the cell or highlighted block of cells that you want to name to open the SpeedMenu, then click Create Name....

or

Click the cell or highlight the block of cells that you want to name, click Block, click Names, then click Create....

- Type the block name in the Name edit field of the Create Name dialog box.
- Click OK.

To complete her second sort more easily, Sarah decides to name all the cells in the database with the block name DATABASE, and to name all the cells that will be sorted in the database as SORTBLOCK. Then, she'll be able to use the block names when specifying the elements of the second sort, and when completing other database management tasks. First, Sarah creates the block name DATABASE.

To create the block name DATABASE:

❶ Highlight the block A1..G36.

❷ Right-click anywhere in the highlighted block to open the SpeedMenu.

❸ Click **Create Name...** on the SpeedMenu. The Create Name dialog box appears with the block address Database:A1..G36 displayed in the Block(s) edit field, as shown in Figure 6-8.

❹ Make sure the Name edit field is active.

❺ Type the block name **DATABASE** in the Name edit field, as shown in Figure 6-8.

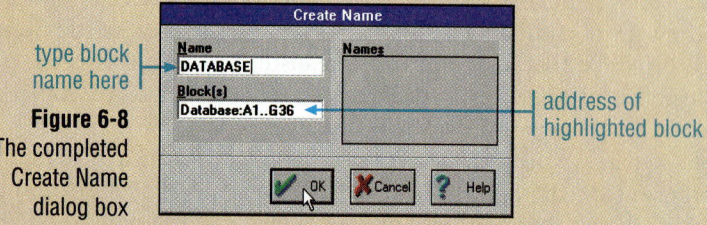

type block name here →

Figure 6-8
The completed Create Name dialog box

← address of highlighted block

❻ Click **OK**.

❼ Press [Home] to make cell A1 the active cell.

Next, Sarah creates the block name SORTBLOCK.

To create the block name SORTBLOCK:

❶ Highlight the block A2..G36. Notice that row 1, which contains the field names, is not included in this block.

❷ Right-click anywhere in the highlighted block to open the SpeedMenu.

❸ Click **Create Name...** on the SpeedMenu. The Create Name dialog box appears with the block address Database:A2..G36 displayed in the Block(s) edit field.

❹ Make sure the Name edit field is active.

❺ Type the block name **SORTBLOCK** in the Name edit field.

❻ Click **OK**.

❼ Press [Home] to make cell A1 the active cell.

Sarah also wants to create a block name for each field name. She decides to follow a common spreadsheet database convention and assign the block name to the first cell below the field name. For example, the field name LASTNAME is in cell A1. The first cell below the field name is cell A2, so Sarah will assign the block name LASTNAME to cell A2.

With one block name for each field name, there will be seven new block names. Sarah could create the seven block names one at a time, but instead she uses the Names Labels... command on the Block menu, which creates block names based on existing labels. The cells to be assigned the block names must be adjacent to the cells containing the labels.

Sarah wants to create block names for cells A2 through G2 based on the field names in cells A1 through G1.

To create the block names for cells A2 through G2:

❶ Highlight the block A1..G1. This block is the row containing the field names, which are the labels that will be used as the basis for the block names.

❷ Click **Block**, click **Names**, then click **Labels...**. The Create Names From Labels dialog box appears with the block address Database:A1..G1 displayed in the Blocks edit field.

TROUBLE? If the Create Names dialog box appears instead of the Create Name From Labels dialog box, you clicked Create... instead of Labels.... Click the Cancel button and repeat Step 2.

❸ In the Directions settings, click the **Down radio button** to specify that the blocks to be named are located in the row below the labels. See Figure 6-9.

Figure 6-9
The Create Names
From Labels
dialog box

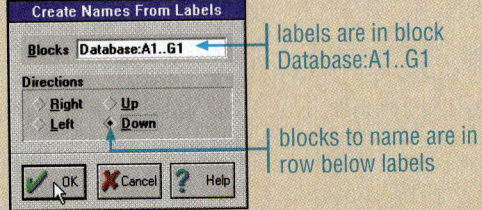

labels are in block
Database:A1..G1

blocks to name are in
row below labels

❹ Click **OK**.

❺ Press **[Home]** to make cell A1 the active cell.

Sarah wants to check to make sure that the block names based on the field names were created correctly. To do this, she decides to use the Goto command.

The Goto Command

Quattro Pro's Goto (pronounced as two words: *go to*) command on the Edit menu enables you to move quickly to any location in a notebook. Goto is so useful that [F5] is assigned as a shortcut key to open the Goto dialog box. You can specify a cell address, a block name, or a page address as your target location.

Sarah decides to test the location of the block name LASTNAME by moving to that location using the Goto command.

To move to the cell assigned the block name LASTNAME using Goto:

❶ Press **[F5]** to open the Goto dialog box, shown in Figure 6-10.

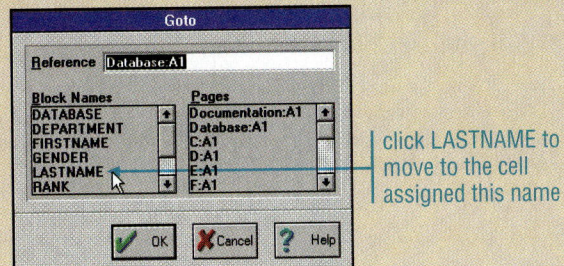

click LASTNAME to
move to the cell
assigned this name

Figure 6-10
The Goto dialog box

❷ In the Block Names list, click **LASTNAME**.

❸ Click **OK**. Notice that cell A2, which is assigned the block name LASTNAME, is now the active cell.

❹ Press **[Home]** to make cell A1 the active cell.

The block names are assigned correctly, so now Sarah can use them to specify the sort for the second list requested by the dean.

Using Two Sort Keys

To prepare the second list for the dean, Sarah sorts the data using two sort keys: rank as the first, and last name as the second. As a result, Quattro Pro will list the records for all faculty members of a particular rank, and then within each rank will sort the records alphabetically by last name.

To sort the faculty data by rank and by last name:

❶ Click **Data** then click **Sort...** to open the Data Sort dialog box.

❷ Click **Reset** to clear the settings from the previous sort.

❸ Click the **Block edit field** to make it active.

Sarah wants to use the block names she created to specify the sort. Recall that [F3] gives you access to block names.

❹ Press **[F3]** to display the Block Names dialog box, shown in Figure 6-11.

list of block names that have been created →

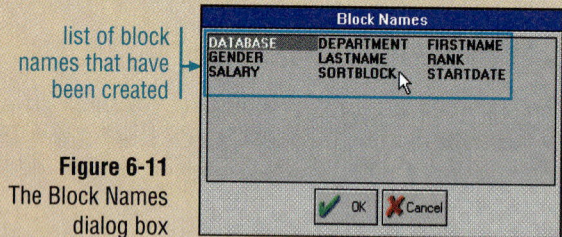

Figure 6-11
The Block Names dialog box

❺ Click **SORTBLOCK** then click **OK**. The Data Sort dialog box reappears with the block name SORTBLOCK in the Block edit field.

❻ In the Sort Key settings, click the **1st Column edit field** to make it active.

❼ Press **[F3]** to display the Block Names dialog box, click **RANK** to specify the RANK field as the first sort key, then click **OK**. The Data Sort dialog box now contains the block name RANK in the 1st Column edit field.

TROUBLE? If the block name SORTBLOCK disappeared from the Block edit field when you pressed [F3], you didn't complete Step 6. Pressing [F3] has the same effect as clicking Reset if (1) the active edit field is not empty, and (2) the contents of the active edit field are not highlighted. Repeat Steps 3 through 7.

❽ In the Sort Key settings, click the **2nd Column edit field** to make it active.

❾ Press **[F3]** to display the Block Names dialog box, click **LASTNAME** to specify the LASTNAME field as the second sort key, then click **OK**. The Data Sort dialog box now contains the block name LASTNAME in the 2nd Column edit field, as shown in Figure 6-12.

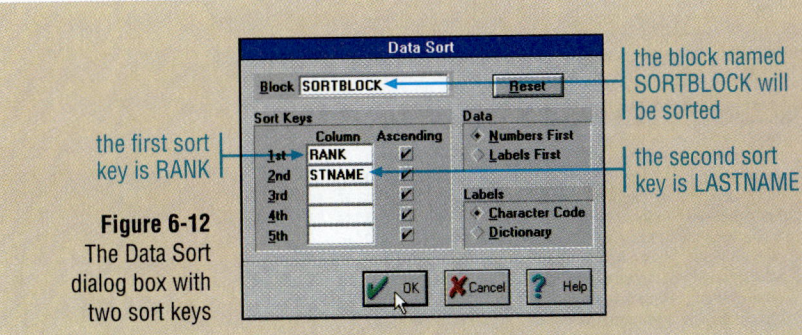

Figure 6-12
The Data Sort
dialog box with
two sort keys

⓾ Click **OK** to sort the records, then press **[Home]** to make cell A1 the active cell. The records now appear sorted by rank, and within rank by last name.

Sarah saves the notebook with the sorted records.

To save the notebook:
❶ Click the **Save Notebook button** (or click **File** then click **Save**).

Sarah is ready to print the sorted database. Just as she used block names to help her sort the data, she can use block names to print the data. Using a block name to specify a print block saves you from having to highlight the block you want to print.

Sarah specifies the block named DATABASE as the print block, then she previews the spreadsheet and prints it for the dean.

To specify the print block, then preview and print the spreadsheet:
❶ Click the **Print button** on the Productivity Tools SpeedBar. The Spreadsheet Print dialog box appears.
❷ Press **[F3]** to display the Block Names dialog box.
❸ Click **DATABASE** then click **OK**. The Spreadsheet Print dialog box reappears with the block name DATABASE in the Print block(s) edit field.
❹ Click **Preview** in the Spreadsheet Print dialog box.
❺ Click **Print** on the Print Preview SpeedBar.
❻ Click the **Close SpeedBar button** on the Print Preview SpeedBar.
❼ Click **Close** in the Spreadsheet Print dialog box.
❽ Press **[Home]** to make cell A1 the active cell.
❾ Click the **Save Notebook button** (or click **File** then click **Save**). Figure 6-13 shows Sarah's printed spreadsheet.

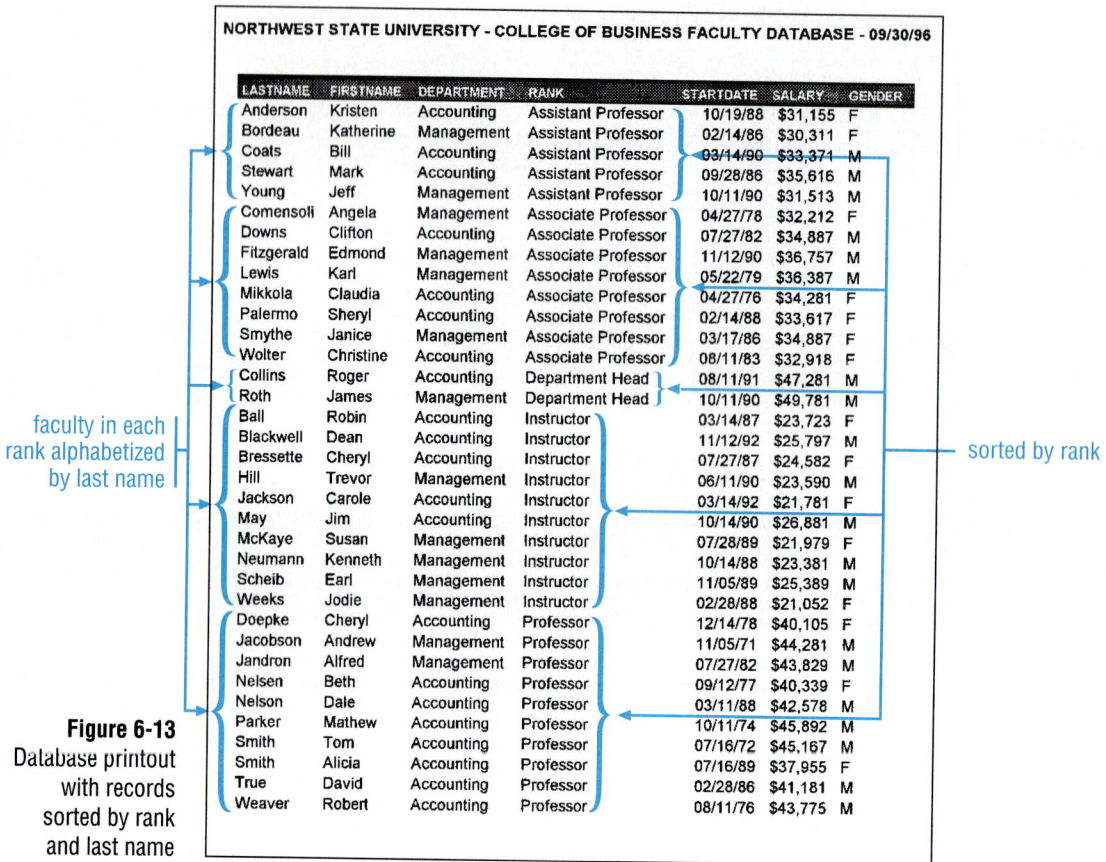

NORTHWEST STATE UNIVERSITY - COLLEGE OF BUSINESS FACULTY DATABASE - 09/30/96

LASTNAME	FIRSTNAME	DEPARTMENT	RANK	STARTDATE	SALARY	GENDER
Anderson	Kristen	Accounting	Assistant Professor	10/19/88	$31,155	F
Bordeau	Katherine	Management	Assistant Professor	02/14/86	$30,311	F
Coats	Bill	Accounting	Assistant Professor	03/14/90	$33,371	M
Stewart	Mark	Accounting	Assistant Professor	09/28/86	$35,616	M
Young	Jeff	Management	Assistant Professor	10/11/90	$31,513	M
Comensoli	Angela	Management	Associate Professor	04/27/78	$32,212	F
Downs	Clifton	Accounting	Associate Professor	07/27/82	$34,887	M
Fitzgerald	Edmond	Management	Associate Professor	11/12/90	$36,757	M
Lewis	Karl	Management	Associate Professor	05/22/79	$36,387	M
Mikkola	Claudia	Accounting	Associate Professor	04/27/76	$34,281	F
Palermo	Sheryl	Accounting	Associate Professor	02/14/88	$33,617	F
Smythe	Janice	Management	Associate Professor	03/17/86	$34,887	F
Wolter	Christine	Accounting	Associate Professor	08/11/83	$32,918	F
Collins	Roger	Accounting	Department Head	08/11/91	$47,281	M
Roth	James	Management	Department Head	10/11/90	$49,781	M
Ball	Robin	Accounting	Instructor	03/14/87	$23,723	F
Blackwell	Dean	Accounting	Instructor	11/12/92	$25,797	M
Bressette	Cheryl	Accounting	Instructor	07/27/87	$24,582	F
Hill	Trevor	Management	Instructor	06/11/90	$23,590	M
Jackson	Carole	Accounting	Instructor	03/14/92	$21,781	F
May	Jim	Accounting	Instructor	10/14/90	$26,881	M
McKaye	Susan	Management	Instructor	07/28/89	$21,979	F
Neumann	Kenneth	Management	Instructor	10/14/88	$23,381	M
Scheib	Earl	Management	Instructor	11/05/89	$25,389	M
Weeks	Jodie	Management	Instructor	02/28/88	$21,052	F
Doepke	Cheryl	Accounting	Professor	12/14/78	$40,105	F
Jacobson	Andrew	Management	Professor	11/05/71	$44,281	M
Jandron	Alfred	Management	Professor	07/27/82	$43,829	M
Nelsen	Beth	Accounting	Professor	09/12/77	$40,339	F
Nelson	Dale	Accounting	Professor	03/11/88	$42,578	M
Parker	Mathew	Accounting	Professor	10/11/74	$45,892	M
Smith	Tom	Accounting	Professor	07/16/72	$45,167	M
Smith	Alicia	Accounting	Professor	07/16/89	$37,955	F
True	David	Accounting	Professor	02/28/86	$41,181	M
Weaver	Robert	Accounting	Professor	08/11/76	$43,775	M

faculty in each rank alphabetized by last name

sorted by rank

Figure 6-13
Database printout with records sorted by rank and last name

Quattro Pro performed this sort by first alphabetizing the ranks in column D, so, for example, all the assistant professors are listed before the associate professors. Within each rank, Quattro Pro sorted the records alphabetically by last name. For example, within the assistant professor rank, Anderson is listed first, followed by Bordeau.

If you want to take a break and resume the tutorial at a later time, you can exit Quattro Pro by double-clicking the Control menu box in the upper-left corner of the screen. When you resume the tutorial, launch Quattro Pro, maximize the Quattro Pro and NOTEBK1.WB1 windows and place your Student Disk in the disk drive. Open the file S6FACUL1.WB1, then continue with the tutorial.

Sarah goes through her in-basket and comes across a memo from the dean, announcing that Jim May, an instructor in the Accounting department, has resigned and that Martin Stein has been hired as his replacement. In addition, the Management department has hired a new assistant professor named Constance Evans. Sarah needs to update her database to delete the record for Jim May and add new records for Martin Stein and Constance Evans.

When Sarah uses the Quattro Pro Sort command, she works with the data using the row and column format in which it appears on the spreadsheet. Sarah prefers to do other data management tasks, such as adding new records to the database, using Quattro Pro's database form, which lets her view the data in a card file format.

Maintaining a Database with Quattro Pro's Database Form

A **database form** is a dialog box that makes it easy to search for, view, edit, add, and delete records in a database. The form displays one record at a time as if it were on an index card, rather than displaying the table of rows and columns you see on the spreadsheet.

REFERENCE WINDOW

Displaying a Database Form

- Click Data then click Form... to open the Database Form dialog box.

- In the Input Range edit field, enter the address of the block of cells containing the database.

- Click OK to display the form.

Sarah now uses the Form command to display one record at a time.

To display a database form:
1. Click **Data** then click **Form...** to open the Database Form dialog box.
2. Make sure the Input Range edit field is active.
3. Press **[F3]** to display the Block Names dialog box.
4. Click **DATABASE** to specify the block containing the database field names and records, then click **OK**. The Database Form dialog box reappears with the block name DATABASE in the Input Range edit field.

⑤ Click **OK** to display the form. The first record in the database is displayed in the Edit Records form, as shown in Figure 6-14.

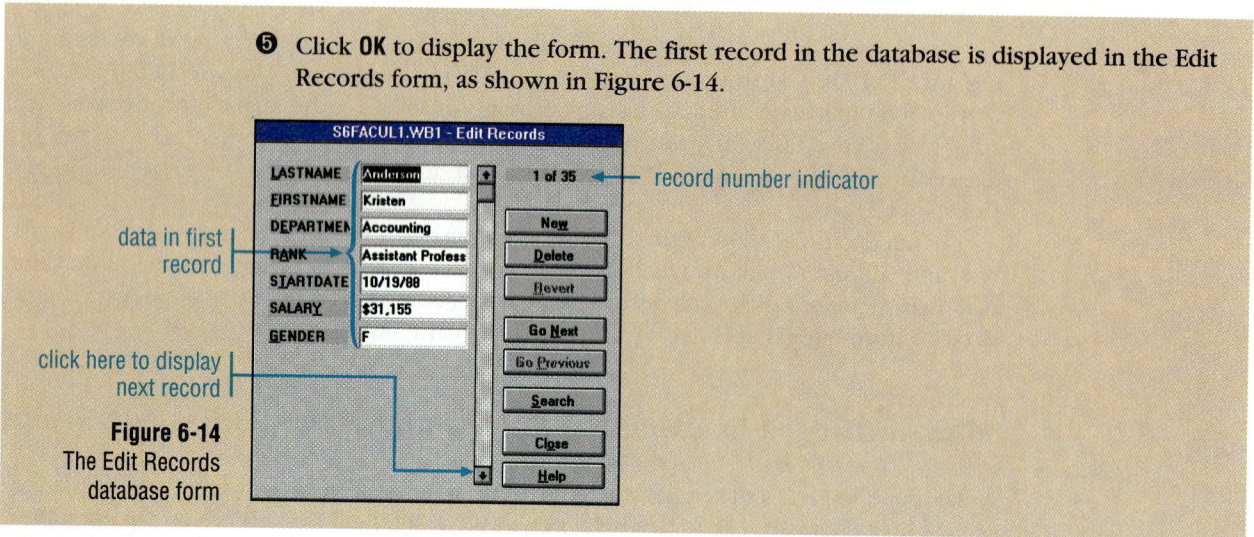

Figure 6-14
The Edit Records
database form

In order to delete the record on Jim May, Sarah must first locate the record. Sarah can use the scroll bar on the database form to search through each of the records until she finds the one she wants, or she can have Quattro Pro search for her. Let's see how to search for individual records using both methods.

Manual Search

You can use the database form to manually scroll through the database one record at a time using the arrow buttons on the vertical scroll bar, or [↑] and [↓] on the keyboard. You can also use the scroll box on the vertical scroll bar to move quickly to a particular record number.

The **record number indicator** in the upper-right corner of the database form shows the number of the record displayed in the form and the total number of records in the database. In Figure 6-14 the record indicator shows "1 of 35," indicating that the current record is the first record in the database and that the database contains a total of 35 records.

Let's practice using the scroll arrow buttons and arrow keys to scroll through the database records.

To practice manually scrolling through the database:
❶ Click the **down arrow button** at the bottom of the vertical scroll bar, or press [↓] to display the next record in the database. The record number indicator shows that record 2 of 35 is displayed. See Figure 6-15.

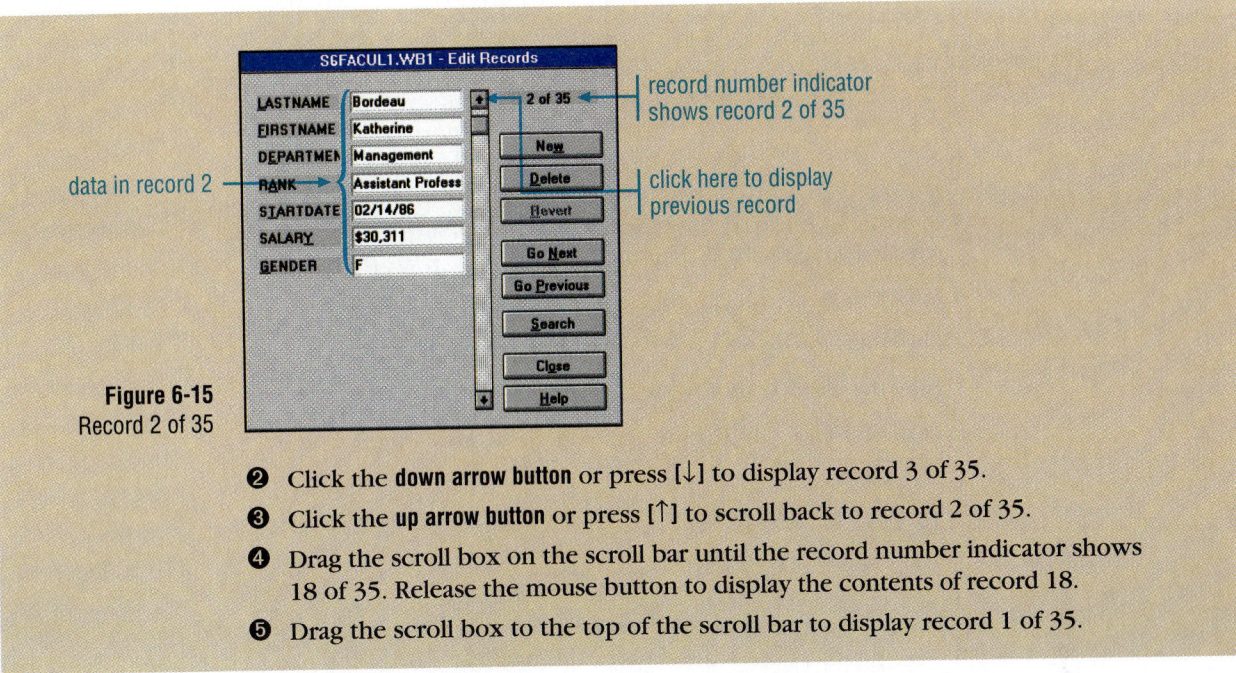

Figure 6-15
Record 2 of 35

❷ Click the **down arrow button** or press [↓] to display record 3 of 35.

❸ Click the **up arrow button** or press [↑] to scroll back to record 2 of 35.

❹ Drag the scroll box on the scroll bar until the record number indicator shows 18 of 35. Release the mouse button to display the contents of record 18.

❺ Drag the scroll box to the top of the scroll bar to display record 1 of 35.

With large databases, locating specific records manually can take time. The alternative is to have Quattro Pro automatically search for records in the database that match the criteria you specify.

Criteria Search

You can use the Search button on the database form to have Quattro Pro search for a specific record or group of records. When you initiate a search, you specify the **search criteria**, or the instructions for the search. Quattro Pro starts from the current record and moves through the database searching for any records that match the search criteria. If it finds more than one match, Quattro Pro displays the first record that matches the search criteria.

The search is not *case sensitive*; that is, it does not matter if you use uppercase or lowercase letters when you enter the search criteria. For example, if you have a record with "Hill" as the last name, you can find it by entering "HILL" or "Hill" or "hill" as the search criteria.

REFERENCE WINDOW

Searching for a Record Using the Database Form

- Click Data then click Form....

- In the Input Range edit field, enter the address of the block of cells containing the database, then click OK.

- Click Search.

- Click Clear to remove any previous search criteria.

- Enter the search criteria in the appropriate edit fields.

- Click Go Next to display the next record that matches the search criteria.

- Click Find Previous to display the previous record that matches the search criteria.

A criteria search is also referred to as a **query** because it finds the answers to questions, or queries, about the data in the database. Let's see how Sarah might query the faculty database.

Suppose Sarah wants to find the date that Trevor Hill started working at the College of Business. She can use the Search button to have Quattro Pro search for the record of the faculty member with a last name of "Hill." Then, when she finds the record, she can look in the STARTDATE field to find out when he was hired.

To search for the record for Hill:

❶ Make sure the record number indicator shows 1 of 35.

❷ Click **Search** to begin entering the criteria. Notice that some of the database form buttons change, the title of the form changes to "Search Records," and the record number indicator displays "Search Mode."

❸ Click the **LASTNAME edit field**, then type **Hill**. The Search Records database form now appears as shown in Figure 6-16.

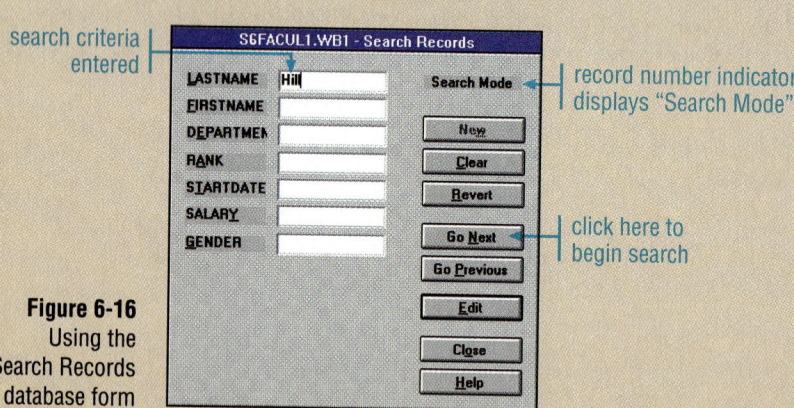

search criteria entered

record number indicator displays "Search Mode"

click here to begin search

Figure 6-16
Using the
Search Records
database form

❹ Click **Go Next** to display the first record that contains Hill as the last name. The record for Trevor Hill appears.

❺ Click **Go Next** again to see if there are any more records containing Hill as the last name. The Search Mode dialog box appears containing the message "No more matching records after this one."

❻ Click **OK** to clear the message.

Sarah can see from the record in the database form that Trevor started on June 11, 1990. Next, suppose that Sarah needs to find the names of the female faculty members with the rank of professor. For this query, Sarah must enter two search criteria: RANK must be Professor and GENDER must be F.

To view the records for all female professors:

❶ Drag the scroll box to the top of the scroll bar to display record 1 of 35.

❷ Click **Search**.

❸ Click **Clear** to clear the previous search criteria.

❹ Click the **RANK edit field**, then type **Professor**.

❺ Click the **GENDER edit field**, then type **F**.

❻ Click **Go Next** to view the record for the first female professor. Record 26 displays the data for Cheryl Doepke, a professor in the Accounting department.

❼ Click **Go Next** again to view the next record that matches the search criteria. Record 29 displays the data for Beth Nelsen, a professor in the Accounting department.

❽ Click **Go Next** to view the next record. Record 33 displays the data for Alicia Smith, a professor in the Accounting department.

❾ Click **Go Next** to view the next record. The Search Mode dialog box appears containing the message "No more matching records after this one."

❿ Click **OK** to clear the message.

Sarah now knows that there are three female professors in the College of Business—Cheryl Doepke, Beth Nelsen, and Alicia Smith.

Next, suppose that Sarah wants to find out which faculty members started with the university before January 1, 1975. She can use the "less than" symbol (<) to specify that she wants to select faculty members whose start date is less than (earlier than) 01/01/75.

To view the records for all faculty members who started before 01/01/75:

❶ Drag the scroll box to the top of the scroll bar to display record 1 of 35.

❷ Click **Search**.

❸ Click **Clear** to clear the previous search criteria.

❹ Click the **STARTDATE edit field**, then type **<01/01/75** to search for all faculty members who started before 01/01/75.

❺ Click **Go Next** to view the record for the first faculty member who meets the criteria. Record 27 displays the data for Andrew Jacobson, who started in the Management department on 11/05/71.

❻ Click **Go Next** to view the next record that matches the criteria. Record 31 displays the data for Mathew Parker, who started in the Accounting department on 10/11/74.

❼ Click **Go Next** to view the next record. Record 32 displays the data for Tom Smith, who started in the Accounting department on 07/16/72.

❽ Click **Go Next** to view the next record. The Search Mode dialog box appears containing the message "No more matching records after this one."

❾ Click **OK** to clear the message.

Sarah remembers part of a radio interview she heard on her way to work. The interview was with a faculty member from the College of Business who recently won first place in a women's local 10K race. She remembers that the woman's last name started with *Ne*, such as in Nesbitt or Nelson. Sarah would like to use her database to find out who won the race. Because Sarah does not know the exact search criteria, she can use a wildcard to replace part of the search criteria.

Using Wildcards

Quattro Pro's database form allows you to use wildcards when you enter search criteria. A **wildcard** is a symbol that stands for one or more characters. The database form recognizes two wildcards: the question mark and the asterisk.

You use the **question mark (?) wildcard** to represent any single character. For example, if you didn't know whether a faculty member's last name was spelled Nels*e*n or Nels*o*n, you could specify Nels?n as the search criteria. The database form would display all records in which the last name started with *Nels*, followed by any single character, and then ending with the letter *n*.

You use the **asterisk (*) wildcard** to represent any group of characters. For example, if you enter *Ne** as the search criteria for the LASTNAME field, Quattro Pro will find all the records containing last names that begin with *Ne*, regardless of the letters that follow. If you use **son* as the search criteria, Quattro Pro will find all the records containing last names that end with *son*, regardless of the letters at the beginning of the last name.

Sarah decides to use the asterisk wildcard to find all the female faculty members whose last names start with the letters *Ne*.

To search for all female faculty members whose last names start with *Ne*:

❶ Drag the scroll box to the top of the scroll bar to display record 1 of 35.

❷ Click **Search**.

❸ Click **Clear** to clear the previous search criteria.

❹ Click the **LASTNAME edit field**, then type **Ne*** to specify last names that start with *Ne*.

❺ Click the **GENDER edit field**, then type **F**.

❻ Click **Go Next** to view the record for the first female faculty member whose last name starts with *Ne*. The record for Beth Nelsen is displayed. Beth could be the person who won the 10K race.

❼ Click **Go Next** to view the next record that matches the search criteria. The Search Mode dialog box appears containing the message "No more matching records after this one."

❽ Click **OK** to clear the message.

Sarah found only one female faculty member whose last name starts with *Ne*, so Beth Nelsen must be the faculty member who won the women's 10K race. Now Sarah wants to delete Jim May's record from the database.

Maintaining Data in a Quattro Pro Database

An important data management task is maintaining the accuracy of the database by deleting records, adding new records, and changing the data in existing records. The process of maintaining the accuracy of the data is often referred to as **updating**.

Deleting Records

To delete a record using the database form, you display the record then click Delete. Quattro Pro removes deleted records from the spreadsheet.

REFERENCE WINDOW

Deleting a Record Using the Database Form

- Click Data then click Form....
- In the Input Range edit field, enter the address of the block of cells containing the database.
- Click OK.
- Scroll or search through the database to display the record that you want to delete.
- Click Delete then click Close.

Sarah must locate the record for Jim May before she can delete it.

To locate and delete the record for Jim May:

❶ Drag the scroll box to the top of the scroll bar to display record 1 of 35.

❷ Click **Search**.

❸ Click **Clear** to clear the previous search criteria.

❹ Click the **LASTNAME edit field**, then type **May** as the search criteria.

❺ Click **Go Next** to display the first record that matches the search criteria. The record for Jim May appears in the database form.

❻ Click **Delete** to delete the record.

❼ When you see the message "Are you sure you want to delete the row? No undo possible" click **Yes**.

Quattro Pro deletes the record for Jim May from the database by removing that row from the spreadsheet. The next record, the one for Susan McKaye, appears in the database form. Sarah will check the spreadsheet to verify the deletion after she adds the new records for Martin Stein and Constance Evans.

Adding New Records

The New button on the database form adds a new blank record to the database. You can then enter data into the form to add a new record. Quattro Pro adds the record to the spreadsheet by inserting a row after the last record. If you want to keep your database in alphabetical order, you need to sort it again after you add records.

REFERENCE WINDOW

Adding a Record Using the Database Form

- Click Data, then click Form....
- In the Input Range edit field, enter the address of the block of cells containing the database.
- Click OK.
- Click New.
- Enter the information for the new record, then click Close or scroll to another record to insert the new record in the database.

Let's work along with Sarah as she adds the records for Martin Stein and Constance Evans to the database.

To add the record for Martin Stein to the faculty database:
❶ Click **New** to create a new record.
❷ Type **Stein** in the LASTNAME edit field.
❸ Press [Tab] to move to the FIRSTNAME edit field, then type **Martin**.
❹ Press [Tab] to move to the DEPARTMENT edit field, then type **Accounting**.
❺ Press [Tab] to move to the RANK edit field, then type **Instructor**.
❻ Press [Tab] to move to the STARTDATE edit field, then type today's date using the format MM/DD/YY, for example, 09/30/96.
❼ Press [Tab] to move to the SALARY edit field, then type **20562**.
❽ Press [Tab] to move to the GENDER edit field, then type **M**. The database form now appears as shown in Figure 6-17. The record for Martin Stein is record 36.

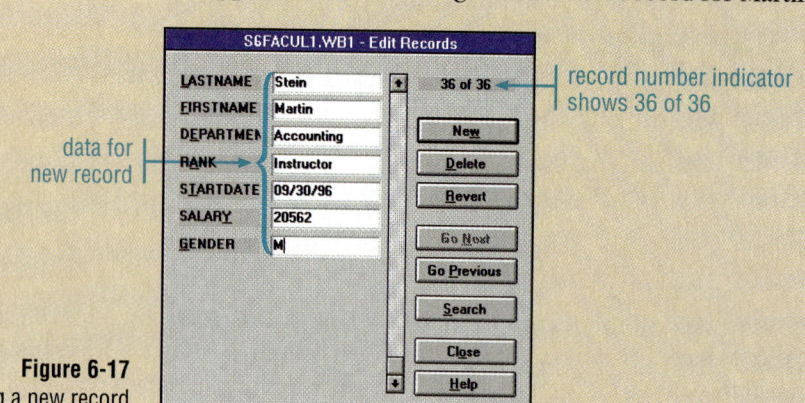

Figure 6-17
Adding a new record

Next, Sarah adds the record for Constance Evans.

To add the data for Constance Evans:

❶ Click **New** to create another new record.

❷ Type **Evans** in the LASTNAME edit field.

❸ Press [Tab] to move to the FIRSTNAME edit field, then type **Constance.**

❹ Press [Tab] to move to the DEPARTMENT edit field, then type **Management.**

❺ Press [Tab] to move to the RANK edit field, then type **Assistant Professor.**

❻ Press [Tab] to move to the STARTDATE edit field, then type today's date using the format MM/DD/YY, for example, 09/30/96.

❼ Press [Tab] to move to the SALARY edit field, then type **32652.**

❽ Press [Tab] to move to the GENDER edit field, then type **F.**

❾ Click **Close** to close the database form and save the records.

Sarah wants to verify that the record for Jim May was deleted, and that the records for Martin Stein and Constance Evans were added.

To verify the changes to the database:

❶ Scroll the spreadsheet and make sure the record for Jim May was removed.

❷ Scroll to the bottom of the spreadsheet and verify that row 36 now contains the record for Martin Stein and row 37 contains the record for Constance Evans.

Because Sarah created block names for use in her database, she needs to update the block names to reflect the changes in the database.

Updating Block Names

Quattro Pro does not automatically update block names when you add or delete records in a database, so you should check any block names and adjust them if necessary. Further, if you delete the first record in the database, Quattro Pro will delete the block names created from the field names.

To update a block name to reflect the addition of new records, highlight the rows in the block—including the rows for the new records—then use the Create Name dialog box to reset the new block address to the old name.

REFERENCE WINDOW

Updating a Block Name After Adding Records

- Press [F5] to open the Goto dialog box.

- Click the block name in the Block Names list, then click OK.

- Scroll the spreadsheet until you can see the bottom of the high-lighted block.

- Press and hold [Shift] then press [↓] to adjust the highlighted block until it matches the modified database.

- Right-click anywhere in the highlighted area to open the SpeedMenu, then click Create Name....

- Click the block name in the Names list then click OK.

Sarah needs to update the DATABASE and SORTBLOCK block names to include the two new records.

To update the block names DATABASE and SORTBLOCK:

❶ Press **[F5]** to open the Goto dialog box.

❷ Click the block name **DATABASE** in the Block Names list, then click **OK**. The block named DATABASE is highlighted.

❸ Using the vertical scroll bar, scroll the spreadsheet until you can see the bottom of the highlighted block in row 35. Notice that the block does not include the new records for Martin Stein in row 36 and Constance Evans in row 37.

❹ Press and hold **[Shift]** and press [↓] twice to extend the highlight to include rows 36 and 37, then release [Shift].

❺ Right-click anywhere in the highlighted area to open the SpeedMenu.

❻ Click **Create Name...** in the SpeedMenu to open the Create Name dialog box. The adjusted block address Database:A1..G37 is displayed in the Block(s) edit field, as shown in Figure 6-18.

adjusted block
address is
Database:A1..G37

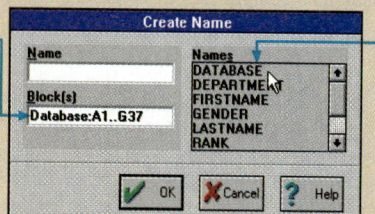

click DATABASE to display
it in Name edit field

Figure 6-18
Updating the block
name DATABASE

❼ Click **DATABASE** in the Names list. The block name DATABASE is displayed in the Name edit field.

❽ Click **OK**. Quattro Pro updates the block address for DATABASE.

❾ Repeat Steps 1 through 8 for the block name SORTBLOCK. Recall that the original address for this block is A2..G35. The updated address should be A2..G37.

Now that the block names have been updated, Sarah can use them in future work with her database. For example, she can use SORTBLOCK to resort the database with the two new records.

Before she sorts the database, however, Sarah notices that the new records are not formatted in the same way as the other records. The dates Sarah entered in the STARTDATE field appear as Quattro Pro serial numbers, and the data entered in the SALARY field is not formatted as currency.

Sarah decides to format the STARTDATE and SALARY data by copying cell properties.

Copying Cell Properties

You can copy the formatting in one cell to another by using the Paste Special... command on the Edit menu. The Paste Properties button on the Productivity Tools SpeedBar gives you easy access to this command. You copy the formatted cells to the Clipboard, highlight the cells you want to format, then paste only the cell properties. The highlighted cells then share the same formatting.

REFERENCE WINDOW

Copying Cell Formatting

- Highlight the cell or block of cells with the formatting you want to copy.

- Click the Copy button on the notebook SpeedBar.

- Highlight the cell or block of cells you want to format.

- Click the Paste Properties button on the Productivity Tools SpeedBar.

Sarah copies the STARTDATE and SALARY formatting to the new rows.

To copy the STARTDATE and SALARY formatting to rows 36 and 37:

❶ Highlight block E35..F35.

❷ Click the **Copy button** 🖻 on the notebook SpeedBar.

❸ Highlight block E36..F37, as shown in Figure 6-19.

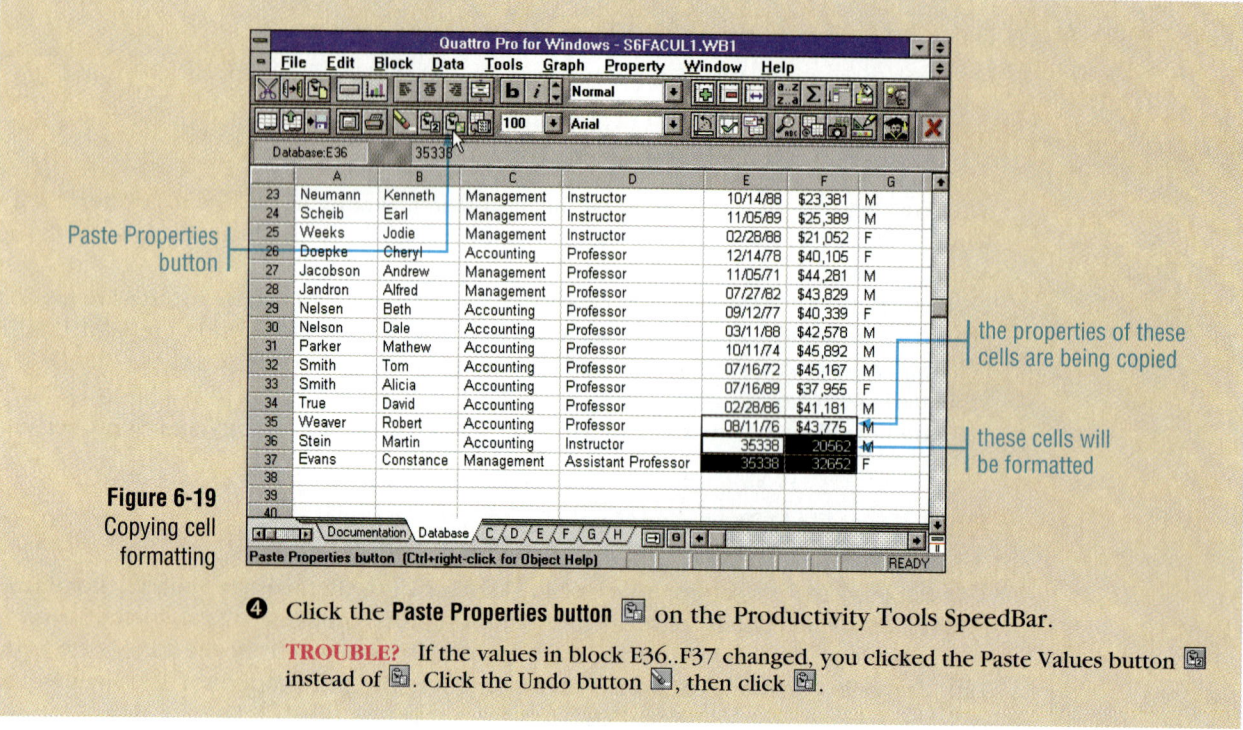

Paste Properties button

the properties of these cells are being copied

these cells will be formatted

Figure 6-19
Copying cell formatting

❹ Click the **Paste Properties button** 🔲 on the Productivity Tools SpeedBar.

   TROUBLE? If the values in block E36..F37 changed, you clicked the Paste Values button 🔲 instead of 🔲. Click the Undo button 🔲, then click 🔲.

Finally, Sarah sorts the database again by rank and last name, and prints a copy of the updated database for the dean.

To sort the database:

❶ Click **Data** then click **Sort...** to open the Data Sort dialog box.

❷ Click **Reset** to clear the sort settings.

❸ Click the **Block edit field** to make it active.

❹ Press **[F3]**, click the block name **SORTBLOCK** in the Block Names dialog box, then click **OK**. The Data Sort dialog box reappears with the block name SORTBLOCK in the Block edit field.

❺ In the Sort Key settings, click the **1st Column edit field** to make it active.

❻ Press **[F3]**, click the block name **RANK** in the Block Names dialog box, then click **OK**. The Data Sort dialog box reappears with the block name RANK in the 1st Column edit field.

❼ In the Sort Key settings, click the **2nd Column edit field** to make it active.

❽ Press **[F3]**, click the block name **LASTNAME** in the Block Names dialog box, then click **OK**. The Data Sort dialog box reappears with the block name LASTNAME in the 2nd Column edit field.

❾ Click **OK** in the Data Sort dialog box to sort the records.

Sarah saves the notebook with the sorted database file, then prints the spreadsheet.

To save the notebook then preview and print the spreadsheet:

❶ Press [Home] to make cell A1 the active cell.

❷ Click the **Save Notebook button** 🖫 (or click **File** then click **Save**).

❸ Click the **Print button** 🖨 on the Productivity Tools SpeedBar. The Spreadsheet Print dialog box appears.

❹ Press [F3], click **DATABASE** in the Block Names dialog box, then click **OK**. The Spreadsheet Print dialog box reappears with the block name DATABASE in the Print block(s) edit field.

❺ Click **Preview** in the Spreadsheet Print dialog box.

❻ Click 🖨 on the Print Preview SpeedBar.

❼ Click the **Close SpeedBar button** ✖ on the Print Preview SpeedBar, then click **Close** in the Spreadsheet Print dialog box.

❽ Press [Home] to make cell A1 the active cell.

❾ Click 🖫 (or click **File** then click **Save**). Figure 6-20 shows Sarah's printed report.

Figure 6-20
Database printout with two new records

NORTHWEST STATE UNIVERSITY - COLLEGE OF BUSINESS FACULTY DATABASE - 09/30/96

LASTNAME	FIRSTNAME	DEPARTMENT	RANK	STARTDATE	SALARY	GENDER
Anderson	Kristen	Accounting	Assistant Professor	10/19/88	$31,155	F
Bordeau	Katherine	Management	Assistant Professor	02/14/86	$30,311	F
Coats	Bill	Accounting	Assistant Professor	03/14/90	$33,371	M
Evans	Constance	Management	Assistant Professor	09/30/96	$32,652	F
Stewart	Mark	Accounting	Assistant Professor	09/28/86	$35,616	M
Young	Jeff	Management	Assistant Professor	10/11/90	$31,513	M
Cornensoli	Angela	Management	Associate Professor	04/27/78	$32,212	F
Downs	Clifton	Accounting	Associate Professor	07/27/82	$34,887	M
Fitzgerald	Edmond	Management	Associate Professor	11/12/90	$36,757	M
Lewis	Karl	Management	Associate Professor	05/22/79	$36,387	M
Mikkola	Claudia	Accounting	Associate Professor	04/27/76	$34,281	F
Palermo	Sheryl	Accounting	Associate Professor	02/14/88	$33,617	F
Smythe	Janice	Management	Associate Professor	03/17/86	$34,887	F
Wolter	Christine	Accounting	Associate Professor	08/11/83	$32,918	F
Collins	Roger	Accounting	Department Head	08/11/91	$47,281	M
Roth	James	Management	Department Head	10/11/90	$49,781	M
Ball	Robin	Accounting	Instructor	03/14/87	$23,723	F
Blackwell	Dean	Accounting	Instructor	11/12/92	$25,797	M
Bressette	Cheryl	Accounting	Instructor	07/27/87	$24,582	F
Hill	Trevor	Management	Instructor	06/11/90	$23,590	M
Jackson	Carole	Accounting	Instructor	03/14/92	$21,781	F
McKaye	Susan	Management	Instructor	07/28/89	$21,979	F
Neumann	Kenneth	Management	Instructor	10/14/88	$23,381	M
Scheib	Earl	Management	Instructor	11/05/89	$25,389	M
Stein	Martin	Accounting	Instructor	09/30/96	$20,562	M
Weeks	Jodie	Management	Instructor	02/28/88	$21,052	F
Doepke	Cheryl	Accounting	Professor	12/14/78	$40,105	F
Jacobson	Andrew	Management	Professor	11/05/71	$44,281	M
Jandron	Alfred	Management	Professor	07/27/82	$43,829	M
Nelsen	Beth	Accounting	Professor	09/12/77	$40,339	F
Nelson	Dale	Accounting	Professor	03/11/88	$42,578	M
Parker	Mathew	Accounting	Professor	10/11/74	$45,892	M
Smith	Alicia	Accounting	Professor	07/16/89	$37,955	F
Smith	Tom	Accounting	Professor	07/16/72	$45,167	M
True	David	Accounting	Professor	02/28/86	$41,181	M
Weaver	Robert	Accounting	Professor	08/11/76	$43,775	M

two new records →

If you want to take a break and resume the tutorial at a later time, you can exit Quattro Pro by double-clicking the Control menu box in the upper-left corner of the screen. When you resume the tutorial, launch Quattro Pro, maximize the Quattro Pro and NOTEBK1.WB1 windows and place your Student Disk in the disk drive. Open the file S6FACUL1.WB1, then continue with the tutorial.

■   ■   ■

After lunch the dean returns from a meeting regarding equal pay for male and female faculty members. The dean wants to compare the salaries of male and female faculty members in the College of Business, so he asks Sarah to calculate the average pay of the faculty members.

Sarah thinks about the dean's request and decides that she can first list all the data for female faculty and then use the @AVG function to calculate their average salary. She will then list all the data for male faculty and calculate their average salary.

Extracting Records from a Database

In this tutorial, you have manually scrolled through the database to find records, and you have used the database form Search button to find records that match specific search criteria. When you use the database form, you can view only one record at a time, even if more than one record matches the search criteria. If you want a list of all the records that match the search criteria, Quattro Pro can extract them and present them in a separate part of the spreadsheet.

The **Query command** on the Data menu contains an extract option that copies all the records matching the search criteria to a specified section of the spreadsheet, where they are displayed in a list. When you extract records, you must define three areas on the spreadsheet: the database block, the criteria table, and the output block. Figure 6-21 shows a simplified example of these three areas (for a sewing center).

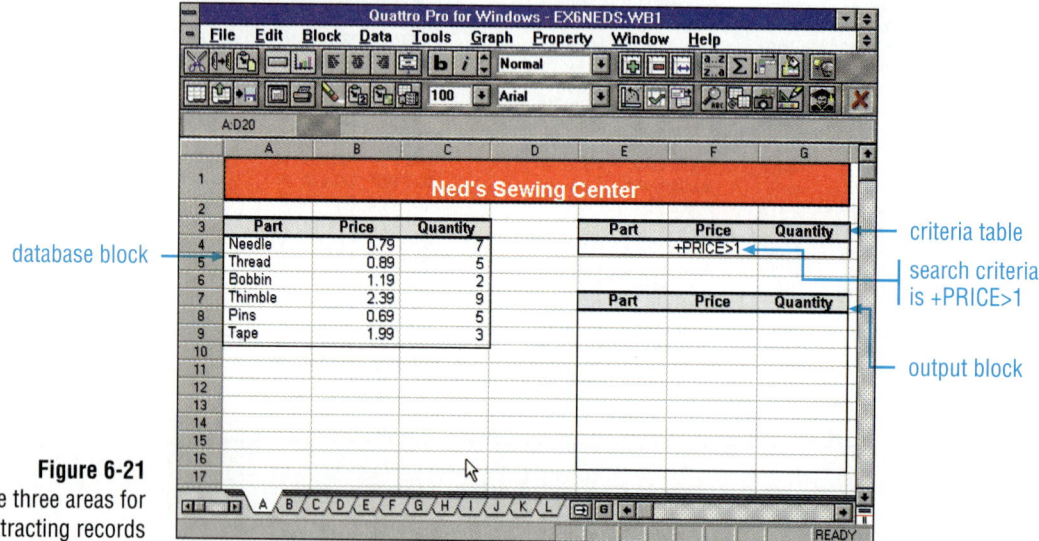

Figure 6-21
The three areas for extracting records

The **database block** includes the row with the field names and the rows that contain the database records. In Figure 6-21, the database block includes cells A3 through C9.

The **criteria table** is an area of the spreadsheet where you enter the search criteria. In Figure 6-21, the criteria table is the block of cells E3..G4. Cell F4 contains the criteria +PRICE>1 which means "search for records with a value greater than 1.00 in the Price field." Although you can put the criteria table anywhere you want, the two best locations are directly above the database block or directly above the output block.

The **output block** is the area of the spreadsheet where Quattro Pro lists a copy of the records that match your search criteria. You create the output block by copying the field names to a blank area of the spreadsheet and including enough empty cells below the copied field names so that Quattro Pro has space for the copies of the records it extracts. In Figure 6-21, the output block is E7..G17. Note the empty cells in the output block.

It's a good idea to create block names for both the block containing the criteria table and the output block. Then you can use the block names to simplify the process of extracting records.

Sarah wants to extract all the records for female faculty members so she can calculate their average salary. She must create the criteria table and the output block before she can use the Data Query command. Let's see how she does this.

Creating a Criteria Table

Sarah decides to use an additional spreadsheet page for the criteria table and output block for her list of female faculty members. Sarah uses the Block Copy command to copy the field names in cells A1 through G1 to page C. Because she is using the Block Copy command, she can copy all the property settings for the block at the same time. The property settings include column widths, which will save her the trouble of setting column widths on the new page.

To copy the field names to page C for use in the criteria table:
❶ Highlight cells A1 through G1 to select the field names.
❷ Click **Block** then click **Copy....** The Block Copy dialog box appears.
❸ Click the **To edit field** to make it active, then press **[Home]** to move the insertion point to the start of the edit field.

❹ Delete the page name Database, then type the page name **C**. The To edit field should contain the block address C:A1..G1.

❺ Click the **Model Copy** check box.

❻ Click **OK**. The field names are copied to page C.

❼ Click any cell to remove the highlighting.

❽ Click **page tab C** to switch to page C and view the copied field names.

Now Sarah enters the search criteria for the records to be extracted.

Entering Search Criteria in a Spreadsheet

The dean wants Sarah to find the average salary for female faculty members and for male faculty members. Sarah wants to list the records for female faculty members on this spreadsheet page. She enters "F" under GENDER in the criteria range to specify that Quattro Pro should extract only the records for female faculty members.

To enter the search criteria:

❶ Make sure page C is the active page.

❷ Click cell **G2** to make it the active cell.

❸ Type **F** then press **[Enter]** to enter the search criteria, as shown in Figure 6-22.

criteria table is
block A1..G2

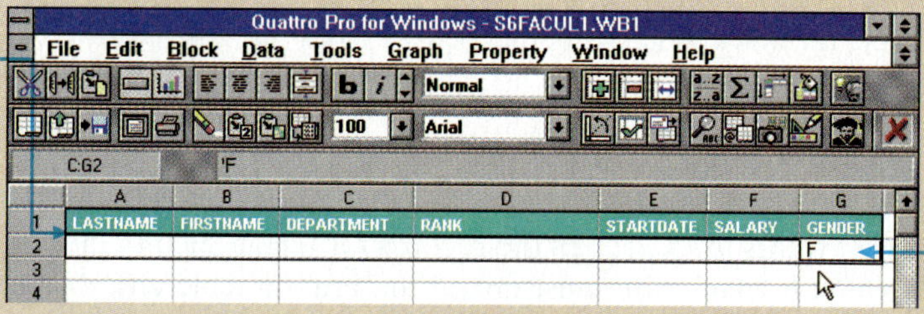

Figure 6-22
Entering the
search criteria in
the spreadsheet

search criteria

Next, beginning at cell A1, Sarah highlights the block of cells that includes the field names and the row containing the criteria (if there is more than one row containing criteria, all these rows would be included in the highlighted block). She then creates the block name CRITERIA for this block.

To create the block name CRITERIA:

❶ Highlight cells A1 through G2.

❷ Right-click anywhere in the highlighted area to open the SpeedMenu.

❸ Click **Create Name...** on the SpeedMenu to open the Create Name dialog box. The block address C:A1..G2 is displayed in the Block(s) edit field.

❹ Click the **Name edit field**, then type **CRITERIA**.

❺ Click **OK**.

Next, Sarah creates the output block.

Creating an Output Block

If you place a criteria table on a different page from the page containing the database, the best place for the output block is directly below the criteria table. You should leave enough blank rows below your criteria table so that you can add more criteria rows later if you need them. When creating an output block, you create another set of field names with empty rows below them to hold the extracted records. Quattro Pro allows you to specify the output block address as just the block containing the field names. Using this method, you have not limited the number of rows available in the output block.

Sarah decides to place the field names for the output block in row 7 under the criteria table. This leaves plenty of room under row 7 for the list of extracted records.

To copy the field names to the output block:
❶ Highlight cells A1 through G1.
❷ Click the **Copy button** 🔲.
❸ Click cell **A7** to make it the active cell.
❹ Click the **Paste button** 🔲 to copy the field names to cells A7 through G7.

Next, Sarah assigns the block name REPORT to the field names in block A7..G7. She will use this block to specify the output block.

To create the block name REPORT:
❶ Highlight cells A7 through G7.
❷ Right-click anywhere in the highlighted area to open the SpeedMenu.
❸ Click **Create Name...** on the SpeedMenu to open the Create Name dialog box. The block address C:A7..G7 is displayed in the Block(s) edit field.
❹ Click the **Name edit field**, then type **REPORT**.
❺ Click **OK**.
❻ Click any cell to remove the highlighting.

Sarah has set up the database, the criteria table with the search criteria, and the output block. Now she uses Quattro Pro's Data Query command to extract the matching records from the database.

Using the Data Query Command

The Query command on the Data menu opens the Data Query dialog box, where you enter the block addresses of the database block, the criteria table, and the output block. The block names you've created make this simple, because you can just press [F3] and select the appropriate block name. Then, for the specified criteria, you can locate records, extract records, or delete records.

Sarah is ready to extract the records from the database.

To extract the records for all female faculty members:

❶ Click **Data** then click **Query...** to display the Data Query dialog box.

❷ Make sure the Database Block edit field is active.

❸ Press [F3], click **DATABASE** in the Block Names dialog box, then click **OK**. The Data Query dialog box reappears with the block name DATABASE in the Database Block edit field, as shown in Figure 6-23.

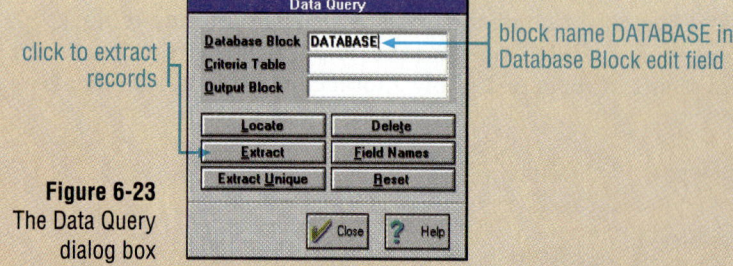

click to extract records

block name DATABASE in Database Block edit field

Figure 6-23
The Data Query dialog box

❹ Click the **Criteria Table edit field** to make it active.

❺ Press [F3], click **CRITERIA** in the Block Names dialog box, then click **OK**. The Data Query dialog box reappears with the block name CRITERIA in the Criteria Table edit field.

❻ Click the **Output Block edit field** to make it active.

❼ Press [F3], click **REPORT** in the Block Names dialog box, then click **OK**. Notice that you need to specify only the block containing the field names of the output block.

❽ Click **Extract** to list copies of the records that match the search criteria.

TROUBLE? If a dialog box with the message "Too many records for output block" appears, your block named REPORT has too many rows in it. Click OK, click Close, then adjust the block name REPORT to refer to just block A7..G7. Repeat Steps 1 through 8.

❾ Click **Close** to return to the spreadsheet.

❿ Scroll the spreadsheet to see the extracted records, shown in Figure 6-24.

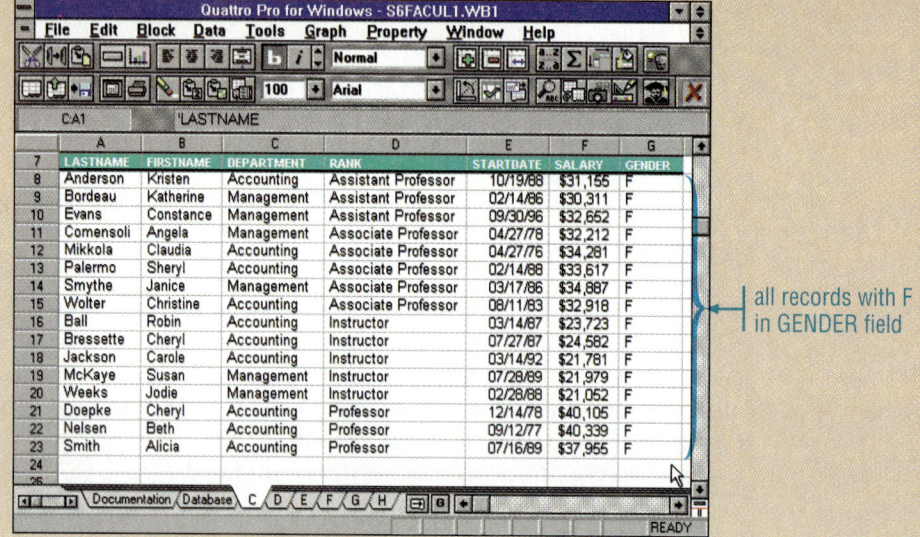

all records with F in GENDER field

Figure 6-24
The extracted records for the female faculty members

Sarah has successfully extracted the records for all female faculty members. Now she uses the @AVG function to calculate their average salary. She decides to enter an identifying label in cell D24, then to enter the formula to calculate the average salary in cell F24, in the SALARY column.

To calculate the average salary for female faculty members in the College of Business:

❶ Click cell **D24**.

❷ Type **AVERAGE SALARY:** then press **[Enter]**.

❸ Click the **Bold button** [b].

❹ Click cell **F24**.

❺ Type **=@AVG(** to begin the formula.

❻ Highlight block F8..F23 to select the cells you want to average.

❼ Press **[Enter]** to complete the calculation and display the result.

❽ Click the **Style list drop-down arrow button** to display the list of styles, then click **Currency0** to format the value in cell F24 as currency with no decimal places.

Sarah's calculation shows that the average salary for female faculty members in the College of Business is $30,847. She prints a copy of her report for the dean.

To print the average salary report for female faculty members:

❶ Click the **Save Notebook button** [▦].

❷ Highlight cells A7 through G24.

❸ Click the **Print button** [🖨] on the Productivity Tools SpeedBar. The Spreadsheet Print dialog box appears.

❹ Click **Print** in the Spreadsheet Print dialog box. The printed output is shown in Figure 6-25.

Figure 6-25
The average salary report for female faculty members

NORTHWEST STATE UNIVERSITY - COLLEGE OF BUSINESS FACULTY DATABASE - 09/30/96

LASTNAME	FIRSTNAME	DEPARTMENT	RANK	STARTDATE	SALARY	GENDER
Anderson	Kristen	Accounting	Assistant Professor	10/19/88	$31,155	F
Bordeau	Katherine	Management	Assistant Professor	02/14/86	$30,311	F
Evans	Constance	Management	Assistant Professor	09/30/96	$32,652	F
Comensoli	Angela	Management	Associate Professor	04/27/78	$32,212	F
Mikkola	Claudia	Accounting	Associate Professor	04/27/76	$34,281	F
Palermo	Sheryl	Accounting	Associate Professor	02/14/88	$33,617	F
Smythe	Janice	Management	Associate Professor	03/17/86	$34,887	F
Wolter	Christine	Accounting	Associate Professor	08/11/83	$32,918	F
Ball	Robin	Accounting	Instructor	03/14/87	$23,723	F
Bressette	Cheryl	Accounting	Instructor	07/27/87	$24,582	F
Jackson	Carole	Accounting	Instructor	03/14/92	$21,781	F
McKaye	Susan	Management	Instructor	07/28/89	$21,979	F
Weeks	Jodie	Management	Instructor	02/28/88	$21,052	F
Doepke	Cheryl	Accounting	Professor	12/14/78	$40,105	F
Nelsen	Beth	Accounting	Professor	09/12/77	$40,339	F
Smith	Alicia	Accounting	Professor	07/16/89	$37,955	F
			AVERAGE SALARY:		$30,847	

Now Sarah extracts the records for all male faculty members so she can calculate their average salary. To extract the data for all male faculty members, Sarah simply changes the search criteria from "F" to "M" in the criteria table. It is not necessary to delete the records from the previous extract because Quattro Pro will automatically clear any previously extracted records from the output block.

To extract the records for all male faculty members:

❶ If necessary, scroll the spreadsheet so you can see cell G2.

❷ Click cell **G2** to make it the active cell.

❸ Type **M** then press **[Enter]** to enter the search criteria.

❹ Click **Data** then click **Query...** to display the Data Query dialog box. All the correct block names are still in the edit fields.

❺ Click **Extract** to list copies of the records that match the search criteria in the cells below the output block.

❻ Click **Close** to return to the spreadsheet.

❼ Scroll the spreadsheet to see the extracted records, shown in Figure 6-26.

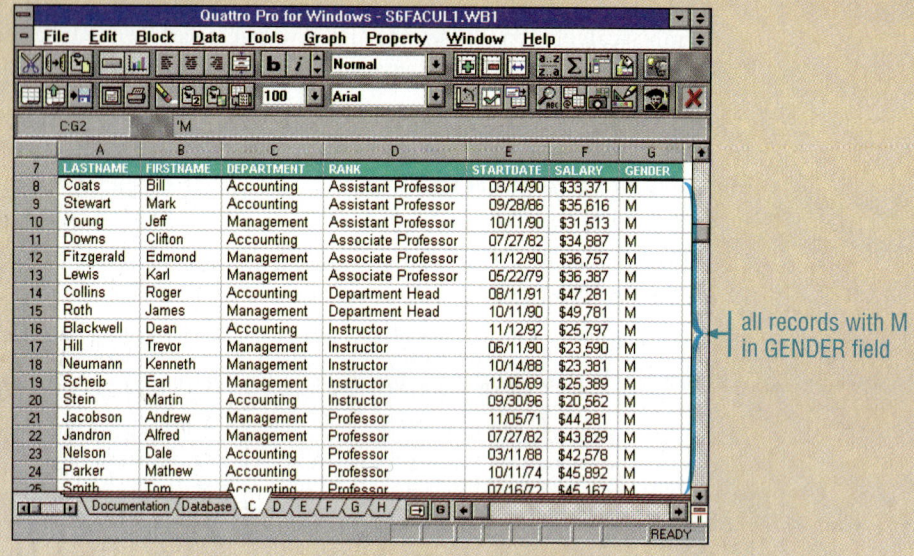

Figure 6-26
The extracted records for the male faculty members

all records with M in GENDER field

Sarah must now create a new formula to calculate the average salary for male faculty members. She scrolls to the bottom of the list and enters an identifying label in cell D28, then enters the formula to calculate the average salary in cell F28, in the SALARY column.

To calculate the average salary for male faculty members in the College of Business:

❶ Click cell **D28**.

❷ Type **AVERAGE SALARY:** then press **[Enter]**.

❸ Click the **Bold button** b.

❹ Click cell **F28**.

❺ Type **=@AVG(** to begin the formula.

❻ Highlight block F8..F27.

❼ Press [Enter] to complete the calculation and display the result.

❽ Click the **Style list drop-down arrow button** to display the list of styles, then click **Currency0**.

The average salary for male faculty members in the College of Business is $36,551. Again, Sarah prints a copy of her report for the dean.

To print the average salary report for male faculty members:

❶ Click the **Save Notebook button** 🖫.

❷ Highlight cells A7 through G28.

❸ Click the **Print button** 🖨 on the Productivity Tools SpeedBar. The Spreadsheet Print dialog box appears.

❹ Click **Print** in the Spreadsheet Print dialog box. The printed output is shown in Figure 6-27.

Figure 6-27
The average salary report for male faculty members

NORTHWEST STATE UNIVERSITY - COLLEGE OF BUSINESS FACULTY DATABASE - 09/30/96

LASTNAME	FIRSTNAME	DEPARTMENT	RANK	STARTDATE	SALARY	GENDER
Coats	Bill	Accounting	Assistant Professor	03/14/90	$33,371	M
Stewart	Mark	Accounting	Assistant Professor	09/28/86	$35,616	M
Young	Jeff	Management	Assistant Professor	10/11/90	$31,513	M
Downs	Clifton	Accounting	Associate Professor	07/27/82	$34,887	M
Fitzgerald	Edmond	Management	Associate Professor	11/12/90	$36,757	M
Lewis	Karl	Management	Associate Professor	05/22/79	$36,387	M
Collins	Roger	Accounting	Department Head	08/11/91	$47,281	M
Roth	James	Management	Department Head	10/11/90	$49,781	M
Blackwell	Dean	Accounting	Instructor	11/12/92	$25,797	M
Hill	Trevor	Management	Instructor	06/11/90	$23,590	M
Neumann	Kenneth	Management	Instructor	10/14/88	$23,381	M
Scheib	Earl	Management	Instructor	11/05/89	$25,389	M
Stein	Martin	Accounting	Instructor	09/30/96	$20,562	M
Jacobson	Andrew	Management	Professor	11/05/71	$44,281	M
Jandron	Alfred	Management	Professor	07/27/82	$43,829	M
Nelson	Dale	Accounting	Professor	03/11/88	$42,578	M
Parker	Mathew	Accounting	Professor	10/11/74	$45,892	M
Smith	Tom	Accounting	Professor	07/16/72	$45,167	M
True	David	Accounting	Professor	02/28/86	$41,181	M
Weaver	Robert	Accounting	Professor	08/11/76	$43,775	M
			AVERAGE SALARY:		$36,551	

Sarah saves and closes her notebook, then exits Quattro Pro.

To save and close the notebook then exit Quattro Pro:

❶ Click the **Documentation page tab**.

❷ Press [Home] to make cell A1 the active cell.

❸ Click the **Save Notebook button** 🖫.

❹ Click **File** then click **Close** to close the notebook.

If you are not going to proceed to the Tutorial Assignments, you also need to exit Quattro Pro.

❺ Click **File** then click **Exit** to exit Quattro Pro.

The dean looks over Sarah's reports and they discuss the results. The average salary for male faculty members in the College of Business is $36,551. This is significantly higher than the average salary of $30,847 for female faculty members. The dean is pleased with Sarah's capable managing of the salary data. To continue his salary analysis, he'll have to consult with a statistician, but Sarah has provided him with the initial data that he needs.

Questions

1. What is a Quattro Pro database?
2. A(n) _____ consists of one or more fields in the same row that describe a particular person, place, or object.
3. The following block was sorted using three keys. Which field was used as the first sort key? Which field was used as the second sort key? Which field was used as the third sort key?

CLASS	LASTNAME	FIRSTNAME
EN211	Baker	Joseph
EN211	Smith	Carol Ann
EN211	Smith	Jim
SP312	Andrews	Carole
SP312	Casselman	Timothy

4. What is a database form?
5. You can use the _____ button on a database form to enter data that detemines which records will be found when you click Go Next or Go Previous.
6. The _____ wildcard represents any group of characters.
7. A database block consists of: _____ .
8. The _____ consists of one row containing the field names and one or more rows of data used to select the records to be extracted from the database.
9. Quattro Pro copies extracted records to blank cells below the field names of the _____ block.

Tutorial Assignments

Sarah needs to update the faculty database, and has asked you to help her.
1. Open the notebook T6FACUL2.WB1.
2. Save the file on your Student Disk as S6FACUL2.WB1.
3. Revise the documentation on the Documentation page as follows:
    a. Change the filename in cell B4 to S6FACUL2.WB1.
    b. Put your name in cell B5.
    c. Put the current date in cell B6 (do not use an @function).
    d. Use cells B9, B10, and B11 as needed to complete the statement of purpose for the notebook.
    e. Save the notebook again to save these changes.
For the spreadsheet on the Database page:
4. Using the database form, add the following data for a new faculty member:
    Last name = Gerety
    First name = Peter
    Department = Management
    Rank = Assistant Professor
    Start date = Today's date
    Salary = 30524
    Gender = M

5. Use the database form to determine how many faculty members hold the rank of professor in the Management department. Write down your answer.

6. Use the database form to determine how many female faculty members earn more than $35,000 per year. Write down your answer.

7. Use the database form to determine how many faculty members hold the rank of associate professor in the College of Business. Write down your answer.

8. Close the database form.

9. Format any cells in the new record that need formatting.

10. Update the block names DATABASE and SORTBLOCK to reflect the addition of the new record.

11. Sort the records in the block SORTBLOCK in alphabetical order by last name.

12. Preview the spreadsheet and make any necessary format changes.

13. Save the notebook again.

14. Print the updated database.

15. Close the notebook.

16. Submit your answers to Tutorial Assignments 5, 6, and 7, and your printed database.

Case Problems

1. Creating a List of Back-ordered Inventory Items at OfficeMart Business Supplies

You are an assistant buyer at OfficeMart Business Supplies, a business supply retail store. Your boss, Norman Ebenshade, has created Quattro Pro notebooks containing the product and pricing data for inventory items purchased from each primary vendor.

Norman is preparing his monthly order for EB Wholesale Office Supplies, one of OfficeMart's suppliers. Norman has asked you to print a list of all back-ordered EB Wholesale products so he can include them on the order.

1. Open the notebook P6INVENT.WB1 and maximize the notebook window.

2. Save the file as S6INVENT.WB1.

3. Revise and complete the documentation on page A as follows:
    a. Change the filename in cell B4 to S6INVENT.WB1.
    b. Put your name in cell B5.
    c. Put the current date in cell B6 (do not use an @function).
    d. Use cells B9 and B10 as needed to complete the statement of purpose for the notebook.
    e. Use cell D14 to describe the purpose of the EB_Wholesale spreadsheet.

For the EB_Wholesale spreadsheet:

4. Create the block names DATABASE and SORTBLOCK, as described in the tutorial.

5. Create block names based on the field names, as described in the tutorial.

6. Copy the field names to a criteria table on page C. (*Hint:* Use the Block Copy command and place the field names in block A1..H1.)

7. Enter the search criteria in the criteria table. (*Hint:* You want to extract a list of all items with a status of back-ordered. Refer to the status codes listed at the top of the spreadsheet.)

8. Create a block name for the criteria table.

9. Copy the field names to an output block on page C. (*Hint:* Place the field names in block A7..H7.)

10. Create a block name for the field names in the output block.

11. Extract the records for all back-ordered items.

12. Highlight the output block field names and the extracted records. Preview the extracted records and make any necessary formatting changes for the printout.

13. Print the highlighted block.

14. Save and close the notebook.

2.   Creating an Invitation List for Shih Tzu Fanciers of America

Jennifer Santarelli is the membership coordinator for the Shih Tzu Fanciers of America (STFA), a nonprofit organization for owners, fanciers, and breeders of Shih Tzu dogs. The organization maintains a membership list in a dBASE file. (A **dBASE file** is a database file created using the dBASE III or dBASE IV database management software.) The list includes the first name, last name, address, city, state, and zip code for approximately one thousand current members.

The New Mexico Chapter of the STFA is planning a Shih Tzu Fanciers picnic lunch. They want to invite all STFA members in nearby states, and they have asked Jennifer to send them a list of all current members in the surrounding states. In this Case Problem, you'll help Jennifer import the dBASE file, save the records as a Quattro Pro notebook, and extract the records for all members who live in the surrounding states.

E
1. Open the P6MEMBR.DBF dBASE file from your Student Disk:
    a. Click the Open Notebook button (or click File then click Open...) to display the Open File dialog box.
    b. Click the File Types list drop-down arrow button to display the File Types list.
    c. Scroll through the list of file types until you see the dBASE (*.DBF) file type. Notice that Quattro Pro also lists the dBASE II (*.DB2) and dBASE IV (*.DB4) file types.
    d. Click dBASE (*.DBF) to select this file type. The File Types list box now reads dBASE (*.DBF), and a list of all dBASE files appears in the File Name list.
    e. Double-click the filename P6MEMBR.DBF to open the file as a Quattro Pro notebook.

E
2. Save the file as a Quattro Pro notebook with the filename S6MEMBR.WB1:
    a. Click File then click Save As... to display the Save File dialog box.
    b. Click the File Types list drop-down arrow button to display the list of file types. Scroll through the list until the file type QPW (*.WB1) appears, then click QPW (*.WB1) to select it. The File Name edit field changes to *.WB1.
    c. Click the File Name edit field to make it active.
    d. Press [HOME] to move the insertion point to the beginning of the edit field.
    e. Press [Del] to delete the asterisk (*) character.
    f. Type S6MEMBR (using either uppercase or lowercase letters) so that the File Name edit field contains the filename S6MEMBR.WB1.
    g. Click OK to save the notebook on your Student Disk.

E
3. Insert a new page A:
    a. Press [Home] to make cell A1 the active cell.
    b. Click Block, click Insert, click Pages, then click OK.
4. Put the page name "Documentation" on the page tab for page A.
5. Put the page name "Database" on the page tab for page B.

For the spreadsheet on the Documentation page:
6. Following the documentation conventions you've used in other notebooks, create the appropriate notebook documentation on the Documentation page. (*Hint:* Set the column width of columns A and C to 16, and the column width of column D to 48.)
7. Save the notebook again.

For the spreadsheet on the Database page:
8. Format the database spreadsheet:
    a. Adjust the column widths so that the field names fit in the columns. (*Hint:* Highlight the block in row 1 containing the field names, then use the Fit button.)
    b. Center and bold the field names.
    c. Add a color of your choice to the block containing the field names to visually distinguish them from the data.
9. Create the block names DATABASE and SORTBLOCK, as described in the tutorial.
10. Create block names based on the field names, as described in the tutorial.
11. Sort the records using zip code as the first sort key and last name as the second sort key.
12. Save the notebook again.

For the spreadsheet on page C:

13. Copy the field names to a criteria table on page C. (*Hint:* Use the Block Copy command.)

14. Enter the search criteria. (*Hint:* The cells should contain NM, AZ, UT, CO, TX, and OK. Type each state abbreviation in a separate cell in the state column of the criteria table.)

15. Create a block name for the criteria table. (*Hint:* Include the field names and every row containing a state abbreviation.)

16. Copy the field names to an output block on page C.

17. Create a block name for the field names in the output block.

18. Extract the records.

19. Highlight the output block field names and the extracted records. Preview the extracted records and make any necessary formatting changes for the printout. (*Hint:* Print in landscape orientation to fit complete records on each page.)

20. Print the highlighted block.

21. Save the notebook again.

For the spreadsheet on the Documentation page:

22. Revise the documentation to reflect the changes you've made to the notebook.

23. Save the notebook again.

24. Highlight the documentation. Preview the documentation and make any necessary formatting changes for the printout. (*Hint:* Print in portrait orientation.)

25. Print the documentation.

26. Save and close the notebook.

27. Submit copies of your printouts.

3. Creating a Current Membership List for Shih Tzu Fanciers of America

This Case Problem is a continuation of Case 2 above. You must have completed Case 2 before doing this Case.

The board of the Shih Tzu Fanciers of America (STFA) has asked Jennifer to prepare a report on the current membership, listing the members who live in Los Angeles and New York City.

1. Open the S6MEMBR.WB1 notebook.

For the spreadsheet on the page D:

2. Copy the field names to a criteria table on page D. (*Hint:* Use the Block Copy command.)

3. Enter the search criteria. (*Hint:* The cells should contain the names of the cities Los Angeles and New York. Type each city name in a separate cell in the city column of the criteria table.)

4. Define a block name for the criteria table. (*Hint:* Include the field names and every row with a state abbreviation in it.)

5. Copy the field names to an output block on page D.

6. Define a block name for the field names of the output block.

7. Extract the records.

8. Highlight the output block field names and the extracted records. Preview the extracted records and make any formatting changes that are necessary before printing. (*Hint:* Print in landscape orientation to fit complete records on each page.)

9. Print the highlighted block.

10. Save the notebook.

For the spreadsheet on the Documentation page:

11. Revise the documentation to reflect the changes you've made to the notebook.

12. Save the notebook again.

13. Highlight the documentation. Preview the documentation and make any formatting changes that are necessary before printing. (*Hint:* Print in portrait orientation.)

14. Print the documentation.

15. Save the notebook again.

Index

TASK	MOUSE	MENU	KEYBOARD
@Functions, type in a formula *QP 152*	See Reference Window: Typing an @Function in a Formula		
@Functions, select with @Functions button *QP 154*	See Reference Window: Using the @Functions Button to Place an @Function in a Formula		
@IF *QP 165*	See Reference Window: Using @IF to Display Results Based on Specified Conditions		
@PAYMT *QP 161*	See Reference Window: Using @PAYMT to Calculate a Monthly Payment		
@ROUND *QP 169*	See Reference Window: Using @ROUND to Round the Stored Results of a Formula		
Active cell, make a cell the *QP 21*	Click the cell		Use `←`, `→`, `↑`, `↓` to move to cell
Active cell, make cell A1 the *QP 56*			`Home`
Active cell, use Goto to make a cell the – see Goto			
Active notebook page, make a page the *QP 20*	Click the page tab of the new page	Click Edit, Goto..., page in Pages list box, OK	`F5`, `Alt` `P`, scroll to page in Pages list box, `Enter`
Active notebook page, make Graphs page the – see Graphs page, change to			
Active notebook page, return to from Graphs page – see Graphs page, return from			
Active spreadsheet – see Active notebook page			
Block names, create *QP 239*	See Reference Window: Creating a Block Name		
Block names, create from labels *QP 241*		Select block of labels, click Block, Names, Labels..., select Direction (click Right, Left, Up, or Down), OK	Select block of labels, `Alt` `B`, `N`, `L`, select Direction (`Alt` `R`, `Alt` `L`, `Alt` `U`, or `Alt` `D`), `Enter`
Block names, use in dialog boxes *QP 242*			`F3`
Block names, update *QP 254*	See Reference Window: Updating a Block Name After Adding Records		
Cell contents, print *QP 136*	Click ▦, ▦, click Cell formulas, OK	Click File, Print..., Options..., Cell formulas, OK	`Alt` `F`, `P`, `Alt` `O`, `Alt` `C`, `Enter`
Center cell contents *QP 113*	Click ▦	Click Property, Current Object..., Alignment, Center, OK	`F12`, `Ctrl` `PgDn` 3 times to select Alignment, `C`, `Enter`
Center label across columns *QP 114*	Click ▦	Click Property, Current Object..., Alignment, Center across block, OK	`F12`, `Ctrl` `PgDn` 3 times to select Alignment, `B`, `Enter`
Centering the printout *QP 134*	Click ▦, ▦, Center blocks, OK	Click File, Page Setup..., Center blocks, OK	`Alt` `F`, `T`, `Alt` `C`, `Enter`
Clear cell contents but retain property settings *QP 78*	Right-click cell or block, then click Clear Contents	Click Edit, Clear Contents	`Del` or `Ctrl` `B` or `Alt` `E`, `A`

TASK	MOUSE	MENU	KEYBOARD
Clear cell contents and property settings *QP 78*	Right-click cell or block, then click Clear	Click Edit, Clear	Alt E , E
Close the notebook *QP 35*	Double-click notebook Control menu box ▣	Click File, Close	Alt F , C or Ctrl W
Color a block *QP 126*	Right-click block, then click Block Properties..., Shading, Color 1, Color 2, Blend, OK	Click Property, Current Object..., Shading, Color 1, Color 2, Blend, OK	F12 , Ctrl PgDn 2 times to select Shading, 1 (use arrow keys to select Color 1), 2 (use arrow keys to select Color 2), B (use arrow keys to select Blend), Enter
Column width, change *QP 50*	Drag the right edge of column border C ↔ D or right-click column border, click Block Properties..., Column Width, enter width in Column Width edit field, click OK	Select column, click Property, Current Object..., Column Width, enter width in Column Width edit field, click OK	Select column, F12 , Ctrl PgDn 9 times to select Column Width, enter width in Column Width edit field, Enter
Column width, best fit *QP 50*	Click ▦	Select column, click Property, Current Object..., Column Width, Auto Width, OK	Select column, F12 , Ctrl PgDn 9 times to select Column Width, Alt A , Enter
Copy cell contents *QP 62*	Highlight cells to be copied, click ▣. Highlight destination cells, click ▣	Highlight cells to be copied, click Edit, click Copy. Highlight destination cells, click Edit, click Paste	Highlight cells to be copied, Alt E , C . Highlight destination cells, Alt E , P
Copy cell properties *QP 255*	See Reference Window: Copying Cell Formatting		
Copy spreadsheet structure *QP 87*	See Reference Window: Copying Blocks to Other Pages		
Database, extract records from *QP 259*	See Reference Window: Extracting Records from a Database		
Database, sort data *QP 236*	See Reference Window: Sorting a Block of Cells		
Database form, adding a record with *QP 252*	See Reference Window: Adding a Record Using the Database Form		
Database form, criteria search with *QP 248*	See Reference Window: Searching for a Record Using the Database Form		
Database form, deleting a record with *QP 251*	See Reference Window: Deleting a Record Using the Database Form		
Database form, display *QP 245*	See Reference Window: Displaying a Database Form		
Edit cell contents *QP 22*	Select cell, click input line		Select cell, F2
Exit Quattro Pro for Windows *QP 35*	Double-click application Control menu box ▭	Click File, Exit	Alt F , X or Ctrl Q

TASK	MOUSE	MENU	KEYBOARD
Font style bold, use *QP 111*	Select cell, click **b**	Select cell, click Property, Current Object..., Font, Bold, OK	Select cell, F12 , Ctrl PgDn 1 time to select Font, Alt B , Enter
Font style italic, use *QP 112*	Select cell, click *i*	Select cell, click Property, Current Object..., Font, Italics, OK	Select cell, F12 , Ctrl PgDn 1 time to select Font, Alt I , Enter
Font point size, select *QP 112*	Select cell, click ⬍ or right-click block, click Block Properties..., Font, Point Size list box drop-down arrow, then click point size, OK	Select cell, click Property, Current Object..., Font, Point Size list box drop-down arrow, then select point size, click OK	F12 , Ctrl PgDn 1 time to select Font, Alt P , ↓ , use arrow keys to select point size, Enter
Footer on printout *QP 132*	Click ▭, ▤, complete Footer edit field, click OK	Click File, Page Setup..., complete Footer edit field, click OK	Alt F , T , Alt F to complete Footer edit field, Enter
Format cells *QP 109*	See Reference Window: Formatting Cells		
Format cells with Style list *QP 80*	Select cell, click Style list drop-down arrow ⬇, click style		
Format numbers *QP 116*	See Reference Window: Formatting Numbers		
Formulas, entering *QP 66*	See Reference Window: Entering a Formula		
Goto *QP 241*		Click Edit, Goto..., complete Reference edit field, click OK	F5 , complete Reference edit field, Enter
Graph, adding or editing graph titles *QP 214*	See Reference Window: Adding or Editing Graph Titles		
Graph, change axis title font size *QP 204*	In graph window right-click axis title, click Axis Title Properties..., Text Font, select typeface from list, click OK	In graph window select axis title, click Property, Current Object..., Text Font, select typeface from list, click OK	In graph window select axis title, F12 , Ctrl PgDn 3 times to select Text Font, Alt T , use arrow keys to select typeface, Enter
Graph, change line marker style *QP 207*	In graph window right-click line, click Line Series Properties..., Marker Style, select from examples, click OK	In graph window select line, click Property, Series..., Marker Style, select from examples, click OK	In graph window Alt P , E , use arrow keys to select series, Enter , Ctrl PgDn 2 times to select Marker Style, use arrow keys to select marker, Enter
Graph, change pane color *QP 219*	In graph window right-click pane, click Graph Pane Properties..., Fill Style, Solid, Fill Color, select from palette, click OK	In graph window click Property, Graph Pane..., Fill Style, Solid, Fill Color, select from palette, click OK	In graph window Alt P , P , Ctrl PgDn 3 times to select Fill Style, S , Ctrl PgUp 2 times to select Fill Color, use arrow keys to select color from palette, Enter
Graph, change title font size *QP 203*	In graph window right-click title, click Graph TitleBox Properties..., Text Font, select typeface from list, click OK	In graph window select title, click Property, Current Object..., Text Font, select typeface from list, click OK	In graph window select title, F12 , Ctrl PgDn 2 times to select Text Font, Alt T , use arrow keys to select typeface, Enter

TASK	MOUSE	MENU	KEYBOARD
Graph, create *QP 209*	See Reference Window: Creating a Graph Using the Graph New Command		
Graph, format bars in a *QP 218*	In graph window right-click bar, click Bar Series Properties..., use Bar Series Object Inspector, click OK	In graph window select bar, click Property Series..., use Bar Series Object Inspector, click OK	In graph window `Alt` `P`, `E`, use arrow keys to select series, `Enter`, then use Bar Series Object Inspector, `Enter`
Graph, format horizontal grid lines in a *QP 217*	In graph window right-click line, click Y-Axis Properties..., Major Grid Style, Line Style, select from examples, click OK	In graph window, Click Property, Y-Axis..., Major Grid Style, Line Style, select from examples, click OK	In graph window, `Alt` `P`, `Y`, `Ctrl` `PgDn` 7 times to select Major Grid Style, `Alt` `L`, `Tab`, use arrow keys to select line style, `Enter`
Graph, format lines in a *QP 205*	In graph window right-click line, click Line Series Properties..., use Line Series Object Inspector, click OK	In graph window select line, click Property, Series..., use Line Series Object Inspector, click OK	In graph window, `Alt` `P`, `E`, use arrow keys to select series, `Enter`, use Line Series Object Inspector, `Enter`
Graph, format X-axis labels *QP 204*	In graph window right-click x-axis, click X-Axis Properties..., use X-Axis Object Inspector, click OK	In graph window click Property, X Axis..., use X-Axis Object Inspector, click OK	In graph window, `Alt` `P`, `X`, use X-Axis Object Inspector, `Enter`
Graph, format Y-axis values *QP 204*	In graph window right-click y-axis, click Y-Axis Properties..., use Y-Axis Object Inspector, click OK	In the window click Property, Y Axis..., use Y-Axis Object Inspector, click OK	In graph window, `Alt` `P`, `Y`, use Y-Axis Object Inspector, `Enter`
Graph, insert on spreadsheet *QP 221*	See Reference Window: Inserting a Graph on a Spreadsheet		
Graph, name a *QP 200*	See Reference Window: Renaming a Graph		
Graph, select type *QP 213*	See Reference Window: Selecting a Graph Type		
Graph, view *QP 192*	In notebook window, right-click floating graph, click View	Click Graph, View, select graph name in Select Graph list, click OK	`F11`, `Alt` `S`, use arrow keys to scroll to graph name, `Enter`
Graph Expert *QP 196*	See Reference Window: Creating a Graph with the Graph Expert		
Graphs page, change to *QP 194*	Click ▣		
Graphs page, return from *QP 194*	Click ▣		
Graph window, open *QP 201*	See Reference Window: Opening the Graph Window to Edit a Graph		
Graph window, close *QP 208*	Click Close	Click graph window Control menu box ▣, Close	`Ctrl` `F4`
Group of pages, creating *QP 92*	See Reference Window: Creating a Group of Spreadsheet Pages		
Group of pages, deleting *QP 95*		Click Tools, Define Group..., complete Define/Modify Group dialog box, click OK	`Alt` `T`, `G`, complete Define/Modify Group dialog box, `Enter`
Group mode, activating *QP 93*	Click ▣		

TASK REFERENCE
QUATTRO PRO 5.0 FOR WINDOWS
Italicized page numbers indicate the first discussion of each task.

TASK	MOUSE	MENU	KEYBOARD
Header on printout *QP 32*	Click ▫, ▣, complete Header edit field, click OK	Click File, Page Setup..., complete Header edit field, click OK	`Alt` `F`, `T`, `Alt` `H`, complete Header edit field, `Enter`
Help, Object *QP 33*	Press and hold `Ctrl`, then right-click object		
Help system *QP 34*		Click Help, Contents	`F1`
Highlight a block of cells *QP 60*	Position pointer, press and hold mouse button, drag mouse to select block, release button		Hold down `Shift` and use arrow keys to select block
Inserting a column *QP 75*	See Reference Window: Inserting a Row or Column		
Inserting a row *QP 75*	See Reference Window: Inserting a Row or Column		
Landscape print orientation *QP 30*	Click ▫, ▣, Landscape, OK	Click File, Page Setup..., Landscape, OK	`Alt` `F`, `T`, `Alt` `D`, `Enter`
Launch Quattro Pro 5.0 for Windows *QP 8*	Double-click Quattro Pro for Windows icon		
Left-align cell contents *QP 113*	Select cell, click ▣	Select cell, click Property, Current Object..., Alignment, Left, OK	Select cell, `F12`, `Ctrl` `PgDn` 3 times to select Alignment, `L`, `Enter`
Line segments, add *QP 123*	See Reference Window: Adding and Removing Line Segments		
Line segments, remove *QP 123*	See Reference Window: Adding and Removing Line Segments		
Margins on printout *QP 133*	Click ▫, ▣, complete Margins edit fields, click OK	Click File, Page Setup..., complete Margins edit fields, click OK	`Alt` `F`, `T`, select Margins edit fields with `Alt` `T`, `Alt` `E`, `Alt` `L`, `Alt` `R`, `Alt` `O`, and `Alt` `B`, `Enter`
Maximize the notebook window *QP 9*	Click ▲ on the notebook window		
Maximize the Quattro Pro for Windows window *QP 9*	Click ▲ on the application window		
Object Inspector, Active Block *QP 31*	Right-click any cell in block, click Block Properties...	Select cell, click Property, Current Object...	Select cell, `F12`
Object Inspector, Active Notebook *QP 31*		Click Property, Active Notebook...	`Shift` `F12`
Object Inspector, Active Page *QP 31*	Right-click page tab	Click Property, Active Page...	
Object Inspector, graph objects *QP 202*	See Reference Window: Using Graph Object Inspector		
Open a notebook *QP 13*	Click ▣	Click File, Open, complete File Name edit field, click OK	`Alt` `F`, `O` or `Ctrl` `O`, complete File Name edit field, `Enter`
Page break, delete manual *QP 224*	See Reference Window: Deleting Manual Page Breaks		

TASK	MOUSE	MENU	KEYBOARD
Page break, insert manual *QP 224*	See Reference Window: Inserting Manual Page Breaks		
Portrait print orientation *QP 130*	Click ▣, ▣, Portrait, OK	Click File, Page Setup..., Portrait, OK	`Alt` `F`, `T`, `Alt` `P`, `Enter`
Print Preview *QP 128*	See Reference Window: Using Print Preview		
Print graph *QP 208*	Select graph, then click ▣	Select graph, click File, Print, Print	Select graph, `Alt` `F`, `P`, `Enter`
Print spreadsheet *QP 25*	Select print block, then click ▣	Select print block, click File, Print, Print	Select print block, `Alt` `F`, `P`, `Enter`
Right-align cell contents *QP 113*	Select cell, click ▣	Select cell, click Property, Current Object..., Alignment, Right, OK	Select cell, `F12`, `Ctrl` `PgDn` 3 times to select Alignment, `R`, `Enter`
Row height, change *QP 57*	Drag the bottom edge of row border ▣ or right-click row border, click Block Properties..., Row Height, complete Row Height edit field, click OK	Click Property, Current Object..., Row Height, complete Row Height edit field, click OK	`F12`, `Ctrl` `PgDn` 8 times to select Row Height, complete Row Height edit field, `Enter`
Save notebook with a new filename *QP 16*		Click File, Save As..., complete File Name edit field, click OK	`Alt` `F`, `A`, complete File Name edit field, `Enter`
Save notebook with the same filename *QP 24*	Click ▣	Click File, Save	`Alt` `F`, `S` or `Ctrl` `S`
SpeedFill a block of cells *QP 60*	See Reference Window: Using SpeedFill to Complete a Series		
SpeedSum *QP 77*	Click Σ		
Undo *QP 23*	Click ▣	Click Edit, Undo	`Alt` `E`, `U` or `Ctrl` `Z`
Zoom Factor, changing *QP 107*	See Reference Window: Changing the Zoom Factor		